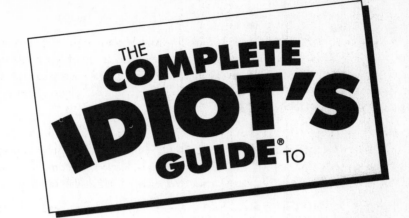

THE **COMPLETE IDIOT'S GUIDE®** TO

# Understanding Catholicism

## Third Edition

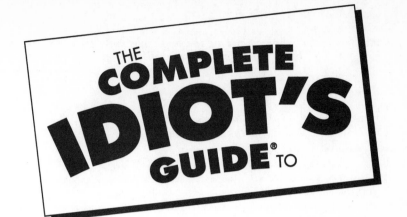

THE
COMPLETE
IDIOT'S
GUIDE® TO

# Understanding
# Catholicism

## Third Edition

*by Bob O'Gorman, Ph.D., and
Mary Faulkner, M.A.*

ALPHA

A member of Penguin Group (USA) Inc.

*This book is dedicated to all who have been and are the people who make the Catholic Church. This is whose story we try to tell.*

## ALPHA BOOKS

Published by the Penguin Group

Penguin Group (USA) Inc., 375 Hudson Street, New York, New York 10014, U.S.A.

Penguin Group (Canada), 10 Alcorn Avenue, Toronto, Ontario, Canada M4V 3B2 (a division of Pearson Penguin Canada Inc.)

Penguin Books Ltd, 80 Strand, London WC2R 0RL, England

Penguin Ireland, 25 St Stephen's Green, Dublin 2, Ireland (a division of Penguin Books Ltd)

Penguin Group (Australia), 250 Camberwell Road, Camberwell, Victoria 3124, Australia (a division of Pearson Australia Group Pty Ltd)

Penguin Books India Pvt Ltd, 11 Community Centre, Panchsheel Park, New Delhi—110 017, India

Penguin Group (NZ), cnr Airborne and Rosedale Roads, Albany, Auckland 1310, New Zealand (a division of Pearson New Zealand Ltd)

Penguin Books (South Africa) (Pty) Ltd, 24 Sturdee Avenue, Rosebank, Johannesburg 2196, South Africa

Penguin Books Ltd, Registered Offices: 80 Strand, London WC2R 0RL, England

## Copyright © 2006 by Bob O'Gorman and Mary Faulkner

International Standard Book Number: 1-59257-535-8
Library of Congress Catalog Card Number: 2006922335

08  07  06      8  7  6  5  4  3  2  1

Interpretation of the printing code: The rightmost number of the first series of numbers is the year of the book's printing; the rightmost number of the second series of numbers is the number of the book's printing. For example, a printing code of 06-1 shows that the first printing occurred in 2006.

*Printed in the United States of America*

**Note:** This publication contains the opinions and ideas of its authors. It is intended to provide helpful and informative material on the subject matter covered. It is sold with the understanding that the authors and publisher are not engaged in rendering professional services in the book. If the reader requires personal assistance or advice, a competent professional should be consulted.

The authors and publisher specifically disclaim any responsibility for any liability, loss, or risk, personal or otherwise, which is incurred as a consequence, directly or indirectly, of the use and application of any of the contents of this book.

Most Alpha books are available at special quantity discounts for bulk purchases for sales promotions, premiums, fund-raising, or educational use. Special books, or book excerpts, can also be created to fit specific needs.

For details, write: Special Markets, Alpha Books, 375 Hudson Street, New York, NY 10014.

**Publisher:** *Marie Butler-Knight*
**Editorial Director:** *Mike Sanders*
**Managing Editor:** *Billy Fields*
**Executive Editor:** *Randy Ladenheim-Gil*
**Development Editor:** *Megan Douglass*
**Senior Production Editor:** *Janette Lynn*
**Copy Editor:** *Amy Borrelli*
**Book Designers:** *Trina Wurst/Kurt Owens*
**Cover Designer:** *Bill Thomas*
**Indexer:** *Jennifer Rushing-Schurr*
**Layout:** *Ayanna Lacey*
**Proofreader:** *John Etchison*

# Contents at a Glance

**Part I:**  **What's a Catholic?**  1

1 Can You Judge a Catholic by the Cover?  3

*Catholicism is a religion with a rich tradition of ritual and ceremony. It's both romantic and mysterious. This chapter offers an opportunity to learn more about what makes a Catholic tick, what practices and beliefs are uniquely Catholic, and how Catholics have influenced the culture in which you live.*

2 The People: Many Faces, Many Flags  15

*To talk about Catholics is to talk about all the peoples of the world. Literally, there is not a patch of land on this planet that is not under the jurisdiction of a bishop or pastor. We'll take a look at an African American Mass, a Mexican cemetery, and a New Mexican pueblo.*

3 Catholicism: It's a Big Tent  25

*How can political opposites such as Patrick Buchanan and Cesar Chavez both be Catholic? Like the diversity of its cultural expressions, the Church is also expressed through many different types of spirituality. We'll look at a variety of ways the Catholic religion is played out in the world.*

4 The Vatican: The Church That's a Country  37

*This chapter will describe the structure of the Vatican city-state and give you the basic rules and regulations that hold this global religion together, forming a faith that is both diverse and unified.*

5 The '60s: Seeds of Revolution  51

*Have you heard of Vatican II? Do you know that it revolutionized 400 years of the practices and beliefs of the Catholic Church? Just what went on when the council fire was lit? Did it scorch Catholicism or purify it for the third millennium?*

**Part 2:    Putting the "Ism" in Catholicism: Becoming Catholic, Becoming Different        65**

6   "It's Elementary, My Dear Watson"        67
*The ceremonies and rituals of Catholicism are rooted in the
rich traditions of the indigenous people of Old Europe, and
draw from the Jewish, Greek, Roman, and Celtic worlds as
well. This is an opportunity to see how these early traditions
combined to create the magic, mystery, and mythology of
"modern" Catholicism.*

7   The Bible        81
*What is the difference between the "Catholic Bible" and other
Bibles? What are the Catholic beliefs about the Bible? Is it
true that Catholics don't read the Bible?*

8   Jesus: Spirit of a New Religion        95
*Were Catholics always called "Catholic"? Weren't Jesus
and the apostles Jews? Learn where Catholics come from.
Learn the deep roots of Catholic spirituality and how the
desert experience of solitude and sanctity got started.*

**Part 3:    The Sensuous Side of Catholicism: How Catholics Experience God        109**

9   Catholic Imagination: The Sacred Space of Ritual        111
*Catholicism is both a whole-brained and full-bodied religion.
How is it both religious and spiritual in nature? Learn about
the beads, bells, books, and candles of Catholics. Read some of
the prayers and songs that celebrate the Catholic spirit.*

10  Jesus: The Original Sacrament        123
*Sacraments are important to Catholics. Just what is a sacra-
ment? Catholics insist that Jesus is fully present in the bread
they call a host—how can that be? What do they really mean
by this hocus-pocus?*

11  Seven Sensual Sacraments        133
*Some Christian denominations have one sacrament. Some
have three. Catholics hold out for seven. What are these
various sacraments? Would you know what to do if you
attended a Catholic wedding or were asked to come to the
baptism of a Catholic friend's child?*

12 Who Is Mary?     151

*One of the most distinctive marks of Catholics is their devotion to Jesus' mother, Mary. Why is she so special to Catholics? How has she influenced Catholic life? Learn about the sightings of this woman at various places around the world and what draws millions of people to her shrines. How seriously do Catholics take these events?*

**Part 4:**     **Imagination and Prayer**     **163**

13 Feeding the Imagination     165

*Besides going to church, Catholics have a lot of external objects of worship around their homes, or in their pockets: rosaries, holy cards, statues, etc. Learn what a rosary is and what it means to Catholics. Some say this is the worship of idols. Hear how Catholics defend themselves against this.*

14 Catholic Prayers and Music: Tangible Poetry     177

*Did you know that Gregorian chant works at many levels to awaken the spirit and prepare the soul for worship? Just what is a rosary? Get in on the popularity of contemplative prayer.*

15 The Mass: The Catholics' Big Dinner Party     191

*Why has the Mass been the central ritual and gathering for Catholics for 2,000 years? What is all that standing and kneeling about? Can a non-Catholic guest feel okay about just sitting down and watching? What is all the hoopla about Communion? Is that real wine? What parts can you participate in and what parts can't you if you're not part of the tribe?*

**Part 5:**     **Catholic Identity: How Are Catholics Wired?**     **205**

16 It's a Tribe     207

*To an outsider, Catholics are often seen as having a superiority complex, as if theirs were the only true Church. Do Catholics really believe this? What is their esprit de corps that so many envy? Enter the world of Catholics: their parish life, their colleges, and their charitable institutions. Learn how to join the tribe and what it takes to maintain your status.*

17  The Teaching Church: More Than Just a Slap with
the Ruler                                                              219
*Learn about the two great sources of Catholic teaching:
Scripture and tradition. Find out how they work together
to create a distinctive Catholic profile. What about new ideas?
Who rocks the cradle of religious thought? How do you sort
the wheat from the chaff?*

18  The Catholic Church's Best-Kept Secret: Social Justice    231
*Catholics have a serious side that makes them take the
comings and goings of the world to heart. Is there a Catholic
sensibility that makes justice in the world a moral imperative? What is the difference between working for justice and
charity? The U.S. Catholic Church is becoming less European
and more Latin, and with this comes new gifts.*

19  The Teachings of the Church: Moving Beyond Sin            247
*Get the scoop on sins both large and small and find out if
there is really such a thing as Catholic guilt. We'll also
explore all about free will, the Devil, sexuality, and the
"consistent ethic of life." Catholic teachings concern not only
their members, but are often addressed to the world as a
whole. Learn what the Church is teaching and why it has
such an influence.*

20  The Church: Moving from Steeple to People                 259
*From* The Flying Nun *to* Bing Crosby *and* The Bells
of St. Mary's, *the public has certain ideas about nuns and
priests. This chapter will help you understand religious
orders. How are Jesuits different from Dominicans? What
do Franciscans do differently than Benedictines? Learn about
the bureaucrats and the Church's chain of command and
where the laity stands within the hierarchy in all this.*

Part 6:    **The Church's History**                                   273

21  The Roman Establishment                                   275
*Meet Constantine and find out how the Church moved
from underdog to top dog in the Roman Empire. Meet
St. Augustine, St. Patrick, and St. Boniface and learn
how Catholicism became French, English, Irish, German,
and Polish.*

22  Division, Debauchery, and Reform: The Church's
    Second Millennium                                    287
    *Catholicism had its dark side. Learn all about the scandals of*
    *the Middle Ages and how Christianity separated into Protes-*
    *tantism and Catholicism. Are Catholics really Christian?*
    *Learn how the Church got into trouble and how it learned*
    *from its mistakes.*

23  The Birth of the Church in the New Land              299
    *The conquistadors and Franciscans carried Catholicism*
    *to the New World. Learn about the miracle at Guadalupe*
    *that made Catholicism the religion of the people. How was*
    *a new race of people created? How is this new race shaping*
    *Catholicism in the United States?*

24  Catholics Earn Their Citizenship                     311
    *When Catholics first came to the United States, they were not*
    *welcome. See how each wave of immigrants brought their*
    *version of the Catholic story, and how they learned to pull*
    *together. Can a Catholic really be a good American? Did you*
    *know that 50 percent of U.S. Catholics are Hispanic?*

Part 7:  **A Look to the Future**                         **327**

25  Catholic Sexuality: The Church's Dirty Little Secret?  329
    *We look at the abuse and the attempted cover-ups by the*
    *Church's leaders and then face the question: how could this*
    *happen? We explore the history of Catholic sexuality and the*
    *development of a clerical culture to see its relation to a climate*
    *of abuse. We will examine a new sense of ownership of the*
    *religion people seem to be claiming out of this catastrophe and*
    *what it means to reclaim Catholicism.*

26  Face-to-Face in the Third Millennium: The Church
    Looks to the Future                                  339
    *You will discover that Catholics are a people in process, and*
    *here you'll learn how cultural shifts in consciousness are*
    *changing the way its members relate to the Church and how*
    *the Church relates to the world. Meet the new generation of*
    *Catholics, who are the sons and daughters of the old Roman*
    *Empire and the sons and daughters of the conquistadors and*
    *Indians. How will they carry the message into the future?*

**Appendixes**

A  Glossary                            355

B  Recommended Reading                 367

   Index                               377

# Contents

**Part 1: What's a Catholic?**    **1**

**1 Can You Judge a Catholic by the Cover?**    **3**

Why You Might Be Interested ............................................4

What Catholics Believe ....................................................5

  *Nicene Creed* ................................................................5

  *The Catholic Spirit* ........................................................5

  *The Richness of Catholic Tradition* ..................................7

  *Aren't All Catholics the Same?* ........................................8

  *You Know You're Pre–Vatican II If ...* ............................8

Same Church Different Pews ..............................................9

  *A New Perspective on an Old Church* ..............................10

What You Have to Do ....................................................10

  *From Law to Loving Response* ........................................11

The Classic Definition ....................................................12

**2 The People: Many Faces, Many Flags**    **15**

Would I Know One If I Saw One? ....................................15

  *Day of the Dead* ..........................................................16

  *An African American Mass* ............................................17

  *A Native American Parish* ..............................................18

  *The Taos Pueblo Catholic Church* ..................................19

So Where Would I Find a Catholic? ..................................20

  *The Americas: Close to Home* ........................................20

  *The Rest of the World* ..................................................22

  *Worldwide Catholic Population by Continent and Future*

    *Projections* ..............................................................23

**3 Catholicism: It's a Big Tent**    **25**

Image: The Power of the Press ..........................................25

  *Opus Dei: Working It Out with God* ................................26

  *Pro and Con* ................................................................27

  *Voice of the Faithful: Speaking Out* ................................28

  *Pro and Con* ................................................................29

From Bing to Bono ........................................................29

  *The Good Priest* ..........................................................30

  *Rock Star Meets Rock of the Church* ..............................30

From Bishop Sheen to Dan Berrigan ........................................31
   *The Good Ambassador* .................................................*32*
   *Religious Outlaw* ........................................................*32*
From Cesar Chavez to Clarence Thomas ..............................34
   *Grapes of Wrath* .........................................................*34*
   *Dirt Poor in Georgia to the Supreme Court* ..................*35*

**4   The Vatican: The Church That's a Country                    37**

Just Who Is the Pope? ...........................................................38
   *Upon This Rock ...* ....................................................*38*
   *Papal Thumbprints* ....................................................*39*
   *Infallibly Speaking ...* ...............................................*40*
   *What's His Address?* ..................................................*41*
   *Smoke Signals* ...........................................................*42*
   *Changes in Papal Election Process* ..............................*43*
   *The Beloved John Paul II* ...........................................*43*
   *New Pope in a New Millennium* .................................*44*
The Big Church and the Little Church ...................................45
Rules and Regulations ...........................................................45
   *The Ten Commandments* ............................................*46*
   *The Six Precepts* ........................................................*46*
   *The 1,752 Canons* ....................................................*47*
   *The Beatitudes* ..........................................................*47*
   *Conscience, Virtue, and Grace* ...................................*48*

**5   The '60s: Seeds of Revolution                               51**

The Stillness Before the Storm ..............................................52
   *Vatican II: A Radical Departure and a Rebirth* ...........*52*
   *Lighting the Council Fires* ..........................................*53*
   *The Altar Rail Comes Down, the Priest Turns Around* ....*55*
   *The Rosary Gives Way to the Bible* ............................*56*
Church as Listener ................................................................56
   *Science and Faith Reach a Compromise* .....................*57*
   *From the Sanctuary to Selma* .....................................*57*
Ecumenism: Catholics' Relationship to Other Christians ......58
   *Ecumenism Begins at Home* .......................................*58*
   *Expanding Interfaith Relationships* ............................*59*
   *We Throw Open Heaven's Gate: Religious Liberty* .......*59*
Conscience Reigns Supreme ..................................................60

A Painful Side Effect of Vatican II: Loss of Tradition ..............60

*Mea Culpa, Mea Culpa, Mea Maxima Culpa* ..........................61

*Shifting Prayers and Practices* ......................................61

*The Saints Suffer* ...................................................62

*Dress Code: Defrocking the Clerics* .................................62

*Numbers Tell the Story* .............................................63

**Part 2: Putting the "Ism" in Catholicism: Becoming Catholic, Becoming Different**    **65**

**6 "It's Elementary, My Dear Watson"**    **67**

Ritual: The Old Religion, Roots, and Renewal ........................68

*Elementally Speaking* ...............................................69

*A Visit to Antiquity* ...............................................69

"Yada, Yada, Yada" ..................................................71

*Paradise Lost, and Paradise Found* .................................72

*The Covenant* .......................................................73

*Moses Receives the Law* .............................................74

*A Summary of Jewish Influence* ......................................75

Influences of the Greeks, Romans, and Indigenous Peoples ....75

*The Greeks Decapitate the Mind from the Body* .......................75

*Roman Power and Might* ..............................................77

*Indigenous Peoples of Western Europe* ...............................78

*Cultural Influences* ................................................79

**7 The Bible**    **81**

Sacred Scriptures ...................................................81

*The Old Testament* ..................................................82

*The New Testament* ..................................................84

The Canon: How Are We Sure What Texts Are Sacred? ........86

*Catholic Beliefs Regarding the Bible* ...............................87

*What Place Does the Bible Hold for Catholics?* ......................88

*Catholics Can and Do Read the Bible* ................................89

All God's Children ..................................................90

*Correcting Mistakes of the Past* ....................................90

*Anti-Semitism* ......................................................90

*"In Our Time"* ......................................................91

*It's About Time* ....................................................92

**8   Jesus: Spirit of a New Religion                                      95**

How We Know What We Know About Jesus ........................96
*The Wellspring of Galilee* ...............................................*96*
*Jesus the Jew* ...........................................................*97*
The Key Stories of the Christians ...................................97
*Jesus' Birthday: Christmas* ...........................................*98*
*His Mission, Death, and Resurrection* ..........................*98*
*Pentecost: The Birthday of the Church* ........................*100*
Was Jesus the First Catholic? ......................................101
*The Core Beliefs* ....................................................*102*
*The Calling* ...........................................................*102*
Catholics Separate from the Jews ................................104
*The Martyrs* ..........................................................*104*
*Designing the Structures* ...........................................*106*
*The Desert Fathers and Mothers* ...............................*107*

**Part 3:   The Sensuous Side of Catholicism: How Catholics
Experience God                                      109**

**9   Catholic Imagination: The Sacred Space of Ritual        111**

What Is Ritual and Why Do Catholics "Do" It? ...................112
*Feeling the Faith* ...................................................*112*
*Walking and Talking with Jesus* ...............................*113*
The Theology of Catholic Ritual ...................................113
*Now You See Him, Now You Don't: How God Is Present* ..........*114*
*Catholic Symbol/Protestant Word* ...............................*114*
*Catholic Crucifix and Protestant Cross* .......................*116*
*The Touchy-Feely Stuff* ...........................................*116*
Imagination: Tasting, Touching, Smelling God ..................117
Sacred Elements: Air, Earth, Fire, and Water ..................118
*Earth: Ashes to Ashes and Dust to Dust* .......................*118*
*Air as Holy Spirit* .................................................*119*
*Holy Water and Holy Oil* .........................................*119*
*Fire, Symbol of Transformation* ................................*120*
When No One Is Watching ..........................................121

**10   Jesus: The Original Sacrament                             123**

Omnipresence: The Catholic Sacramental Principle ............124
Church as Sacrament ................................................125
*The Church, Jesus' Sensible Side* ..............................*125*
*Sacrament: Mediating Grace—Really!* ...........................*126*

Religion: The Marriage of Form and Spirit ...........................127
*Getting from Here to There* ...............................................127
*Community: The Kingdom of God Is Within (Us)* ..................128
*Sacramental Awareness* ...................................................129
Ignatius Loyola's Spiritual Exercises: A Journey into
Sensual Imagination ......................................................129

**11 Seven Sensual Sacraments** **133**

Baptism: More Than Just Water on the Head ......................134
*Water on the Head* ........................................................134
*Who Can Baptize?* .........................................................135
*The Origins of Baptism* ..................................................136
Eucharist: First Holy Communion ...................................136
*Eucharist: A Catholic's Thanksgiving* ...............................137
Confirmation: It's No Longer a Slap on the Face ................137
*Origins of the Sacrament of Confirmation* ..........................138
*Oil and Words and the Holy Spirit* ..................................138
*The Seven Gifts* .............................................................139
*Ménage à Trois:* It's More Than Just Two in a Marriage .........139
*I Do! I Do!* ...................................................................140
*A Covenant Relationship* ................................................140
*Forever Is a Long Time* ...................................................141
Holy Orders: More Than Just Oil on the Fingers ................142
*In the Beginning …* .......................................................142
*The Ceremony* ...............................................................143
*A Few Good Men* ...........................................................144
Penance: More Than Just a Kick in the Pants ....................144
*Confession Is Good for the Soul* ......................................145
*Sin, the "S" Word* .........................................................145
*The Little Black Box* ......................................................146
*Guilt: The Gift You Leave Behind* ...................................147
Anointing of the Sick: More Than a Simple Good-Bye .........148
*Three for the Price of One!* ..............................................148
*Healing Body and Soul* ...................................................149
*Transformation for the Community* ...................................149

**12  Who Is Mary?**                                                                     **151**

Do Catholics Worship Mary? ...............................................152
Mary, the People's Choice ...................................................152
  *Mary: Myth and Legend* .................................................*152*
  *Virgin and Mother: Not a Problem* .................................*153*
  *"Now and at the Hour of Our Death ..."* ........................*154*
Mary's Incomplete History ...................................................154
Council of Ephesus .............................................................155
  *Theotokos: Mother of God* ...............................................*156*
Apparitions: Here, There, and Everywhere ............................156
  *Lourdes: Healing Waters* ................................................*157*
  *Fatima: World Peace* .......................................................*158*
  *Our Lady of Guadalupe: Patron of the Americas* .............*158*
Feasts and Devotions to Mary ..............................................158
  *Immaculate Conception of Mary: December 8, and Mary's*
    *Birthday: September 8* .................................................*158*
  *The Annunciation: March 25, and the Visitation: May 31* ......*159*
  *Mary, Mother of God: January 1* ...................................*159*
  *The Assumption: August 15* ..........................................*160*
  *Our Lady of Guadalupe, Mother of the Americas:*
    *December 12* ................................................................*160*
  *May Altars* ...................................................................*160*

**Part 4:  Imagination and Prayer**                                           **163**

**13  Feeding the Imagination**                                                **165**

Sacramentals: Little Sacraments ..........................................165
  *Catholic Stuff: Statues, Holy Cards, and the Saints Go*
    *Marching In!* ................................................................*166*
  *Church Bells Chiming* ...................................................*168*
Sacramental Gestures .........................................................170
  *The Sign of the Cross* ....................................................*170*
  *Blessings for Everything!* ...............................................*171*
  *Hands, Knees, Heads, and Hats* ....................................*171*
  *Superstition or Sacred Tradition?* ..................................*172*
The Liturgical Calendar: Sacred Time ..................................173
  *Celebrating the Seasons* ................................................*174*
Celebrating the Final Journey ..............................................175

**14  Catholic Prayers and Music: Tangible Poetry**                    **177**

Personal Prayer ..................................................................178
The Rosary .......................................................................179
   *Origins of the Rosary* .....................................................*179*
   *How to Say the Rosary* ...................................................*180*
   *The Prayers of the Rosary* ...............................................*181*
   *The Twenty Mysteries of the Rosary* ..................................*182*
   *When Is the Rosary Said?* ...............................................*184*
Monasteries, Mysticism, and Contemplative Prayer ..............184
   *Mystic Roll Call!* ...........................................................*184*
   *Monasticism: The Great Getaway* ......................................*185*
   *Mysticism Today* ...........................................................*186*
Liturgy of the Hours ........................................................186
Sacred Music ...................................................................188
   *How Sacred Music Functions* ...........................................*188*

**15  The Mass: The Catholics' Big Dinner Party**                     **191**

Celebration or Sacrifice: What Is the Mass? ........................192
The Liturgy of the Word ...................................................193
   *Gathering: The People Arrive* ...........................................*193*
   *Proclaiming: The Word of God* .........................................*194*
   *Reflecting: a Word to the Wise* .........................................*194*
   *The Prayers Go Out Over the Land* ...................................*195*
The Liturgy of the Eucharist ..............................................195
   *There's No Free Lunch!* ..................................................*195*
   *Blessing the Bread* .........................................................*196*
   *Breaking the Bread* ........................................................*198*
The Eucharist: Feeding the Flock .......................................199
   *Is It Real, or Is It "Memorex"?* ........................................*199*
   *The Meaning of Sacrifice* .................................................*200*
Here's the Church, and Here's the Steeple, Open the
Doors, and See All the People! .........................................201
   *Sacred Spaces* ...............................................................*201*
   *Putting on Your Glad Rags* ..............................................*202*
   *Who's Who at a Catholic Mass* .........................................*203*
   *Guess Who's Coming to Dinner: Is It Just for Catholics?* .........*204*

**Part 5:** **Catholic Identity: How Are Catholics Wired?** **205**

**16** **It's a Tribe** **207**

Where the Tribe Meets .................................................................207
*Center for Belonging* ...............................................................*208*
*Center for Prayer and Sacraments* ........................................*208*
*Launching Pad to the World* .................................................*209*
Catholics' Social Face .................................................................210
*Catholic Health Care: More Than Chicken Soup for the Soul* ....*210*
*Catholic Colleges: Rocking the Cradle of Thought* .................*211*
*Catholic Charities: More Than Just a Handout* .....................*212*
*Missing the Mark* ...................................................................*212*
Getting In and Out of the Tribe ...............................................213
*Joining Catholicism, Not a Quick Study* ...............................*213*
*Excommunication* ....................................................................*215*
*Maintaining Status: How Catholic Do You Have to Be?* ..........*216*
*Broken Relationships: Recovering Catholics* ...........................*216*

**17** **The Teaching Church: More Than Just a Slap with the Ruler** **219**

The Sources of the Church's Teaching: Scripture and
Tradition .....................................................................................220
*Keeping the Faith* ...................................................................*220*
*Tradition: More Shall Be Revealed* ........................................*220*
*The Catechism* .........................................................................*221*
Theology: Faith Seeking Reason ...............................................222
*Classical Theology* ..................................................................*223*
*Getting Grounded: Contemporary Theology* ...........................*224*
Bargains from the Border: Liberation Theology and Base
Communities ...............................................................................224
*The Mirror of Change* ............................................................*225*
*Church in the 'Hood* ...............................................................*226*
*Prophetically Speaking ...* .......................................................*227*
Stirring the Pot of Change .........................................................228
*The Dynamic Triangle: The People, Theologians, and Bishops* ....*229*

**18** **The Catholic Church's Best-Kept Secret: Social Justice** **231**

Lucy's Enlightenment ................................................................231
Charitable Work and Social Activism ......................................232
*Justice: A Community Effort* ...................................................*233*
*Bishop Lobbyists* .....................................................................*233*

Religion and Politics: Beyond Polite Conversation ...............234
  *God and Caesar* ..........................................................*234*
  *Empowering the Laity* .................................................*235*
The Nine Themes in Catholic Social Teaching ....................236
  *The Dignity of Every Person and Human Rights* ....................*239*
  *Solidarity, Common Good, and Participation* .......................*239*
  *Family Life* ...............................................................*240*
  *Subsidiarity and the Proper Role of Government* ...................*240*
  *Property Ownership in Modern Society: Rights and
    Responsibilities* .....................................................*241*
  *The Dignity of Work, Rights of Workers, and Support for
    Labor Unions* .........................................................*241*
  *Colonialism and Economic Development* ............................*241*
  *Peace and Disarmament* ...............................................*242*
  *Option for the Poor and Vulnerable* .................................*242*
Dorothy Day and The Catholic Worker Movement .............243
  *Dorothy Day's Legacy for Today's Catholic Worker* .................*244*
Conclusion: The Church Today .........................................244

**19  The Teachings of the Church: Moving Beyond Sin          247**

Sin: Missing the Mark ......................................................248
  *Categories of Sins: Specks and Logs* ................................*248*
Human Sexuality: "Male and Female He Created Them" ......250
  *Birth Control: The Church's Big Headache* ..........................*250*
  *Natural Family Planning: It's Not Your Grandma's
    Calendar* ..............................................................*251*
  *Homosexuality: Yes and No* ...........................................*252*
The Seamless Garment ......................................................253
  *Euthanasia: Say No to Dr. Death* ...................................*254*
  *Can War Be Justified?* ...............................................*254*
  *Abortion: When Life Begins* ..........................................*256*
  *Capital Punishment: A Call to Reconciliation* ......................*257*

**20  The Church: Moving from Steeple to People          259**

A Call to Hierarchical Communion .....................................260
The Unified Church ..........................................................261
  *Who's Who in the Church* .............................................*261*
  *Bishops: Shepherds of the Flocks* ...................................*262*
  *The Roman Curia* ......................................................*262*
Vocation: No Family Is Complete Without One ...................263
  *Priests: The Guys on the Front Line* .................................*263*

Religious Orders: Know Your Players ...........................264

*Becoming Monks, Nuns, and Brothers* ........................265

*Benedictines: Behind Closed Doors* ............................266

*The Rule of St. Francis* ............................................266

*Dominicans: Telling It Like It Is* ..............................267

*Jesuits: The Pope's Foot Soldiers* ..............................268

Lay Vocation: What About the Rest of the Folks? .................268

*There Is a Job for Everyone* .....................................269

*Faith in Action* ....................................................270

## Part 6:   The Church's History                              273

### 21   The Roman Establishment                               275

From Underdog to Top Dog ......................................275

*Constantine: The Church Gets a Break* .......................276

*Augustine: Lover and Loser* .....................................278

Christianity Comes to Your Hometown ........................280

*Monasticism: Attraction Rather Than Promotion* .............280

*St. Patrick: Three Cheers for the Irish* .......................281

*German Christianity* ..............................................283

From Rationality to Mysticism ..................................284

A New Empire Is Born ...........................................284

### 22   Division, Debauchery, and Reform: The Church's Second
Millennium                                                    287

Catholic and Orthodox: The Church's Y1K Problem ...........288

Catholicism's Dark Side ..........................................289

*Crusades: Holy War or War on the Holy?* ....................289

*Good Out of Evil* .................................................290

*Inquisition: Ask Me No Questions, and I'll Tell You No Lies!* ....291

*Indulge Me, One More Time* .....................................292

Problems, Protest, and Protestants .............................293

*Martin Luther: The Hammer Heard 'Round the World* ..........294

*Henry VIII: Love and Marriage* ................................294

Trendy Trent: Going to Reform School .........................295

*Scripture and Tradition Upheld* ................................295

*Lines Drawn: Them and Us* ......................................295

The Church Turns Its Face to the New World ..................296

**23 The Birth of the Church in the New Land** **299**

Colonization: Ready or Not, Here We Come! ........................300
*Europe Comes to Mexico* ......................................*300*
*The Beliefs of the Indigenous People* .......................*302*
*Spanish America* ..............................................*302*
*Missions and Conversion* ......................................*304*
A New People Emerges ............................................305
*The Brown Lady of Guadalupe* ................................*305*
*La Nueva Raza: The New Race* ...............................*307*
Cultural Contributions to Today's Catholicism ..................308

**24 Catholics Earn Their Citizenship** **311**

Catholicism and Colonial America: There Goes the
Neighborhood! ..................................................312
*Breaking Into the Protestant Club* ...........................*312*
*Catholics and the Revolution* .................................*313*
Coming in Droves: The Immigrant Experience ....................314
*Potatoes, Poverty, and Discrimination: The Irish in America* ....*314*
*Sauerkraut and Sausages: Germanic Education and Liturgy* ....*315*
*Poles: Pierogi and Patriotism* ...............................*316*
*Italians: Pasta and Festa* ....................................*317*
*African Americans: Soul Food, Clapping, and Justice* .............*318*
A Checkered Church Solidifies ..................................320
*Catholic Prosperity* .........................................*321*
*The Loss of Innocence* .......................................*322*
Catholics Come of Age ..........................................323
*Movin' on Up* ................................................*323*
*The Transference of Leadership: The Baton Is Passed* ...........*324*

**Part 7: A Look to the Future** **327**

**25 Catholic Sexuality: The Church's Dirty Little Secret?** **329**

Sex, Lies, and Vatican Tapes ...................................330
*"Safe" Sex: Cover-up by Bishops* .............................*330*
*Is Sex Abuse a Catholic Issue?* ..............................*330*
Our Legacy: Dualism and the Mind/Body Split ....................331
*The Soul of a Cleric: Anthony and Augustine* .................*331*
*Celibacy's Slippery Slope* ...................................*332*
*Spawning Ground for Sin Legislation* .........................*332*
*Sex Education: "Thou Shalt Not ..."* ..........................*333*

Clericalism: The Secret Culture .................................................334
 *The Power of Secrecy* ........................................................*334*
 *Bishops: Stewards and Shepherds* ......................................*335*
 *Peeking Under the Cleric's Robe* .......................................*335*
 *Protecting Patriarchal Power* .............................................*336*
Sexual Imagination (Thou Shall ...) ......................................337
 *The Paradox: Lousy Laws, Good Sex* ..................................*337*

**26 Face-to-Face in the Third Millennium: The Church Looks to the Future**   **339**
Recap: Past, Present, and Future ............................................340
 *The Tectonic Plates Shift* ..................................................*340*
The Church Is One ................................................................342
 *The Church's Unified Vision* ...............................................*342*
 *Unified Vision Interrupted* .................................................*342*
 *Women in the Wings* .........................................................*342*
 *Letting Justice Roll Down* ..................................................*343*
The Church Is Holy ...............................................................344
 *Spirit on the Rise* .............................................................*344*
The Church Is Catholic ..........................................................345
 *Universal: All Over the Map* ...............................................*346*
 *Speaking a Universal Language* ..........................................*346*
The Church Is Apostolic .........................................................347
 *Partnership: From Power Over to Empowerment* ...................*348*
 *Sharing the Bread* .............................................................*348*
The New Generations: Passing the Cup .................................349
 *Post–Vatican II Generation: Anglos* ....................................*350*
 *The Latino Generation* ......................................................*351*
 *Quantum Generation: Generation Q: Identity Chosen,*
  *Not Commanded* ............................................................*352*
Incarnation: Celebrating Life ................................................353
In Conclusion ......................................................................353

**Appendixes**

**A Glossary**   **355**

**B Recommended Reading**   **367**

 **Index**   **377**

# Foreword

During the confirmation proceedings of Justice Samuel Alito, the Senate Hearing Committee probed his life extensively to learn about him as a person and as a judge in order to see how he might vote as a Supreme Court Justice. His family background and education were scrutinized. Opinions he rendered on the bench were reviewed. Theoretical cases were presented to see the direction he would take in solving them. Some members of the committee challenged his answers on incendiary issues in hopes of getting him to commit one way or other on them. Unlike other hearings of Supreme Court nominees, character witnesses were also introduced at his hearing. In essence, the hearings were an effort to uncover Judge Samuel Alito's Weltanschauung, his worldview, and what exactly in it is influencing him.

*The Complete Idiot's Guide to Understanding Catholicism, Third Edition,* can rightly be called a Weltanschauung—an all-encompassing worldview of Catholicism and the principal parts that make up its whole. It delves into history, case studies, precedents, and traditions. It reviews the development of theology and how we have come to understand God, a sacramental life, and the role Mary plays in the Church. It discusses the theology, philosophy, sociology, and anthropology that are needed to understand its teachings, its leaders, and its culture. It explores its revered tradition of spirituality, recalling the contribution of saints, as well as addressing popular religiosity and pluralism that are generated at the grass roots.

Wherever there are inspiring theology, philosophy, and spirituality, there is also a burning desire to restore human dignity and champion social justice. All of this, and more, is contained in this book.

Although Judge Samuel Alito is one individual person, if we looked deeply into his soul, we would find that over time there were two or three other conflicting voices within him causing conflicts, doubts, mistakes, and regrets. This is part of life, and it is also an integral part of the life of the Catholic Church. To truthfully understand the whole of Catholicism, its inner conflicts, flaws, and regrets are likewise contained in this book.

One other very important observation about this book is in order here. When I was a young priest, I used to drive through farmlands on the way to my parents' home. Even though the scenery was absolutely beautiful, it had a sameness to it. One day, while driving the same road, the rays of the sun were such that I noticed for the first time a picturesque country church and its quaint cemetery. Suddenly the whole countryside took on a new look. I had a Gestalt, an "ah ha" experience of seeing what I had always seen, but now in a new light. The church and its cemetery popped out at me in 3-D, creating new forms of life out of an old setting.

Due to an extensive education, I have studied and experienced much of what is in this book. Thanks to the way it presents Catholicism, I have had many new refreshing "ah ha's" never before experienced. Well-educated Catholics as well as those knowing nothing about the Catholic Church who read this book are in for the same awesome experience.

—Rev. Eugene Hemrick

Director of the National Institute for the Renewal of the Priesthood at the Washington Theological Union

# Foreword

The best way of introducing this marvelous book, which I know will enrich the life of anyone who reads it, is by exploring it in terms of why I love being a Catholic. This is the religion of my parents and ancestors, and it connects me with the very origins of my life and existence.

Being a Catholic is great fun, and this book celebrates the fun of this religion. Jesus started his public ministry with the feast at Cana—enjoying himself with family, friends, and other guests. Throughout his life, he loved going to the festivals in Jerusalem and having a good time with anyone and everyone. Mexican Catholicism is festive. It allows us to experience in very vivid ways the deepest mysteries of our faith, of God's love for us, of the life of Jesus, the Son of God made human for us, Mary, the sorrowful mother, and the saints who were sinners like us but achieved great virtue. For every mystery of the faith, there is a festive and elaborate celebration allowing us to enter into the mystery as if it was taking place in our own backyard.

Catholicism is colorful, it's sensual, it's emotional, it's dramatic, and it's fun. As this book helps you see, you can take part and benefit from the great celebrations of the faith like Guadalupe, Christmas Posadas, Midnight Mass, Ash Wednesday, Holy Week rituals, Day of the Dead, and many others. These popular festive celebrations allow anyone and everyone to enter into a collective mystical experience of the sacred as it is present among us here and now today.

The book tells you how Catholics have so many ways of being in touch with God throughout the day wherever we happen to be. Medals, holy cards, scapulars, rosaries, holy water, candles, home shrines, and other simple things put us in immediate contact with God, just like the picture of a loved one in my wallet helps to put me in their presence even when they are far away or even gone to heaven. These simple objects allow us, as the book points out, to touch God and feel God's touch even when we don't know much about God.

I love being a Catholic because much more than a religion, it seems to be a large, extended family—or as the book says, a tribe! We find ourselves at home wherever we go in the world, and even though the language and some of the details may be different, the basic symbols are the same and we immediately recognize ourselves to be among family. When people travel or migrate to other countries, we can immediately find a religious home in a local Catholic church.

I love being a Catholic because our Catholic story, as this book does such a good and balanced job of saying, is so human and divine at the same time. Human because of the many crazy, stupid, weird, and even cruel things we have done, as well as the many heroic acts and movements of charity, mercy, and compassion. Through all this weakness, I see all the good and beautiful things the Church has done throughout history and continues to do today: orphanages, lepresoriums, schools, universities, hospitals, community-organizing, social justice initiatives, visitation of the sick, aid to immigrants, and so on.

*The Complete Idiot's Guide to Understanding Catholicism, Third Edition,* is wonderful and stimulating. It is brief while exposing substantial matter in an attractive way. I am honored to have been asked to introduce this book, which will definitely reach many more people than some of the best theological works or even the official catechism of the Catholic Church. It is written in a simple and attractive way, it is easy and exciting to read, and the authors have managed to distill and condense very technical matter into a very cohesive book.

—Father Virgilio Elizondo
The Mexican American Cultural Center, San Antonio, Texas

# Introduction

The book you are about to read is perhaps one of a kind—the only book of this breadth about the Catholic Church written from the perspective of the people. This isn't an official rulebook about Catholic laws and rules—it is about *Catholic culture*. It's written by two cradle Catholics, both professionals in the Church but not ordained clergy. We did not seek an *imprimatur*, the official approval stamp of the Church, because the focus of this book is on the practice of the religion by the people in the pews. It isn't being offered as a definitive teaching of Church law—for that, readers are directed to the *Catechism of the Catholic Church*. However, the book contains an accurate account of beliefs and practices as well as offering an explanation of the meanings. For example, it tackles matters like what is ritual and why do Catholics prefer it to preaching, the belief in sacred "presence," and what is church, anyway? Is it a building with a steeple, an organization in Rome, or a community of people—or all three?

*The Complete Idiot's Guide to Understanding Catholicism, Third Edition*, is doing what the title suggests, making a complex and sometimes incomprehensible religion understandable—hopefully with perspective and humor, something no one has attempted to do before. In doing that we offer a comprehensive discussion of the Church, detailed in the following paragraphs, and also provide a fair look at areas where the tension between laity and clergy is the greatest.

This book offers a look inside the experience of being Catholic. It hopes to increase understanding about a religion that is known all over the world, yet is still mystifying and even downright baffling to many. It contains a history of the Catholic Church—its beginnings in the Middle East, its growth in Europe, its arrival into the Americas, and its trip north to the United States, where the book has its prime focus. It includes a fascinating look into the rich sacramental life of the Church and an exploration of basic beliefs and how they came to be part of Catholic doctrine. It explains the various offices of the Church from the parish to the Vatican and how each works to create a unified Catholic Church—but a Church that also has many different ways of expressing faith.

The story of the modern-day Church hinges on the Second Vatican Council, which took place in the early 1960s. Both authors grew up in the pre–Vatican II years and have seen many of the changes from the council as well as proposed changes that have fallen by the wayside. Much of what continues to constitute Catholicism in the cultural imagination and in the minds of Catholics, too, is rooted in the pre–Vatican II Church. Despite the common misunderstanding that all Catholics think alike or that the Church never changes, councils show differently. It is impossible to understand today's Catholic Church without looking at it both before and after the only council of modern time—the only Church council since 1870.

A similar point of differentiation exists between the Church's lay members and the clergy—often leaving members and leaders existing in parallel universes. At the same time, not all clergy think alike. You have those who are pushing for change, those who want to keep things as they are, and those who want to roll things back. In a Church whose membership is at least 50 percent female, and the majority of its male population is married and raising families, but with an all-male, celibate clergy, differences of opinion and of priority are going to happen! And one must consider that this is a worldwide Church that includes members from every continent, with all their inherent cultural diversity, levels and types of education, and forms of governing. That Church leadership has managed to keep us all, if not on one page, at least singing out of the same hymnal is a miracle in itself.

For most of the 2,000-year history of the church, the hierarchy, speaking through its office, has been the official voice. And it remains the official voice, but its ability to effectively speak for its diverse population is a challenge today. Dialogue between the people and their leaders is increasing in some geographic areas and being impeded in others. For the most part, members who disagree with how the hierarchy does business aren't willing to walk; they see Church as the *people*—all of the people. Rather than seeing "the Church" as a third party or as an institutional entity of the leaders, these folks see the people as the living, breathing Body of Christ, which the buildings and administrative offices serve. If the hierarchy closes ranks, it may find the majority of its members still in the circle and still holding different views! Someone once said that you can throw people out of the family, but you can't throw them out of the family tree. The Church is like that.

In presenting this story, we maintain that differences are normal and make for a healthy, vigorous organization. Legitimate debate has (at least) two sides and both have merit. This book does not attempt to answer age-old questions but to present a balanced look at areas of contention where it has reached the level of public awareness. There are those who uphold tradition and those who push for change; it is the very dance of creation!

Our second edition looked at the Church from the perspective of its humanness—a Church in process. This third edition will continue in that spirit, looking at the journey through compassionate eyes and at least a little wisdom.

# What You'll Discover in This Book

The book is divided into seven parts:

**Part 1, "What's a Catholic?"** provides a profile of Catholics and a peek at their practices and prayers. You'll get inside the workings of the Vatican and learn all about the Church's revolution, Vatican II.

**Part 2, "Putting the 'Ism' in Catholicism: Becoming Catholic, Becoming Different,"** explores the roots of Catholicism in the earth, the Bible, and in Jesus, and Catholicism's emergence as a religion.

**Part 3, "The Sensuous Side of Catholicism: How Catholics Experience God,"** lets you in on the way Catholics taste, touch, hear, smell, and see God through their sacramental practices and how Catholics experience Jesus. In this part, you'll learn all about Mary and Catholics' relationship to her.

**Part 4, "Imagination and Prayer,"** takes you into the world of Catholics, their statues and holy cards, their liturgical cycle of seasons, their Rosary, their sacred music, their contemplative life, and most important, the Mass.

**Part 5, "Catholic Identity: How Are Catholics Wired?"** looks at the center of Catholic life: its parishes and its schools and charities. You'll find out about key Catholic teachings and who determines them. You'll learn about the Church's best-kept secret, its powerful teachings on social justice. You'll meet the hierarchy of the Church as well as its foot soldiers.

**Part 6, "The Church's History,"** begins with a visit to the Roman Empire and looks at important people who had a hand in shaping the early Church. You will see the Church grow and struggle through the Middle Ages. You'll hear all about the miracle that brought Catholicism to the New World.

**Part 7, "A Look to the Future,"** takes up the challenges that the Church faces in the third millennium. First, we look at the future for women in leadership. Then you'll see how the center of gravity for the Church moved from Europe to Africa, Latin America, and Asia, and meet a new generation of Catholics who will carry the Church into the future. Finally, we look at the sex scandals that are currently shaking up the Church and shocking the community. We look at deeper issues about Church structure that may (or may not) contribute to a climate where abuse can fester. And we'll look at the potential for a "new" kind of Catholic and a "new" kind of Church to emerge out of the rubble.

In the appendixes, we have included information that will provide you with some interesting and useful details. There is a glossary for you to quickly check terms used in the book. There is a list of the books and sources we have drawn from and others that you might find helpful for further reading.

## Helpful Hints for the Reader

Throughout the text, you will find helpful and interesting information to spice up your journey through Catholicism.

> ### S'ter Says
> The Catholic religion has a language of its own. Information provided in this sidebar will give you a quick grasp of terms that may be new to you.

> ### Epiphanies
> These boxes offer a quick study of interesting Catholic tidbits. Use this information as a resource to impress your Catholic friends.

> ### For Heaven's Sake
> This information is designed to help keep you on the straight and narrow and alert you to common misunderstandings about the Church.

> ### Your Guardian Angel
> The Catholic Church is known for its mysterious practices. These boxes contain suggestions for the reader on how to easily participate regardless of whether you are a believer, along with helpful tips.

> ### Saints Preserve Us
> In these boxes, you'll learn the stories of some well-known and not-so-well-known saints, their feast days, and who and what they watch over.

## Acknowledgments

We've got a lot of people to thank. Some of the ones who were indispensable were Linda Roghaar, our agent; Suzanne LeVert, our primary editor; Jim Mallett, our religious editor; and Dan O'Gorman, our historical editor. We had great technical help from Dean Caskey, our personal photographer; Valerie Harrell, who did our graphics; Cherri Kowalchuk and Matt Lohmeier, our Gen X'ers; and Scott Weiss, who untangled the computer. We had special consultation from Margaret Ann Crain, Jack Seymour, Joe Glab, Sheila Bourelly, and Lynn Westfield. Our perspectives in writing this book were greatly influenced by two people who have made major contributions to the study of Catholicism: Andrew M. Greeley, professor of Social Science, University of Chicago, and Virgilio Elizondo, founder of the Mexico-American Cultural Center, San Antonio, Texas.

Our families and friends helped us, too, including Mary Lou, Tim, John, Lucile (who prayed a lot), Elizabeth, Susan, John, Martha Leigh, Dorothy, Lilyleone, Noris, Claudia (for picking up the slack at the office), Paul Dokecki, and Bob Newbrough (for patience and support), The Ladies of Nashville Circle, and Darby.

Our thanks also go to all the words and thoughts of others both written and spoken that have worked their way into this book.

## Special Thanks to the Technical Reviewer

*The Complete Idiot's Guide to Understanding Catholicism, Third Edition*, was reviewed by an expert who double-checked the accuracy of what you'll learn here, to help us ensure that this book gives you everything you need to know about Catholicism. Special thanks are extended to Rev. James K. Mallett, pastor of Christ the King Church, Nashville, Tennessee.

## Trademarks

All terms mentioned in this book that are known to be or are suspected of being trademarks or service marks have been appropriately capitalized. Alpha Books and Penguin Group (USA) Inc. cannot attest to the accuracy of this information. Use of a term in this book should not be regarded as affecting the validity of any trademark or service mark.

# Part 1

# What's a Catholic?

A pop image of Catholics exists in the world of movies, television, and books: the Irish cop, the spunky nun, and a priest who refuses to break the seal of confession. Nostalgic remembrances, stereotypes, prejudice, and just plain curiosity surround this somewhat mysterious religion. How powerful is the Vatican? What really happened at the Council in the 1960s? We'll look at what is fact and what is fiction regarding Catholics and their practices.

There also exists an image of the Catholic Church as a political, social, and economic force in society. In most cities, there is an abundance of Catholic institutions: schools, hospitals, homes for the aged, and other vital social agencies. The Church exists in many countries and among many nationalities. It has a colorful mix of cultures.

# Can You Judge a Catholic by the Cover?

## In This Chapter

♦ What does it mean to be in the Catholic Tribe?

♦ The essential Catholic beliefs

♦ What about Catholic Spirit?

♦ What Catholics do and don't do

♦ The classic definition of Catholic

Can you identify Catholics by how they look, what they believe, or how they act in the world? One way of answering this question is to point to the great diversity that exists within the religion. Yet Catholicism also exists as a distinct culture, almost tribal. For many it forms a deep identity that goes all the way to the bone; intrinsic to their sense of being. The Catholic Church is the kind of church that if you ever leave it, you never leave it behind; you forever bear its mark.

There is an "insider and outsider" character to the Church, captured by the language, rituals, songs, and beliefs of the religion, all of which serve to make Catholics distinct from other groups. Probably the best answer to the question "Can you judge a Catholic by his or her cover?" is to say sometimes yes and sometimes no.

This chapter highlights how Catholics are both of one mind regarding the beliefs of the religion and also of different minds in how those beliefs are interpreted and expressed in the world. Hopefully it will give you a better sense of who Catholics are today.

# Why You Might Be Interested

The Catholic Church was the common ground for Christian denominations for over a thousand years. It has played a major role in the development of Western culture, and continues to be influential in matters of religion, social institutions, and politics. The recent death of Pope John Paul II occupied the front pages of newspapers all over the globe, and the whole world awaited the election of his successor. (There is more on this prestigious office in Chapter 4.)

The Vatican has diplomatic relations with almost every country in the world and the pope receives weekly visits by heads of state (as well as rock stars and rappers). John Paul II's frequent trips were legendary, drawing dramatic crowds everywhere, from Uganda to Uruguay, from Paris to Papua New Guinea. He traveled to more than 129 different countries, logging more than 750,000 frequent-flyer miles, which is approximately three times the distance to the moon. According to estimates, between his election to the papacy in 1978 and his death in 2004, more than 17 million people attended his weekly audiences in Rome.

Every cityscape around the world reveals churches, hospitals, schools, office buildings, and cemeteries that are statements of the Catholic presence in the culture. Catholicism is a religion with a high media profile. Hardly a week goes by that it's not in the news. From protests of the 1960s, when men and women in Roman collars and black-and-white habits stood with civil-rights protesters in Alabama to the annual journey up the steps of the Supreme Court where Catholics protest the decision legalizing abortion, this faith is visible to the world.

Unfortunately, not all the publicity has been good. In recent years, sex abuse scandals have had a huge impact on Catholics and others as well. Many look to the Vatican and wonder about the silence.

Despite its failures, it's a fascinating faith that has held a vast number of people together for 2,000 years.

# What Catholics Believe

Throughout this book, we'll be exploring the religious beliefs and practices of the Catholic faith in some detail, but a concise version is contained in the creed named for the Council of Nicaea (325 C.E.). It's part of the Liturgy of Catholic Mass, and expresses beliefs most Christians hold in common.

## Nicene Creed

We believe in one God, the Father, the Almighty, maker of heaven and earth, of all that is seen and unseen.

We believe in one Lord, Jesus Christ, the only Son of God, eternally begotten of the Father, God from God, Light from Light, true God from true God, begotten, not made, one in Being with the Father. Through him all things were made. For us men and for our salvation he came down from heaven: by the power of the Holy Spirit he was born of the Virgin Mary, and became man.

For our sake he was crucified under Pontius Pilate; he suffered, died, and was buried. On the third day he rose again in fulfillment of the Scriptures; he ascended into heaven and is seated at the right hand of the Father. He will come again in glory to judge the living and the dead, and his kingdom will have no end.

We believe in the Holy Spirit, the Lord, the giver of life, who proceeds from the Father and the Son. With the Father and the Son he is worshipped and glorified. He has spoken through the Prophets. We believe in one holy catholic and apostolic Church. We acknowledge one baptism for the forgiveness of sins. We look for the resurrection of the dead, and the life of the world to come.

## The Catholic Spirit

Catholics believe the Bible contains sacred revelation from God and from it they draw their faith and morality. Catholics believe God is present in the world and throughout all creation. This is known as God's immanence. At the same time, God is bigger and more inclusive than creation—God is transcendent. Catholics' devotional life centers on bridging that gap and reinforcing God's availability and presence to the people.

The following list shows Catholic characteristics, some of which are shared with other Christians.

♦ A shared history and common traditions

♦ A hierarchical governing structure with obedience to the pope regarding matters of faith

♦ The use of prescribed rituals called sacraments and a strong commitment to Holy Communion

♦ A belief in Mary, the mother of God, as intercessor, and reverence for the saints

♦ A rich tradition of spirituality and contemplative prayer, monasticism, and religious orders

♦ The use of statues, pictures, and other religious and artistic symbols and a shared tradition of music

♦ A deep appreciation for both faith as a set of beliefs that are not approached through pure reason and reason as a means of faith

♦ An emphasis on community as an essential ingredient of the faith journey

♦ A social doctrine based on the dignity of the human person

♦ A sense of responsibility for social justice and outreach

**For Heaven's Sake**

Beware of genuflecting Catholics! They often go down on one knee before taking their seat in church. A Baptist woman was invited by her prospective mother-in-law to attend Mass. She had never been inside a Catholic church, and was trying to take it all in as she followed her mom-to-be up the aisle. Suddenly, without any warning, the mother-in-law stopped and genuflected before entering the pew. The visitor fell over her, knocking her down, and both of them spilled out across the floor. What an introduction to an already formidable situation!

Miracles, personal visions, and other extraordinary religious experiences catch the imagination of the media, but are actually quite rare and must undergo a long and involved documentation to be accepted. Even when they are authenticated, such as the events at Fatima or Lourdes, they do not occupy a central place in Catholic worship. People can believe in them or not. (You can find out more about the miracles at Fatima and Lourdes in Chapter 12.)

Catholics believe in both grace (the gift of God's presence in our life) and our own good nature. Redemption does not come through belief in God alone; faith and good works are necessary as well. One way this belief takes form is through the social action of Catholics. Chapter 17 has much more on this.

## The Richness of Catholic Tradition

Tradition as used in the term *Catholic tradition* has two meanings. For example, there are many traditions such as practices and prayers in the Catholic world. And it is also used to describe official beliefs of the Catholic Church, as in *Catholic tradition*. Catholic tradition is the recorded articles of faith discerned by the Church's teaching authorities. It is drawn from the collective faith experience of the people.

Although Catholic tradition might appear to move slowly, is not static (fixed); it is always dynamic (in process). It is open to the new scholarly work of theologians, new witness of prophetic voices of the people, and the insight of the leadership. While the Church sometimes finds itself at odds with the world of science, in the bigger picture there is the belief that science can (and eventually will) lead to God.

> **S'ter Says**
>
> **Tradition** is both the process of handing down the faith to others and the material that has been handed down. Tradition refers to the Scriptures, Church doctrines, writings of the Church teachers, and the liturgical life of the Church down through the centuries; additionally, tradition refers to the everyday customs and practices of the Church.

"Catholic" and "guilt" are sometimes believed to be synonymous, but the Church is not a "hell-scared" religion. For example, you will find a variety of views regarding the Catholic interpretation of heaven, hell, sin, and redemption, from a narrow perspective to a broader one. Pope John Paul II himself reminded followers that hell was not a piece of real estate, but was the suffering of realizing the full implications of separation from God.

For most clergy as well as the regular folks, evil is recognized as a reality, but the physical world is seen as sacred, rather than "wicked." Creation is good because it is infused with God's sacred Spirit as the Creator and sustainer. His presence as the resurrected Christ dwells with all humanity through the power of the Holy Spirit.

## Aren't All Catholics the Same?

If you ask any Catholic what he or she believes, you will hear as many different answers as people you have asked. Beliefs, like people, come in a lot of different shapes and sizes. Beliefs are about faith, and faith is a process—it grows and changes. Although most Christians hold very similar beliefs, one of the differences between Catholics and other Christians is a faith in the Church itself. Catholics believe that the Church has the divine authority to discern God's will and is the guardian of the basic truths of the religion, described earlier as Catholic tradition.

Catholics believe that the Church is the continuation of Jesus' presence through the Holy Spirit and that the Church holds the authority—through its leaders, the pope and the bishops—to teach and continue to discern the will of God.

Church councils are called periodically for the purpose of discerning, defining, and refining tradition. The most recent one was Vatican II, held in the middle of the twentieth century, for the purpose of refocusing the Church, making corrections in the course set in place in the first Vatican council of 1870 and the council before that, Trent (1545–1563). Vatican II changed how modern Catholics (both leaders and laypeople) interpret traditional beliefs and act upon them—it brought the Catholic Church into modern time.

## You Know You're Pre–Vatican II If …

The impact of Vatican II on Catholic life will be explored further as we go. But for now, the following check list lets you know which side of history you're on.

You're so pre–Vatican II if …

- ◆ You have a St. Christopher medal in your car.

- ◆ You know more than 15 recipes for preparing tuna fish.

- ◆ You bury a statue of St. Joseph upside down in your yard when you are selling your house.

- ◆ You can name all of Ethel Kennedy's kids.

- ◆ You name your first daughter Mary.

- ◆ You reach in your pocket for your handkerchief to cover a sneeze, and your rosary falls out.

- ◆ You still think twice about ordering a steak on Friday.

- You refer to other religions as "non-Catholic."

- You have mistakenly genuflected before taking your seat in the theater.

- You put J.M.J. at the top of your expense report before turning it in to your boss.

- You make the sign of the cross before shooting a basket (oops, that one totally translates into today!).

- You suffer from free-floating guilt.

- You have braided palm leaves stuck behind the corner of the crucifix in your bedroom.

- You have pinned a tissue to the top of your head to go to church.

- You know the difference between a C-rated movie and an X-rated one.

- You have ransomed a "pagan baby."

- You know that a spiritual bouquet isn't something you buy at the neighborhood florist.

# Same Church Different Pews

Catholics today find themselves standing between worlds, or at least standing with a foot in each of two worlds—the pre-Vatican world of a century ago and the post-Vatican world of today. In telling the story of Catholicism, one has to tell overlapping if not parallel stories. This in no way implies a split in the Church, but simply that people of faith find themselves existing in the process of *becoming*—it is impossible that a billion people would be on the same page at the same time! Much of what still defines Catholic identity within the Church and to the world comes from pre–Vatican II practices and experiences. Changes set in motion a little over 40 years ago (a mere blink of an eye in Catholic-time) are still being integrated. Others have fallen by the wayside, or are temporarily off the table. As stated earlier, tradition evolves slowly in the Church—and only by taking the long view can these changes be seen.

For now, you might identify yourself as a traditional Catholic, which usually means adhering to stricter interpretations than the person sitting next to you. Both you and your neighbor are correct. Adherence to tradition and adaptation to change are both necessary for an organization, whether it's a family, a business, or a church. There are both conservative and progressive Catholics.

Eventually opposing viewpoints converge and a bigger truth emerges. To help readers understand the complexities of Catholicism, we'll identify both the conservative and progressive perspectives when they affect the discussion.

## A New Perspective on an Old Church

As you read the following list showing characteristics of the emerging post–Vatican II Church, notice how they aren't really new and they don't change Church doctrine—they are shifts in perspective:

◆ A shift in emphasis from the institution of the Church to the people, harkening back to the communities that were the first-century Church

◆ Reconnecting to the foundation of Catholicism in Scripture

◆ Greater participation in the services and ceremonies by the congregation

◆ Embracing the whole world: its people, their beliefs, culture, social and economic concerns, with an emphasis on world peace

◆ Cooperation with other religions and respect for the validity of their beliefs

◆ A call for an end to anti-Semitism and for a true respect for Judaism

◆ Valuing the role of the individual Catholic layperson as an emissary of Catholic values in society

◆ An end to discrimination of all kinds, recognition of the innate dignity of all people and all creation

◆ Upholding of the individual conscience as the norm for morality

# What You Have to Do

Catholics are required to attend weekly Mass (also called Eucharist), along with six major holy days through the year when attendance is required. They follow the *liturgical* calendar, which reflects the seasons and cycles of the year, connecting religious services with the external events of one's life and to the natural world.

Catholics celebrate seven sacraments, and members are expected to develop their sacramental life by preparing and receiving them according to the prescribed form. They are: baptism, Communion, confirmation, marriage, Holy Orders, penance, and anointing of the sick. (Sacraments are further discussed in Chapter 11.)

Faith is encouraged through a rich prayer life, meditation, Scripture study, and devotions that are held throughout the year, such as Lenten and Advent services. Catholics are required to give money and personal time to support their churches and schools, and to be generous with charities and missions. Catholic teaching and sacramental life impart and strengthen values such as faith, hope, charity, peace, and justice, which members are expected to express through action—living their faith in everyday life.

> **S'ter Says**
>
> **Liturgical** is the word the Catholic Church uses to describe Church practices such as hymns, prayers, and services—from the Greek *leitourgia*, meaning "the work of the people."

## From Law to Loving Response

The impetus of Vatican II is toward Catholics making moral choices based on discernment rather than strict adherence to law. And as stated earlier, not every Catholic is comfortable with this change. Obeying a set of laws offered consolation—almost a guarantee you were living a moral life. Those who oppose these changes are concerned that picking and choosing creates what they refer to as "cafeteria" Catholics.

Others say the old model, which emphasized obedience to rules to avoid sin, treated Catholics like children and led to a minimal kind of faith.

The new way which emphasizes finding the most loving response to life's dilemmas requires more engagement with the gospel message and Church tradition, and counts on individuals to be faithful in their discernment.

The concept of finding the most loving response is being tested most directly in the areas of contraception and abortion, where the gap between law and practice is substantial. The Church clearly defines contraception and abortion as morally wrong. However, statistics show there is little difference between the use of birth control and abortion among Catholic couples and non-Catholics.

Conservatives in the Church maintain that laxity in obedience to laws such as these has grave moral consequences. Progressives believe that law must be tempered—that circumstances count. Regardless of one's position, discussion on important matters is not approached lightly, nor are personal decisions made without wrestling with the consequences. By seriously holding the line on morality, a Catholic is extremely conscious of what it means to cross it—thus avoiding what is called a slippery slope.

Meanwhile, science and technology press forward, presenting challenges about the basic dignity and right to life that did not exist previously. Examples of today's moral challenges include surrogate parenthood, in vitro fertilization, stem cell research, organ transplants, life support systems, and dying with dignity, along with political/moral issues such as abortion, capital punishment, nuclear weapons, and AIDS.

---

### Epiphanies

In 1995, 49 percent of Catholics considered themselves pro-choice on the matter of abortion, and 41 percent considered themselves pro-life. Three years later, those figures were nearly reversed, with 48 percent of Catholics calling themselves pro-life and 41 percent calling themselves pro-choice. This shift mirrored the national shift in the same direction. Catholic beliefs are not all that different from the culture at large.

---

Church leaders once made decisions about these types of concerns and the followers simply obeyed the rules. The moral baton has been passed, and people must now work to resolve and be responsible for issues in the context of the Church's faith structures, regulations, and rules. Catholics use prayer, meditation, and reflection on the teachings of the Church as a way of coming to decisions and establishing moral priorities.

# The Classic Definition

Having taken a quick look at what lies ahead, let's now consider a textbook definition of the Catholic Church. In doing so, it will give you a better sense of the importance of the papal office. The pope is the central symbol under which the diverse Catholic Church unites.

Catholicism is actually comprised of some 22 different churches that are all in communion with the pope. Each professes the same truths, but expresses these beliefs in slightly different practices or rites. Twenty-one of these are commonly referred to as the Eastern Rite Churches. The one Western Rite, often called Roman, is the largest. It is officially called the Latin Church and is the primary focus of this book.

### S'ter Says

**Ecclesiastical** is a term used to describe church stuff. Just as "civil" describes things that relate to government, ecclesiastical describes things that belong to an established institutional church.

Next let's consider the word *church*. The Catechism, the official book of definitions, says church is a convocation or assembly of people, gathered together for religious purposes; however, the term is used in several ways.

- Church is a building where members gather for religious services, as in "We went to church to pray."

- Church describes the group of people gathered together to support one another on the faith journey, as in "The church gathered clothing to aid flood victims of Hurricane Katrina."

- Church is the governing authority that unites all the parishes throughout the world, as in "The Catholic Church has declared a new saint."

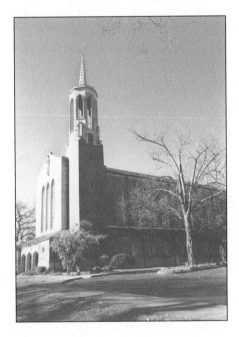

*Christ the King Church, Nashville, Tennessee.*

*(Courtesy of H. L. [Dean] Caskey)*

The word "catholic" was first used by Ignatius of Antioch around the year 110 C.E. It is from the Greek word *katholikos*, which means "toward the whole." Ignatius was suggesting that the Church is a gift offered by Christ for all people.

Now that you've had a bird's-eye view of Catholicism, we will go on to look at the variety of people and cultures in the Catholic Church.

## The Least You Need to Know

- ◆ The Catholic Church is the largest single denomination in Christianity.

- ◆ A major rebirth happened to the Church in the middle of the twentieth century, known as the Second Vatican Council (or Vatican II).

- ◆ There is diversity of thought within the Catholic religion. There is an official collection of beliefs called *Catholic tradition*, but practicing Catholics differ in how that is interpreted and observed.

- ◆ Outreach, charity, and social justice are central to Catholicism.

- ◆ Catholicism is both a culture and a religion.

# The People: Many Faces, Many Flags

## In This Chapter

- ◆ Visit a Mexican cemetery
- ◆ Attend an African American Mass
- ◆ Look in on a Native American Parish
- ◆ Facts and figures about the Catholic population

Right from the beginning, the mission of the Catholic Church has been to make the religion available to all people. As you learned in Chapter 1, "catholic" means moving toward wholeness or, as it is often interpreted, "universal." That describes the Church very well, as it includes many nationalities and exists in every country in the world.

## Would I Know One If I Saw One?

The Church draws on a rich cultural heritage. Beyond the stereotypical image of a Catholic lies a diverse palette of cultural expressions of the religion. Particularly since Vatican II, the Church has encouraged various cultures to include their unique music, art, dance, dress, and values in the

Mass and other religious ceremonies. This process is called enculturation. It has resulted in expressions of Catholicism that differ greatly from those that many "traditional" Catholics are accustomed to. These expressions may surprise you.

## Day of the Dead

On November 1st the Church celebrates the feast of *All Saints Day* to honor the dead in heaven. The following day, November 2nd, All Souls Day is celebrated and prayers are offered for all the souls in *purgatory*. In Mexico and parts of the southwestern United States, these feasts are celebrated as Dia de los Muertos or Day of the Dead. Dia de los Muertos combines ancient Mexican traditions with the Catholic celebration introduced by the Spanish 500 years ago.

> ### S'ter Says
>
> **All Saints Day** is also known as the feast of All Hallows. The night before became known as All Hallows Eve, or Halloween. So when the "spooks" come to your door, they are honoring an old tradition as well as having a good night of fun.
>
> **Purgatory** is the condition of the soul of a person who at the time of death has not completely repented for wrongdoing. They rely on the living to "pray them into heaven."

In the Mexican Catholic culture, death is seen as a part of the cycle of life, and it's believed that ghosts come back to earth to renew bonds with the living. Families prepare altars at home and in the cemeteries where vigils are kept day and night to welcome these souls. Altars can also be found in many businesses and public buildings, and in some towns the church builds an altar in the square for "homeless" or forgotten spirits that will have no place else to go, and no one to welcome them.

### For Heaven's Sake

Check your local newspaper to find out if there are Day of the Dead celebrations in your part of the country. You might find them at a local museum or cultural center. You might use this day to visit the cemetery where someone you love is buried. You might honor them with a small altar at home on which their picture is displayed.

Markets are filled with bright orange marigolds, candy skulls, and figures of skeletons that are sold to grace home altars and graves. Families buy Pan de Muerto (Bread of the Dead) and other edibles that they place on the altar and serve to visitors. Flower petals are strewn between the cemeteries and homes to show the spirits the way, where their favorite foods await them on the altars.

The Day of the Dead is the time for the whole family to come together for a celebration, visiting together, and cleaning the gravesites and tend the cemetery. Each family tells stories to share the events of the past year with the spirit of the loved one.

The celebration serves as a reminder that death comes as a natural part of life. It also dispels fear of death by poking fun at it. Skeletons are used as decorations, and the children play with them. There are sugar skulls to eat with one's own name written on them. A favorite game is to write a humorous obituary of a prominent townsperson who is still very much alive, and read it out loud. Everyone enjoys a good laugh. The next day people gather at the church where Mass is offered for the dead.

> **Epiphanies**
>
> Marigolds are called *flor de muerto*, or flower of death, and Mexican Catholics use them to decorate altars and graves at the feast of the Day of the Dead. Some say the flowers smell of incense and bones. Others say the cycle of life and death is shown in the marigolds' bright orange color, which is reminiscent of the sunrise and sunset.

## An African American Mass

Although African Americans make up a smaller percentage of the Catholic population in the United States, they have unique celebrations and worship services, and their cultural statement is strong. With the renewal of Catholic liturgy in the middle of this century, particular ethnic expression of the Mass was encouraged, offering quite a contrast to the uniformity that was the custom.

If you attend a Catholic African American Mass, expect to participate in a 2-hour ceremony. African American spirituality celebrates a sense of God's presence everywhere, and it is met with a powerful emotional response. Sunday Mass is a family gathering, which brings together the gifts of all the people. Musically, hand clapping, tambourines, drums, and foot tapping set the tone. Everybody—the choir, the readers, the priest, and the servers—all move in the African rhythms that have been held sacred for generations. The congregation praises the Lord with body and soul. Several choirs made up of people of different ages join in song. The music varies from traditional hymns to spirituals to

> **Your Guardian Angel**
>
> Learn more about the African American branch of the Catholic family by reading one or more of the several African American Bibles available. These Bibles feature devotions that celebrate the social experience and cultural heritage of black Christians. Many have illustrations that depict Jesus and the apostles as Africans.

contemporary songs. It is an expression of the African American soul: alive and spontaneous.

The priest delivers the Gospel, speaking to the people with drama and passion. He usually talks about things that reflect the lives of the people: black pride, racism, poverty, and social and family values. Responses from the people punctuate the message: "Hallelujah! Thank you, Jesus!" Hands wave throughout the church. At the sign of peace, the time during the Mass when worshippers exchange handshakes, all move throughout the church, greeting and hugging every member.

Often, members of the congregation furnish the art displayed in the church, which reflects their lives and experiences. African colors of red, black, and green adorn the altar and are worn as vestments by the priest as a sign of black pride and solidarity with the African people. Although the celebration typically lasts 2 hours, the parishioners generally remain after the service to visit and conduct church business. The rich cultural heritage of the African American people is expressed within the honored traditions of Catholicism.

## A Native American Parish

When the Spanish arrived in the area now known as New Mexico, they found the native people living in permanent earth structures made of mud bricks in villages all along the Rio Grande. The Spanish called these settlements *pueblos* and named each of them for a saint who then became the patron saint of the village. Nineteen of these pueblos (considered parishes) still exist, and each one boasts a Catholic church. Over the years, the Native American people have adapted Christian practices and symbols to their native beliefs, creating a unique cultural blend of both religions.

> **S'ter Says**
>
> The word **vespers** means "evening star," and Catholics use this term to describe prayers traditionally said at sundown. Vespers are the sixth of seven prayers said throughout the day and night in the Catholic Church.

Native parishes offer traditional Mass on Sundays and holy days, and on the feast days of the patron saints, native dances and ceremonies become part of the religious ceremonies. These dances are prayers, not performances. One in particular, called the Deer or Matachina Dance, is a traditional, symbolic animal dance and is performed at San Ildefonso Pueblo on January 23. The night before the feast, *luminarios* (paper sacks partially filled with sand and containing a candle) glow, and their soft light illuminates the village.

In the large plaza, the Catholic Church stands at one corner and an adobe-style *kiva*, a traditional native temple, stands in another. Fiesta *vespers* are held in the church at sundown. Afterward, people gather around juniper fires burning in the town square. They hold an all-night vigil in honor of the feast day. The medicine man, in traditional dress, makes a brief appearance, preparing the space for the festivities that will soon follow. Men dressed in traditional Native American costumes drum and chant.

At first light of day, figures appear on the horizon of the hill just outside of the town. They seem to be walking on stick legs, and they wave heavy antlers over their heads. They are the deer men. They descend in a noisy procession accompanied by painted and feathered costumed dancers. The drums accompany ancient songs that honor the deer and buffalo. A Mass is offered in the church as part of the ceremonies.

## The Taos Pueblo Catholic Church

Taos Pueblo is said to be one of the oldest towns in the United States, populated continuously since the 1400s. The Native Americans in Taos have created a religious system that combines their own deeply spiritual beliefs with Catholicism in a unique way.

*San José de Gracia Catholic Church in Las Trampas, New Mexico.*

*(Courtesy of Bob O'Gorman and Mary Faulkner)*

In the center of the village sits the Catholic Church that the villagers still refer to as the "new" church, even though it was built more than 150 years ago. The church has no electricity, but is lit by gas lamps along the walls. In the center of the altar in the place where you would usually find a crucifix is a large statue of the Earth Mother. She is dressed in a beautiful satin gown, the color of which changes to match each season. In the spring, for instance, she wears green. The other statues and the altar are draped in a similar fabric. A large casket covered with matching cloth stands at the side of the altar. The casket is where Christ resides and is a reminder to the congregation, which is mostly Native American, that Christ died for them, and it serves to remind the congregation that a lot of them died for Christ, too.

# So Where Would I Find a Catholic?

You can find Catholics everywhere. In its long history, Catholicism has become a global religion. Although there are certain regions that have high Catholic populations, there are no countries that do not include some Catholics in their populations.

## The Americas: Close to Home

There are several lively Catholic centers in North and South America. The Catholic Church in Canada, for instance, exists under two separate but parallel hierarchies: French-speaking and English-speaking. Overall, Catholics account for more than 43 percent of the total Canadian population, about 14 million people. The majority of Canadian Catholics live in the province of Quebec; French-speaking Catholics comprise more than 95 percent of Quebec city's population.

Farther south, Mexico City became a diocese of the Catholic Church in 1530. A very Catholic country, with 95 million Catholics (almost 90 percent of the population), Mexico's unique history makes its relationship with the Catholic Church interesting. In 1820, Mexico won its independence from Spain, which conquered it in 1521. When it overthrew Catholic Spain, Mexico also overthrew the rule of the Catholic Church. The Catholic Church was not allowed to operate with full legal rights after the war of independence. Only as recently as 1992 have Mexico and the Vatican established full diplomatic relations.

Another heavily Catholic nation to the south is Nicaragua in Central America. Its four million Catholics make up more than 70 percent of the total population. The history of Catholicism in Nicaragua goes back to the Spanish conquest in 1524.

**Your Guardian Angel**

Spanish-speaking communities in the United States are served by the Institute of Hispanic Liturgy, a national organization of liturgists, musicians, artists, and pastoral agents. It publishes liturgical material and promotes the development of liturgical spirituality among Hispanics. The Mexican-American Cultural Center in San Antonio, Texas, is a center where Hispanic leadership is developed and cultural materials are available.

Cuba's relationship with Catholicism began in 1514, and Cuba today has a Catholic population of over nine million, which comprises about 85 percent of the total population. When communist Fidel Castro took control of the government in 1959, he nationalized Catholic schools and expelled more than 100 priests. The visit of Pope John Paul II highlighted the Catholic presence on this island and invigorated the Church. In response to the popularity of this visit, the government improved its relationship with the Church.

The Caribbean nation of the Dominican Republic has been a Catholic country since Columbus arrived there in 1492. Today the Catholic population of 8.5 million represents about 95 percent of the total population, and Catholicism is the state religion.

The largest Catholic population in the world lives in the South American nation of Brazil. First celebrating the Mass in 1500, Brazil is a country in which a significant number of clergy and lay Catholics have been active in movements for social reform. More than 137 million Catholics, making up 77 percent of the population, call Brazil home.

Because of the tightly woven relationship between the colonial governments and the Church in Latin America, politics and religion have remained closely connected. As a result, many Church leaders, both clerical and lay, take an activist role in the politics of Latin Americans.

Compared with Brazil, the United States has a relatively small Catholic population of just 71 million people, or 24 percent of the total population. Here's where most U.S. Catholics live:

♦ Los Angeles has 4.2 million Catholics, making up 38 percent of the population.

♦ Chicago has 2.4 million Catholics, representing 40 percent of the population.

♦ Pre-Katrina New Orleans had 488,000 Catholics, making up 36 percent of its population.

◆ Boston has two million Catholics, representing 52.3 percent of its population.

◆ New York City has 4.3 million Catholics, which is 42 percent of its population.

◆ El Paso has 656,000 Catholics, which represents 81 percent of the population.

## The Rest of the World

Here is a random selection of Catholic populations around the world.

| Country | Catholic History | Catholic Population | Percent of Population |
|---------|------------------|---------------------|-----------------------|
| Belgium | Introduced to Catholicism as early as the year 325. It was a Catholic land from about 730. | 7.8 million | 75 percent |
| Czech Republic | Christianity spread by the martyrdom of Prince Wenceslaus in 929. Continuous parish system since the thirteenth century. | 2.7 million | 26.8 percent |
| Croatia | Christian since the seventh century. Independent republic in 1991, formerly under Yugoslavia. | 4 million | 88 percent |
| Iceland | An island republic first visited by Irish hermits in the 700s. Catholicism was officially accepted about the year 1000. | 6,000 | 2 percent |
| Ireland | This island received Catholicism from St. Patrick in the middle of the 400s. | 3.5 million | 88 percent |
| Poland | Presence of Church from later ninth century. First bishop 968. Suffered through two world wars and the rise of Communism. Birthplace of John Paul II. | 34.7 million | 89.8 percent |
| Philippines | The Spanish introduced Catholicism in 1564. | 71 million | 80.9 percent |

| Country | Catholic History | Catholic Population | Percent of Population |
|---|---|---|---|
| Uganda | Catholic missionaries arrived in 1879. In its short history of Catholicism, 22 of its first converts were martyred. These people were declared saints in 1964. | 9 million | 33 percent |
| Australia | The first Catholics in the country were Irish convicts sent by the British. | 5.3 million | 26.4 percent |
| Israel | It all began here. | 74,900 | 1.2 percent |

## Worldwide Catholic Population by Continent and Future Projections

There are 1.12 billion Catholics in the world, or about 20 percent of the world's population. Nearly one in every five people in the world is Catholic.

◆ Africa: 140 million; 18 percent

◆ Asia: 130 million; 4.3 percent

◆ North America: 82 million; 25 percent

◆ Latin America: 400 million; 83.5 percent

◆ Europe: 270 million; 36.4 percent

◆ Oceania: 9 million; 26.8 percent

Presently 70 percent of Catholics live in what is termed "the developing world." It is projected that by 2050 Catholics will come overwhelmingly from these countries and that traditionally Catholic countries such as Poland and Italy will suffer large declines in numbers.

By 2050 Catholic populations are projected to increase by 146 percent in Africa, 63 percent in Asia, 42 percent in Latin America and the Caribbean, and 38 percent in North America. Europe is expected to decline by 6 percent; its share of Catholics is projected to drop from one fourth in 2004 to one sixth in 2050.

The overwhelming shift toward the developing world will mean devoting greater energy to issues that affect the lives of Catholics there—poverty, hunger, AIDS, inequitable access to health care, economic inequality, and war. One can expect more aggressive measures to ensure that priests from the developing world attain positions of ecclesiastical power, eventually including the papacy, and the Church will have to rely on youth from the developing world to fill the ranks of priests and nuns. The Catholic Church faces major challenges in balancing the needs of its growing developing-world population and those of its traditional but declining populations in Europe.

As you can see, Catholicism comes in many colors, shapes, and sizes, and this religion continues to change dramatically. There is also a great diversity in how it is practiced. Paradoxically, the diversity of the Catholic Church is sustained by following the same leadership—the office of the pope in Rome. In the following chapter, we'll look at some well-known Catholics who represent a wide range of individual spiritual expression.

## The Least You Need to Know

- There's no such thing as a typical Catholic.

- The Catholic Church is a cultural mixing bowl of color, music, art, dance, and tradition that continues to emerge anew.

- Inhabiting every region of the globe, Catholics comprise nearly one in every five people.

- What started out as mainly a European Church is now worldwide.

# Catholicism: It's a Big Tent

## In This Chapter

- Catholics put faith into action
- Catholic organizations reflect great diversity
- From rock concerts to the U.S. Senate, Catholics speak out
- The public face of the Church: the good and the bad of it

Spirituality is the heart of religion. It is both what we believe and how we put those beliefs into action. Catholics do not lack creativity or passion in how they express the values that are important to them. For a Church that is often characterized by an image of strict uniformity, these diverse approaches to Catholic life show that quite the opposite is true. In this chapter, you'll look at two Catholic organizations that are almost polar opposites of one another, and read about individuals who reflect the variety found among rank-and-file Catholics.

## Image: The Power of the Press

The popular novel *The Da Vinci Code* (Doubleday, 2003), by Dan Brown, quickly swept the country catching the imagination of millions. It wasn't as well received by Opus Dei, the Catholic organization portrayed in the book as secretive and archaic. Statements on the Opus Dei website, numerous articles, and television interviews have addressed the image problem caused by the work of fiction.

Since stories of sex abuse and cover-ups in the Catholic Church began breaking in 2002, the stories won't go away. The Church has been on the front page of newspapers and magazines, and featured in television programs across the nation and around the world for the last four years. Struggling to move past its tarnished image, it has been accused of failing to deal with the crimes against members at the expense of maintaining the reputation of the organization.

---

### Epiphanies

Comedian and practicing Catholic Stephen Colbert of *The Colbert Report* (Comedy Central) appeared on Ash Wednesday with his forehead appropriately smudged. Before getting his own show, Colbert did a regular bit, "This Week in God" or (TWiG), on *The Daily Show*, featuring the "God Machine" and a satirical rundown of "everything God did this week." When his show spun off, Colbert quipped: "God has an exclusive licensing agreement with *The Daily Show*. We're trying to get the Devil for our show." Colbert doesn't feel that it's likely he'll run out of material for his provocative religious spoofing; he believes we're having a religious pandemic: "There's so much religion in public life. It's everywhere." Colbert "wishes our founding fathers had been a little clearer in that First Amendment."

---

In this section you'll look at two organizations that show very different expressions of Catholic faith. One organization is Opus Dei (Work of God), and it has a favored place in Vatican policy; the other, the Voice of the Faithful (VOTF), articulates dissent and operates outside the favor of Rome. Both draw on long-standing traditions in the Church.

## Opus Dei: Working It Out with God

Opus Dei (Latin for "Work of God") was founded in Spain in 1928 by a Roman Catholic priest, Josemaría Escrivá. It is an organization of both lay and clergy dedicated to spreading the Gospel message by putting faith to work in the world. It emphasizes the intrinsic spirituality of ordinary working people, maintaining that work itself is spiritual. Opus Dei offers encouragement and training for members on incorporating Christian principles into their daily work through spiritual development, workshops, retreats, spiritual direction, and doctrinal instructions.

Pope John Paul II canonized the founder of Opus Dei on October 6, 2002, only 27 years after his death. His fast rise to sainthood is exceeded only by that of St. Francis of Assisi. Current membership in Opus Dei includes 84,000 people from every continent.

The organization espouses one main vocation—that of service. There are a variety of positions within the organization under three main categories:

◆ Supernumeraries are married men and women dedicated to raising their families as a vocation. Currently about 70 percent of members fall under this heading.

◆ Numeraries practice celibacy and devote all their earnings to the organization. Most live in centers and have secular jobs. Others work as professionals in the organization. These members follow the practice of corporal mortification, which will be discussed later in this chapter. They make up less than 20 percent of the membership.

◆ Numerary Assistants are the women of Opus Dei, attending to the domestic needs of the organization.

## Pro and Con

Critics of Opus Dei are concerned with rigid training, cultlike methods such as aggressive recruitment, secrecy, and separation from family. Others point to ultraconservative and regressive practices, such as relegating women to traditional roles not in accordance with their abilities or education. Others question the political agenda, and some of the more extreme acts of physical mortification which include a cordlike whip which resembles macramé, used on the buttocks or back once a week, and the use of a cilice, a spiked chain worn around the upper thigh for 2 hours each day, except for Church feast days, Sundays, and certain times of the year.

The organization replies that membership is voluntary, the organization respects freedom, and it evidently is offering something people want—a way of expressing their spirituality in the world as everyday citizens. Many Church officials and scholars have said that Opus Dei has a revolutionary theological doctrine. Others praise it for the opportunities it provides.

Regarding Opus Dei's use of physical mortification, officials say it follows traditional Church practices. Members are encouraged to make sacrifices during particular times of the year (such as Lent), including outreach to the poor, fasting, or physical discipline. These practices are performed under the direction of a spiritual advisor and are not used in a way that would jeopardize health.

Critics say inconsistencies surrounding this organization have become "a sign of contradiction," an indication that it falls outside the norm. Response from inside the organization says more people love Opus Dei than don't.

The spirituality of Opus Dei is one of belonging. Similar to religious orders, it offers lay members the opportunity to experience the mystery and power of being on the inside. Unlike religious orders that were primarily instituted as an alternative voice to Rome, Opus Dei exists under the wing of Rome. It has been given the status of prelature—an office within the Church structure. It offers an alternative to the world, rather than to the organization.

Information can be found at www.opusdei.org or by contacting the Opus Dei Information Office at info@opusdei.org or 212-532-3570.

## Voice of the Faithful: Speaking Out

Voice of the Faithful (VOTF) is a worldwide movement of concerned mainstream Catholics formed in response to the clergy sexual abuse crisis. Their mission statement reads: *To provide a prayerful voice, attentive to the Spirit, through which the Faithful can actively participate in the governance and guidance of the Catholic Church.*

VOTF began in the immediate wake of the sex abuse scandals as they were swamping Boston and the rest of the country. News stories were breaking daily and people needed a place to sort through it all. VOTF's first mission was to listen. In January 2002, 25 people gathered at St. John the Evangelist Church in Wellesley, Massachusetts, and 4 years later there are 30,000 members meeting in churches around the world.

VOTF goals are:

◆ To support those who have been abused

◆ To support priests of integrity

◆ To shape structural change in full accordance and harmony with Church teaching

Rather than focusing on individuals within the Church, VOTF is looking at the organization itself and asking the question: *Does the Church structure create a climate that supports abuse and the subsequent cover-ups?*

Virtually all experts agree that power inequities and secrecy are the two factors that most directly contribute to the likelihood of abuse—in this case, sexual abuse. VOTF has identified a culture of power and secrecy in the Church that has a direct relationship to the sex scandals and subsequent cover-ups that immeasurably increased the problem.

## Pro and Con

The Catholic Church's field of operation has been described as an accountability-free zone—"feudal—a complete power down model. The hierarchy (bishops and above) basically function to protect their position to the detriment of priests and people. Even the 'good' bishops seldom speak out against the organization."

Calls for accountability by VOTF have resulted in bishops tagging them as "suspicious," accusing them of a "hidden agenda."

VOTF's agenda for reform in the organizational structure of the Church includes:

◆ Establishing an ongoing dialogue with bishops

◆ Hiring lay administrators to attend to diocesan business

◆ Publishing financial records

A bill seeking to repeal a 1954 exemption for churches of a law requiring nonprofits to publish their financial accounts recently passed the Massachusetts Senate but failed in the House.

Apparently VOTF seems to know its stuff, and more than a little about Church stuff, too. A survey conducted in October 2005 shows that almost 87 percent of members have college degrees, and a quarter of these have degrees in Canon law or Scripture study. Eighty-five percent belong to a parish—half sit on parish councils or occupy other positions in their local church. In its short history, VOTF has become an alternative source for news. It receives calls every day from the press around the world asking for comments on any number of Catholic-related news stories.

The spirituality of VOTF follows the prophetic tradition of calling leaders to accountability by speaking out. It also puts universal values to work by protecting the most vulnerable in the flock. Members of VOTF know that whether or not they will succeed in their goals of establishing dialogue with bishops and creating accountability, by speaking out they are expressing their faith.

VOTF can be found online at www.votf.org, or contact John Moynihan at 617-558-5252 (e-mail: jmoynihan@votf.org).

# From Bing to Bono

Music, television, and film both shape and reflect social values—transmitting much of today's spiritual message. During the 1950s, the message was about living right.

During the 1990s, the message became more about doing right. Two important stars of these eras had one thing in common: one became the poster child for "Catholic priest" and what it meant to be a good Catholic. The other is a rock star, the Gen X poster child, expressing Catholic spirituality in the spirit of social justice.

## The Good Priest

Harry Lillis, better known as the singer and actor Bing Crosby, was born in 1903 in Tacoma, Washington. His first recording was "I've Got the Girl" in 1926, which began his career as a top pop vocalist for the next 50 years. He starred in 55 films and earned three Academy Award nominations, winning best actor in 1945 for his portrayal of a priest, Father O'Malley, in *Going My Way*.

*Going My Way* made a deep impression on the Catholic imagination in the 1940s and on the public's imagination of Catholics as well.

In this idyllic version of priestliness, Father O'Malley solves every problem great and small, from the finances of St. Dominic's to the threat of street gangs—and he does so with a cool nonchalance. The film's presentation of a nonsexualized version of male power created a paradigm for priests for generations to come. His black clerical dress topped with a straw hat created a mixture of religious restraint and jauntiness. Father O'Malley was a priest and a real okay guy at the same time.

The spirituality of the film and the music celebrates a hope-filled belief that right acting and right thinking will produce right results. To borrow from the old poem, "God is in his heaven and all is right with the world." The spirituality is focused on the accomplishment of goals as a virtue rather than the journey. It shows a world in which reason, order, and logic will prevail. Virtually everyone knew the songs, which celebrated self-improvement, urging listeners to get an education. This "you can do" thinking was both personally and culturally uplifting.

## Rock Star Meets Rock of the Church

The spokesperson and front man for U2 (a rock group from Ireland), Bono, was born in Dublin in 1960 in the midst of the violence of the Catholic and Protestant clash. Bono's father was Catholic and his mom Protestant, and he felt like an outsider to both. Today he doesn't claim either but his penchant for justice is steeped in the values of his Catholic upbringing. Bono has said he will work as long as it takes to end poverty and disease among the poor—he considers this his spiritual mission.

In the article "Bono's American Prayer" by Cathleen Falsani appearing in *Christianity Today* (March 2003), Bono said he prays frequently, says grace before meals, and follows where the Spirit leads him. "If it's in the back of a Roman Catholic cathedral, in the quietness and the incense, which suggest the mystery of God, of God's presence, or in the bright lights of the revival tent, I just go where the life is ... where I feel the Holy Spirit."

Bono's lyrics are a fusion of politics, religion, and rock. His signature pink-tinted sunglasses and straw cowboy hat don't match the dress code among the religious and politically "right," but his commitment and charismatic enthusiasm for mission has brought the normally staid evangelical community on board. He did it by entering their world and talking their language—Scripture—pointing out that Scripture has no fewer than 2,103 references to taking care of the poor!

When the rocker met Pope John Paul II in 1999, the unlikely pair bonded over the issue of justice for the poor. In a *Los Angeles Times* interview, Bono attributed "Catholic guilt" as the possible source of his passion for social justice. Bono gave the Holy Father his "fly" pink sunglasses which the pontiff promptly wore, and the pope gave him a rosary with a crucifix designed by Michelangelo, which Bono has worn on stage every performance since—until recently. In an April 2, 2005, concert following the death of the beloved pontiff, Bono removed the rosary, kissed the crucifix, and hung it over the microphone as he and the band left the stage. Bono says the pope is "the best front man the Catholic Church ever had—a great showman."

Bono's spirituality isn't an antisectarian statement, but is for the most part the result of growing up feeling the terrible impact of *sectarianism*. He is distrustful of organized religion, but says, "I'm a believer, but I don't set myself up as any kind of Christian. I can't live up to that. It's something I aspire to, but I don't feel comfortable with that badge." Bono says he wants to avoid becoming a poster child for Christ when people should be looking to the Savior, not some rock star, for their example.

> **S'ter Says**
>
> **Sectarianism** is the belief that one particular religion is superior to all others. It is characterized by rigid adherence to a set of beliefs and intolerance of other people or religions.

# From Bishop Sheen to Dan Berrigan

Two very important characteristics of the Catholic Church are its philosophical side and its passion for justice. During the 1950s, the leadership of the Church focused on the reasoning side of the equation; in the 1960s, there was a cultural explosion into the realm of social justice. The two personalities represented here capture the extraordinary cultural and spiritual changes going on in this country. It gives insight into the difference between the pre-Vatican Catholic and the Catholic that evolved out of the Vatican II 1960s. It illustrates how and why this is a defining moment in consciousness both in the organizational Church and its members.

## The Good Ambassador

In the mid-1950s, a common topic of conversation among Catholics and non-Catholics alike often centered on Bishop Fulton J. Sheen's phenomenally popular national weekly television show, *Life Is Worth Living*. Mingling religious ideas with secular life, Sheen became a kind of pop culture icon for the Church in 1950s America.

He moved Catholicism into mainstream American life. He was redefining the Church in the world by telling Catholic stories that had shared meaning both with other Christian communities as well as Judaism. Sheen's approach to faith always provoked thought, popularizing philosophy. He preached against the evils of atheistic communism, and he focused Catholic spirituality in the 1950s on that mission. Working with his sharpest tools—logic, reason, and humor—he was the premier anticommunist.

**Your Guardian Angel**

Pray for world peace! In the 1950s, it was common for Catholics to pray for the conversion of Russia at the end of every Mass. Catholics still pray for world peace regularly.

Sheen's spirituality saw a thoughtful approach as the best cure for family and social difficulties and the breakdown of morality in the culture. In his carefully crafted talks, he made reasoning work for the common folks, not just for the educated.

## Religious Outlaw

The turbulent 1960s revealed a liberal, activist side of Catholicism. At the center of this awakening was Daniel Berrigan, a *Jesuit*, one of the first clerics in the Church to draw the media's attention to the moral dimension of the political protest against the United States' role in the Vietnam War. In 1968, he and his brother Philip, also a priest, stormed the building housing draft records in Catonsville, Maryland. Using homemade napalm, he torched hundreds of files within 10 minutes.

He was sentenced to 3 years in prison, and went underground for several months. using his time on the lam to publicly teach and lecture, showing up at various antiwar protests. His every move made sensational news. After a speech at Cornell University, he eluded the FBI by slipping out a side door in a larger-than-life papier-mâché puppet of an apostle. After 18 months in prison, Berrigan was paroled in 1972.

> **S'ter Says**
>
> **Jesuit** is the common name for a religious order of priests and brothers in the Catholic Church. The official name is the Society of Jesus, and hence the initials after a member's name are "S.J."

Dan Berrigan's radical leftist beliefs created great controversy within the Catholic Church. He pressed the Church's theory of just war to the limits, and many say he pushed it past the limits. Berrigan believed that "the death of a single human being is too great a price to pay for the vindication of any principle."

To this day the political activism of Dan Berrigan and others is seen by some Catholics as the true principles of the Church, and by others as totally inappropriate radicalism. Indeed, those who are incensed by such politics consider clerics like the Berrigans to be traitors hiding behind the religious collar. Those who agree with their motives and their methods consider them to be brave saints. Regardless of where you come down on the issues, the Berrigans focused Catholic spirituality in the 1970s on confronting injustice.

### Epiphanies

Martin Sheen, who played the U.S. president in the NBC series *The West Wing*, considers being a peacemaker not a role, but a calling. In a *Los Angeles Times* interview (Teresa Watanabe, March 2, 2003), he said, "Spirituality is not safe. It leads you down uncharted waters. If it didn't cost you anything, you'd have to question its value." Sheen professes belief in a "nonviolent Jesus," dedicating himself to the cause of peace and spirituality. His first protest was at the age of nine when he organized caddies to strike for wages. He opposed the Star Wars missile defense program with the Berrigan brothers, marched with Cesar Chavez, and protested U.S. aid to El Salvador's right-wing government. Born Ramon Estevez, he connects with the poor and oppressed, with whom he shares a common history. He works in soup kitchens and visits prisons and juvenile detention halls. Sheen attends Mass regularly, and carries a rosary in his pocket.

# From Cesar Chavez to Clarence Thomas

Although theology and Church beliefs are often defined in the Vatican chambers and universities, the average Catholic learns his religion in the home and transmits it by the way he lives in the real world. Two Catholic men, both from poor beginnings, developed very different ways of expressing their spirituality and helping their fellow workers during two different political eras (one in the 1960s and one in the 1990s). One chose the way of self-reliance, and the other chose community action.

## Grapes of Wrath

Cesar Chavez was born in 1927 in Yuma, Arizona. His family worked its small farm until 1939, when unpaid taxes forced them into the migrant labor stream. The year 1952 found Chavez working in a lumberyard in the San Jose barrio called Sal Si Puedes, which means, ironically, "get out if you can." There he met a Catholic priest who worked with migrant farm laborers. This priest immersed Chavez in the social activism side of the Catholic Church, particularly the pope's teachings on the right of labor to organize. Chavez also came under the influence of a community organizer who taught him how to apply the Church's social philosophy to the community around him.

### Your Guardian Angel

Look for the union label on all your grapes! Chavez and the many others who worked with him fought a long and hard battle to get better pay and working conditions for the migrant laborers who picked crops. They formed a union. You can join in the support of the dignity of the workers by buying union grapes.

In 1962, Chavez began organizing California's migrant workers into a union. His strategy was economic boycott. In 1968, Chavez led a boycott of table grapes. The response of the Church and community groups in boycotting supermarkets who carried nonunion grapes resulted in contracts for the union for 85 percent of the table grapes market. Although his methods were political and economic, Chavez espoused a fundamental and absolute affirmation of the dignity of the human person and a firm commitment to non-violence. He based his philosophy on the teachings of Jesus, St. Francis, Gandhi, and Martin Luther King Jr.

Chavez himself was a deeply religious man, thanks in large part to the influence of his mother. Fasting and daily Mass accompanied his protests. He named one of his largest marches a *peregrine* (pilgrimage, a religious term signifying the holy walk of a people). In addition to the union banner and the United States flag, he and his followers carried banners depicting the Mexican Lady of Guadalupe and the Aztec eagle. His actions on behalf of justice gave new meaning to the concept of spirituality to his generation and the ones that followed. This spirituality consisted of a profound conviction of the absolute value of each individual, a firm commitment to nonviolence, and untiring work on behalf of the dispossessed.

## Dirt Poor in Georgia to the Supreme Court

Despite growing up in poverty and facing racial oppression, Clarence Thomas, who is now a Supreme Court justice, took advantage of the sacrifices that his family made for him to receive a good education. Thomas's family sent him to Catholic schools whose teachers taught him that with hard work and self-reliance, he could overcome the obstacles of discrimination. In the end, he would, but the road was never easy. Although he entered a Catholic seminary, he dropped out because of intolerable racial remarks made by classmates at the time of Martin Luther King Jr.'s death.

### Epiphanies

There are many biblical references to the poor, and it is clear that the God of the Scriptures loves the poor, but not the condition of poverty. God's people, especially the leaders, are given the responsibility to care for the poor. They are a necessary part of bringing God's reign, and are a constant reminder that God's will is not yet fully accomplished. Their presence reminds the faithful of the responsibility we have for one another. The help of the poor is the hope of the Church.

Thomas attended the Jesuit Holy Cross College, graduating cum laude, and was elected to Alpha Sigma Nu, the Jesuit national honor society. From there, he received his law degree from Yale University, and then went on to serve the government in legal positions under conservative Republican administrations at the state and national levels. He was nominated and approved as a justice of the United States Supreme Court in 1991.

Thomas's conservative views on public policy evolved from his grandfather's self-reliance and independence. His grandfather was anti-welfare, holding that "Man ain't got no business on welfare as long as he can work." Thomas's independence of spirit and strong belief in hard work and self-reliance articulate an American belief that everyone can succeed and speak to the spiritual belief that humans can overcome the odds and excel.

---

**Epiphanies**

John Fitzgerald Kennedy, the only Catholic elected to the presidency of the United States, broke an enduring stereotype of Catholics as being unthinking, superstitious, clannish, and separatist. Prior to Kennedy, a Catholic could not expect to sit in the chair that administers the highest office of the United States, indeed of the world. One of the key battles to overcome was the lack of public acceptance and the fear that Catholics could not be trusted because of their loyalty to the pope and to Rome. In a memorable 1960 speech before the greater Houston Ministerial Association, Kennedy called upon the best in Catholic intellectual thought to show that good Catholic beliefs did not interfere with good citizenship.

---

This chapter has shown how a variety of Catholic beliefs are played out in the public arena. Some are traditional and some push at the established boundaries and understandings of what it means to be a Catholic. When both ends of the spectrum are respected, there is a creative tension between them that shapes the Church and the culture in which it exists, and it comes to life through the faith expression of its members.

The next chapter explains more about how these beliefs are shaped. You'll learn about the Church's structure and guiding principles.

## The Least You Need to Know

- Spirituality is the way we express our values to the world.

- Coming from the same Catholic principles, there are a wide variety of spiritual expressions and a wide variety of people to express them.

- Spirituality plays out not only in different forms of religious practice, but also in a variety of arenas: politics, music, and the nightly news, for example.

- Paradoxically, the Catholic commitment to unity is strengthened by the diverse faith expressions of the members.

# Chapter 4

# The Vatican: The Church That's a Country

## In This Chapter

- Who is the shepherd of this very large and potentially unwieldy flock?
- Does infallibility mean the pope knows *everything?*
- Explore Vatican City: the country within a country
- Understand the Church's organizational structure and the source of its power, and how leadership is passed
- The basic rules and regulations Catholics live by

The Catholic Church is a study in contrasts. It consists of more than a billion members throughout the world, but it has the ability to speak with one voice. It is made up of thousands of parish churches, yet these communities of worship all follow the same faith. How is this unity accomplished? That's the focus of the chapter, which starts by introducing you to the leader of this massive organization: the pope.

# Just Who Is the Pope?

Pilgrims from all over the world travel to fill the square outside this man's window every day and wait hours to catch a glimpse of him. Dignitaries from every country request an audience with him. On his worldwide visits, millions of people gather to cheer and witness his presence. Seldom does a week go by that there isn't international coverage on his whereabouts or pronouncements.

Who is the man who commands this much attention? It is the pope, the leader of one of the biggest and most complex organizations in the world: the Catholic Church. In Latin, the word *pope* means "papa" or "father." The pope is the spiritual father or head of the Church. He is the focal point of unity among its members and aspires to be a symbol of peace and unity for the world. The Vatican has diplomatic relations with most countries in the world.

*Pope John Paul II was the first non-Italian elected pope in almost 500 years. This popular pope came from Poland.*

*(Courtesy of Photofest/Icon Archives)*

# Upon This Rock ...

All of this attention and power in the hands of one man may seem extraordinary. It may seem less so when you consider that Catholics believe that his office is the storehouse for the truths of the Church.

Since the ninth century, *pope* has been the designated title of the bishop of Rome, Vicar of Christ, a title the pope shares with all other bishops, referring to the claim that they stand as representatives of Jesus Christ and act with his authority in the Church. Catholics have traditionally claimed St. Peter as the first bishop of Rome and trace the succession of popes in a direct line back to this apostle. They believe the authority of the Church rests on the commission given by Jesus to Peter found in Matthew 16:18–19:

> You are Peter, and upon this rock I will build my Church, and the gates of hell shall not prevail against it. I will give you the keys of the kingdom of heaven, and whatever you bind on earth will be bound in heaven, and whatever you loose on earth will be loosed in heaven.

New scholarship explores the Church's historic connection to St. Peter, making the matter of linear descent a debatable issue. There certainly was no formal papal office in the first centuries of the Church. Originally, *apostolic* described the early communities that were formed during the lifetime of the apostles. Only one of the six of these first communities was in the West—Rome. The other five—Antioch, Philipi, Ephesus, Corinth, and Thessalonica—were in the East. These large communities were geographical centers for groups of smaller communities. Official teaching depended on what the larger communities, representing the smaller ones, agreed on. This process developed as a way of securing the teaching of Jesus, keeping it separate from the personal revelations that were popular in communities—which had a more charismatic character. The early Church communities mentioned here were not hierarchal, but operated by the principle of agreement.

## Papal Thumbprints

Popes have a strong influence on the Catholic religion; however, *not all popes interpret Church tradition the same.* Different popes place different emphasis on how much collegiality there will be during their reign—for example, Pope Pius IX emphasized the differences between the Church and the world at Vatican I, and Pope John XXIII removed barriers, "opening the windows" to the world at Vatican II. Pope John Paul II had a unique style. He espoused a conservative doctrine, yet traveled the world for liberal social causes and held audiences with pop artists like Bob Dylan and Bono. Popes leave a personal mark on the Church. Traditionalists cry heresy when questions about long-held treasured beliefs are questioned, and progressives push the boundaries. Just where that balance is struck depends on who's in the Vatican sitting on St. Peter's chair.

Catholics believe the task of authentically interpreting the Word of God has been entrusted by Christ to the Pope and to the bishops in communion with him. This teaching authority is known as the *Magisterium* (from the Latin for "teacher") of the

Church. The Church's Magisterium exercises the authority it holds from Christ to the fullest extent when it defines dogmas, that is, when it proposes, in a form obliging the Christ's followers to an irrevocable adherence of faith, truths contained in divine revelation or also when it proposes, in a definitive way, truths following from divine revelation.

## Infallibly Speaking ...

Catholics believe that the pope exercises the infallibility that Christ grants the Church. The pope proclaims the faith of the church. That is why the office of the pope is infallible. Papal *infallibility* means that the pope cannot make a mistake when defining what the Church believes to be a doctrine—a formal belief of faith or morals for the Catholic Church. The pope speaks infallibly only when he claims to be using his authority according to an established process. This infallibility is also present in the body of bishops when, together with the pope they proclaim a supreme teaching. This infallibility is put into effect above all by the Church in an Ecumenical Council, such as Vatican II.

Today, as well as throughout history, questions arise from the people and from the clergy that eventually stir the theological waters. Issues are debated, and those that make it up to the top are finally wrangled out among the bishops. The pope eventually rules on what is acceptable and what is not. We talk more about this process in Chapter 17.

> **S'ter Says**
>
> **Infallibility** is a gift of the Holy Spirit to protect the Church's teachings from error. Papal infallibility is the Church belief that when the pope defines what the Church believes to be a doctrine of faith and morals, that definition must be held by the whole Church. It is the Holy Spirit who grants the Church infallibility. **Magisterium** is from the Latin word for "teacher" and refers to the teaching authority and function of the Church.

Infallibility is often a misunderstood doctrine by non-Catholics and by Catholics as well. Infallibility does not apply to every comment the pope makes, but is reserved for decisions about doctrine, and follows a formal process of pronouncing. In other words, there are rules around infallibility. It is rarely used. Since the doctrine of infallibility was defined by Vatican I, Mary's assumption into heaven, defined in 1950, is the only doctrine to be proclaimed an article of faith. Chapter 12 discusses this in more detail. In other words, rather than being some mystical power of the pope, infallibility means the Church *allows* the office of the pope in communion with the bishops to be the voice in deciding what will be accepted as formal beliefs in the Church.

The pope works with the bishops in a shared decision-making process called collegiality. The pope, along with the bishops, make decisions about doctrine—what will be taught and what won't. As previously mentioned, how much collegiality, or shared power, will depend on the pope's leadership style. Bishops, for the sake of unity, "officially" yield to the politics of the particular leader. Bishops can and do have different opinions and sometimes voice concerns, but it is generally done with great respect to the Vicar of Peter. One doesn't become a bishop by being a "wild card." Remember, the pope is a bishop, but wields more power than the other bishops.

## What's His Address?

The pope, bishop of Rome, resides in the Vatican—short for Vatican City State. It is from here that the central government or the Holy See (from the Latin seat) of the Church operates. Vatican City is the smallest sovereign state in the world, covering an area no larger than 108.7 acres. The Basilica (or church) of St. Peter is the focal point of Vatican City. It's the mother church of Catholics and the largest church in the Christian world. About 1,000 people live in the Vatican, and another 4,000 work there every day. In addition to being the home of the spiritual leader of the Catholic Church, the Vatican has an enormous library of sacred books and a vast collection of religious art.

*St. Peter's Basilica in Rome, Christianity's largest church, is the mother church of Catholics.*

*(Courtesy of Alinari/Art Resource, New York)*

At one time, the small city-state of the Vatican comprised several states in central Italy known as the Papal States, including the city of Rome. Although the size of the Vatican is now greatly reduced, it still maintains the essential character of a country. For example, The Holy See has formal diplomatic relations with 174 countries and over 30 international organizations, including the United Nations and the World Trade Organization; it issues its own stamps and coins, and there is a remnant of the papal army represented by colorful Swiss guards who maintain a vigil that at least symbolically guards the pope.

## Smoke Signals

The pope is elected by the *College of Cardinals* during a council called together no sooner than 15 days and no later than 20 days after the death of his predecessor. Cardinals are high-ranking bishops appointed to their position by the pope. (Pope John Paul II appointed 114 of the 117 cardinals that would elect his successor.) All cardinals under the age of 80 are eligible to take part in the election of the new pope. Traditionally vote is by secret ballot, but a voice vote is permitted.

> **S'ter Says**
>
> The **College of Cardinals** is a collection of special bishops with the title "cardinal" that offers counsel to the pope, elects new popes, and governs the Church in between popes. There are approximately 180 members of the college.

There is much ritual and pageantry surrounding the election of a new pope. Recent changes to the process are discussed in the following paragraphs—but the custom of sending smoke signals to announce the election results remains intact. The Cardinals are sequestered from the outside world. Rounds of voting that fail to produce the necessary majority are burned in a small stove inside the chapel area, along with straw that will make dark smoke. The dark smoke announces to the waiting crowds that a pope has not yet been elected. When the necessary majority is acquired, the ballots are burned without straw, producing the white smoke that signifies election of the pope.

## Changes in Papal Election Process

Pope John Paul II changed 800 years of tradition in the papal election process. (Note: this change does not constitute an infallible statement; it isn't a doctrine. It is a law that governs the process, and while it is a noteworthy organizational change, it can be changed again.) For the last 800 years it has required a two-thirds majority to elect the pope. In 1945 Pope Pius XII made a small but important change in the election process, making it a two-thirds-plus-one majority so that a candidate couldn't influence the process by voting for himself. Cardinals had to stay with the election process until this majority was accomplished—which often required endless days of voting.

Pope John Paul II changed the papal election law in 1996. In a Papal Bull entitled *Universi Dominici Gregis,* he dropped the "plus one"—eliminating the fail-safe measure of the extra vote—and made other changes that paved the way for the pope to be elected by a simple majority.

The new process is less time-consuming. It is a step toward democracy, but comes at the risk of politicizing the procedure. It moves the Church away from the long-standing tradition of consensus-style decision-making that the two thirds plus one often demanded. It increases the likelihood of electing a leader that reflects the views held by the majority, but might silence the very important minority voice that could stop the process in the old regulations.

## The Beloved John Paul II

Karol Wojtyla grew up in the southern Polish village of Wadowice skiing, playing soccer, and considering a career in show business—skills that would take him far, but in a different direction than he could imagine at that time! He was a teenager in 1939 when German tanks invaded Poland, and during World War II and the Nazi occupation he worked as a laborer, studying theology by flashlight. In 1944, following a crackdown on religious teaching, he was forced into hiding. Many of his friends went to concentration camps. Following the war he was ordained a priest in 1946. By 1964 he was archbishop of Krakow and three years later he became a cardinal.

Wojtyla, the first non-Italian pope in 450 years, was elected in 1978, becoming Pope John Paul II. During his long career he saw many political changes, including the fall of communism in Eastern Europe and the end of apartheid in South Africa, where he met with President Nelson Mandela. Pope John Paul II survived an assassin's bullet in 1981 and lived to forgive the man who fired it. And he gave the world the Popemobile—the glass-sided bulletproof car from which he stood and waved to the crowds.

A spirit of outreach and conciliation characterized him. He visited Fidel Castro, the Communist leader of a traditionally Roman Catholic Cuba, and was the first pope to visit Egypt, a mainly Muslim country. He expressed sympathy with the plight of the Palestinians, and spoke of his sadness at the Church's role in anti-Semitism and the persecution of Jews by Christians. Despite increasing frailty he kept working, making an emotional trip to his native Poland in 2002, and voicing his opposition to the war in Iraq in 2003.

In 1998 he marked his twentieth year as pope, making him the longest-serving pontiff of the twentieth century, but his health was noticeably failing. The once-strong skier managed to hang on for another seven years, before taking a final wave good-bye to the people standing in St. Peter's Square below his window. His love of the theater from his youth was apparent in his charismatic style. That quality combined with a genuine love of people often overrode the controversy about his hard-line stand on Church doctrine. He died at the Vatican on April 2, 2005, at the age of 84.

---

**Epiphanies**

Pope trumps king! The pope's funeral on April 8, 2005, forced the rescheduling of the marriage of Britain's Prince Charles to Camilla Parker-Bowles, which had been planned for that same day—causing some to wonder if Henry VIII, the "errant" king who left the Catholic Church on the issue of his re-marriage and started his own church, rolled over in his grave that day!

---

## New Pope in a New Millennium

Pope Benedict XVI, elected on April 19, 2005, became the first pope elected under the new procedure. At the age of 78, he is the oldest person to have been elected pope since Clement XII in 1730. He served longer as a cardinal before being elected pope than any pope since Benedict XIII (elected 1724). He is the ninth German pope, the last being the Dutch-German Adrian VI (1522–1523). The last pope named Benedict was Benedict XV, an Italian who served from 1914 to 1922, during World War I.

Joseph Alois Ratzinger was born in 1927 in Bavaria, Germany, of a working-class family. In accordance with the law, at 14 he was conscripted into the Hitler Youth. It is reported he was an unenthusiastic member who refused to attend meetings.

He began his career as a university theologian before being made an archbishop. Ratzinger is considered to be a primary architect of Vatican II. He was made a cardinal by Pope Paul VI in 1977, and appointed the prefect of the Congregation for the Doctrine of the Faith by Pope John Paul II in 1981. Cardinal Ratzinger was a close friend and associate of Pope John Paul II and one of the most influential men in the Vatican. Pope Benedict XVI speaks German, Italian, and French fluently, and English, Spanish, and Latin slightly less fluently. He can read ancient Greek and classical Hebrew.

# The Big Church and the Little Church

Beginning at ground level, the Church is divided into parishes (local districts) that are under the direction of their pastor. Parishes are grouped into a diocese, under the direction of a bishop.

The diocese is the ruling structure of the Church, and all the parishes within the diocese follow the guidelines established by their bishop. (Remember, bishops operating together form the ruling body of the whole Church, and even the pope is a bishop (although he is granted the head leadership role). A group of dioceses are grouped into provinces or archdioceses that are governed by an archbishop. Archbishop is a title representing a slight bump up from bishop, but an archbishop is still a bishop.

| Structure | Geographical Divisions |
| --- | --- |
| Pope | Vatican (the Diocese of Rome) |
| Cardinals/Archbishops | Archdioceses (or Provinces) |
| Bishops | Dioceses |
| Priests | Parishes |

Catholics primarily identify themselves by their parish, and parish life is discussed in Chapter 16.

# Rules and Regulations

Catholics follow the Ten Commandments. In doing that, special emphasis is placed on what is called the twofold law of love of God and neighbor, which Jesus said was the most important commandment. Other important sources for Catholic teaching come from the Bible's Sermon on the Mount, where Jesus pointed out the importance of compassion.

**For Heaven's Sake**

Don't get caught up in the rules! Remember the twofold law. Love is the first law, and motivates one toward good. "You shall love the Lord your God with all your heart, with all your soul, with all your mind, and all your strength." (Mark 12:30, Deuteronomy 6:5) Likewise, "Love your neighbor as yourself." This is the basis for the whole moral law.

## The Ten Commandments

The Ten Commandments are also called the Decalogue, which comes from the Hebrew phrase meaning "10 words." Taken from the Old Testament Scriptures Exodus 34:28 and Deuteronomy 4:13 and 10:4, the Ten Commandments are believed to have been given to Moses by God on Mount Sinai.

Many of the requirements set down in the commandments are not unique to the Jewish people; they can also be found in other texts of the ancient Near East. Nowhere else, however, are they so clearly and concisely stated or expressed so personally. As described in the Scriptures, God gives the Ten Commandments directly to the Jewish people in *His own voice*. It is said that they were written by God's own hand on two tablets of stone, the first containing the commandments that directly refer to our relationship to God and the second governing our relations with one another. The Ten Commandments constitute the foundation of Christian law and ethics.

Here are the Ten Commandments as they appear in Catholic teaching:

1. I am the Lord your God. You shall not have strange gods before me.
2. You shall not take the name of the Lord thy God in vain.
3. Keep holy the Sabbath.
4. Honor your father and your mother.
5. You shall not kill.
6. You shall not commit adultery.
7. You shall not steal.
8. You shall not bear false witness against your neighbor.
9. You shall not covet your neighbor's spouse.
10. You shall not covet your neighbor's goods.

The Ten Commandments play an important role in a Catholic's life. One of the first tasks of a young Catholic is not only to memorize them, but also to understand what it means to live by them.

## The Six Precepts

In addition to the Ten Commandments, the Church has six rules, called *precepts*, that members must adhere to:

1. Attend Mass on Sunday and on the six other established holy days of obligation.

2. Observe the fast days as established by the Church.

3. Confess any grave sins at least once a year.

4. Receive Communion at least once a year, preferably during the Easter season.

5. Contribute to the support of the Church.

6. Observe the Church's laws concerning marriage.

## The 1,752 Canons

From the very earliest times up to the present, the Church has compiled a complex system of rules called *Canon law*. These rules are compiled and reviewed regularly. Currently there are 1,752 Canon laws defining operational principles and internal structures, and describing the rights and obligations of members in relationship to their religious life.

> **S'ter Says**
>
> The term **canon** comes from the Greek word *kanon*, which means a "measuring stick." It is used to describe the rules governing the Church, or Church law.

Canon law affects the everyday Catholic by establishing the perimeters on how the faith should be lived. For example, Canon law regulates the sacramental life of the Church, determines how and when marriages take place, sets the rules for fasting, states the requirements for church attendance, and establishes the process by which leaders and teachers are chosen. For the most part, Canon law is Church law, not moral law, which is contained in the Ten Commandments.

## The Beatitudes

The spirit of the Church is expressed in the Beatitudes, which lie at the heart of the teachings. They provide examples of Jesus' love for the people and provide a map for Christian life. They sustain hope and proclaim the blessings and rewards of life in Christ. The Beatitudes teach that true happiness is not found in riches or well-being, fame, power, or material achievement, but in our good relations with one another. The following Beatitudes are taken from the New Testament of the Bible in Matthew (5:3–12) and are Jesus' teachings from the Sermon on the Mount:

- Blessed are the poor in spirit, for theirs is the kingdom of heaven.

- Blessed are those who mourn, for they shall be comforted.

- Blessed are the meek, for they shall inherit the earth.

- Blessed are those who hunger and thirst for justice, for they shall be satisfied.

- Blessed are the merciful, for they will receive mercy.

- Blessed are the pure in heart, for they shall see God.

- Blessed are the peacemakers, for they shall be called the children of God.

- Blessed are those who are persecuted for righteousness' sake, for theirs is the kingdom of heaven.

- Blessed are you when people revile you and persecute you and utter all kinds of evil against you falsely on my account. Rejoice and be glad, for your reward is great in heaven, for in the same way they persecuted the prophets who were before you.

As we began this section, we pointed out that Jesus came to bring us the law of love that he expressed as love of God and neighbor. The Ten Commandments, the six laws of the Church, and all Catholic rules and regulations are for the purpose of instruction—they inform conscience. The individual ultimately stands responsible for his or her actions.

## Conscience, Virtue, and Grace

Catholics believe that moral conscience is present at the heart of a person. This belief follows the covenant relationship between God and the people established in Hebrew Scripture: "This is the covenant I will make with the house of Israel after that time, declares the Lord. I will put my law in their minds and write it on their hearts. I will be their God and they will be my people." (Jeremiah 31: 31–38)

Catholics believe that when you listen to your conscience, you hear God speaking. The Church teaches that each person has the right and responsibility to make personal moral decisions, and must not be forced to act against what he or she determines to be right action. Such interference violates the principle of free will. The Church also recognizes the wisdom of educating the conscience and sees this as a lifelong process.

The Church teaches there are three primary qualities, or virtues, that are characteristic of our soul, or the presence of the Holy Spirit of God within us—faith, hope, and love.

- ◆ By faith we intuitively understand that there is a God and actively seek to know and do God's will.

- ◆ Through hope we desire God regardless of the circumstances of our life at any given moment.

- ◆ Charity allows us to experience God's love, love ourselves, and love our neighbors.

Here are four additional or key virtues acquired through practice. They develop the inner compass:

- ◆ Prudence is *following* our "inborn" common sense.

- ◆ Justice is respecting others' rights and working for the common good.

- ◆ Courage ensures endurance in our pursuit of good.

- ◆ Temperance moderates our pursuit of life's pleasures, assuring balance.

Catholic spiritual life is honed by practicing these virtues in everyday interactions in the community with family, friends, and the society as a whole. To be a practicing Catholic doesn't just mean attending Mass on Sunday, or simply knowing about these virtues, but following these principles to the best of one's ability. The emphasis is on practice! The Church is the people of God always *striving* to live according to spiritual principles. To do this well, we need regular doses of grace.

Grace has many definitions. In the covenant sense, grace is the gift of God's presence or faithfulness to us, His promise of constant and unfailing love for us even when we fail to get it exactly right.

We've looked at the heart of the Catholic Church and the organizational structure that holds that core in place. In the next chapter we'll look at a shift in this organizational structure and some new challenges Catholics have been given to live their religious principles.

## The Least You Need to Know

- ◆ The Catholic Church expresses its unity through the office of the pope.

- ◆ The doctrine of infallibility is powerful, but seldom used.

- ◆ Traditions around electing the pope have changed, and we've said good-bye to Pope John Paul II and hello to Pope Benedict XVI.

- ◆ The Church bases its moral laws on the Bible and tradition, for the purpose of helping the faithful be faithful!

# The '60s: Seeds of Revolution

## In This Chapter

◆ Pope John XXIII opens the windows and the Church gets a good airing out

◆ Catholicism enters the third millennium with a new face and a new attitude

◆ We mend our fences and become better neighbors

◆ How we lost a few of our favorite things, and how we feel about that

The Second Vatican Council, called Vatican II, took place from 1962 to 1965. During those years, the pope summoned Church leaders to begin to reform and update Church policy and practice.

Young Catholics have most likely heard their parents and grandparents refer to being a pre–Vatican II Catholic, almost like they belonged to a totally different Church. Indeed this pivitol event molded a new Catholicism—it set the Church in a new direction. Tensions between progressives and conservatives that began at that tumultuous time in history continue to characterize Catholicism today. This chapter tells the story behind this tension and its creative contributions.

# The Stillness Before the Storm

Just as the bland sweetness of Wally and Beaver Cleaver represented the surface of America of the 1950s on television, growing up Catholic in the 1940s and 1950s for many had a similar innocence and order to it. It involved attending a Catholic grade school, which was most likely located right across the street from the public school. Other than a brief encounter at the crosswalks, the Catholics didn't mix much with the public school kids. They had their own ball teams, textbooks, library, and, of course, their own church.

Girls wore blue jumpers and white blouses for school. They kept their heads covered while they were in church, pinning on a tissue with a bobby pin in the absence of a proper scarf or hat. They always wore dresses to church and wore gloves on Sunday. Boys wore shirts and ties to school and suit coats to Mass. The sisters who taught school wore starched habits and long ropes of rosary beads that jangled (giving fair warning of their arrival) as they glided down clean, waxed corridors. The answers to all moral questions were neatly contained in the *Baltimore Catechism*, the little paperback book that held all the rules and beliefs of the Church. Every Catholic child memorized it.

The popular images of this time in history were merely a thin veneer covering long simmering issues of social, political, and spiritual unrest that emerged in the latter half of the 1950s and the early 1960s. For better or worse, the world would never be the same again.

## Vatican II: A Radical Departure and a Rebirth

Beginning with the Civil Rights Movement, followed by political assassinations and a growing anti-war sentiment, the America of the 1960s was in the throes of cultural and social revolution. As if the political questions being raised were not enough to shake the very ground of being, the Catholic Church chose this moment to come together to raise many of the same issues in the arena of religion that were being asked in the political world. Pope John XXIII, elected in 1958, prophetically called a *council* to update the Church and to open it up to the modern world.

His time at the helm was indeed short—a brief five years—yet he came to occupy a particularly crucial place in history. This very energetic man had an instinctual connection to the people and a far-reaching vision for the Church. His warmth, simplicity, and charm won the hearts of Catholics, Protestants, and non-Christians alike, and he bridged a religious and cultural gap. By stretching out his hand in friendship to non-Catholic Christians, calling them "separated brethren," Pope John made history. He showed us that the walls that divided Christians could be broken down and that it was possible to align the Church's life with the worlds of science, economics, and politics. Under his leadership, the Church was to become more Catholic and less Roman, making a huge leap toward that distant and elusive goal of Christian unity.

The Council opened on October 11, 1962. By this time, the pope knew of his own fatal illness. His death came more than 3 years before the council ended. The council continued without him, and the changes that were effected are still unfolding, influencing, and changing the face of Catholicism in the post-modern world.

> **S'ter Says**
>
> A **council** is an assembly of bishops from the whole Church called together by the pope to make decisions. The preceding council, Vatican I, was held from 1869 to 1870.

## Lighting the Council Fires

Church councils are rare; there had been only 20 in the nearly 2,000 years of Catholic history. Simply by summoning Vatican II, Pope John caused a major impact. Added to that, it was the first council called for the purpose of initiating change from within—looking at Church policy rather than marshaling the Church against hostile forces such as a rising heresy, or threatening political climate.

There were more than 900 million Catholics at the time of Vatican II, making it the world's largest religion. The revolution begun by Pope John XXIII with Vatican II put into motion ideas and forces that would come to affect a major portion of the world's population. The Church's revolution brought it into the world and onto the front pages of newspapers, often outranking the secular concerns of the day. The Church's monolithic and absolutist character was forever changed.

> **Your Guardian Angel**
>
> Do justice, love kindness, and walk humbly. A prophetic message from the past given to the Jewish people by Micah is as pertinent to the Church today as it was then: "What does Yahweh require of you but to do justice and to love kindness, and walk humbly with your God?" (Micah 6:8)

Prophets have always had a place in religious history. We know their names from the Old Testament: Isaiah, Amos, Micah, and Elijah, to name a few. Their voices often cried out for change. Perhaps the most revolutionary mark of Vatican II was its acknowledgment of Catholicism's modern-day prophets. It recognized that those who had difficulty with the Church, even those who had left it, might well have had good reasons for doing so.

Pope John invited the bishops to Rome to speak freely. He encouraged what he called "holy liberty." The bishops, who had long considered the pope as the sole source of power and authority in the Church, discovered that they, and not just the pope, constituted the leadership of the Church.

---

### Epiphanies

A story that captures the spirit of the changing times in both the arena of politics and religion involves Jacqueline Kennedy's visit to Pope John XXIII. He asked his secretary what would be the proper way to address her. The secretary replied, "Mrs. Kennedy or just Madame, since she is of French origin and has lived in France." Waiting in his private library, the pope went over the options, trying to decide which one to use: "Mrs. Kennedy, Madame; Madame, Mrs. Kennedy." Then the doors opened, and the First Lady entered. He stood up, extended his arms, and cried "Jacqueline!"

---

In the 5 years of the council, Church leaders pounded out a new definition of the Church and a new way for the Church to relate to the world. The new model of Church drew its power from the Old Testament covenant relationship between God and his creation. "People of God" became the defining image.

Internally, a major goal of Vatican II was to be less focused on its institutional structure and more focused on its people. It invited all Church members to more active participation. Internally, the Church began to not only see itself as an institution that organized and ruled people, but equally as a community of people with co-responsibility.

Externally, the Church shifted from seeing itself as the only means of salvation to improving its relationship to the larger community—the whole people of God. It began to take down many of the walls that existed between Catholics and the rest of the world. In doing this, the council addressed the following areas of the Church:

- Liturgy: the prayers, songs, and the Mass
- The role of the laity: from spectators to participants
- The role of the Church in the political and social world
- Religious freedom and respect for other spiritual paths

Core issues of Catholic identity were fundamentally challenged; the rules changed. We'll take a look at these changes next.

## The Altar Rail Comes Down, the Priest Turns Around

To the average Catholic, the changes in Church ceremony after Vatican II were nothing less than shocking. The altar was moved forward. The priest now faced the people during Mass, and the altar railing came down. Members of the congregation walked up to the altar and read the Scripture at Mass. The Mass was no longer said in Latin, and during the service, members of the congregation turned to one another with a handshake. Even the priest left the altar to walk up and down the aisle and greet members of the crowd by name.

Like the culture around it, the Church reflected the atmosphere of informality that characterized the 1960s. Worshippers wore jeans to church, and sometimes folk music played in the background. In some churches, you might have seen a bareheaded young woman and her longhaired boyfriend carrying the Communion bread and wine up to the altar to be consecrated. Perhaps most striking of all, the priest handed the bread of Communion to Church members rather than placing it on their tongues. In the past, only the priest, whose hands had been consecrated, was allowed to touch the Communion host.

Prior to Vatican II, a "father-knows-best" attitude prevailed throughout the Church. All decisions were made on the highest level by the pope and handed down to the bishops, who handed them down to the priests. In the parish, the priest made the decisions and handed them down to the people. Now, in the post–Vatican II Church, laity were invited to participate in Church governance through *parish councils.*

> **S'ter Says**
>
> A **parish council** is a group of Church members whose job it is to plan and secure the resources for the mission of the parish.

Councils composed of both priests and lay members of the Church were also established to work with the bishop at the level of the diocese. The spirit of collegiality was similarly expressed as bishops were invited into a more collaborative relationship with the pope than had ever existed in the history of the Church. Although many people still tend to think that the pope holds all authority in the Catholic Church, in reality Vatican II changed all that.

## The Rosary Gives Way to the Bible

Vatican II changed the people's relationship to the Bible as Catholic education began to focus Scripture reading and reflection. A ceremony called Liturgy of the Word became a well-attended regular feature of parish life, in many cases replacing the Rosary as a favorite devotion.

Today, many people share their faith in small gatherings in homes reading and reflecting on Scripture—a tradition that departs radically from what had always been the "Catholic way." As you will read in Chapter 7, the Catholic religion is based in the Bible, but private interpretation of the Scripture was discouraged. The sacraments continued to be a mainstay of Catholic spiritual life, and adding Scripture enriched the faith experience of Catholics.

# Church as Listener

Perhaps the most revolutionary concept to come out of Vatican II was a new relationship to the culture. The Council reversed centuries of Church antagonism toward the world and gave it a new direction—to listen and learn from the times.

In the spirit of Vatican II, the Church issued a long overdue apology to Galileo and removed 400-year-old sanctions against him, recognizing him posthumously as a great scientist. Although this apology may seem totally bizarre to the present-day reader, it represented a complete change in Church policy. Popes, like kings and queens and many other political and religious leaders, traditionally did not—and still do not—apologize. To do so showed a complete change of protocol. This expression alone represented one of the most remarkable and revolutionary changes of identity that resulted from Vatican II.

---

**Epiphanies**

Galileo (1564–1642), Italian mathematician, physicist, and astronomer, was one of the first men to emphasize scientific observation rather than philosophical speculation to learn how the natural world works. He invented many instruments and was able to apply mathematical laws to determine that the Earth moves around the sun rather than the reverse, which was the popular belief of Europeans and the Church of his day. He was brought before the Church authorities in 1633, where he was forced to take back his teachings and was put under permanent "house arrest." As he left the court, it is said he murmured, "and yet it moves," referring to the Earth's revolution around the sun.

---

## Science and Faith Reach a Compromise

One of the ways the Church has begun to reflect its new role as listener is by paying attention to some of the visionaries in its ranks. Pierre Teilhard de Chardin, who lived from 1881 to 1955, was a visionary who bridged the gap between the two worlds of science and religion in his writings and teachings in modern time. He was a paleontologist and a French Jesuit theologian.

Chardin's writings ended the mind/body duality for both the secular world and the Church. His positive vision helped to set aside conflicts between religion and science and inspired the spiritual journeys of many men and women in search of a worldview that is beyond the conflicts of dualism.

Chardin told of his two loves, one for the world of matter known by science and the other for the world of spirit revealed by faith. He said that at one time they were like two stars that divided his allegiance. Through his love and devotion to both science and religion, he eventually reconciled the two, seeing matter and spirit as indivisible and evolving together.

## From the Sanctuary to Selma

The world the Church stepped into was in massive turmoil over almost every social issue: race relations, international relations, and sexual relations. The Council gave the green light to active involvement in the world's culture and suddenly priests were advocating for social and political change from their pulpits, activities almost unheard of in the United States before this time. This radical confrontation with the real world was shocking to many Catholics, who turned on the 6 o'clock news and not only saw young people arrested and dragged off by police but also their beloved nuns, priests, and bishops in handcuffs.

Catholics began to look below the surface to examine the very structures of the society. There was a shift in focus from charity to justice, and from personal sin to social sin. Rather than simply helping the poor, Catholics began to push their leaders to look at the causes of poverty.

 **For Heaven's Sake**

"Take away from me the noise of your songs; to the melody of your harps I will not listen. But let justice roll down like waters, and righteousness like an ever-flowing steam." (Amos 5:23–24)

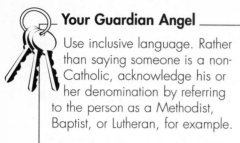

Social justice became a core focus—to be a Catholic was to be involved with the issues of the world and to seek justice (more on this in Chapter 18). Church leaders talked, wrote, and preached about peace, justice, racism, poverty, nuclear war, and ecology. In Latin America, clergy seeking justice for their people risked torture and death to challenge what they considered to be unjust authorities.

# Ecumenism: Catholics' Relationship to Other Christians

Ecumenism is a term that describes the unity of all Christian believers and the Vatican II Council declared that the term *Church* included all Christians, not just those who practiced the Catholic faith. Prior to Vatican II, Catholics divided the world into two distinct categories: Catholics and non-Catholics. After Vatican II, in the spirit of John XXIII, they referred to other Christians as "separated brethren," a marked shift in the Church's belief that it was the only true Church.

## Ecumenism Begins at Home

Ecumenism has very practical consequences for average Catholics. In the past, the Church placed major restrictions that discouraged marriage between Catholics and others. For example, if a Catholic married a Protestant, the service was often performed in the privacy of the priest's office rather than in the church. Very little public recognition was given to "mixed" marriages.

Today, not only can mixed marriages take place in the sanctuary, but often the priest also invites the partner's minister or rabbi to participate in the ceremony. With the permission of the bishop, the marriage can take place before another Christian minister or rabbi. Today it would not be uncommon for the partner of a Catholic to participate in Catholic Church services and functions, including being a member of the parish council.

Many commissions and dialogues have been established to improve communication and bring about greater understanding among all Christians. Preachers from other Christian faiths have been invited to speak in Catholic churches. Cooperative ventures in social justice efforts such as Room at the Inn, a program to house homeless people in the winter, bring many churches together to open their doors to each other as well as to the needy.

## Expanding Interfaith Relationships

Vatican II not only took a more open stance toward other Christians, it also reached out to mend relationships with other faiths, particularly the Jewish people, removing prayers from the liturgy that implied Jewish culpability in the death of Jesus. For centuries past, these prayers and the attitudes they represented contributed to anti-Semitism on the part of the Catholic Church and many Catholics.

Additional efforts have been made in the religious education curriculum to revise prejudicial stands toward the Jews and to teach about the Hebrew faith. This new attitude has led Church scholars to encourage a deeper respect for sacred Hebrew literature, referring to the Old Testament as the "Hebrew Scriptures" or "The First Testament." These writings are now recognized as important to the faith not just as an introduction to the "Christian Scripture" or New Testament.

A major effort of the Church since Vatican II has been to re-evaluate the Catholic Church's role in the Holocaust. Pope Pius XII has been criticized by many for failure to take a stand against Nazi Germany's persecution of the Jews. Pope John Paul II spoke out on this matter, offering an apology to the Jewish people for the Church's conduct. Clearly, much more investigation and explanation is necessary before any moves toward reparation can be meaningful.

In addition to attempts to repair relations with the Jewish people, the Church has reached out to Muslims, meeting with Muslim leaders and delegations in Rome and around the world. Pope John Paul II has spoken to large gatherings of Muslims in Morocco, Indonesia, Mali, and elsewhere. Formal dialogues have been held from time to time with Islamic organizations to promote good relations between the Christian world and the Islamic world.

Within Catholic monastic life, the hand of friendship has been extended to members of Buddhism, Hinduism, Confucianism, Taoism, and Shinto. Buddhist and Catholic monks have joined together in practices and studies of the mystical life. Thomas Merton, a popular twentieth-century Catholic mystic, met with Buddhists to talk about the mystical life and social justice issues during the Vietnam War before he died in Thailand in 1968.

## We Throw Open Heaven's Gate: Religious Liberty

Vatican II issued "The Declaration on Religious Liberty." In this important paper, the council declared that all people have the right to religious freedom. This means that all men and women should be free from coercion regarding religious choices. No one can be forced to act against personal convictions in choice of religion and practices.

This document held particular importance to U.S. Catholics, because the United States was the first Western country to be constitutionally founded on religious freedom. During his campaign for president, John F. Kennedy made it clear that Catholics championed this separation.

"The Declaration on Religious Liberty" also had a profound effect on Catholic missionary activity. No longer was it acceptable to disregard the beliefs of others. As a result, mission efforts have been much more concerned with sharing beliefs rather than imposing the Catholic faith.

# Conscience Reigns Supreme

Catholic teaching has always taught that you must obey your conscience. Vatican II strengthened that stand. Prior to Vatican II, Catholics generally would seek and follow the advice of their priest in moral matters. Since Vatican II, they have been urged to search their own hearts and minds to come to their own informed moral decisions. Likewise, priests were encouraged to approach the confessional with compassion rather than judgment.

# A Painful Side Effect of Vatican II: Loss of Tradition

Although Vatican II brought positive changes to the lives of Catholics, many of the faithful felt a deep loss as traditional and beloved beliefs and practices were altered or dropped altogether in an effort to update the Church. In addition, the Church lost some of its uniqueness. Once so clearly defined by their difference from other faiths, and characterized by separation from the world, many Catholics were left with a vague sense of the Church being "less Catholic" than it used to be.

### For Heaven's Sake

Take responsibility for yourself and your actions. The post–Vatican II Catholic Church emphasizes personal responsibility for moral decisions, which means that you cannot simply follow directions. You must seek instruction, pray and meditate, and make your own moral choices.

## Mea Culpa, Mea Culpa, Mea Maxima Culpa

*Mea culpa, mea culpa, mea maxima culpa* is Latin for "I am sorry, I am sorry, I am heartily sorry." It was a line from a prayer said at the beginning of the Mass, but it also spoke to the sentiment of many Catholics who regretted the loss of their Latin prayers. Until Vatican II, all Catholics heard the Mass in this ancient language. Thus, it was possible to attend Mass in any Catholic church in the world and hear the prayers said in exactly the same way. In the pre–Vatican II days, uniformity was the rule, and diversity and individuality were discouraged.

Likewise, Church music was written and performed in Latin; when the language of the Mass was changed to the vernacular, meaning the language of the country, the music changed, too. The choir had been a central gathering point for many in the Church, and as traditional music such as Gregorian chant, classical music, favorite hymns and psalms that had been sung in Latin was suddenly deemphasized and the congregation was urged to sing, many felt a painful loss of their religious identity.

Catholics traditionally abstained from eating meat on Friday to honor the day Christ died—a practice that was intrinsic to Catholic identity. Vatican II changed the status of many dietary rules, making them voluntary rather than absolute.

Today, dietary restrictions have been relaxed so that Friday meat abstinence is urged only during Lent (the 40-day period of preparation for Easter) and fasting before Communion can be limited to 1 hour before reception. Some wonder if this relaxation does not take the "Holy" out of "Holy Communion," make Catholics forgetful of the Lord, and diminish the celebration of Easter.

**Your Guardian Angel**

Make Friday your fish day. Every Catholic over the age of 50 knows at least 10 recipes for tuna casserole. Here is a favorite one: mix one large can drained tuna fish with one can cream of mushroom soup, add 2 cups cooked macaroni or rice, and top with crushed potato chips. Bake for 20 minutes in a moderate oven. Deeeeeelicious!

## Shifting Prayers and Practices

Many other practices and prayers once considered an integral part of the Catholic faith and ritual either have been eliminated or their importance has been diminished. You can read more about them in Parts 3 and 4.

These ceremonies, practiced faithfully for decades, gave Catholics a clear image of what it meant to belong to a particular tribe of people—to be Catholic. For many people, the loss of these ceremonies has resulted in the blurring of their image of what it means to be Catholic.

Attendance at Mass has dropped and, as the definitions about sin have been softened, people no longer line up outside the confessional on Saturday afternoon, as was once the weekend ritual. Catholicism lost its absolutism, and for many it also lost its certainty.

## The Saints Suffer

Popular and long-standing devotion to saints was also up for reassessment. Catholics have a saint for every day of the year, and a saint is designated as the patron of almost everything from countries to careers to conditions. As the Church attempted to clean up its roster, determining which had a historical basis and which were simply part of the folk legends of the people, many were removed from the records. In doing this, Church leaders discovered that the people were not willing to let the saints go.

Regardless of whether there was a historical basis for these saints, the virtues represented in the stories about them were important to the people. They had become part of the fabric of Church mythology, and the Church leaders could not unravel it. St. Christopher, a beloved character in Catholic mythology and popular with non-Catholics, too, was one of the saints who was declared to be no longer part of the official directory. However, devotion to him has continued. Today, as always, people keep St. Christopher medals in their cars and feel protection under his care.

## Dress Code: Defrocking the Clerics

After Vatican II, the familiar dress of nuns and clergy were relaxed. Many nuns moved out of the convents into other living arrangements; some even took secular jobs. There has been a mixed response to these changes. Catholics liked the fact that their religious leaders could be so easily identified and that the greater community showed them respect. Many people feel the change in dress code resulted in a general lack of regard for the Church and its leaders. Others feel that the old style of dress set religious leaders apart too much and emphasized separation of the religious leaders from the people they were to serve.

## Numbers Tell the Story

Numbers tell the story of the changing face of the Church. In the pre–Vatican II days, a large parish typically would have four or five priests. Today, very few parishes have more than one in residence. Often the parishes are much larger. There has been a big exodus of priests, nuns, and brothers from the Church ministry since the 1960s, and the number of people entering religious life has dropped. This downsizing of clerical ministers is seen both as a sign of the times and a result of Vatican II's strict adherence to celibacy. Many persons had expected a change in this regulation.

*Sister Mary Catherine, CSJ (Congregation of St. Joseph), in the traditional pre–Vatican II habit of her order.*

*(Courtesy of Bob O'Gorman and Mary Faulkner)*

The reduction in religious vocations is a great challenge the Church faces in the post–Vatican II time. Many feel that the shortage will eventually cause the Church to rethink its stand on celibacy and on the ordination of women. In addition, a major focus of the council was toward giving more responsibility to the people. The reduction in Church staff has certainly resulted in more participation by the lay members of the Church.

*Here Sister Mary Catherine appears in a post–Vatican II style of dress.*

*(Courtesy of Bob O'Gorman and Mary Faulkner)*

We've just taken a quick look at the Church both before and after Vatican II. Now we're going to go back in time to the beginnings of the religion and see how it developed. We'll look at its roots, the Bible, Jesus, and the beginning of his followers' journey.

## The Least You Need to Know

◆ Vatican II was an important turning point for Catholics; it directed the institution to be inclusive and identified all as the "people of God."

◆ The Church focused the religion less on institutional structure and more on the people.

◆ Better relations between Catholics and Protestants, Catholics and Jews, and Catholics and the rest of the world were fostered.

◆ In updating the Church, some traditions that were important to many Catholics were lost.

◆ The Church continues to work through the changes brought on through the council of Vatican II—essentially updating Church thinking from the last 100 years.

# Part 2

# Putting the "Ism" in Catholicism: Becoming Catholic, Becoming Different

In *Fiddler on the Roof*, the character Tevia sings about a very important word, "tradition." As with our Jewish forebears, tradition is an important part of Catholicism. Tradition is the composite teachings of the Church, compiled over the last 2,000 years, and Catholics believe that both the revelations within tradition as well as the Bible must be taken into account as faith directives. For many Protestants, the focus must be on Scripture alone.

Catholic tradition, as you will see, is deep and wide, going to the center of the earth as well as stretching to its four corners. Just what constitutes official Catholic teaching (Catholic tradition) and traditional practices? These issues are the core of religion and are as alive and elusive today as they were yesterday—which can mean 2,000 years ago in this very old Church. At the same time, the story of this religion is the story of the progressive development called tradition. You'll learn about all this in Part 2.

# Chapter 6

# "It's Elementary, My Dear Watson"

## In This Chapter

- ◆ The roots of Catholicism are in the earth
- ◆ Catholicism draws its identity from the Jewish Scripture
- ◆ Greek learning gives Catholicism a heady start
- ◆ Catholics gain power and might from the Roman tradition

In this chapter, you'll see how the Catholic religion came upon the scene within the context of human history. We'll explore the experiences, images, and stories that make up the ritual, creed, and code of the Catholic Church. You might be surprised to find the sources of its ritual in the ceremonies of ancient people. We'll look at the culture and religion of the Jews, Greeks, Romans, and Celtic people and see how they influenced the formation of the early Church and how their influence is still present in the modern Church.

The Church's official birthday is Pentecost, the day the Scriptures tell us the followers of Jesus went out into the community to tell of their experience with him. But the story has much deeper roots than that.

The Church is a composite of many quite ancient rituals that speak to the heart, mind, and actions of its members.

# Ritual: The Old Religion, Roots, and Renewal

One of the hallmarks of Catholics is their long tradition of ritual and ceremony. In order to understand the religion, it helps to understand how rituals work to transmit spiritual truths. We don't know exactly how that happens, but we do know that rituals work to reveal deep spiritual meanings to those who participate in them.

**For Heaven's Sake**

Watch your language! The word *pagan* can be a derogatory term. If you're talking about someone who believes in more than one god, you may be better off using the word polytheistic.

Earth is the first church. To get to the core of the Catholic religion, we're going to go on a very deep journey into the heart of our planet. The roots of this old tradition go to the very beginnings of the human story: back to birth, death, and regeneration. Ever since humans conceived of some power or spirit beyond themselves, they have enacted and re-enacted elementary themes of life and death in what is called ritual. Ritual began as our way of reinforcing what we intuitively knew.

The term *Judeo-Christian* describes Catholics' connection to the Jewish religion and acknowledges our common history. Yet even farther back than this tradition is a culture developed by the people who lived in the Fertile Crescent, an ancient region made up of what is today the Middle East, Turkey, and Greece. The people of this culture, sometimes called *pagans*, had well-developed societies, raised children, built towns, made pottery, worked with metal, said prayers, and enjoyed productive, artistic lives. Some were monotheistic, believing in one God, and others were polytheistic, believing that God takes many forms. Many of these tribal people were assimilated into Judaism and Christianity. The tribal religions of Europe survived for hundreds of years into the Christian era and a cultural exchange went on between the two cultures that influenced Church practices and rituals we still use today.

Pagan is a word that was originally used as a derogatory term to describe one who lived in the country (the "sticks") rather than the city. Another term for pagan would have been country bumpkin. The meaning was further shortened to describe anyone who is not a Christian, Moslem, or a Jew, as these religions developed in the cities. The term *pagan* is often used to describe the religions of the Greeks and Romans—distinguishing them from Jews or Christians, and is sometimes applied to indigenous cultures today. *Heathen* originally described those who lived on the heath. It is now applied to the people regarded as worshipping "false gods." In light of modern scholarship, both terms are considered culturally insensitive.

## Elementally Speaking

To revisit these people and explore their faith is vital to the understanding of Catholicism because, fundamentally, all religion is about understanding who we are and our connection to the Creator, as well as understanding the way humans have interacted in the world throughout history. The word *religion* comes from the Latin *religare*, which means "to bind back, to bind together." Understanding religion, then, means connecting to the past and learning the story of the communities of people on earth who came before us—and reconnecting to the whole of creation. Their simpler, peaceful societies are an important contribution to the human story. We can't go forward until we go backward and connect their stories with our own.

> **S'ter Says**
>
> **Religion** concerns what exists beyond our comprehension. It is different from philosophy in that it operates from faith or intuition rather than reason.

For many thousands of years, it was believed that all physical matter was composed of four elements: earth, air, fire, and water. These elements symbolized God's real presence in creation. The seasons and cycles of nature translated to our own human spiritual process. Our creativity was connected to the Creator and reflected in the earth's abundance. Crops planted in the earth would be nourished by the sun and rain and would produce food. Winter was like a death: inevitable and a part of life. Nature shut down and regenerated itself again in spring. To die was to be reborn. Ceremonies celebrating the seasons of the year were deeply rooted in the human psyche; they affirmed that life would continue.

## A Visit to Antiquity

Imagine you're a member of a tribe living thousands of years ago. Summer is ending. The days grow shorter. A distinct chill fills the morning air. The vines no longer produce their fruits. You're concerned about the food supply. (Remember that this is before the age of microwaves and corner grocery stores. When the food is gone, it's gone!) If the winter is as long and cold as it was the previous year, will there be enough food? Will the old people and the children stay warm enough; will they survive the winter? Winter connects us to thoughts of death, but also to spring's renewal.

Today, as well as in ancient times, rituals and rites explore these themes. In the past, drummers gathered in a circle outside the cave and beat their drums in rhythms that matched the human heartbeat to make the spirit strong for winter. Then dancers circled the fire, echoing the beat and pounding the experience of hope renewed, moving it up through the legs into the body and into their hearts.

### S'ter Says

The words **ceremony** and **ritual** are often used to describe the same thing: a formal act or set of formal acts established by custom or authority as proper to a special occasion, such as a wedding or other formality. They describe the process by which we observe something that we want to honor as important or sacred.

Hope is strengthened through the rhythms of *ritual* and enactment of *ceremony*. In Baptism, for example, we light the candle, which is our ritual fire. We are immersed in water, and through it we are born into the new life of the Spirit just as God once gave us physical life through our mother. We are connected in a sacramental way to God's renewing Spirit. We are reborn.

Within the Catholic Church, the rituals and ceremonies celebrate not the passing of seasons as they did in ancient times, but rather the physical presence of Christ on earth. His availability to human beings, walking and talking with them in their everyday experiences, is a key belief for Catholics. They believe he showed us that God is, was, and will always be present to His people. We can realize His presence through all of creation. We can understand that we are loved and cared for in all ways. God is in the earth, providing food, shelter, and all the material things we need to sustain us.

Catholics connect to the earthly presence of God by enacting rituals. Through rituals, they're able to physically touch and be touched by God's presence. The Communion bread is made of the wheat that grows in the fields. The Communion ritual says: "I am here with you. This is my body. I will feed and nourish you. This is how I am intimate with you." This earthy ritual manifests the physicality of God.

Rituals are tribal events. They're acted out in a community. It is only when we find a connection to the symbols of hope with others that we become certain of their validity. (We explore Catholic ritual and how it works in Chapter 9.)

# "Yada, Yada, Yada"

As we stated earlier, Catholics share a common history with the Jews. In Hebrew, the word for faith is *yada*, which the Greeks translated as *gnoskin (gnoskein)*, meaning "to know." For Judeo-Christians, *yada* (knowing) is something we do more with our hearts than with our minds. *Yada* comes from having earthy experiences, not by standing back from the world at an intellectual distance. Indeed, faith and knowing are action words that require a lot of living to achieve. A Catholic's faith is expressed through action in the world, and its roots stem from the Jewish tradition of *yada*.

To strengthen and develop this faith, both Jews and Catholics look to Scripture. The term *Bible* is commonly used to designate the sacred writings of the Christians, but it contains both the Jewish and the Christian Scriptures. In fact, the word *Bible* comes from the Greek *ta biblia*, meaning "the books," which describes its contents rather accurately. When the term was translated into Latin, the plural was dropped, making it the singular "The Book" we know today. (Chapter 7 explores the Bible further.)

**For Heaven's Sake**

The Old Testament is old, but not out-of-date. It is called old in relationship to the New Testament that begins with the life of Christ. The stories continue to give us fresh meaning and insight, and are integral to the religious understanding of Christians.

---

**Epiphanies**

The abbreviations B.C. (before Christ) and A.D. (*Anno Domini*, which means "in the year of our Lord") have been in existence a long time and are widely accepted by the entire world, but they are strictly Christian in origin. Many believe these abbreviations are insensitive to non-Christians. Sometime in the last century, people began using the new terms B.C.E. (before the common era) and C.E. (common era). Jewish people, Moslems, Buddhists, Hindus, and many other religious groups agree that these new terms are more accurate for all people. We'll use them in this book.

---

To Catholics and Jews, Scriptures are inspired, meaning that they have divine origin and provide guidance and comfort as well as the special sense of connection with the divine. Scriptures contain common themes, stories, and characters that give an identity to a religion and by which a religion can interpret the unfolding events of the day. These stories and characters provide a mirror in which people look to see who they are and where they came from, as well as where they are headed.

# Paradise Lost, and Paradise Found

A culture's creation story gives you the basics on what the people of that culture believe about God, the world, and themselves. The Judeo-Christian creation story begins in the Garden of Eden.

Genesis, the first book of the Jewish Scripture, explains that God has been involved in a huge project called Creation. God created the earth, the sea, the sky, the animals, Adam (the first man), and Eve (the first woman). In this book, God places humans in a beautiful garden and cares for their needs. The humans walk and talk with God on a regular basis. Right from the beginning of the story, God is shown to be personal and caring.

**For Heaven's Sake**

Don't think the Genesis creation story is the only one available. There are more than 20,000 known creation stories. Virtually every group of people has a story about how the world was created and how its culture came into being.

God puts only one stipulation on Adam and Eve. He tells them not to eat the fruit of a certain tree. A serpent, representing evil, enters the garden and tempts them to eat the forbidden fruit. As they eat the fruit, they immediately experience terrible consequences. They are cut off from the very close relationship they enjoyed with God, and they are, as the Scripture says, "cast out of the garden." However, later in Genesis, God promises the people that He will not forget them.

The human journey depicted in Genesis begins in travail and loss, but also with promise of reunion. Christians believe that Jesus brings the long-sought-after reunion with God, the reunion God promised. Here's what the story of Genesis means to Catholics' understanding of their relationship to God and relationships among men and women on earth:

- Creation has a master plan. It has meaning.

- We are created in God's image, which means we are intelligent, compassionate, and creative.

- There are sacred laws and rules that we must follow.

- We have free choice, and our choices carry responsibility.

- God is compassionate and will stay with us. He has a covenant relationship with the people.

The creation story in Genesis conveys a sense both of loss and of promise. This theme runs throughout Christianity. In Judaism, it is expressed as the covenant relationship between God and the people. Christians believe Jesus fulfills the covenant.

# The Covenant

The idea of the *covenant* is the central theme in the Hebrew Scriptures of the Old Testament. In the covenant relationship between God and the Jewish people, God promises to stay faithful to His people, and the people promise their faithfulness to Him. This theme of covenant is expressed in the following stories.

In the story of Noah (found in Genesis 9:9–11), God sends a flood to punish the people. Noah is saved because God judged him and his family to be just. When the flood is over, God places a rainbow in the sky as a symbol of His promise to the people, the animals, and the earth that He will never send another flood to destroy them:

**S'ter Says**

A **covenant** is made of two separate agreements. Each party agrees to abide by certain rules of the covenant. If one party fails to keep the covenant, the other party is still obligated. This makes a covenant different than a contract, because in contracts default can take place. Covenants have no default.

> I will establish my covenant with you and with your descendants after you; and with every living creature that is with you, the birds, the cattle, and every wild animal with you; all that came out of the ark, even the wild animals. I establish my covenant with you. Never again shall all living things be destroyed by the waters of the flood; never again shall there be a flood to destroy the earth." And God said, "This is the token of the covenant; I set it between me and you and every living creature that is with you, for all generations to come. I will set my rainbow in the clouds, and it shall be a token of the covenant between me and the earth." (Genesis 9:9–13)

In a later story, God tests Abraham by asking him to offer his son, Isaac, as a sacrifice. Abraham is grief-stricken but obeys God and prepares to kill his son. God stops him and forms a covenant, promising Abraham that because he has obeyed, he will become the father of a great nation and that the land of Canaan will be its permanent possession. (Genesis 22:1–19)

## Moses Receives the Law

At Mount Sinai, God seals a special covenant with the entire people of Israel through Moses as He gives Moses the law. Catholics believe in the covenant relationship as it is presented in the Hebrew Scriptures. Both Judaism and Catholicism are based on the understanding that God is constant and available and that we have a choice in entering into relationship with Him. To be in this relationship means we have the responsibility to live in accordance with His laws.

Law is the second central theme of Jewish identity. The Ten Commandments are the core of Jewish law. God gave them to the people through one of their leaders, Moses. Jews do not experience the law as an external obligation, but as an expression of God's care. God gives His people the law as an act of love, as His side of the covenant. The people respond to it as their side of the covenant. It is through obeying the law (right action) that the Jewish people know of God's love.

The Jews were a wandering nomadic people who had no homeland. They carried the presence of God with them on an object called an ark. The ark housed the Scriptures that contained the law, their covenant with God. Eventually, when they established a homeland, the Ark of the Covenant was placed in the holiest part of the temple. The temple, then, became the place where Jews could be in physical contact with the sacred relationship that was signified by God's law.

---

### Epiphanies

The Ark of the Covenant resided in the most holy place in the Jewish temple. It was entered on one day only per year, the Day of Atonement (Yom Kippur). Access was restricted to one person, the high priest. The ark itself was a small box made of acacia wood, overlaid with gold. Two long bars, also made of the same wood overlaid with gold, carried it. It contained three sacred items of the Jewish religion: the two stone tablets of the law given to Moses, Aaron's rod that budded, and the golden pot of hidden manna. Catholics keep the Communion bread in a similarly sized box, which they call the *tabernacle*. The tabernacle occupies a place of honor near the altar.

---

The Hebrew Scriptures talk of "knowing the Lord." This means that God takes the initiative, and the people respond to this encounter as it happens in events, in relationships, and in creation. In other words, such knowledge is gained here and now, not in an otherworldly way. Knowledge of the Lord is knowledge of the law and demands obedience to God's will.

In following this tradition, a Catholic's knowledge of God is not a fixed possession but is an activity. Knowledge develops in the life of the Catholic as lasting obedience and reflection. Faith is not a defined set of beliefs; it is an ongoing relationship with God.

## A Summary of Jewish Influence

These important aspects of Catholic identity come from the Hebrew Scriptures:

- **Monotheism.** The belief in one all-knowing God is central to both Catholicism and Judaism. Unfortunately, monotheism carries with it an intolerance of other religions.

- **God's presence.** Judaism's central theme is the covenant between God and the people. Faith is a living response.

- **Free will.** Catholics and Jews believe that we are all personally responsible for our actions. Actions bear consequences.

- **Moral law.** The Old Testament forms the basis for Christian morality as it does for the Jewish people.

The key difference between Judaism and Catholicism is that Catholics believe that Jesus came as the fulfillment of the Old Testament covenant Scriptures.

# Influences of the Greeks, Romans, and Indigenous Peoples

Although the influence of the Jewish faith is most easily recognized because Catholics and Jews share common sacred writings, two prominent cultural philosophies (the Greek and the Roman) also affected the formation of the early Church. Less prominent, yet equally important, were the indigenous peoples of the Middle East and their understanding of mystery.

## The Greeks Decapitate the Mind from the Body

What is called the Golden Age of Greece had been in full glory, influencing Jerusalem and the surrounding areas, for at least 300 years before Christianity. The view of the world held by the ancient Greeks is paradoxical. On the one hand, they contributed much of what is considered Western civilization in the way of art, education, health, philosophy, and mathematics; Greek order and beauty as well as Greek love of thought are the foundation of our understanding of culture.

On the other hand, the official religion of Greece was one based in power struggles and domination in which the god Zeus established and maintained his supremacy through acts of cruelty and barbarism. Greek philosophy was based on the belief that humans are ruthless, grasping, and self-centered. The Greeks had a very strict class system that required force to uphold—a force the Greeks believed was natural and right. The most influential thinker of the time was Plato. His perfect society was one in which the strong dominated the weak, and it became the model for Greek culture.

Plato was a Greek philosopher who lived 400 years before Christ. His thinking greatly influenced both the Greek and Roman world at that time and for the next 1,500 years. The Church reflected Plato's teachings in its own way. Plato believed that the human soul is eternal and that learning occurs when the soul remembers its former life. It then becomes one with the eternal perfect idea.

Plato believed God was the ideal form of good and that the goal of humans was to become more like God. His ideal world was composed of incorruptible, perfect forms held as ideas. The physical world contrasted sharply and was considered inferior to his perfect world of ideas.

Plato's philosophy is dualistic in that it sharply divides reality into two separate parts: either mind or matter, rather than both mind and matter. The shift in thinking from either/or to both that has occurred in more recent eras may seem like a small shift now, but it had major impact on the cultural development of the *Western world*.

> **S'ter Says**
> The **Western world** separates from the Eastern world in Istanbul, Turkey. Lands to the east are called the Eastern world, and to the west lies the Western world.

This duality between the spiritual world and the physical world began to infiltrate the Church right from the beginning. As Christianity moved out of the Jewish world and into the Greek world, it met the dualistic mind. According to Plato's philosophy, to progress toward accomplishing union with God, we must move away from the imperfection of the material world of the physical body into the more perfect world of the mind. This philosophy put Christians at war with the physical body. Rather than being sacred in itself, the body was considered an impediment to the spiritual nature.

## Roman Power and Might

Although the Greeks certainly left a philosophical mark on the development of Western civilization, Rome ruled the world by the time of Christ. This was the world in which the Church developed. "All roads lead to Rome" was a saying of the time. Roman roads flowed both ways. As people and goods flowed into Rome from elsewhere, Roman ideas and Roman soldiers traveled outward, influencing all areas of the known world. When you think about it, Catholicism spread largely because of the work of Roman road-builders.

The Romans borrowed much from Greek culture. In addition, they developed technology, architecture, administration, trade, and law. This combination established the foundations of Western civilization. However, some of the destructive elements of Roman rule were found in its militaristic mentality. The Romans developed a competitive, patriarchal culture in which the greatest value was placed upon accomplishment in battle, physical strength, and fearlessness. In addition, self-denial and service to the state were ways to achieve excellence in this society.

The warrior aspect of the Roman world influenced the culture at the time of the early Church in three main ways. First, Rome ruled by its undisputed power and might. What it decreed became law. Second, Rome was able to back up its laws with the authority of its military. Finally, Rome had a hierarchical ranking system upon which all militaries are formed.

In its first 100 years, the new Church struggled for survival in the midst of Roman chaos. As we shall see in Chapter 21, when Catholicism became the religion of the Roman Empire, the Church modeled itself on Greek ideas and the Roman sense of law.

The Church adapted a hierarchical and patriarchal ranking system for its clergy, placing them above the people they served. At the top of the hierarchy was the bishop of Rome, as Rome was the center of all things. Roman influences brought strength and unity to the newly developing Church, and created problems as well.

Two major concepts that were woven into the Church in its early years are patriarchy and hierarchy. Patriarchy is a society led by older men having authority over members. Hierarchy describes a ranking system where a group of persons or things are arranged in order of rank, grade, or class, and thus are accorded privilege.

Problems inherited from the patriarchal and hierarchical paradigm are the social, religious, and ecological forms of domination it created. This worldview supports and promotes the strong conquering the weak, the rich exploiting the poor, males ruling over females and children, and human society dominating the earth. It found racial expression in the dominance of light-skinned people over dark-skinned.

In the hierarchical worldview, each order has sovereignty over those below it. Power flows from the top down, exclusively. It can be contrasted to a communal worldview using a circle. The circle represents the Divine and contains all the other groups. The eight pieces of the pie represent each of the kingdoms: mineral, plant, animal, child, woman, man, saints, and angels. The circle worldview is relational; all the groups meet in the center. It is based in equality and shared power.

The hierarchical worldview is less relational as each individual kingdom only touches the one next to it. The early Church formed in communities that are represented by the communal paradigm. As the Church became increasingly influenced by Roman politics, its institution developed according to the hierarchical form.

*The hierarchical and communal worldviews.*

*(Courtesy of Bob O'Gorman and Mary Faulkner)*

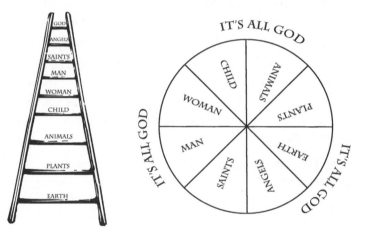

## Indigenous Peoples of Western Europe

Anyone who has family roots in central and western Europe probably shares a common heritage. Tribal people living on the edge of the Roman world existed more than 3,000 years ago across most of Europe. They were constantly being taken into the empire as it expanded into their lands. Many were captured and served as slaves, joining the households of their captors. Although the tribes were in no way unified, they shared similar beliefs, languages, and practices.

Each tribe was distinct from the others and had its own community identity and its own gods, laws, and customs. Unlike the Romans and the Greeks, these people had an integrated worldview. They did not separate religion from the activities of daily life, but they instead celebrated God's mystical presence in the natural world. The concept of the presence of God in daily life was a reality to them, because their gods and goddesses lived with them in nature.

What the indigenous people contributed to the early formation of the Catholic Church was a mystical understanding of the world in which logic and order did not always prevail. This understanding is the basis of a faith structure that believes in God's presence through His son, Jesus Christ. Such a belief defies science and cannot be thoroughly substantiated by history. In many ways, the Catholic Church, although it has a highly developed theological base, remains what is called a mystery religion. What is meant by that is that Catholics fully accept that many of their doctrines cannot be understood or accepted other than by faith.

## Cultural Influences

The influence of other traditions and cultures on the development of the early Catholic Church is outlined in the following chart.

| Cultural Influences | Time Span | Contributions |
| --- | --- | --- |
| Judaism | 1800 B.C.E.–70 C.E. | Love of the law, patriarchal structure, monotheism, God present to His people, a rich written tradition in the Hebrew Scripture |
| Greek | 332 B.C.E.–141 C.E. | Love of thinking, dualism, hierarchical structure, a better world awaits us elsewhere, authority outside of self, a loss of intuitive knowing |
| Roman | 63 B.C.E.–600 C.E. | Authority, militaristic enforcement of the rules, hierarchical structure, ability to reach many people through Roman expansion |
| Indigenous | 3000 B.C.E.–300 C.E. | Love and loyalty to leaders; mystery, tribes, myth, and symbol; real presence of God in the world; community; intuitive knowing |

Now that you understand the major points that surrounded the beginning of the Catholic Church, you're ready to see just how it developed into a major world religion. But first let's take a look at the source for Catholics' story of their religion: the Bible.

## The Least You Need to Know

- ◆ To get to the origins of the Catholic religion, you need to revisit history and look at the many cultural influences that affected it.

- ◆ At the heart of the Catholic religion is its ceremonies with their elementary expressions of earth, air, fire, and water as sacred.

- ◆ Judeo-Christian is a term used to describe the shared world of Jews and Christians. Catholics draw on the Hebrew Scripture for a basic understanding of their religion.

- ◆ The Greeks gave us Plato and his belief that things of the material world are bad, and things of the spiritual world are good, and that these two worlds are separate.

- ◆ At the time of Christ, Rome ruled the known world and was a warrior culture. The Roman character of power and might had a profound influence on the Church.

- ◆ Indigenous people influenced the Catholic Church's mythology and the understanding of God's real presence.

# Chapter 7

# The Bible

## In This Chapter

- ◆ Jews, Christians, and Muslims share a common Scripture base

- ◆ The Old Testament speaks through at least four basic voices

- ◆ Four different communities of people wrote the Gospels known as Matthew, Mark, Luke, and John

- ◆ A Catholic view of the Bible

The last chapter showed how the stories of the Old Testament formed the basis for Catholics' relationship to God and to the world. This chapter offers a further glimpse into that storehouse of sacred information and highlights some of the differences between Catholic sacred Scripture and that used by other faith traditions. It answers questions like: who wrote the sacred texts? What were their reasons for writing them? How did the Church decide on what would be included as sacred texts?

## Sacred Scriptures

The *Bible* is the sacred book or Scriptures of Jews, Christians, and Muslims. Our discussion will focus on the Scripture from the Hebrew and Christian perspective; however, readers are encouraged to investigate the Koran, the sacred book of Islam. The Bible as we know it today is divided into two

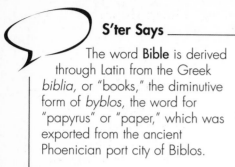

**S'ter Says**

The word **Bible** is derived through Latin from the Greek *biblia*, or "books," the diminutive form of *byblos*, the word for "papyrus" or "paper," which was exported from the ancient Phoenician port city of Biblos.

**Your Guardian Angel**

The Bible is a faith history. The stories teach how to handle life's experiences. The events in the Bible are the recorded wisdom of those who have gone before. Through these stories, experiences are kept alive, and important moments are preserved.

parts. The first part, the Hebrew Scriptures or the Old Testament, is the written record of the Jewish people from Abraham (1800 B.C.E.) until Maccabees (168 B.C.E.). The second part of the Christian Bible is the New Testament, which contains the life and work of Jesus, as well as the faith experience of the early Christians until about 100 C.E.

The word *testament* means "agreement" and refers to the belief that God, the Creator of life, has initiated a personal relationship with His creatures. The Old Testament is the Christian name for the covenant God made with the Hebrew people that they would be His special people in whom He would reveal His love. Christians believe that in Jesus, God has revealed Himself in a new way. They believe Jesus is both human (completely accessible to everyone) and divine (fully acting as God). The teachings about Jesus are a new testament—a new covenant. Catholics believe the Bible is the word of God, inspired by the Holy Spirit and written by humans. They consider both testaments as one Bible, not two.

Like all good stories, the Bible has a plot. The basic plot revolves around God's love for the people and His willingness to be with them. It begins in Genesis with God speaking, "Let there be light." It ends in the Book of Revelation with a prayer, "Come Lord Jesus!" In between, there is a constant dialogue between God and the people, rich stories, and an amazing cast of characters.

## The Old Testament

The Old Testament (or Hebrew Scriptures) is not called "old" because it is out-of-date; it refers to its position as coming before the "new" testament. It's an essential part of sacred Scripture for Catholics, and they believe the books that comprise it are divinely inspired. The Old Testament is more than a book of history or culture. It is a book of religion: Israel's witness to its encounter with God and its faithful response to him. As the faith journey of the Jewish people, the Old Testament is a sacred history to both Jews and Christians. They turn to these stories for guidance in life's events. Ultimately, the stories disclose the meaning of human life. The 46 books of the Old

Testament contain a wealth of teaching on God, as well as wisdom about the affairs of human life. They are a treasure house of prayers.

The Old Testament was formed gradually; its books were composed over many centuries. The *Pentateuch* is the first five books of the Old Testament: Genesis, Exodus, Leviticus, Numbers, and Deuteronomy. The Hebrew name for these five books is *Torah*. Torah is a difficult word to capture in translation, but a close meaning is "law," and a better one might be "teaching." It contains the divine guidance given by God for the historical pilgrimage of the Jewish people. The teachings stand for all time. Most of all, Torah is an expression of God's care. It is summed up in the phrase: "I will be your God, and you will be my people." As such, then, the law of God is the Jews' expression of care and response.

> **S'ter Says**
>
> **Pentateuch** is a word based on a Greek term referring to "the book of the five scrolls" (the *pentateuchos biblos*), also known as the **Torah**. Moses commanded that the Torah be placed in the Ark of the Covenant. The Book of Joshua and the Torah were placed in the ark, and these sacred books were kept there during the wilderness journey.

Jewish, Protestant, and Catholic scholars agree that the books known as the Pentateuch are a composite of several sources. Years of study have determined four main literary strands, which are identified as follows:

♦ A Judaean source, using the divine name Yahweh and written about 950 B.C.E.

♦ A North Israelite source that favors the use of the divine name Elohim and was written about 850 B.C.E.

♦ A source reflecting the style and theology of the period of Josiah's reform about 650 B.C.E. and later

♦ A source from the time of the Babylonian Exile, 550 B.C.E.

These different strands, each having a different perspective on the stories, were woven together in a final form that emerged in about 400 B.C.E. (For more information on the themes and stories referenced here, we suggest consulting a more detailed resource such as Bernhard Anderson; see Appendix B.) The Old Testament ends in what some have described as an incomplete drama. According to the beliefs of many Jewish people, it leads to the Talmud (the authoritative writings of Jewish tradition) and a continued wait for the Messiah. According to the Christians, the story leads to Jesus Christ who came not to destroy, but to fulfill the law.

# The New Testament

The New Testament is the story of God's son Jesus Christ, his teachings, the story of his death and resurrection, and the Church's first 100 years of life. Like the Old Testament, the New Testament also developed gradually. As Christian communities began to spread to other parts of the Roman Empire, specifically the lands around the Mediterranean basin, the followers of Jesus took with them their memories of their time with him. They had been firsthand witnesses to the events, and they taught others about Jesus' life and works from their experiences. However, they wrote none of it down. As the first witnesses were dying, it became apparent that someone had to record the information.

> **S'ter Says**
>
> The **epistles** of the New Testament are writings of Apostles to churches founded in particular parts of the Mediterranean world as well as to individuals. The epistles dealt with concerns and false teaching that needed immediate correction. Some were written in response to questions from the particular church. They comprise more than one third of the New Testament. Paul wrote the majority of them.

The first written material consisted of the letters written by Paul to the various faith communities; the early Christians circulated these letters. Paul was a convert to the new religion. He was the first missionary, founding churches all over the Mediterranean. He wrote letters to these communities offering guidance. These letters were written about 52 C.E. to 64 C.E. and are the earliest works of the New Testament. His letters, called *epistles*, offer valuable and practical instructions to the new Church for living out Christ's teachings.

Next came the Gospels, which are the books of Matthew, Mark, Luke, and John. The Gospels form the heart of the New Testament. *Gospel* is a word meaning "good news," in Old English from Greek. The Gospels of the Bible contain important stories of Jesus' life and teaching. Between the years 70 C.E. and 100 C.E., the community acknowledged four Gospels to be the most authentic because they appeared to be written by those who were most intimately connected with the apostles. Scholars believe they were developed in four major communities of the Christian world. Mark was written in Rome, Matthew in Jerusalem, Luke in Antioch, and John in Ephesus.

The communities that produced the New Testament material operated as writers and editors, and they were inspired in this regard. The roles of the writers (evangelists) were understood to be the following:

   ◆ **Selectors.** From the many things Jesus did, they chose what they wanted to include and emphasize.

◆ **Arrangers.** They organized the material in blocks, often by themes rather than chronologically.

◆ **Shapers.** They adapted their sources and told the stories in ways that would emphasize what they wanted to stress.

◆ **Theologians.** They reflected on the meaning and significance of the events in light of their belief in God and in Jesus.

Matthew, Mark, and Luke constitute the *Synoptic Gospels*. That means the communities identified with these names are looking at the same events and describing them in similar ways. Scholars generally agree that all four Gospels were written in Greek and drew on the stories that were being told about Jesus and his life.

> **S'ter Says**
> Synoptic means seeing with one lens. Matthew, Mark, and Luke all give a common view of Jesus, and they are called the Synoptic Gospels. John has a different perspective.

The community represented by John's Gospel reports several incidents not mentioned in the other stories. Likewise, some of the events mentioned in the Synoptic Gospels do not appear in John. They give a different order to the events and different dates for the Last Supper and Crucifixion. It is generally believed that John's material was written after the Synoptic Gospels. This community may or may not have been aware of them when they wrote their own account of Jesus' life.

All the Gospels differ from one another in terms of author, time of writing, audience, and purpose. Although each Gospel is a separate and unique portrait of Jesus, no one Gospel tells us everything we need to know about him. To gain a fuller understanding of Jesus, we must consider all four Gospels together.

Around 70 C.E., a companion of the apostle Peter named Mark, sometimes referred to as John Mark, most likely wrote the Gospel attributed to the community of Mark. It is the earliest Gospel and is called "the Gospel of action" because Jesus is always on the move. It emphasizes the humanity and suffering of Jesus and portrays him as the unrecognized Messiah. It was directed toward Gentile members of the Church living in Rome.

> **For Heaven's Sake**
> Don't make the mistake of thinking that the four evangelists—Matthew, Mark, Luke, and John—wrote all their own material. The Gospels were a composite of writings gathered by their respective communities.

A Gentile doctor around 85 C.E. possibly represented the community that wrote Luke. This Gospel stresses the central role of the Holy Spirit in Jesus' life. It shows Jesus' compassion, mercy, and concern for sinners in the miracle stories. It is the first part of a two-part work; part two is the Acts of the Apostles (the story of the beginning of the Church). It appears to have been written for Gentile Christians, and perhaps for well-to-do ones, at that. Its message seems to be about the universality of Christianity. It shows women and poor people in important roles.

Matthew, written around 90 C.E. for Jews who were converting to Christianity, emphasizes Jesus as the fulfillment of promises made by God in the Hebrew Scriptures. It demonstrates Jesus' role as a teacher and preacher and talks about the responsibilities of Jesus' followers.

John was probably written by the community of followers of this beloved disciple of Jesus around 95 C.E. It reflects theological sophistication and is considered to be more poetic and more spiritual in nature than the other accounts. It presents Jesus as "the Word of God" and highlights God's presence as flesh and blood with us—his incarnation. It urges the reader toward faith, emphasizing that faith comes from God and is most present when the believer is without visible evidence of God. John creates poetic and memorable images of Jesus, such as the Vine and the Good Shepherd.

# The Canon: How Are We Sure What Texts Are Sacred?

The Canon of the Bible refers to the definitive list of the books that are considered to be divine revelation and are included in the text. Slightly different books were selected for the Catholic Canon than for the Protestant Canon. Catholics include 46 books in the Old Testament, and Protestants have 39. Both groups accept 27 books for the New Testament, for a total of 73 and 66 books, respectively.

How did the disciples' writings come together to form the New Testament Canon, the collection of books that the Church acknowledges as genuine and inspired Holy Scripture? The leaders, guided by the authority of the Spirit, determined which books God inspired. The actual Canonization process took a long time. There were many questionable Gospels and epistles circulating. Careful, prayerful, and deliberate examination proved which books were genuine and which were false. Pope Damasus at the Council of Rome in 382 listed the books of today's Canon. At that time, the Canon was closed, and no more books were entered. Here's what it includes:

**The Old Testament**

◆ **The Pentateuch.** Genesis, Exodus, Leviticus, Numbers, and Deuteronomy

◆ **The historical books.** Joshua, Judges, Ruth, 1 and 2 Samuel, 1 and 2 Kings, 1 and 2 Chronicles, Ezra, Nehemiah, Tobit, Judith, Esther, and 1 and 2 Maccabees

◆ **The wisdom books.** Job, Psalms, Proverbs, Ecclesiastes, the Song of Songs, the Wisdom of Solomon, and Sirach (also called Ecclesiasticus)

◆ **The prophets.** Isaiah, Jeremiah, Lamentations, Baruch, Ezekiel, Daniel, Hosea, Joel, Amos, Obadiah, Jonah, Micah, Nahum, Habakkuk, Zephaniah, Haggai, Zachariah, and Malachi

**The New Testament**

◆ **The Gospels** according to Matthew, Mark, Luke, and John

◆ **The Acts of the Apostles**

◆ **Thirteen letters attributed to Paul,** written to particular communities and individuals in the following cities: to the Romans, and 2 Corinthians, Galatians, Ephesians, Philippians, Colossians, and 1 and 2 Thessalonians

◆ **Letters to individual Christian leaders** (the first three are called the Pastoral Letters): 1 and 2 Timothy, Titus, and Philemon

◆ **One biblical sermon,** for which neither the author nor the audience is explicitly mentioned: Hebrews

◆ **Seven epistles** that are attributed to early apostles and written to more general audiences: the Letter of James; Peter 1 and 2; John 1, 2, and 3

◆ **The Letter of Jude**

◆ **The Apocalypse** in the Book of Revelation

# Catholic Beliefs Regarding the Bible

Catholics hold these beliefs regarding the Bible:

◆ The Bible contains both the Hebrew Scriptures and the Christian Scriptures as one book.

◆ The sacred Scriptures are the inspired word of God. God is the author because He inspired the human authors of the Bible.

◆ The Catholic Church accepts and honors the 46 books of the Old Testament and the 27 books of the New Testament, considering them inspired.

◆ The four Gospels occupy a central place in the Bible because Jesus Christ is their focus.

◆ The unity of the two testaments reveals the whole of God's plan.

There are no copies of the original Scriptures. The early manuscripts were written on scrolls and later copied by monks. When Latin became the commonly used language, the manuscripts were translated into Latin from Greek and Hebrew texts.

The Septuagint is the third century B.C.E. Greek translation of the Jewish Scriptures from Alexandria, Egypt, and was used heavily in the early Church. It contains texts that are not included in the Hebrew Canon, and is still used by Catholics, which is what accounts for the difference between the Catholic and Protestant bibles.

Since Vatican II, new translations of the Bible are available for Catholics, and Bible study is encouraged. New research continues to add to the body of knowledge around these sacred texts. Today, Bibles are composed by the collaboration of Jewish, Catholic, and Protestant scholars. Rather than a means of separation, the Bible has become an interfaith event.

## What Place Does the Bible Hold for Catholics?

Catholics constantly find nourishment and strength in the Scriptures. The four Gospels hold a unique place in the Church and are read each time that the Mass is offered.

The Catholic Church understands that in sacred Scripture, God speaks in a human way. To interpret Scripture correctly, you must listen for what the human authors wanted to say and what God wanted to reveal through their words. To do this you must know something about the culture, writing style, and times in which it was written.

The Church distinguishes between two interpretations of Scripture: literary and spiritual. The literary (or scholarly) meaning is discovered by following the rules of sound interpretation. The spiritual meaning comes through understanding the allegorical, moral, and symbolic levels of the Scriptural stories.

Scriptures are understood to have parallel (allegorical) meanings for Catholics: thus, the crossing of the Red Sea could be a sign of Christ's victory and also of Christian baptism. They are also understood in the moral sense by leading us toward right action. Finally, the symbolic level reveals an ultimate spiritual or mystical meaning.

The Catholic Church teaches that interpreting Scripture is ultimately up to the judgment of the Church. It believes that it is the task of Scripture scholars to work toward a better understanding and explanation of the meaning of sacred Scripture.

## Catholics Can and Do Read the Bible

Despite stories to the contrary, the Catholic Church has never forbidden reading the Bible, but because of the complexity of the Scripture, it has warned against private interpretation as stated above. At times these warnings were expressed very strongly. The wisdom of this is apparent in that Catholics have a deep understanding of the Gospel message, yet have avoided fundamentalist distortions. Such interpretation starts from the principle that the Bible, being the word of God, is free from error and should be read and interpreted literally in all its details. "Literal interpretation" applies a word-for-word understanding that does not take into account historical scholarship about origins and development of the texts.

◆ Fundamentalism is absolutist; it rejects questions and demands adherence to rigid doctrinal points of view.

◆ It treats biblical text as if it had been dictated word for word by God, rather than the inspired word of God expressed in human language by humans.

◆ It pays no attention to the literary forms and to the human ways of thinking in the biblical texts, many of which extend over long periods of time and reflect very diverse historical and cultural situations.

◆ It places undue emphasis on literal accuracy and fails to take account of symbolic or figurative meaning, particularly in regard to historic matters, events, or (supposedly) scientific truth.

◆ It is often narrowly bound to one fixed translation, whether old or present day. It denies the complexity of the text in its original Hebrew, Aramaic, or Greek form.

◆ It fails to consider how the first Christian communities themselves understood the impact produced by Jesus of Nazareth—the essence of his message—thus it misrepresents the Gospel itself.

◆ Its narrow point of view and noncritical reading can reinforce prejudice, racism, and sexism that are contrary to the Gospel.

◆ It falsely holds out certainties, where life offers complexities. A fundamentalist approach attracts people who naively look to the Bible for quick answers.

# All God's Children

Catholic theology and teaching is rooted in Scripture and draws its life from it. Scripture is used to gain insight into one's life, to appreciate the past and better understand today's world, and hopefully move us closer to being one people. The character of Scripture is dynamic. It presents a variety of viewpoints and offers insight. It isn't meant to wrap up "truth" and hand it to the reader; rather, it is a faith story—if not always of human faithfulness to God, always of God's faithfulness to the people. In showing what God has done in the past, it symbolizes what He can be counted on to do in the future. Catholics don't believe that Scripture should become the basis of excluding people from God's love. While in the past Christians, Catholics included, have appropriated the Old Testament and considered it an unfinished revelation, today the Church is correcting this mistake and other theological errors that have occurred throughout history that have created and sustained anti-Semitism.

## Correcting Mistakes of the Past

It's important to understand that Jewish Scripture records God's word as revealed to Israel, and it needs no supplement, nor fulfillment. Its principle message is that the covenant made with God in the past has relevance today—it has shaped and continues to shape the concepts and values of three great religions that acknowledge its authority: Judaism, Christianity, and Islam. Scripture, however, has been used to justify anti-Jewish prejudice. Efforts are being made to correct mistakes of the past and to boldly foster better relations between Catholics and all world religions.

## Anti-Semitism

Anti-Semitism never was part of Catholic doctrine, even before the Second Vatican Council denounced it. Nonetheless, Christian anti-Semites have often turned to Christian Scripture to justify their actions. Although there are unquestionably anti-Jewish statements in the New Testament, when all things are considered, most Jews don't consider the Scriptures to be the biggest problem. It's how the New Testament has been used to legitimize or provoke anti-Semitism. Following is a list of attitudes, many of which are drawn from Scripture, that prevail in Christianity and continue to create and sustain anti-Semitism:

- The claim that Jews are responsible for the murder of Jesus. This is exemplified by I Thessalonians 2:14–15:

    "For you, brethren, became imitators of the churches of God in Christ Jesus which are in Judea; for you suffered the same things from your own countrymen as they did from the Jews, who killed both the Lord Jesus and the prophets, and drove us out, and displease God and oppose all men."

- Claims that the Jewish covenant with God has been superseded by a new covenant.

- Criticisms of the Pharisees.

- Criticisms of Jewish detachment or separatism.

- The penchant for Christians to want to convert Jews.

## "In Our Time"

The Vatican II document called "Nostra Aetate," literally meaning "in our time," is a call to Catholics and all Christians to heal 2,000 years of hatred and vilification of Jews done "in the name of God," and to end the disparities between Catholics, Jews, Muslims, and other religious traditions today. It was one of the most publicized documents of the council, passing by a vote of 2,221 to 88 of the bishops attending, and was proclaimed on October 28, 1965, by Pope Paul VI. The document contains five essential statements of faith:

- It begins with a statement of the unity of all people both in their origins and their destination. It describes questions that have haunted humankind throughout history, and how various religions have struggled to provide answers.

- It specifically mentions some of the answers Hindus and Buddhists have provided to these age-old questions, stating: "The Catholic Church rejects nothing that is true and holy in these religions. She regards with sincere reverence those ways of conduct and of life, those precepts and teachings which, though differing in many aspects from the ones she holds and sets forth, nonetheless often reflect a ray of that Truth which enlightens all men."

- It declares that the Catholic Church regards the Muslims with esteem and cites specific truths that Catholics (and other Christians) share with Islam: worship of One God, the creator of heaven and earth, merciful and omnipotent, who has spoken to humans; the Muslims' respect for Abraham and Mary, and the great respect they have for Jesus, whom they consider to be a prophet and not God. It urges all Catholics and Muslims to forget the hostilities and differences of the past and to work together for mutual understanding and benefit.

◆ It describes the "New Covenant" bond that ties Christians to Jews. It states that even though some Jewish authorities and those who followed them called for Jesus' death, the blame for this cannot be laid at the door of all those Jews present at that time, nor can the Jews in our time be held as guilty; "the Jews should not be presented as rejected or accursed by God." The declaration also decries all displays of anti-Semitism made at any time by anyone.

◆ It states that we are all created in God's image, and that it is against the teaching of the Church to discriminate against, show hatred toward, or harass any person or people on the basis of color, race, religion, way of life, and so on.

"In Our Time" received its fair share of praise and some criticism. Forty years of history has revealed both its prophetic wisdom and its shortcomings. Despite pros and cons, its symbolic significance provides a prophetic and inspirational direction to the Church.

## It's About Time

The address given by Pope John Paul II during a March 2000 ceremony in St. Peter's was the most well-known example of his efforts to improve relations between Catholicism and Judaism. He publicly pleaded for pardon and forgiveness from God for the transgressions of Catholics in the past. He took personal responsibility for what had occurred at the hands of "sons and daughters of the Church" and acknowledged that Jews in the past had suffered grievous wrongs not merely by Christians, but also in the name of Christianity.

Although few could deny the responsibility of the Catholic Church for so many "sins" against the Jews, there were those who objected to such public contrition. There is general agreement that John Paul II did more than any pope to improve relations between Judaism and Christianity. At the same time, it is commonly accepted that some of his actions raised further questions. For example, he beatified Edith Stein, who converted to Catholicism from Judaism, designating her as a Catholic martyr despite the fact she was killed because of her Jewish birth. In his signed remarks, he attributed anti-Semitism to neo-paganism, seemingly ignoring its footing in centuries of Christianity. Criticism clouded John Paul's attempts to canonize Pope Pius XII. Both during the pre-war years as cardinal secretary of state and his World War II papal ministry, Pius XII's actions seem to be done more to appease the Nazis—preserving the "power and prestige" of the Church at the expense of individuals. History will no doubt shed light on these controversies and in the spirit of ending religious strife both sides of the debate will be taken to higher ground.

Now that you have a fairly basic understanding of the Bible as the faith source for Catholics, let's move on and meet the one from whom Catholicism truly emerged: Jesus.

## The Least You Need to Know

- ◆ The Old and New Testaments work together to create the whole Bible for Catholics.

- ◆ The Bible was written over a long period of time and has many authors; it is the faith story of the people and was inspired by the Holy Spirit and written by human hands.

- ◆ The four Gospels work together to give us different perspectives of Jesus' life and work.

- ◆ By the end of the fourth century, the Church decided which books were authentic and which were not and closed the Canon. No new books can be added.

- ◆ Catholics do not believe in simply a literal interpretation of the Bible.

- ◆ Pope John Paul II proclaimed the Church's responsibility for anti-Semitism and called on it to heal relations with Jews and other religious traditions, giving Catholics a fuller appreciation of the Old Testament.

# Jesus: Spirit of a New Religion

## In This Chapter

- ◆ How the Catholic Church is rooted in the life and times of Jesus
- ◆ The Christian stories: Christmas, Easter, and Pentecost
- ◆ The persecution of the early Church, underground catacombs, and the desert retreat
- ◆ Protecting the Gospel: the movement from charismatic communities to organization

As well established and powerful as the Catholic Church may seem today, it had a rocky start, and its history is a long and fascinating one with lots of ups and downs. This chapter focuses on Jesus and shows how his simple message became a religion, how this religion became organized, and how it survived persecution. You'll also learn how the Catholic mystical tradition took root and grew in the desert almost 2,000 years ago, nurturing the spirit of the Church.

# How We Know What We Know About Jesus

As you read in Chapter 7, followers of Jesus compiled the historical references to Jesus and his teachings, but they weren't formally written down until a generation or two after his death. They are interpretations of the experiences his followers had of him and their accounts of his teachings as told to the communities who recorded them.

**Your Guardian Angel**

For many years, it was the custom to capitalize all pronouns that refer to Jesus: He, Him, His. One of the major developments of Vatican II was to emphasize the human side of Jesus. As a result, religious writers now generally use lowercase pronouns when referring to Jesus. The reasoning behind this is to recognize Jesus' likeness to us.

Very few facts are known about the actual history of Jesus. We know that a man named Jesus lived and preached in Galilee, a region in northern Israel, and in Jerusalem. He was crucified in Jerusalem, probably on a combination of charges of religious blasphemy and treason against the Roman authorities. The rest of what is known about Jesus comes to us through the stories that his followers told about him and what they believed the stories to mean. It's a matter of faith.

## The Wellspring of Galilee

Jesus is the name of a Jewish preacher and teacher who lived and taught in Galilee. Jesus is a Latin version of the Greek *Iesous*, itself a form of a Hebrew name, *Y'shua*. "Christ" is more of a title than a name. It comes from the Greek word *Christos*, which in Greek means "the anointed one," translated from the Hebrew word *messiah*. Messiah is a term used to describe a figure of great importance chosen or "anointed" by God. As Jesus' name already shows, he lived in the Jewish, Greek, and Roman worlds.

**For Heaven's Sake**

Don't judge a book by its cover. There was a saying in Jerusalem at the time of Jesus: "Can anything good come out of Galilee?" Jesus was more than something good: he was the son of God, and he was from Galilee.

Unlike Jerusalem, Galilee was not a particularly important cultural or religious center for the Jews. In fact, Jews who lived so far away from the temple in Jerusalem were thought to be ignorant and lax in religious matters. In the society of the time, Jews of Jerusalem scorned a Galilean Jew like Jesus.

Yet, in its own way, Galilee was a natural geographic region to spawn a new religion. It was a natural crossing place for international travel routes, and people of many nations gathered there: Phoenicians,

Syrians, Arabs, Greeks, and Asians, as well as Jews. These international contacts meant that ideas flowed in from the four corners of the known world. Its distance from Jerusalem, where the Jewish law and teachings prevailed, gave it a freedom of thought that would not have been available nearer the temple. Its people were relatively unschooled in Jewish law, but were ruled by common sense and wisdom. The people practiced a Jewish faith that was simpler and more spontaneous than the more conservative faith of the Jerusalem intelligentsia, and these qualities greatly influenced Jesus' teachings.

## Jesus the Jew

Jesus himself was a bit of a character. Growing up with diverse people and cultures, he naturally attracted people from a variety of social ranks into his inner circle. Whether or not he intended to, he broke class and cultural rules, bringing fishermen, tax collectors, and women into his ranks. But make no mistake: Jesus was born, lived, and died a Jew. Like the other members of his religious community, he was faithful to God by observing the law and temple rituals.

What did the people find so interesting about Jesus and his teachings? He claimed to have a special relationship with God, in which he said everyone could share. The relationship he spoke of was simple and direct—captured in the very intimate way he addressed God as *Abba* ("my dearest daddy").

According to the stories, Jesus was not as concerned that the "little guy" followed the law as he was about the leaders following it—a point he challenged them on. He talked about "the reign of God" as a time when the evils of society would be transformed—poverty, hunger, illness, and other injustices would be addressed. He not only talked about a law of love, he lived it—spending time together with his friends and with the growing band of loyal followers, reaching out to include others, feeding and caring for the poor. And he also spent his time in prayer to God.

# The Key Stories of the Christians

All religions have their great stories. Chapter 6 outlined several that were important to the Jews, such as Adam and Eve and the creation story, Abraham and the covenant, and Moses and the law. Christians base their understanding of God in those same stories and have additional ones that tell of the life and times of Jesus and his followers. Three in particular form the basis of the Christian religion. They are the birth of Jesus, his death and resurrection, and his continued presence in the lives of the people, as celebrated in the coming of the Holy Spirit at Pentecost.

# Jesus' Birthday: Christmas

The story goes that Jesus was born in Bethlehem of simple parents named Mary and Joseph—a young couple from Galilee. It's clear right from the start that something very important was happening in this story. For example, the night Jesus was born, the story says angels suddenly appeared in the night sky and burst into song. Shepherds heard them and came to the place where they found the couple and a new baby. They bowed, knowing instinctively that they were in the presence of a "great one." News of his birth soon traveled far and wide. Kings and wise men from distant lands saw a star in the eastern sky, and they came in search of him.

Jesus' father, Joseph, made a living with his hands as a carpenter. We assume that Jesus grew up working in his father's shop. Jesus did not receive a formal education. However, when he visited the temple in Jerusalem at the age of 12, the story says that he impressed the Jewish scholars with his knowledge and understanding of Jewish law. We don't hear much more about him until he began his public life of preaching at the age of 30. Most of the events of his public life took place in and around Galilee and on the road to Jerusalem. His life ended at the age of 33.

---

### Epiphanies

Christmas takes its name from the central act of Catholic worship, the Mass. Christmas means "Christ's Mass," derived from the Old English *Cristes mæsse*, a ritual that celebrates his birth as a human. It is often abbreviated *Xmas*, because *X*, the Greek letter chi, is an abbreviation for Christ. Most languages, except English, use a word signifying nativity or birthday of Christ to designate the feast of Christmas: in Latin, **Dies Natalis;** in Italian, **Il Natale;** and in French, **Noël.** Wherever you are and whatever language you speak, what is being celebrated is the birth of Christ. The way this event is commemorated and renewed in Catholicism is the Mass. Legend says that Christ was born moments past midnight on December 25, and Catholics celebrate this occasion by the tradition of midnight Mass.

---

# His Mission, Death, and Resurrection

From the beginning of his public life, Jesus both astonished and confused those who heard him speak. To the Jewish religious leaders, he was an uneducated upstart, a hayseed from the boondocks of Galilee, and they were puzzled by the attention he was getting. He welcomed the downtrodden and exiled people of the society, and at the same time people of means were mysteriously joining his ranks, too—he was gaining momentum. Commoners, if not astounded by his wisdom, were attracted by his message and his deeds—caring for the poor and sick. His message was calling the authority of the religious leaders into question, and pushing the political buttons of the Romans, too. Curiosity was giving way to concern among both political and religious leaders, and it wasn't long before the whole "Jesus thing" began rubbing the wrong people the wrong way.

The Romans were increasingly putting the squeeze on the Jews, as they strengthened their empire in this part of the world. The growing popularity of the "oddball" message of this itinerant preacher worried Jewish leaders—it was drawing attention to them and might seem subversive to the Roman authorities. The Jewish leaders didn't need any more trouble. It is worth noting here that Jesus and most of his followers were operating as Jews in a Jewish culture inside the Roman world. It isn't indicated by the Scriptures that he was trying to start a religion or a revolution. However, sincerity combined with action is a powerful mix.

The stories say he worked *miracles*. His first occurred at a wedding feast in Cana where he turned jugs of water into wine to prevent the embarrassment of his host, who had run out of wine for the guests. His followers, some of them fishermen, say he told them where they should place their nets to catch the most fish—and it worked. And even more amazing, he talked to the sea and the sea obeyed him—and further, it was said he walked on water! There was another story going around about a basket of fish and a couple loaves of bread feeding 5,000 people who had gathered to hear him speak. His ability to heal people, even bringing them back from the dead, got him the most recognition. After three years of preaching, teaching, and amazing the crowds in Galilee, he was gaining a lot of respect. It was then that Jesus decided to head for Jerusalem to celebrate Passover. He went from the outskirts of the Jewish world, where even though his fame was growing he was off the screen for the most part, to Jerusalem, where he was bound to draw a lot of attention to himself.

> **S'ter Says**
>
> A **miracle** is an event that breaks through the laws of nature. Miracles are extraordinary happenings that provide a glimpse of God at work.

Jerusalem was the symbol of established power for the Jews. Everything about it had religious significance. It was the holy city, the site of the Temple, and the reference point of Jewish identity and belonging. It was also elitist and the center of the powers that oppressed and excluded many of its people. Jesus took his message, which attacked the very concept of superiority, to Jerusalem. With his maverick ideas and eccentric ways, he forced the leaders' hand, and they played it. The authorities had him arrested on two counts, charging him with political sedition because of how he challenged Roman power, and religious blasphemy because he claimed he was the Son of God. Whether it made matters worse or not, he claimed that he had a special relationship with God—one in which we all share. He said we are all God's children!

Jesus' trial was swift, and he was sentenced to die by an extraordinarily cruel yet common method of Roman execution—crucifixion. Most of his followers abandoned him at the hour of his death; only a handful remained with him. They took him down from the cross and hid his body in a cave. This day is known in the Christian tradition as "Good Friday." Three days later, when the women came to anoint him for burial, they were shocked to discover an empty tomb. Even more astonishing, the story says an angel appeared and told them that Jesus had "risen"! From this first experience of the risen Jesus a new and most important feast began for Christians—the celebration of Easter Sunday. Between the Jewish feasts of Passover and Pentecost, several more people reported seeing him. The last account said he ascended into the sky. That is the end of the story of the historical Jesus.

---

### Epiphanies

Crucifixion was a method of capital punishment practiced by the Greeks and Romans in ancient times. It was used frequently in putting down Jewish opposition to the Roman conquest of Israel. The Romans used wooden beams crossed like a T. Typically the one to be executed was scourged (whipped) and required to carry the cross to the site of the execution. The prisoner was either nailed or tied to the cross. Death came by asphyxiation. Crucifixion was abolished when the Roman Empire became Catholic centuries later.

---

## Pentecost: The Birthday of the Church

Fifty days after Jesus' death, his followers—who were grieving, still in shock, confused, and fearful—gathered together to celebrate Pentecost in the room where they used to meet with him for meals. Earlier he had told them to wait there because he would send his Spirit to be with them—but they had no idea what that meant.

A sudden storm began to rattle the shutters on the windows, and it grew dark. The room started glowing, and tongues of fire appeared over each of their heads. Strangely, they felt the fear leave—it was replaced with a sense of mission. They reported feeling especially powerful when they left the room and went down into the street and began talking with people—telling them their stories. Jerusalem was filled with thousands who were gathered there for the religious ceremonies of Pentecost. To their amazement, they could understand the apostles, each in their own language.

It was bold. Given that he was so recently put to death, talking about it was risky. They began with the most unbelievable part of the series of events—by saying that Jesus had been raised from the dead and had walked among them and that he was the Messiah, the Son of God. The story says that 3,000 people were baptized as a conversion to Jesus' teaching. Jesus' followers were further encouraged by this response and decided to actively pursue bringing about the vision he had talked about so often—the "reign of God." As you shall soon see, although the followers had undergone a change, the society in which they began to preach had not.

Jesus Christ's followers began to believe he was both a living human being and the divine Son of God. They believed he was the one promised by God—the Messiah sent to fulfill the promise of the law, bringing news of mercy and forgiveness to the people.

Jesus' popular ministry challenged the accepted social and religious rules of the day. For one thing, it embraced sinners and social outcasts. For another, it was rather simple and straightforward—promoting love, tolerance, and kinship. The heart of it was: "All people, especially the poor and rejected, are invited to come into the kingdom of my Father." It revealed a new understanding of God as well as insights into the human struggle. Almost all societies have an "in" group and "out" group. Most have their particular classifications that determine who is a success and who is a failure, what it means to be good or bad, normal and abnormal—their ranking system. Jesus' core message of unity—that all are one in the Father—challenged the bottom-line cultural assumption of his day. Hitting at both the spiritual and political arenas, it angered both the Jewish leaders and the Roman authorities.

# Was Jesus the First Catholic?

On the surface, Jesus' ministry seemed to be a failure. He did not liberate the people from Roman oppression. Many who had been part of his following either didn't understand what he was saying or they just lost interest and continued living their lives in very much the same way as they had before they knew him. A handful, however, were inspired to keep it going. They realized building the kingdom was an inside job—it meant restoring human dignity. They also recognized it as a bottom-to-top approach, as it was to the down-and-out that Jesus delivered his "good news," telling them they were God's sons and daughters. Those that got the message banded together in small groups keeping his memory alive and his work going.

## The Core Beliefs

Here are Jesus' main ideas:

- ◆ The law of the Old Testament is based in forgiveness and love.

- ◆ The kingdom of God is within us.

- ◆ Everyone can have a personal relationship with God.

- ◆ Social class, education, and economics have little to do with God's love.

Jesus' core message was and continues to be that God is available to everyone. Jesus' followers believed that the real presence of God they had experienced in Jesus continued in spirit after he was physically gone. Nearly 2,000 years later, there are a lot more workers and still plenty of work to go around. The Church teaches that the memory continues to live in how we respond to the world's injustice and inequities—how we keep the faith when everything around looks and feels like "Good Friday."

## The Calling

Jesus' followers did not immediately formalize a Church. They lived in communities and met mostly in homes. They were simply called disciples at this time. Only later would they be called *Christians*. Their mission was to bring the "reign of God" to others the way that Jesus had brought it to them. Early writings use these terms in describing the followers: a household, a family, God's assembly, a new creation, and the body of Christ.

> **S'ter Says**
>
> The followers of Jesus were first called **Christians** in Antioch around 40 C.E., and it was used as a derogatory term. Christians didn't adopt the name until the next century.

You met Paul in the last chapter. An early convert and a leading missionary, Paul spread the teaching of Jesus throughout the Mediterranean world. He established Christian communities from Syria to Turkey, Greece, and Rome. Paul's most lasting influence has been felt through his writings to the communities, which, as we have noted, were the earliest and most extensive writings in the New Testament. His letters are passionate and full of concern for the fledging Church.

The three main spiritual ministries the followers dedicated themselves to were: celebrating God's gift of life, teaching, and serving.

♦ **Celebration.** Jesus celebrated life in relationship with God and with the people. He did this as he gathered with the common folks, sharing meals and enjoying camaraderie. His followers remembered how special these times were, and they wanted the spirit of this celebration to be a part of their communities.

♦ **Teaching.** Jesus taught how good and loving God is. Perhaps this is best captured by the prayer he taught his followers: the Our Father, which is also known as the Lord's Prayer:

> Our Father, who art in heaven,
> hallowed be thy name;
> thy kingdom come,
> thy will be done,
> on earth as it is in heaven.
> Give us this day our daily bread,
> and forgive us our trespasses,
> as we forgive those who trespass against us;
> and lead us not into temptation,
> but deliver us from evil. Amen.

The God of Jesus was intimate and accessible. His followers gathered the memories of his teachings and passed them on in the same spirit.

♦ **Serving.** Jesus served the people, caring for their physical and spiritual needs. He healed the sick, cured the deaf and blind, and fed the hungry. His followers wanted to carry on these important ministries and maintain the spirit of service.

Jesus had spoken of returning. At first his followers thought he meant soon, and during prayer services someone would leave the congregation, go out and look up at the sky to see if he was coming. When the person reported back that Jesus was not coming, the service would continue. Weeks turned into months and slipped into years. Eventually, they came to understand that he was not coming back in their lifetimes as they thought he would, but that he was with them in spirit always.

**Your Guardian Angel**

Catholics end the Lord's Prayer with the line "deliver us from evil." They don't say, "For Thine is the kingdom, the power and the glory forever," as is the Protestant custom. So if you're attending a Catholic service and are used to the Protestant version, don't get confused by this.

# Catholics Separate from the Jews

As mentioned earlier in this story, the Jewish people had been oppressed by the Romans for many years. Despite the suffering, their resistance continued. As a result of these ongoing "uprisings," in 70 C.E. the Romans ordered the Jewish Temple destroyed—crushing the rebellion and much of Jerusalem with it. This struck at the heart and soul of the Jewish people. During the next few years, Jewish leaders met to reorganize, and some of this reorganization included expelling sects of Judaism they identified as heretical. When the Jews tightened ranks, Jesus' followers found themselves outside the circle. Outcasts already, they further split from the Jewish religion and the two became separate.

We can answer our opening question about whether Jesus founded the Catholic Church by saying there was no institutional Catholic Church at the time of Jesus, or for many years after. The early followers of Jesus were considered to be members of a sect of Judaism, until they were forced out. At that time they became a new community.

## The Martyrs

Despite this less-than-momentous beginning (having been thrown out of the family home, so to speak), the followers of Jesus created a new identity. The title "Christianity" was first used as a derogatory name. The new religion appealed largely to the urban poor, women, noncitizens, social outcasts, and slaves—most of the followers were from the non-Jewish world. The essence of the "Gospel" message was that they did not need money or education to belong to the kingdom. These factors combined with the humiliating death of their leader made Christians a good target—a scapegoat for the Romans, and martyrdom was woven into their identity from the beginning. Like their leader, several of his closest disciples were also put to death.

The idea that no man or woman was a slave in God's world had enormous appeal among the downtrodden. They liked the idea of Jesus being a common man—a *martyr* with a message. They liked his promises of a better tomorrow and refuge from pain and suffering. The new, available God had infinitely more appeal than the distant gods of Greek and Roman mythology, who were seen to be on the side of the rulers and didn't offer much of anything to the people. These early converts formed communities, giving whatever resources they had in exchange for a little security and a hopeful message.

Roman authorities, sensing there was more to this thing than met the eye, began to view them as a threat to their power. Increasingly, in the Roman state, the lines between the emperors and the gods they worshipped had blurred. Roman leaders began to think of themselves as divine and they required homage such as that given to the gods be paid to them. Christians were more and more often and in greater numbers refusing to bow to Roman authority or burn incense before the emperor's statue—even making public statements that there was only one God. At first Christians became the targets of mockery, but as the Romans realized that the Christian ideas were taking root, mockery turned to violence.

Technically, Christianity was an outlawed religion, although the authorities didn't always enforce the law against it. However, whenever acts of civil disturbance against the Romans erupted, regardless of who was behind them, they blamed Christians. Roman punishments were severe. Christians were sometimes forced into arenas with *gladiators* or wild animals, which usually resulted in death, and they continued the cruel practice of crucifixion. On and off for 300 years the early Church endured persecution, and these martyrs became the first saints of the early Church.

> **S'ter Says** _____
>
> **Martyr** is Greek for "witness," and describes people killed because of their religious beliefs. The Church considers martyrdom to be the highest form of witness to the faith; therefore, martyrs go straight to heaven. **Gladiators** were slaves (including Christians) and prisoners of the Romans who were trained for the sport of hand-to-hand combat, as well as fighting wild beasts. The result of this combat was often death.

> **For Heaven's Sake** _____
>
> Don't think that the candles on the altar are just for decoration! The Church lights candles at every Mass, and it was customary that a relic of the saints (a fragment of their bones) be contained in the altar as a reminder of the early martyrs. The altar is a holy place.

Rather than scaring people away, however, stories of the bravery of the early Christians became the source of many conversions. They were an inspiration to others who wanted to know more about this religion for which so many would willingly die.

Greeks and Romans cremated their dead. Jews and Christians were allowed burial, but they had to do it outside the city limits. Following the Jewish tradition, early Christians buried their dead in cemeteries called catacombs—an extensive subterranean system of tunnels and vaults outside Rome as well as other cities. Besides serving as burial grounds, they became hiding places for Catholics fleeing persecution. Today, catacombs are honored as shrines to the saints and martyrs.

| Saints Preserve Us |
|---|
| **St. Stephen, December 26, Patron of Stonemasons**<br><br>St. Stephen, a disciple of Christ, was the first martyr. He was described as "full of grace and fortitude," and the effect of his work was great among the people. He was accused of blasphemy against Moses and against God and was brought before the authorities who condemned him to death by stoning. Kneeling down before his murderers, he cried out with a loud voice saying, "Lord, do not lay this sin against them." He was stoned to death in 35 C.E. His feast day is December 26, and he is the patron of stonemasons. |

## Designing the Structures

After an extraordinary beginning, the young Church was alive and breathing. Although the Roman Empire was still the controlling force as Catholicism started, it was losing its position as a world power. Many forces contributed to its downfall: increased invasions by warring tribes, the outrageous cost of maintaining the military, and the growing decadence of the aristocrats. As taxes continued to increase alarmingly, more people grew disenchanted with the state and turned instead to spiritual matters. The sense of community, morality rooted in love and kindness, along with the social systems that characterized the new Church made it an attractive package compared to the chaos of an empire in decline and trying to outguess the whims of failing leaders.

The faith expression of these early communities was a spontaneous, charismatic testimony. They didn't have much structure or many rules—members did what needed to be done as they saw it needed to be done! They were led by the Spirit in their praise, and by common sense in their work. Other like communities were springing up at the same time, and all were claiming to be the authentic followers of Jesus, and all were preaching a different version of his "message." Spontaneity was good, but it was becoming clear that more care was needed to protect both the message and the messengers of this growing movement, or risk losing its essential truth.

The goals of the Church founders were to carry on the work and keep the teachings consistent. Local communities were grouped with other communities in the region under the guidance of leaders that they called *bishops*. The order of bishop followed the Jewish model of elder, and the essence of the position was service. Ordination was by proclamation as leaders were recognized by their communities and chosen for their abilities or special gifts of the Spirit—later by laying on of hands. The distinction between ordained and nonordained wasn't solidly defined.

> **S'ter Says**
>
> **Bishop** is from the Greek word *episcopos* and means "overseer." A bishop is in charge of the Church in a local area.

Lines of authority and offices of leadership were slowly established. Gradually, larger churches in metropolitan centers such as Rome, Antioch, and Alexandria gained authority over smaller ones. Rome's position as capital of the empire as well as its financial prosperity made it a good choice for headquartering the new operation. In addition, the followers believed that Jesus had selected Peter to lead them (as we discussed in Chapter 4), and the story goes that he had lived and died in Rome.

Over the next 300 years the Church shifted from movement to institution. As you probably know, in all organizations there is a trade-off in making that shift. Some of the spontaneity and joy that characterize its early stages are sacrificed for stability and systematic growth. The Church didn't escape this, but at the same time, the Spirit was at work. While the institutional structures were being built, a parallel movement of a different nature was happening.

The contemplative or mystical side of the Church was taking root and sprouting in the midst of the desert. It has remained a vital part of the Church throughout history, quietly tending to the Spirit, and breathing life into the institution. As you will notice even today, there are members who find themselves drawn to the charismatic side of the organization and those who maintain the system—they are two sides of a coin.

## The Desert Fathers and Mothers

During these early years of the Church's growth, a movement called the Desert Fathers and Mothers developed in the Egyptian desert. Rejecting everyday life with its many earthy and tedious concerns and distractions, and wanting to follow their newfound and deeply felt faith, many of the members of the new Church established communities in the desert where they meditated, prayed, and studied.

Anthony, living in the middle of the third century, is credited with this movement. He was the son of Christian parents, and from early in his life, he felt a calling to give his possessions away and go to the desert and pray. He lived the life of a hermit for many years, devoting himself entirely to prayer and meditation. As the violence and chaos of the Roman Empire made living a life of the Spirit more difficult there, many Christians sought solace. They gravitated to the desert and found Anthony and the small communities that were gathering around him.

With this movement, an important tradition of monasticism and the contemplative life began within the Church and would grow over the next centuries to become a strong core of Catholic life. Many of the early Christian thinkers who lived in these communities helped define and clarify Church teachings, and their writings were crucial to establishing the spirituality of the Church.

We'll leave this part of the story for now, and pick it up later in Chapter 20. The next chapter examines how the present-day Church keeps the message of Jesus alive and how it keeps his spirit present through ceremonies, rituals, and celebrations.

## The Least You Need to Know

- Jesus invited all people to participate in "the reign of God," an invitation to intimate relationship with God, to feel loved, and to extend this invitation to others.

- The followers of Jesus formed communities as a way of keeping his presence alive and bringing the reign of God to the people.

- The Church began as a persecuted community, and yet it attracted new members who were inspired by the faith of the martyrs.

- The organizational side and the contemplative tradition are integral to the foundation of the Church; together they form its body and soul.

# Part 3

# The Sensuous Side of Catholicism: How Catholics Experience God

Catholics believe God is present in all things. Sacraments awaken sacramental memory, the presence of God deep within us. They mark significant events in the spiritual life, celebrating and connecting the one receiving the sacrament to God's presence in life's events—birthing, nourishing, sustaining, and bonding the community of his followers. Their purpose is to develop sacramental awareness by sharpening the ability to sense the presence of God every day.

God's revelation is an inspiration, the Spirit of God becoming available to humans. Jesus is the sacrament of God; the Church is the sacrament of Jesus; and Mary is the people's sacrament. We'll learn all about these sacraments in the following chapters.

# Chapter 9

# Catholic Imagination: The Sacred Space of Ritual

## In This Chapter

◆ Why Catholics love ritual

◆ How Catholic worship differs from Protestant worship

◆ How religion gets into the bones

◆ The what, why, and how of Catholic imagination

When you ask older Catholics what they like about Vatican II, they might give you any number of answers—a new ownership of the church, parish councils, turning the altar around where the priest faces the people, and more. When you ask them what they miss since Vatican II, they'll all say the old ritual! When Catholics return to the Church even after a long absence, if you ask what brought them back, they'll all say ritual! As this chapter shows, ritual is a central part of Catholic worship, but some of the emphasis has shifted to accommodate new practices such as greater emphasis on Scripture. The reactions mentioned earlier reflect the love of ritual that Catholics have—and how they miss even the smallest changes in their sacramental life.

# What Is Ritual and Why Do Catholics "Do" It?

Catholic ritual can seem mysterious and intimidating to a visitor—and for seasoned Catholics, too. It is complex and opens many levels of knowing. First of all, ritual means doing some symbolic action in a special place on regular occasions. On the surface, Catholic ritual engages the senses (sound, sight, smell, touch) and it evokes emotion. At a much deeper level, it opens the religious imagination, the deep place in the human psyche where we connect with the sacred. In this chapter, we'll explore the very complex practice of Catholic ritual, and gain insight into how Catholics use it in their worship to strengthen their faith.

> **S'ter Says**
>
> A **ritual** is a solemn, fixed set of symbolic actions performed in a particular environment at regular, recurring intervals—a ceremony.

First, let's clear up some confusing terminology. In talking about ritual, the word *sacrament* is used to refer to one of the seven sacraments of the Catholic Church. Sacramentals refer to the individual objects and practices that are used in the devotional life of the Church, such as statues, holy water, candles, and more. The term *sacramental* is used to identify all the devotions and worship practices of the Church, as in the sacramental life of the Church. All of it combines to create the "sacra" mental or sacred mind, a unique Catholic sensibility that experiences the world as holy. Now, more about how this all works in developing and expressing Catholics' faith.

## Feeling the Faith

Catholics sometimes refer to their religion as "the faith," but the religion itself isn't faith. Faith is trusting in someone or something without having proof. It comes as the result of a spiritual experience—a moment in time when the sacred reaches through into the material world, and God's presence is felt. Religion gathers the faith experiences of the followers, assists in interpreting these experiences, and codifies them into rules and regulations. This collection of wisdom is passed from generation to generation through the rich sacramental life of ritual and ceremony.

Catholics rely more on ritual and ceremony than most other Christian religions, and it is often what others are most leery of—even wondering if it is superstition, or worse, idolatry. However, Catholic rituals have a specific intention—to reconnect through the imagination to the experiences of the original faith communities and to feel the presence of Jesus here and now as they did then and there. So while ritual takes the front seat in Catholic worship (even ahead of preaching), it is informed by a sacramental theology and adheres to Catholic tradition. In a very broad way, you can say that the Catholic ritual has three components:

♦ Feeling: experiencing the spiritual.

♦ Thinking: reflecting on the meaning of the experience.

♦ Being: responding with action.

Ritual creates an experience in which faith is felt, insight is gained, and religion literally comes to life in worshippers. To understand where Catholics got the idea to do it this way, we'll go back to the faith experiences of that early community that became the Church.

## Walking and Talking with Jesus

The followers of Jesus had an intimate experience with him. They walked, talked, fished, and ate meals together—all while they listened to the stories he told. He had a unique message. For one thing, he showed more concern about people than rules. He told them life on earth could be different, and he showed them how by their experiences together. We know the rest of the story—most of them failed to "get it." They floundered throughout their time with him, even abandoning him at the end. In a way that's totally understandable. The terrible events of his death and his subsequent appearances were beyond human comprehension.

Later, when they reflected back on these times and the things Jesus taught them, they no doubt felt some of the old excitement and wanted to share it with the others—to somehow keep it going. They got together for meals with friends as they had done so often with him, retold the stories, and followed his example by caring for the poor. Whether or not they ever fully understood his message isn't clear, but the experiences held them together and the work went on. In essence, they created the early ritual Catholics follow today. Rituals are symbolic enactments of important events—a way of keeping something alive.

# The Theology of Catholic Ritual

Catholics have a profound belief in God's glorified nature and also in his sacred presence in the world—not metaphorically, but actually. At the same time, they understand that we are all engaged in the process of bringing the reign of God to fruition, and we aren't finished yet. God knows the disciples didn't "get it," but that they (and we) continue to try to make it happen—this is the faith journey. Catholic rituals and ceremonies celebrate faith and renew it. They strengthen the faithful as they work for the reign of God.

Rituals aren't performances by the priest—they require the involvement of the congregation. By following carefully guided sacramental form and believing together, Catholics enter the world of religious imagination and the realm of sacred time. They experience connection to God and to one another and, importantly, a sense of connection to the bigger community of God's people—meaning the whole of humankind. It's through this sense of union Catholics feel called or inspired to a prayerful response. Most often this involves action expressing love and concern for family, friends, society, and the earth itself.

## Now You See Him, Now You Don't: How God Is Present

All religions are about the business of connecting people with God, and in their own way each wrestles with God's availability to his creatures and how to best span the gap. The classical terms used to talk about this issue are *transcendence* and *immanence*. Transcendence refers to how far away or different God is perceived to be from creation. Immanence refers to how close or alike God is perceived to be to creation.

All classical religions offer basic positions on this issue. Christianity goes further with its insistence on Jesus' nature being both human and divine—both immanent and transcendent.

> **S'ter Says**
>
> **Transcendence** describes the belief that God exists on a higher plane, such as heaven. God is beyond humans' ability to perceive. **Immanence** describes the belief that God exists throughout all of creation and that humans can experience God's presence on earth. Catholics believe that both are true.

Within Christianity itself there are different perceptions of closeness or transcendence. Protestants and Catholics have similar ideas about God; however, the Protestant religions tend to emphasize God's transcendent nature more than his immanence, while Catholics place a stronger emphasis on God's human and immanently present nature. *Where* the emphasis is placed is a theological or doctrinal matter; worship is *how* that emphasis is transmitted.

## Catholic Symbol/Protestant Word

As you attend a Catholic Mass, it's obvious that something different is going on than in Protestant services. With all the smells, bells, holy water, and more, Catholic worship can seem superstitious to those who are not familiar with it. The roots of this misunderstanding go back in history to the different worlds in which these two religions began.

*The Cathedral of the Incarnation, Nashville, Tennessee.*

*(Courtesy of H. L. [Dean] Caskey)*

Catholic worship was developed at a time when a symbolic understanding of the world prevailed. Religion was celebrated mainly through ritual and ceremony. Catholic rituals are rooted in their Middle Eastern Jewish history and the history of the indigenous tribes of old Europe drawing its symbolic character from these sources. The symbolic mind perceives likeness; it sees how things connect. It is relational, and that is reflected in Catholics' emphasis on God's immanent presence. Fifteen hundred years later, as the Protestant religions arrived on the scene, the world was changing; it was becoming more literate and more literal, too. An engine driving this change in the culture was the printing press, and in religion it was particularly driven by the diligence of one man—Gutenberg and the printing of the Bible.

Protestant worship focuses on the Bible—and it draws on the literal mind for its understanding of the sacred. The literal mind is analytical—it understands things through differentiation, by how something is distinct from something else. Thus, Protestantism uses words and concepts to talk about God, and emphasizes how God is different from objects, events, experiences, and people. It relates more to God's otherness—His transcendent nature—and the message of Scripture is transmitted through preaching more than ritual.

Image and symbol is the first language of Catholics and the message of Scripture is transmitted through ritual. Catholics use analogy to talk about God—experiencing and expressing how God is like things. These may not seem like huge differences, but it locates Catholics and Protestants in different parts of the brain.

# Catholic Crucifix and Protestant Cross

The cross is perhaps the most powerful symbol of Christianity. It shows the essential difference between these two faith expressions, which can be summed up as tangible experience (Catholic) contrasted to abstract concept (Protestant).

Catholics use religious symbols to generate an experience—an emotional response—and their crosses are called crucifixes. They have the image of the crucified Jesus on them. It's difficult to escape the reality of his human suffering and death when you see him as a real person hanging on the cross. This arcs into another area of difference between these two religions—Catholic devotion to Mary. She is important to Catholics because she gives Jesus his human nature, thus his strongest connection to us. Through Mary, Jesus is flesh and blood, like us—our brother. We know his pain as he knows ours. The cross transmits the same idea, but it does it at the level of thought, not automatically generating a physical or emotional reaction.

> **Epiphanies**
>
> The magical term "hocus-pocus" comes from the most sacred moment in Catholic ritual: the consecration of the bread as the body of Christ by speaking the words "This is my Body," which in Latin is "Hoc est enim Corpus Meum."

# The Touchy-Feely Stuff

Words and phrases are the gateway to the world of thought, and all the touchy-feely stuff of Catholicism is the gateway to the symbolic world of religious imagination. This is what we meant when we said that the worship style of Catholics and Protestants put them in different parts of the brain.

Stimulating the senses engages the imagination side of the brain. The analytical mind slows down—literally. The pulsations in the brain slow down, and it stops thinking for a while. Ritual, with its familiar music, chanting, bells, the smell of incense, candles flickering, and more, engages the senses; it calms the mind and opens the imagination. Those quiet moments feed Catholic imagination and ground the "concept" of God's presence—making it physically real. The smells, sounds, images, and tastes are the tools of ritual, but they are not used in a haphazard way. Rather, they are encoded with 20 centuries of carefully compiled theology of God's presence to nurture a sense of the sacred.

Jesus made a physical connection with his followers when he broke bread at the Passover meal and assured his friends that through this ritual of breaking bread together he would always be with them. He imprinted their memory with his presence through the senses—the wheat and grapes and the experience of being together when he said, "Do this in memory of me." That memory is encoded in the communal mind of everyone who believes the message of the story. Through that embodied memory, the flesh and blood manifestation of God continues to walk among us.

# Imagination: Tasting, Touching, Smelling God

The "bits and pieces" of ritual are called sacramentals. They are the sacred objects that are used to stimulate the senses, moving you out of the analytical mind and into the mind of sensing and feeling called Catholic imagination. In those gaps between our thoughts we can gain insight. Prayer is talking to God; meditation is when God speaks to us. The meditative state of ritual allows you to enter parts of the brain that haven't been conditioned by disappointment and fear.

In those moments, at a very practical level, it is possible to get free of the everyday pressures such as rent, tuition, a date for the prom, illness, and our other concerns, and for a transcending moment or two actually hold hands with God. Or more appropriately, ritual creates a time and space where God breaks through our "normal" state of awareness and makes His presence known (He's been there all along). In those moments God reaches out and holds our hand, even if only briefly. This experience was captured in Michelangelo's painting in the Sistine chapel where Adam, symbolizing humankind, and God's fingers touch.

Ritual changes our consciousness. It refreshes the mind and renews the spirit. This isn't a new discovery; it's what people have known intuitively since the beginning of time. It's only in our modern world that we need laboratory evidence to understand its value. Today, as people meditate, scientists can measure the chemicals in the body and verify the interconnection between state of mind and the physical body. Serotonin and endorphins are released into the bloodstream and flow to every cell in the body. The immune system is strengthened, blood pressure normalizes, and a thousand other chemical imbalances are corrected. Physical health is improved, the mind clears, and the spirit is lifted.

Likewise, contemplation of God's love and immanent presence in our life allows significant miracles to happen. In spiritual terms, qualities such as hope, courage, fortitude, wisdom, understanding, faith, and love are experienced. It doesn't take long before the mere whiff of incense or the jingle of a bell opens the pathways. Ritual is what encodes religion into the body and bones of Catholics, not merely as a metaphor, but in reality.

# Sacred Elements: Air, Earth, Fire, and Water

Catholic ritual is rooted in the earth. It draws its symbols from the elemental forces of nature expressed as air, earth, fire, and water. It creates a sacramental understanding of the material world and at the same time connects believers to the presence of God in the world in His *material* form. In using these very basic substances as both transmitters and substance of religious truths, a Catholic develops a sacred relationship to the world and to the events of life—earthly struggles are affirmed and the earth itself is sanctified. It puts teeth into the biblical reference to humans being made of dust. Catholics are making the statements of Nicea real—God transcendent and God present here and now in material form.

As stated in the first paragraph in this chapter, Catholics love their rituals, and following are some of the most treasured.

## Earth: Ashes to Ashes and Dust to Dust

Ash Wednesday signals the beginning of Lent, the 6-week period before Easter when we know from Scripture that the death of Jesus is imminent. Service starts with Mass and will include the Ash Wednesday ritual—the most attended event of the year. People come to have their foreheads smudged with ashes.

Ashes are prepared for this ceremony by burning last year's palm leaves (explained in the next paragraph). At the appointed time people come to the altar and the priest dips his thumb into a small glass vial containing the chalky black substance and rubs a cross on each forehead giving the biblical reminder, "Remember that you are dust, and unto dust you shall return." (Genesis 3:19) Through this symbolic act the faithful are connected to the life and death of Jesus and the reality of one's own death as well.

Rituals are like wheels within wheels—they have layer upon layer of symbol. For example, the palm branches that are burned for Ash Wednesday are also sacramentals. They're used once a year on Palm Sunday, the Sunday before Easter when they are distributed and held during the reading of the Gospel story of Jesus' arrival in Jerusalem where cheering crowds greeted him, placing palm leaves in his path as a sign of honor. In the ritual, palms leaves transmit a lesson of life's transitory nature. They remind the faithful that things can change from one minute to the next—Jesus is greeted as a hero on Sunday and is arrested a few days later. *Don't count on the vanities of this life*, they say. Catholics traditionally take the palm leaves home and keep them behind a holy picture or a crucifix where their message will continue to be imparted.

The rest are burned for the following Ash Wednesday. Often the congregation is asked a week or so before Ash Wednesday to bring their palms back in to be burned. Garry Wills, a Catholic writer, captures the essence of this ceremony's earthiness describing it as a time when the Catholic comes face-to-face with death: "Certain feelings are not communicable. One cannot explain to others, or even to one's self, how burnt stuff rubbed on the forehead could be balm for the mind. The squeak of ash crumbled into ash marks the body down for death, yet makes this promise of the grave somehow comforting." Activities throughout the day slowly brush away the ashes, but by nightfall perhaps a small cinder is left as a reminder of the ceremony.

## Air as Holy Spirit

Incense, that very Catholic practice of filling the church with "holy smoke," is a way of cleansing the space and preparing the congregation for sacrament. In biblical time, the arrival of the Spirit on Pentecost was announced by a wind that rattled the shutters! Incense charged with sacred meaning fills the air of the church. It is drawn in through the breath and fuses with the body. In the Aramaic language of the Near East there is only one word—*Roukh*—that means all these: "breath," "wind," "air," "atmosphere," or "spirit." When Jesus talks about Spirit or Holy Spirit, he is also talking about breath.

Breath is inspiration or intake of Spirit; we draw our life from the substance of God—our very existence depends on Him. All people from the beginning of time have breathed the same air; age through age we are literally connected in and through God's Holy Spirit and it energizes everything we do—it is the ongoing of creation.

Today's quantum physics has added a new dimension to the understanding of air and thus opens us up to a new awareness the presence of God or the Holy Spirit. Science now affirms that there is no such thing as empty space. When attempts to create a vacuum are made in the laboratory, instruments report that the void is actually filled with molecules appearing to bubble up out of nowhere, filling the space. Our belief that the Holy Spirit is present everywhere, constantly moving, changing, shaping, and creating is renewed. God's omnipresence cannot be denied!

## Holy Water and Holy Oil

In science, water is considered the universal solvent; in religion, it washes away sin! One of the first experiences for Catholics is the feeling of water being poured over their head. When this person is an infant, as is most often the case, it can be met with anything from mild irritation to loud protest! Holy water is blessed and set aside during Holy Week ceremonies to be used throughout the year. In addition to baptism, water is used in virtually every Catholic ceremony. You can read more about all the sacraments in Chapter 11.

Holy water can be found in every corner of a Catholic's world. Catholics dip their fingers in it when they enter the church, symbolically washing their hands in a symbolic connection to the rite of baptism. During the Mass the priest will again wash his hands before consecrating the Eucharist. Often a bottle of holy water is kept at home to be used in times of illness or even to bless the house against a storm or other impending danger.

Holy oil is another sacramental that is blessed and set aside for use in administering several of the seven sacraments. Traditionally, oil is used as a healing balm, as a cleansing agent, and as a strengthener. In the church, it is used in Baptism, Confirmation, Holy Orders, and the Anointing of the Sick. The use of oil for anointing has increased in recent time because healing ceremonies have become more popular. In many parishes members come one Sunday a month for prayer and to be anointed with oil to help with physical or emotional healing. The parish also may hold a ceremony for someone who is about to volunteer for service mission or go away to school to be blessed and anointed with oil.

## Fire, Symbol of Transformation

Anyone who has ever stared into a campfire or watched a log burning in the fireplace has been mesmerized by the power and wonder of fire. Fire is used in all Catholic rituals and ceremonies to symbolize transformation. You will encounter it immediately upon entering the church, as the glowing red sanctuary lamp alerts you to the sacramental presence of Jesus Christ on the altar.

Your eye might then be captured by 20 to 50 flickering little candles called vigil lights that are found on metal stands, often in front of a statue. Catholics light a candle for a special intention and kneel to say a prayer. When they leave, the candle is left to burn as a way in which their presence can remain. Catholics don't worship saints, but they do acknowledge their presence and invoke their assistance in presenting a request to God—much as you seek the help of a friend when you are asking a favor of someone important.

Candles are used on the altar during Mass and other ceremonies. You get an idea of the importance of the ceremony by counting them! Perhaps the greatest test of an altar server's ability is in managing the candle lighter that can be 3 feet long.

Fire is used very dramatically at the Easter Vigil Mass at sundown on Holy Saturday. Worshippers gather outside in the dark as the priest lights what is called a new fire using flint and steel. The Easter candle representing the risen (transcended) Christ is lit from this fire and carried in procession into the dark church. It becomes the source for each person's candle and slowly the whole church is alive with new fire.

Catholics begin and end life with fire. At baptism they are given their baptismal candle, which can be saved and used again at other important ceremonies such as First Communion, Confirmation, or Marriage. A vigil light accompanies the casket throughout a Catholic wake and during the funeral Mass.

# When No One Is Watching

Some of the uneasiness others feel about Catholic worship comes from the intimacy of ritual—it is personal and evokes emotion, and not everyone is comfortable mixing religion and emotion. However, Catholics believe that evoking a personal response in people is effective. They believe that faith finds meaning in action. Catholic spirituality encourages, if not requires, reaching out to others through kindness, charity, working for social justice, being a good neighbor, and a thousand other small actions that add up to being a positive, loving person in the world.

Someone once said that the test of spiritual development is measured by what a person does when no one is watching! Rules and regulations create a moral framework—they're the bones of the Church. However, ritual connects you to your heart and soul and flows into your daily encounters. Love is the most important value for Catholics as it is most likely for all religions. Ritual and ceremony is the Catholic's way of assuring that a loving response happens even "when no one is watching!"

## The Least You Need to Know

- ◆ Catholic ritual and ceremony creates an experience through which faith is felt and renewed.

- ◆ Ritual creates a particular religious character and way of responding to the world infused with emotional sensitivity, morality, and ethics.

◆ Catholic ritual uses the elements of air, earth, fire, and water as sacramentals to reinforce God's sacred presence in the here-and-now world where He is involved in the human struggle.

◆ Catholic imagination connects people to God and to one another as a faith community. It evokes emotion and calls believers to active participation in the reign of God by feeding and caring for others as a moral mandate.

# Chapter 10

# Jesus: The Original Sacrament

## In This Chapter

◆ Why Catholics say Jesus is the sacrament of God

◆ How the mysterious and untouchable God becomes touchable and a little more knowable

◆ How ancient spiritual forms connect the faithful to the history and presence of Jesus, to one another, and to all humanity

◆ A 500-year-old mind/body spiritual exercise that is still popular today

All humans search for meaning. This is perhaps the ultimate difference between "man" and "man's best friend." We have an inborn desire to know and understand even the unknowable—and we fearlessly pursue whatever lies beyond our human comprehension. We need to make meaning out of our existence, and that eventually leaves us staring straight into the *mystery*. We sense there is something that holds the *ultimate* of everything we search for—meaning, love, happiness, peace, or whatever is in the pot at the end of the rainbow—but it's always just out of reach.

Since we can't touch that ultimate, and can't fully comprehend it, we do what people have done since the beginning of time—we create symbols to bridge the gap between what we know and what we instinctively sense and seek. Symbols make that connection assuring us in a concrete way that the sacred exists. As you read in the last chapter, sensate symbols get you in touch with your intuition where you connect with your God nature, or indwelling of the Holy Spirit. That's a good place from which to make moral choices!

# Omnipresence: The Catholic Sacramental Principle

The Catholic *sacramental principle* is a reality imbued with the invisible or hidden presence of God. A sacramental vision of the world sees God in and throughout all things, every person, all communities and movements, events, places, objects, the world at large, and the entire cosmos. This hefty belief is at the very heart of the Catholic religion, flowing through all ceremonies, rites, and practices. It leaves no lack of clarity as to its seriousness to Catholics when it comes to God's incarnation into the world through Jesus Christ and God's omnipresence. For Catholics there is no dichotomy between the infinite and the finite, between spiritual and material, transcendent and immanent, eternal and historical. *For Catholics, there is no place where God is not.*

> **S'ter Says**
>
> The Catholic **sacramental principle** sees divine presence in everything, all people, events, and the world itself. It is a foundational principle in Catholic religion.

> **Epiphanies**
>
> In the Catholic world, Jesus Christ is the greatest sacrament—the living encounter between humanity and God and likewise between God and His people.

God created the ultimate sacrament when he sent Jesus to be here with us in human form. Jesus was not a symbol, but was in symbolic form. He walked and talked like a human being, but had a hidden dimension others couldn't quite grasp—being God. Jesus didn't just signify transcendence but was one and the same with the one who sent him—he was transcendent.

The Catholic Church began through a personal connection with the man called Jesus. He brought a completely different experience of God into the picture—the experience of an intimate relationship with "the Father." He even talked to God like a parent, and taught us that we could be intimate with God, too. The Catholic Church is organized around the idea of making this intimate relationship of creature to Creator available on a regular basis.

Catholics refer to Jesus as the sacrament of God because he came as a human being, lived with the people, and ultimately surrendered himself to God—an act that mediated life everlasting. His followers didn't fully understand the meaning of Jesus' presence in a cognitive way. It was a faith experience from the get-go! And now, 2,000 years later, we are still receiving insight into this event. The appreciation of Jesus as sacrament of God was and is recognized in the hearts and minds of his followers—alive through their faith responses. The effect of Jesus as *sacrament* continues to grow in the faith community, drawing followers deeper within where a spiritual and emotional connection with the God presence is felt.

# Church as Sacrament

Church, as the body of faith-filled people, is the chalice or container of this ongoing presence. Church is used in its singular form because of the Catholic belief in the absolute unified nature of humanity—we are all one. Unbridled by linear time, the Divine presence enters into and transforms our human experience. Catholics believe human nature is already sanctified, and it is moving toward full completion with God. The struggles endured on this path constitute salvation history. Church exists as a process of becoming fully human.

Following Jesus' death, the early Catholic community began to better understand him as the flesh-and-blood connection to a mysterious and seemingly elusive God. They reflected on their experiences and the stories others told and felt his presence when they gathered for a meal together and when they reached out to others by helping the poor. The Church (meaning the body of people) therefore is called "the sacrament of Jesus." The presence of the sacred lives in the heart, mind, and spirit of the faithful, gathered in a life of worship and service.

## The Church, Jesus' Sensible Side

Rituals connect us with each other as a living community in the tribal sense where personal identity is second to community or tribal identity. For instance, when a person dies, he or she continues to live as long as the tribe lives. Tribal identity is difficult to understand in our culture with its strong sense of individualism, but family is a good example. When you experience strong family ties (both the good and the bad of it) you understand tribe. In the family, something you've said or done never goes away! Ancestors remain alive, literally through the DNA, and figuratively through the stories and values they transmitted. Thoughts and actions have a biological and physical reality, as you read in the last chapter.

**Your Guardian Angel**

Avoid feeling superior. The Catholic religion does not teach that it is the only true expression of Church. Being a "good" Catholic means being a good global neighbor on all levels, valuing others' culture and religious beliefs.

As we've said before, Catholic ritual is rooted in tribal religion, and they draw their rituals and ceremonies from this ancient time. As the faith community experiences ritual together their bonds are strengthened—not just to each other, but to a wider community. In the world of symbols every person, every concept, every religious expression connects. Judgment, competition, and individualism are exchanged for compassion, cooperation, and communion. In ritual, Catholics touch the *unity of being* that is the promise of God, and they feel at least a little of the peace of mind that goes with this union. In this regard, the Church as a worshipping body becomes the sacrament of God. This is most clearly expressed in the Eucharist—where Catholics gather to eat bread and drink wine and so be one with Christ, the sacrament of God.

Describing the Church as the sacrament of Christ is not to lay claim to any privileged condition. An assertion you may have heard put forth is that the Catholic Church is the one true church. This isn't a true Catholic teaching. It's a misunderstanding perpetrated through bad theology, and just plain human error—we all want to have the right answer! Today, the image of church reaching out to embrace all humankind is more accurate than church as a special community. The power of sacrament and ritual is the increased ability to experience that sense of connection to all humanity, and to the world itself.

**S'ter Says**

*Mediation* means standing between or connecting something or someone to someone else. It is usually employed when two parties are unable to connect to each other directly. They seek the services of a mediator. Because of the belief in the "divide" between the human and the divine, Catholics see Jesus as *the* mediator between God and humans.

## Sacrament: Mediating Grace—Really!

Catholics believe that a sacrament not only signifies grace—God's presence—it causes what it signifies. It is what it says it is and it does what it says it's doing! This is the principle of *mediation*. God is not only present in the sacramental action, but causes something to happen as a result of the sacramental encounter. We know that God is present in creation and in us as his created, and that He transforms us by His presence. Sacramental mediation states that an experience constructed and performed by humans contains sacred presence and makes grace available to those who participate. God is present in the action and "makes something happen" through the action. Mediation is what gives weight to the sacraments and to the ordained priesthood. They become points of focus for the presence and transmission (mediation) of grace not for themselves, but for the community.

There is a tendency to make religion and all its words and definitions very otherworldly, but their real power is in their immediate and practical benefits. Salvation has already happened. *Religion is about remembering that, and helping us get through the many snags of this life.* The results of an encounter with the Spirit can be measured, as we talked about in the last chapter. People experience a letting go of tension, a physical, emotional, and mental renewal. In religious talk their heart is lifted, they feel hope, strength, and love. Whatever the circumstances of their lives before ritual, they come out the other side feeling different about themselves and life. This doesn't mean all problems are gone, but that one's ability to solve, endure, or transcend the difficulties increases. Catholic ritual is an earthy experience of the sacred, for practical results.

**For Heaven's Sake**

Don't worry if you have trouble following this word by word; sacraments and symbols are essentially mysteries that can't be fully explained by rational means. That doesn't mean they aren't real, but that they cannot be understood through the thinking mind. They belong to what is called the numinous—the mystical realm of the spirit—and are best understood intuitively.

# Religion: The Marriage of Form and Spirit

Symbols are a human construct and at the same time they take on a life of their own. They connect to a dimension of human experience that eludes control. At that deep level of consciousness, a reservoir of the sacred exists within us, lying beyond the reach of anything that would attempt to bridle it; and in that holy space, the sacred enters into conversation with us. Religion creates form, and becomes the container for humans' most profound symbols—and symbols breathe spirit into religious form.

## Getting from Here to There

The word *symbol* comes from the Greek noun *symbolon*, and means "pulling together." Symbols bridge the gulf between the concrete experience and the spiritual aspect of the ritual. For example, in receiving the sacrament of confirmation the candidate is anointed with oil; and while the Holy Spirit is not visible, spiritual strength in the form of fortitude, wisdom, understanding, knowledge, and more is imparted. The symbol is the link between the desire to be confirmed and the mystery of the sacrament, actual grace. God's actual presence making one's life really and truly fuller and richer is imparted. Our symbolic nature naturally grasps the significance of ritual. This intuitive mind is relational. It makes connection and continues making connections—taking the participant deeper within and to greater awareness of God's presence. Insight and more grace will be imparted indefinitely.

**Your Guardian Angel**

Help others. To be a Catholic is to reach out to others who are in need. A Catholic cannot ignore or refuse this mission and stay true to the teachings of Jesus.

## Community: The Kingdom of God Is Within (Us)

Communion is the radical awareness that we are all in this thing together. It's through the principle of communion that the Church's insistence on binding its people together becomes understandable. The Church is the symbolic and sacramental presence of God dwelling among us through Jesus Christ—not contained in the bricks and mortar, codes and rules, but in the lives of the people. Catholics believe that as Christians they are called into partnership with the Creator and redeemer through the power of the Holy Spirit to assist in the work of bringing the entire world to the perfection of God's kingdom. Therefore, Catholic identity demands engagement.

One of the four essential characteristics of the Catholic Church is to be all embracing. Catholics engage the world and actively work for transformation of oppressive structures, believing that grace is ultimately stronger than evil. Doctrines of creation, presence, incarnation, and redemption undergird Catholic social policy. Working to bring the kingdom of God into reality is described as "a kingdom of truth and life of holiness and grace, of justice, love and peace" (Vatican II *Pastoral Constitution on the Church in the Modern World*, number 39).

Life and ministry cannot be separated. God has created the human race as a people. The human race suffers as a people, it is redeemed as a people, and is destined for eternal glory as a people. There is no personal individual relationship with God or Jesus Christ established or sustained that isn't integral to the human race. We (all people, all creation) are one. This is what puts the mystery in church, and what gives reason to its doctrines, pastoral practice, moral vision, and prayer life. More about this in Chapter 18.

## Sacramental Awareness

For Catholics, religion is not about becoming spiritual, but rather it is about becoming more aware of your spiritual nature. Jesus made this point the central teaching of his Gospel when he said, "The kingdom of God is within." (Luke 17:21) For Catholics, the major point of Jesus Christ's incarnation was not to see him as different from them, but to recognize his likeness in themselves and others. As the God who took human form to be with the people, he shows them that they have a divine nature, too. Going against the dualism of the time in which he lived and even of our time today, Jesus demonstrated that the sacred and the worldly are not separate and that God exists in all life forms. The mission, should we choose to accept it, is to become more aware of our own divine nature, as well as sacred presence within one another, and to lovingly embrace humanity and the world as a place where God's divinity resides. This awareness fires our moral imaginations and moves us to bring about the kingdom that is within to become enacted on Earth. This is called *sacramental awareness.*

# Ignatius Loyola's Spiritual Exercises: A Journey into Sensual Imagination

We've included these spiritual exercises because of their long history in Church tradition, and because they show how "there isn't anything new under the sun." Today there is an emphasis on healing the mind/body duality in science as well as religion, and many new spiritual exercises abound. St. Ignatius Loyola's visionary approach to spiritual development was ahead of the curve by a scant 500 years! His is a disciplined and systematic approach, and intuitive as well. Most of all it is time tested. The approach he uses was part of the desert traditions of the monasteries and the cloistered life of the Middle Ages. Such practice is a vital part of Catholic life today.

The key phrase for the spiritual exercises of St. Ignatius of Loyola is "allowing the creator to deal with the creature." St. Ignatius set the traditional form of these exercises in 1556, and they are more popular than ever with modern Catholics and others.

The participants in these spiritual exercises attend a retreat center away from their homes and observe silence for 4 weeks, sometimes less. The intention of these retreats is to break through old ideas that we continue to cling to, even when part of our mind knows they aren't true any longer. This is done so that new spiritual insight can feed the mind. Subsequent decisions will be clear and unencumbered by the old

**S'ter Says**

A **spiritual director** is a person trained to work with people spiritually, much like a psychologist works with someone emotionally. Spiritual directors work with individuals, and also with groups of people.

"inordinate attachments," as they are called. Under the leadership of a *spiritual director*, participants are led through meditations and encouraged to "play" with God and Jesus through their imagination. The leader takes the participants on an inner journey of imagination by using biblical stories.

If you were looking for an answer to a question in your life, for instance, you would take this question with you into a spiritual journey and ask Jesus for advice. In your meditation, you might walk with Jesus on the road to Emmaus. The leader would connect you to the experience through the senses, asking questions like: What does the countryside look like to you? What is the temperature there? What does the road feel like to your feet? What are you wearing? What colors do you see? Who, besides Jesus, is there with you? What does it feel like to be there with Jesus?

---

**Saints Preserve Us**

**St. Ignatius of Loyola, July 31, Patron of Retreats**

St. Ignatius of Loyola, patron saint of retreats, was born in 1491 in Spain. After having painful surgery performed on his leg, he began reading devotional books. In a radical transformation, he dedicated himself to Christ. A depression drove him inward where he began to develop his spiritual awareness. He formulated his process into the spiritual exercises that bear his name and are still practiced today. He founded the Jesuit order, and his feast day is July 31.

---

As the senses are engaged by the questions, your imagination is activated, and you go deeper into your inner world. You are directed to imagine asking Jesus for his advice on the situation you are struggling with and imagine Jesus' response. Through this process, you are able to tap the divine spirit that resides within you and receive deep spiritual insight.

St. Ignatius believed that God speaks to us through our imagination. The leader, acting as a guide, does not give advice, but helps direct people into their inner worlds, where the Spirit of God resides and the answers can be found.

In this chapter, we have looked at how God is present to Catholics through Jesus, whom the Church calls the sacrament of God. In the next chapter, we will get into the seven sacraments that mark the life of Catholics.

## The Least You Need to Know

◆ Sacraments are symbols that connect the visible and invisible dimensions, the other world and this one.

◆ Jesus came to show the connection between creation and Creator—to overcome the gap people experienced in their relationship with the divine.

◆ Full realization of the indwelling of the Holy Spirit in the earth and all its inhabitants calls Catholics to work for the reign of God now.

◆ The community of the faithful is a sacrament as it is filled with God's spirit. It is keeper of the mysteries, and a place where God's presence can be experienced now.

# Chapter 11

# Seven Sensual Sacraments

## In This Chapter

- ◆ How the sacraments connect Catholics to the sacredness of everyday life
- ◆ Why Catholics baptize babies
- ◆ Why Catholics don't divorce
- ◆ How a priest keeps confidences
- ◆ How the sacrament of the dead became a sacrament of the living

The seven sacraments form the framework of Catholic spirituality. They celebrate seven significant spiritual events marking key transitions in life, bringing spiritual meaning and power to the individual, and binding Catholics together. They are the heart of the Catholic community.

The sacraments are divided into three groups. The first group is sacraments of initiation: baptism, Holy Eucharist, and confirmation. The second group relates to state of life: marriage and Holy Orders. And the third group is sacraments of healing: reconciliation and anointing of the sick.

It would take an entire book (or more) to adequately cover the sacraments and explain the importance of their place Catholic life and faith. We'll use this opportunity to introduce them to you and hope you will look at the resources in the back of the book and learn more. We'll begin at the beginning—baptism.

# Baptism: More Than Just Water on the Head

Baptism is a rite of initiation, and it starts a Catholic on the faith journey by bonding the child to the community. It is a naming ceremony. Parents will name the child and the child will be named (or claimed) for Christ. It introduces the new Catholic to the community among whom they will live and grow spiritually. Likewise, the community commits to be the baptized person's guide and companion on the journey, offering spiritual mentoring when needed.

Catholics believe in infant baptism, although adults who have not been baptized in another faith receive the sacrament when they enter the Catholic faith. This process, called the Rite of Christian Initiation (RCIA), is described in Chapter 16. Some Catholic churches offer baptism by emersion; however, our discussion will focus on the most common form.

## Water on the Head

At an infant baptism, you might see a young couple presenting their new baby at the *baptismal font*, along with several family members, the godparents, and the priest.

> **S'ter Says**
>
> The **baptismal font** is a large container of water often made of marble and placed at the entrance of the church. At it, the priest or deacon pours the water that is used in the baptism of the candidate entering the church. In some churches there is a pool of water for immersion.

After greeting the people, the priest "signs" the infant with the cross in what Catholics call the imprint of Christ. Scripture is read and the priest anoints the child's forehead, lips, throat, and chest with holy oil as a protection from spiritual harm.

The baptismal water is blessed and poured over the child's head in three distinct gestures while saying the words, "(Child's name), I baptize you in the name of the Father, and of the Son, and of the Holy Spirit." Next he takes perfumed oil to anoint the child as a symbol of the enlightenment of the Holy Spirit.

Godparents stand nearby, holding the child's special candle that has been lit from the Easter candle, which was specially blessed and first lit at the Easter vigil. Godparents are chosen by the parents to sponsor the new candidate as he or she enters the Church. They speak for the child, accepting the faith by responding to a litany of beliefs and reciting the Lord's Prayer. With a solemn blessing, the priest concludes the ritual and congratulates the parents.

*Baptismal font and pool. Here you see a baptismal font in the foreground. Behind it is a shallow pool for immersion. Notice the Easter candle. Cathedral of the Incarnation, Nashville, Tennessee.*

*(Courtesy of H. L. [Dean] Caskey)*

## Who Can Baptize?

Although a priest or deacon usually performs baptism ceremonies at the church, anyone can baptize in an emergency situation (a car wreck, for example). Any person (Catholic or not) can pour the water and say the words. The only requirement is to follow the wishes of the person you are baptizing. Virtually all Christian religions baptize in a very similar way, and the Church recognizes the baptism of Christians from other denominations as valid and would not rebaptize them if they chose to become Catholic.

The Church teaches that children who die before baptism are in God's loving care. It has been taught that babies who died before being baptized go to Limbo. This is a "happy resting place," but not heaven. A Theological Commission appointed by the Pope is reexamining the Church's thinking on the fate of unbaptized babies. Look for the results in the fourth edition of this book.

## The Origins of Baptism

Baptism is rooted is John the Baptist's baptizing Jesus in the waters of the river Jordan. However, it must be noted that John was following Jewish custom. St. Paul understood baptism as both a drowning or a death and rebirth as a new being. Catholics believe that the waters of baptism eliminate all sins. The Church recognizes two other times where baptism is implied. One dates back to the time of the martyrs, and is called baptism by blood, which means anyone killed for their beliefs is considered baptized. The other is baptism by desire, which occurs when someone desires to be baptized, but dies before having the opportunity.

In the first centuries of the Church, adult baptism was the common form of the rite. Joining a new community that wasn't Roman, Greek, or Jewish meant a radical change in one's life. As the religion became part of the Roman Empire, both the numbers of people who were becoming Christian and the way whole pagan tribes converted caused a decline in emphasis on instruction. In a few generations, infant baptism became the norm. Catholics renew their baptismal promises at Easter Mass, acknowledging that faith continues to grow after baptism, and we are always "new."

# Eucharist: First Holy Communion

The Catholic Church uses the term Eucharist in two ways: to describe the celebration of the Mass and to define the sacrament of the Eucharist, also called Holy Communion. Eucharist is the central ritual for Catholics, and it is described in detail in the next chapter. Here we'll talk about First Communion, the time when most Catholics first experience this rite.

Typically, Catholics receive the sacrament of the Eucharist for the first time at about the age of seven at the rite called the First Holy Communion. The Church recognizes that previous to the age of seven a child is not considered morally responsible. The sacrament of reconciliation, discussed later in this chapter, accompanies First Communion, and preparation for the First Communion includes instruction about confession, too. Both sacraments mark the time in a child's life when he or she will begin to assume moral responsibility.

A child's First Communion celebration creates a lifelong memory. Little girls are dressed in white from head to toe including a white veil. Little boys wear white suits, white shirts, and white ties. They enter the church in a procession, taking their place in pews reserved in the front of the church. They're being included in one of the most important rites of the Catholic Church. The ritual then becomes central to their spiritual life. Unlike the first two sacraments, baptism and confirmation, which are received only once, Catholics receive the Eucharist at every Mass. Almost every Catholic has keepsakes of this day tucked away in a box somewhere—a white prayer book, rosary, or holy card.

## Eucharist: A Catholic's Thanksgiving

Eucharist means "thanksgiving," and is rooted in an earlier Jewish ritual where the term described the practice of giving thanks during a meal for God's creation, redemption, and sanctification. Eucharist is a symbol of God's nurturing care, offering both physical and spiritual life to the people in the form of bread and wine. In Chapter 9, we described in detail how ritual awakens deep memory and connects those who participate back through time to all who have performed the ritual. The Eucharist reaches back through the ages to the Last Supper, connecting today's Catholics to the ritual Passover meal when Jesus first blessed bread and wine and instructed his followers to do as he did as a way of remembering him. It is the way Christ remains present and accessible to his Church.

Communion is also an important bonding ritual. Just as a family sits down at the table together regularly to secure their connection to one another and also their identity as a family, Catholic bonds are strengthened through this ritual. United with Christ in the Eucharist, the congregation is unified with each other, becoming one body. Because it is both physical and spiritual food, Communion serves as a reminder of the practice of charity toward others less fortunate, teaching compassion for the poor.

Catholics are encouraged to receive Communion every time they attend the Mass, but they must receive it at least once a year. It is reserved for people who are in full relationship with the Catholic Church, including Orthodox Christians. Usually, if you are a non-Catholic guest at a Catholic Mass, you do not partake of the Eucharist.

# Confirmation: It's No Longer a Slap on the Face

Confirmation increases and deepens the process of initiation into the faith begun at baptism, this time with conscious awareness. Those seeking confirmation must be of age to understand what they are committing to, and must have completed a

**Your Guardian Angel**

If you're invited to a confirmation celebration, it is customary to give the guest of honor a small gift. (May we suggest a copy of *The Complete Idiot's Guide to Understanding Catholicism, Third Edition?*)

rigorous study of the religion. (Although in the Eastern churches confirmation is received in infancy, along with baptism.) It bestows spiritual strength for the next leg of the journey, and also strengthens the bond between the individual and the community. Many parishes require candidates to take part in a service project in their community, such as working for a local agency like Meals on Wheels or Habitat for Humanity. This voluntarism demonstrates the candidate's willingness and ability to take Christian values out into the world.

## Origins of the Sacrament of Confirmation

Confirmation can be compared to the coming-of-age ceremonies found in most cultures. It corresponds to the Jewish rite of passage, bar mitzvah for boys and bat mitzvah for girls, which is the ritual ceremony that marks the thirteenth birthday of a Jewish child, after which they are expected to take full responsibility for moral decisions and conduct. In the United States, the bishop of a diocese can decide to confer the sacrament of confirmation at any age between 7 and 18. The biblical roots of confirmation are in the New Testament story of Jesus' baptism by John, Matthew 3:10–12, and the story of Pentecost, found in Acts 2. You read the story of Pentecost in Chapter 8.

## Oil and Words and the Holy Spirit

Confirmation, the second rite of initiation, is also a naming ceremony. In baptism, the child was given a name. In the sacrament of confirmation, the young adult chooses his or her name, usually that of a saint whose life story reflects values that hold a particular meaning. Candidates choose a sponsor to stand up with them. This part of the ritual uses touch, as the adult sponsor places a hand on the candidate's shoulder, transmitting the physical sense of support. The message is that the youngster is going out into the world, but they are not alone, they are not without support. The sponsor is promising to provide lifelong guidance. Often, one of the baptismal godparents plays this role.

**Your Guardian Angel**

Don't be fearful when you hear the phrase "fear of the Lord"! This gift of the Holy Spirit refers to the Old Testament idea of trembling in awe or wonder in the presence of God. Thus, its deep meaning is reverence for God, not being fearful of God.

Candidates stand in front of the congregation, and the bishop, who usually administers the sacrament, extends his hands over them while saying a prayer. The bishop says the new name as he anoints the forehead of each candidate with chrism (holy oil), followed by a laying on of hands, saying the words, "Be sealed with the gift of the Holy Spirit." The oil the bishop uses represents abundance and joy. Being sealed with oil means to be marked as belonging to Christ. It signifies the one receiving the seal is committing to align his or her will to the will of God. Oil also gives strength to the body. The very name "Christian" means anointed, and this is why the confirmation rite is essentially an oil rite rather than a water rite like baptism. To conclude the rite, the bishop offers the sign of peace, which is a handshake, affirming union with the community.

## The Seven Gifts

Catholics believe that confirmation awakens certain spiritual attributes called the seven gifts of the Holy Spirit, described in the Old Testament: Wisdom, Understanding, Right Judgment, Courage, Knowledge, Reverence, and Fear (awe) of the Lord. Catholics believe that all members are called to share in the priesthood of Christ in that they will be called to publicly and officially profess and mediate the faith of the Catholic Church at times in their lives. Confirmation is the sacrament that opens this "priestly" function.

---

### Epiphanies

Confirmation corresponds to the appearance of the Holy Spirit to the apostles on Pentecost. In the first centuries, when baptism was generally administered to adults, confirmation accompanied it. This is still the case when an adult is brought into the Church today and in the Eastern Rite Catholic Churches. Eventually, as the practice of infant baptism grew, the time between the two sacraments lengthened to include the age of discernment, and it became the tradition of the bishop to administer it.

---

# *Ménage à Trois:* It's More Than Just Two in a Marriage

In a Catholic marriage, three parties are involved: the husband, the wife, and Jesus Christ. Not only is marriage a lasting relationship between partners, it is also considered a covenant relationship, based on the covenant relationship between God and his people. Covenant relationships cannot be broken, and Catholic marriage is for life, with very few exceptions. Therefore, thoughtful preparation and prayer precede the marriage vows. It should be noted that the marriage of two baptized persons is sacramental and thus indissoluble. Other marriages are not, and the church can grant a dissolution when at least one party is not baptized.

## I Do! I Do!

When two Catholics marry, this usually takes place during a special nuptial Mass. Guests who are not forewarned can be surprised at the length of the ceremony! Usually, you will find liturgy books in the seats that will help you follow the service. The wedding party enters the church in a ceremonial way, taking places in the front of the church near the altar. Prayers and Scripture readings for the service have been selected in advance by the couple. The celebration of the Mass begins, and vows are exchanged.

Unlike the other six sacraments, the priest does not administer this sacrament, but rather the couple marry each other. The principle of consent is the central feature. Consent is fulfilled as the parties mutually agree to give themselves to each other: "I take you to be my wife," and "I take you to be my husband." The priest or deacon is the official witness to the consent of the spouses and he gives the blessing of the Church to the ceremony. The best man and maid of honor represent the connection of this marriage to the Church community.

## A Covenant Relationship

A covenant is more than a civil agreement. It is also religious in nature, and religious covenants cannot be broken. Catholics believe that God enters into the covenant relationship with the couple, which means they will be given the spiritual support and insight to maintain the marriage as long as they keep the covenant. In other words, God gives the couple a spiritual guarantee to stay with them and provide the necessary grace to help them grow individually and together over their lifetimes. Their part of the covenant is the promise to hang in there, even when the times are tough, or, more traditionally stated, for better or for worse.

In forming the covenant, the couple enters a partnership with God in creation; this has traditionally meant that the prime intention of Catholic marriage is to have children. From the time of Augustine up until Vatican II, Church teachings specifically stated "The primary end of marriage is the procreation and nurture of children; its secondary end has to do with sexual satisfaction."

Vatican II again restated both of these principles, but recognized the importance of the comforting and bonding aspects of sex, making them of equal importance. This means having children and sexual enjoyment together constitute the primary intention of marriage. The fact that having children is still foundational to Catholic marriage does not mean that couples who can't have children are not fulfilling the contract. This same thing applies to couples who marry later in life, past their childbearing age. Such marriages carry the complete sacramental blessing. As you will learn in Chapter 19, Catholics are not allowed to practice artificial contraception of any kind because it violates one of the ends of marriage.

**For Heaven's Sake**

Look before you leap! Marriage is a lifelong partnership commitment, based in love, for the well-being of the spouses and for the purpose of having and nurturing children. It is absolutely dependent on the free consent of the couple.

## Forever Is a Long Time

Because a sacramental marriage cannot be dissolved, and consent is key, there is a mandatory preparation for it known as the Pre-Cana sessions. These group sessions, typically six in number, include prayers and possibly a retreat weekend in which the religious and spiritual aspects of the marriage relationship are talked about in great detail. The sessions are practical as well. They include communication skills, finances, and lectures about human sexuality and health issues. Although the parish priest coordinates these sessions, parish laypersons facilitate them.

In the case of mixed marriages, where one party is Catholic and the other is not, further instruction and preparation is required. The purpose is to find helpful ways in which the couple can fully express their love and faith with spiritual unity.

The Church does not recognize divorce between any two baptized people of any denomination, nor does it recognize civil divorce of nonbaptized persons, although the church may grant a dissolution (divorce) of a nonsacramental marriage under certain circumstances. It does acknowledge the need for

**Saints Preserve Us**

**St. Elizabeth of Portugal, July 4, Patron of Marital Problems**

St. Elizabeth of Portugal (1271–1336) is invoked against marital problems because she had a reputation around town for interceding as a peacemaker in many marriages. After the death of her husband, Elizabeth joined a convent of the Sisters of St. Claire, which she had founded.

physical separation, such as when there is violence in the marriage. However, the man and woman involved are never free to contract a new union.

The Church also acknowledges situations when an invalid marriage has occurred; where there was not complete consent, or complete consent is compromised because of deception by either one of the couple. In this case, the word annulment is used because the marriage is not dissolved, but declared null—it didn't happen. Annulment is a lengthy and sometimes expensive process, handled by a Church court.

# Holy Orders: More Than Just Oil on the Fingers

Holy Orders is the sacrament by which a man commits his life to serve the faith community. With this commitment, he is granted the responsibility and power to preside over sacred rituals, offering Mass, forgiving sins, giving blessings, administering sacraments, and attending to the spiritual life of the people he serves. Holy Orders is traditionally thought of as a higher calling, and those who accept the call are expected to live up to higher standards than the rest of the folks. The priest becomes a symbol of Christ's presence, which carries both privilege and responsibility.

## In the Beginning ...

In the early years of the Church, there was no ordination, no priests or bishops as we know them today. By the end of the first century, two important offices began to emerge: that of overseer, which would later become the office of the bishop, and that of presbyter, the position that became deacon and priest. In the second century, the terms ecclesiastical and priestly began to identify these roles as something apart from the laity.

The Church recognized Holy Orders as a sacrament in the 1100s.

Although Holy Orders is a "one-time only" sacrament, it is received in levels as three separate ordinations, from deacon to priest to bishop:

◆ **Deacons** are assistants to the bishop and usually work in charities in the parishes where they are assigned. They perform a number of sacramental ministries, especially marriage and baptism.

◆ **Priests** celebrate the Eucharist, the sacrament of reconciliation, and the anointing of the sick. They are appointed as the pastors of parishes.

◆ **Bishops** celebrate the sacraments of ordination and confirmation and appoint priests and deacons to parishes. They oversee the parishes that make up a diocese.

| **Epiphanies** |
| --- |
| There are two types of deacons. Prior to Vatican II, ordination as a deacon was only a stepping-stone on the way to priesthood. A man would be ordained deacon about six months before he was to be ordained priest. Today that step continues for those going on to priesthood. These men are called "transitional deacons." However, the Church has restored the "permanent diaconate" of the early Church as an order of leadership and service in its own right. Presently, only men are candidates for this office. They can be married, but if their spouse dies, they may not remarry. They must be 35 years of age or older. |

## The Ceremony

Only bishops can administer the sacrament of ordination, and the custom is to have three bishops to ordain a new bishop. The ritual of Holy Orders for all three levels follows essentially the same form. It is administered during a special Mass in a cathedral with as many of the faithful taking part as is possible. It is a high celebration, with much pomp and circumstance.

The rites begin with a presentation of the candidates and a ritual "calling forth" of those who will be ordained, symbolizing the enactment of "vocation" or God's calling them to the priesthood. The common term describing a man's decision to enter the priesthood is *vocation*; the word is from the Latin and means "calling," which signifies that God is the one who calls. This is followed by an "instruction" by the bishop, who tells them what is expected of them as they receive this office. The first quality of the priest is his openness and ability to listen to God's will or "call."

The bishop then asks a series of questions to examine the adequacy of the person seeking ordination. As in confirmation, there is a laying on of hands by the bishop. Candidates lie face down on the floor in front of the altar, symbolizing humility, service, and connection to the world, as well as the priesthood. Those being ordained as bishop are anointed with holy oil, given the book of the Gospels, a ring, a special hat (called a miter), and a staff (called a crosier). Priests are presented with a paten, which is a gold plate on which the Communion bread is placed during the Mass, and a chalice, which is the container for the Communion wine. Their fingers are anointed with holy oil because they will be handling the consecrated host. Deacons receive a book of the Gospels.

## A Few Good Men

Ordination in the Catholic Church is reserved for men only. Many women also feel called to the priesthood, and must fulfill this calling through service or ministry by different means. Traditionally, women joined religious orders as nuns, where they often served as teachers and health-care workers, as well as orders where prayer and meditation is the focus. Today, women go to seminaries and prepare themselves for various Church leadership positions. We discuss this process in Chapter 24.

Ordination is considered lifelong, so there is a long process of discernment before one is admitted into the final stages of the process. It can take as long as four or five years of seminary training after college. A seminary is a graduate school that has two purposes: one is academic training, and the other is spiritual formation of the candidate. Not only must a man demonstrate his intellectual ability, but he must also show his spirituality and willingness to serve. The final decision is mutual, based on the personal willingness of the candidate to accept the role, and assessment of his fitness for the priesthood by Church officials.

Celibacy is mandatory for priests and bishops in the Roman Catholic Church. Being celibate means you cannot get married or have sexual relations. Celibacy was instituted gradually over the first thousand years of the Church. The 21 Eastern churches (those in union with Rome) have always permitted marriage before ordination. Only the Latin Church requires celibacy. In addition, married clergy from other denominations who seek Catholic ordination can be accepted as married priests and remain married. Deacons also can be married.

# Penance: More Than Just a Kick in the Pants

Penance, now usually called reconciliation, is also (and perhaps better) known among Catholics as confession. The idea of going into a dark little booth and telling someone your deepest faults seems strange to many. However, most people agree that confession is good for the soul. Great mystique surrounds the role of the priest, and many a good story has been spun about his refusing to break the seal of confession, refusing to betray the confessed, even when testifying in court. Today, most Catholics do not observe the weekly rite of confession, and the setting for the sacrament can include sitting face-to-face with a confessor in a room rather than the little black box. However, this sacrament remains an important part of Church practice. This section looks at the practice today.

## Confession Is Good for the Soul

The sacrament of reconciliation has two parts: confessing your sins and forgiveness by the priest in Christ's name. Confession begins with a time of personal reflection, where Catholics examine the events of their lives, particularly their actions and reactions to the people and situations they are currently experiencing. In reflecting, they might assess themselves in light of the Christian principles most important to them. They determine where they are measuring up to their ideals and where they are falling short. As this assessment is made, they might discover particular thoughts, feelings, or actions that are out of alignment with what they know is right, asking questions such as the following:

- How could I have acted in a more loving way?

- What habit do I have that needs to be changed?

- Where am I having problems in my spiritual life?

- Where do I need healing?

The process eventually leads to identifying patterns of behavior that need to be addressed. While confession once seemed to be focused on cataloging and measuring sins, it has always included a more positive process of self-reflection and moral housekeeping. That is certainly the emphasis today.

## Sin, the "S" Word

Some Catholics fear the Church has gone soft on *sin*, and today it is more likely to be identified as simply falling short of the mark instead of something more evil. The concepts of sin and forgiveness will be discussed in greater detail in Chapter 19.

The point of this sacrament is reconciliation. Following the time of self-reflection, also known as the examination of conscience, the penitent—the one going to confession—either enters the confessional or the reconciliation

> **S'ter Says**
>
> **Sin** is a thought or an action that is contrary to the will of God. If left unchecked, it creates a pattern of problematic behaviors. The sacrament of reconciliation helps uncover the pattern and correct it.

room where they will talk with the priest. Traditionally, the opening line of confession began with "Bless me father, for I have sinned." This is followed by …

- Telling your sins to the priest.

- Expressing true sorrow.

- Making a firm commitment or promise to change your behavior.

In turn, the priest …

- Extends the forgiveness of Christ through the position he holds as a priest in the Church.

- Determines the reparation or penance.

The penitent then …

- Prays the Act of Contrition.

- Performs the penance given (after leaving the confessional).

Penance usually comes in the form of prayers or acts of charity the penitent must do. If reparation is appropriate, that, too, must be done. However, according to the teaching of St. Paul, the sinner is forgiven by God when still in the sin. Confession is the symbolic acting out of this belief. The priest acts symbolically as Christ, forgiving sins through God. His role is symbolized by the stole he wears—part of the priest's vestments.

## The Little Black Box

In the past, it was common to receive this sacrament in the confessional box, as shown in the illustration of a traditional confessional. The priest sat in the middle of three stalls. There was a small, screened sliding door on each side, opening to the other stalls. When the penitent on the right was confessing, the other door was closed so that others could not hear. There were no lights, conversation was whispered, and there was a sense of anonymity.

Today, Catholics have the option of face-to-face confession in a reconciliation room. In this style, a person sits down with the priest and confesses in a more conversational and interactive manner.

In addition to private confession, parishes hold communal penance services to emphasize the corporate nature of sin. Communal services emphasize the social consequences of all sin. In such a service, there are Bible readings and reflections about the correct Catholic response to social issues.

*A traditional confessional. Christ the King Church, Nashville, Tennessee.*

*(Courtesy of H. L. [Dean] Caskey)*

## Guilt: The Gift You Leave Behind

Reconciliation celebrates forgiveness and God's willingness to heal us, and it develops introspection and moral responsibility. The Church teaches that a person becomes responsible for their actions some time between the ages of 7 to 12, as the sense of right and wrong develops. From this age onward, Catholics must receive the sacrament of Eucharist and reconciliation, if necessary, at least once a year. The Church teaches that all sins are forgivable.

The sacrament of reconciliation recognizes that sin creates a block between us and God. The effect of reconciliation is to restore the person to a sense of intimate friendship with God. No sin is entirely private; it affects others. Sin is about broken relationships—between the self and God, self to self, and self to the community. It's not just the penitent who is affected by the sacrament, but also the sense of community and trust within the Church is restored.

Forgiveness absolves guilt. The penitent goes forward, unencumbered by the past, and participates more fully in life. Confession is usually followed by a feeling of peace and serenity, a strengthening of the spirit, and joy.

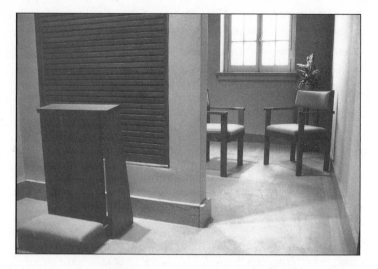

*A contemporary confessional with the option of face-to-face confession, shown by the two chairs, or traditional confession with the screen. The Cathedral of the Incarnation, Nashville, Tennessee.*

*(Courtesy of H. L. [Dean] Caskey)*

# Anointing of the Sick: More Than a Simple Good-Bye

Before Vatican II, this sacrament of anointing the sick was commonly referred to as the Last Rites, or *Extreme Unction*, both suggesting a sense of finality. Many a story has been told of a Catholic waking up from a deep sleep during a serious illness only to find a priest administering the Last Rites. Because this sacrament was the spiritual equivalent of calling 911—or worse, throwing in the spiritual towel—you can imagine the devastating effect this might have had. Even today, chaplains report that when they go to visit a sick Catholic, they are often greeted by a hand signaling stay out, and the proclamation "You don't need to visit me today; I'm feeling just fine!"

### S'ter Says

**Extreme Unction** was one of the former names of this sacrament of anointing of the sick. Extreme refers to the condition of those who are departing, and *unction* means "oil." Receiving the Eucharist is part of the Last Rites. The sacrament of the Eucharist is called *Viaticum* when a dying person receives it. Viaticum is a Latin word meaning "on the way with you."

## Three for the Price of One!

The Last Rites are comprised of the three sacraments of reconciliation, Holy Eucharist, and the anointing of the sick. It was generally administered only at the point of death. The new name, anointing of the sick, makes it clear that this sacrament is about healing.

Under the reformed rite, use has grown to include this sacrament as a healing aid for those who are seriously ill, either physically or emotionally. It is given to people going into serious surgery, the elderly and frail, and even those who are victims of substance addiction and emotional or mental illnesses, as a means of strengthening the spirit and encouraging healing. The sacrament is now received more than one time.

## Healing Body and Soul

The priest lays his hands on the sick and prays silently over him or her. He anoints the forehead with chrism (oil blessed by the bishop on Holy Thursday) praying, "Through this holy anointing may the Lord in his love and mercy help you with the grace of the Holy Spirit." He then anoints the hands of the sick person saying, "May the Lord who frees you from sin save you and raise you up." The practice can be preceded by reconciliation and followed by Holy Eucharist.

The sacrament honors both the physical and spiritual healing presence of Christ. It holds both strengthening and curative powers and brings wholeness and well-being to those who receive it. This sacrament brings the following gifts:

◆ Cures in the form of strengthening, peace, and courage to overcome the diffi-culties that go with serious illness or the frailty of old age

◆ The gift of finding spiritual meaning for health and physical struggles

◆ Preparation and fortification for the final journey

◆ Forgiveness of sins

Just as the sacraments of initiation (baptism and confirmation) begin the Catholic journey with anointing, this last sacrament points to the end of life's journey by strengthening through anointing.

## Transformation for the Community

Since Vatican II, it has become quite common on given Sundays throughout the year to make anointing ceremonies part of the Mass. At these ceremonies, people in need of special healing come forward for anointing. The membership of the Church wit-nesses, prays, and supports the person's healing. In such a setting, an intense transfor-mation can take place when a large group of people prays for those who are sick. The event opens the participants to shifts of consciousness, resulting in a deeper sense of community and awareness of one's personal journey.

As you can see, the seven sacraments are essential to the life of devout Catholics, framing their spiritual life, and bringing strength to the challenges of "regular" life.

In the next chapter, we'll tell you about Mary, who has been called "the people's sacrament."

## The Least You Need to Know

◆ Sacraments mark natural passages and events in the lives of Catholics, giving spiritual and physical support in the life journey.

◆ Catholics practice seven sacraments honoring events from birth until death. They are Baptism, Holy Eucharist, Confirmation, Marriage, Holy Orders, Reconciliation, and Anointing of the Sick.

◆ Sacraments use specific elements and prescribed procedures that draw on both biblical and natural traditions.

◆ Sacraments transmit meaning, give grace, and give spiritual order to the Catholic's life. They represent the presence of the Risen Christ in the Church.

# 12

# Who Is Mary?

## In This Chapter

- ◆ How a simple Jewish girl became the mother of the son of God
- ◆ The stories of many cultures meet in Mary
- ◆ What is Mary's role in the Church?
- ◆ How Mary continues to appear to people all over the world
- ◆ Mary brings comfort to the people

It would be impossible to imagine Catholicism without Mary. Her place in the Church is unrivaled. Just as Jesus is the sacrament of God, and the Church is the sacrament of Jesus, so it would be fair to say Mary is the people's sacrament. From the earliest years to present time, she has been celebrated in prayer, music, song, processions, devotions, and special Masses worldwide. The most famous cathedrals and basilicas in the world were built to honor her. Small roadside shrines where pilgrims hold vigils for her dot the countryside. All of this is testimony to the love that the people hold for her.

Mary is the people's ambassador at large. She is deeply and tightly woven into the Catholic fabric. Many stories about her exist in the popular culture—some are authenticated beliefs of the Catholic Church. In this regard, her stories taunt theology, but they are intrinsic to the lives of many of the faithful. If you've ever used the expression "Hail Mary pass" you know what we mean. We'll distinguish Catholic story from Catholic fact as we go. This chapter will primarily explain the importance of Mary to the faith expression of many (not all) Catholics.

# Do Catholics Worship Mary?

There are two central questions for most people regarding Mary and her place in the Catholic Church: first, who is Mary? And second, do Catholics worship her? Let's begin with the second question.

No, Catholics do not worship Mary. They are devoted to her, they venerate her, and they honor her as the mother of Jesus, but they do not worship her. Catholics worship only God in the three persons of the Trinity: the Father, Son, and Holy Spirit. Mary is revered because of her relationship with God through Jesus. Over time, she has been called the mother of Christ, the mother of God, the new Eve, virgin mother, mediator, co-redeemer, queen of heaven, and mother of the Church. She has many titles, fills many roles, and is a powerful character in a Catholic's spiritual life, but Catholics do not consider her divine, and so she is not worshipped like God. The question then arises: if Catholics do not worship Mary, what is her position in the Church?

# Mary, the People's Choice

It is perhaps easier for the common folk to comprehend her mystery than it is for the experts. For it is to the common people that Mary appears and speaks, and they intuitively understand her. Images, shrines, prayers, poetry, and great churches all over the world are built in her honor. Each year, thousands of pilgrimages are made to the places where she has appeared. Many who make these journeys claim that miracles take place there. Mary's connection to the folk is often a problem to the analytical, intellectual Catholic, but she cannot be explained away.

## Mary: Myth and Legend

While mentioned in the Gospels, she is not central to them. It is perhaps because of the very sketchiness and brevity of biblical references that Mary has grown in the hearts and minds of the people. She is a mystery and, as such, leaves much to the imagination.

The rise of Mary's popularity and the understanding of her roles in the Catholic Church are intricately connected to the cultures in which her legend grew. The gods and goddesses of ancient Greece and Rome were powerful archetypes in the minds of the people up through the first and second centuries. From the very beginning of Catholicism, their characteristics were assimilated into Mary's story.

Every period of history contains images of Mary, and through these images we can see reflections of religious faith. Yet nowhere does there seem to be a complete picture: not in Scripture, not in theology, and not in popular writings. To understand Mary and the position she occupies in the Catholic Church, it is helpful to look at all these sources as well as the beliefs that existed in the pre-Christian cultures of North Africa, Greece, Rome, and Turkey. It helps to see the influence these beliefs had on the way Mary's role in the Church was understood and defined.

For example, images of Mary suspended in the heavens on the orb of a crescent moon with her head surrounded by a circle of stars were popular artistic expressions. These images are based on ancient beliefs and understandings. In the classical world, the moon is the archetypal female symbol. In these artistic representations, Mary, filled by the sun's light, held it in her essence until morning, where she released it to the morning sky, symbolizing her giving birth to the sun.

## Virgin and Mother: Not a Problem

To understand the importance of the belief "Mary, ever virgin," let's look at a series of factors. In the Hebrew Bible, Isaiah first tells us "a virgin will bear a child." (Isaiah 7:14) The Hebrew word, which was translated to "virgin" in the Greek version of the Hebrew Scriptures, is actually *almah*. Properly translated, *almah* doesn't mean "virgin," but "young girl." As the text was translated into Matthew's Greek (Matthew 1:23), *parthenos* is used, which usually is understood as "virgin." Throughout the ages "virgin," rather than "young girl," became integral to the description and understanding of Mary.

In the cultures of North Africa, Greece, Rome, and Turkey where the events of the New Testament took place, the word "virgin" had a different meaning than it does today. Rather than having physical or moral connotations, it meant autonomy. It was a psychological quality signifying freedom of choice. Symbolically, a virgin birth connoted a child's divinity. In other words, gods were born of virgins. Virginity is an important key to understanding Jesus' birth as the Son of God because it told the people in the way they would best understand it, that the child was conceived by divine origin rather than earthly. It said a miracle was taking place. Perhaps even more importantly, Mary's virginity shows us that she used her free will as she said yes to God's request. She gave full consent to making the Incarnation (the birth of God in Jesus Christ) possible.

The importance of Mary's virginity as a symbol of purity developed at the time of Augustine (354 C.E.–430 C.E.), as the Church began to emphasize the difference between the body and spirit. The spirit (our soul) was constantly pitted against the body. Matter (the body) was directly connected to our sexuality and was equated with sin. This dualistic view continued well into the twentieth century. Mary's virginity emphasized her lack of sexuality and therefore portrayed her as sinless. It is this position and worldview that continues to shape the official teaching of the Church on Mary's virginity: "Mary's virginity manifests God's absolute initiative in the Incarnation. Jesus has only God as Father." (Paragraph 503 of the *Catechism of the Catholic Church*.)

At the heart of the teaching about Mary is the belief that God is offering himself to us in the form of Jesus. In order for this gift to be realized, we must accept Jesus into our lives. Mary does so in her freedom and totality, as "ever virgin." Mary is the people's ambassador at large as she enters into this relationship with God. She is the powerful symbol of our complete acceptance of His grace. She is our free and unforced positive response to God's gift—Jesus—when she says for us, "Thy will be done."

## "Now and at the Hour of Our Death ..."

Mary is the "mother of mercy, sweetness, and hope." Mary's role as mother of the son of God gives strength to the living, but her greatest function is in the Catholic understanding of death and redemption. According to Catholics, because Mary is human and has the closest connection to Christ, Jesus cannot refuse her requests. Mary is the merciful one, the one who will not judge, but will simply love. In the last phrase of the Hail Mary, the plea "pray for us sinners now, and at the hour of our death" expresses the popular belief in Mary's mercy and her particular association with death and heaven. Catholics turn to her to plead their case before God's justice. Mary gives God His feminine face in heaven as she did on earth. Mary has a way of touching God's heart. Through her, He becomes tangible as the God of mercy.

# Mary's Incomplete History

Again, who is Mary? The New Testament contains little information about her origins, family, birth, or even how she met Joseph. Joseph was a carpenter who was engaged to Mary. When he discovered she was pregnant, he was concerned for her reputation lest she be treated as an adulteress. An angel appeared to him and told him the child was conceived by God. He married her and became her protector. Was Joseph an older man? He isn't mentioned after Jesus' infancy, and thus we don't know what happened to him. Was Joseph with Mary at the wedding feast of Cana?

How old was Mary at the time of the Annunciation, when the angel came to her and asked her to be the mother of God's Son? Did the Annunciation take place in the usual interval between engagement and marriage? How could a simple Jewish girl like Mary be as familiar with Hebrew Scripture as it appears she is in Luke 1:46–55 (in which Mary repeats the words of the prophet Isaiah and says: "My soul magnifies the Lord")? Did Jesus have brothers and sisters? We are left with many questions.

Mary's parents, Anne and Joachim, were old, possibly past the normal age of child-bearing. Mary's name has been said to be derived from the Hebrew word meaning "myrrh" and from the word for "bearer of light." St. Jerome called her *Stella Maris,* meaning "Star of the Sea." Other sources connect the name Mary with Marah, the place of bitter water in the Exodus story. In this interpretation, her name would mean "stubborn" and even "rebellious." It seems that even her name is a mystery.

# Council of Ephesus

Mary's legends continued to grow, especially around the city of Ephesus in Turkey, where the mother goddess was particularly popular. Pre-Christian legend says Artemis, a representation of the Great Mother, lived in the Arcadian forests, near Ephesus. Later Christian stories place Mary in the same area, living out her old age in Ephesus. It was also in Ephesus that Paul encountered the crowds cheering, "Great is Artemis of Ephesus," as he attempted to preach.

The Council of Ephesus took place in the year 431 C.E. in Turkey. The Church called it to settle the controversy around Mary and clarify Church beliefs regarding Jesus' nature.

The essential questions were: if Jesus was really God, how could he be really human (like us)? Or, if Jesus was really human (like us), how could he really be divine? This issue raised very important questions about Mary. Assuming that Mary gave birth to Jesus, was it proper to say that Mary was the "mother of God" or was it better to say that Mary was only the "mother of Jesus"? To say that Mary is "mother of God" could seem to favor those who claimed that Jesus was divine, but not fully human; to say that Mary is "mother of Jesus" seemed to favor those who claimed that Jesus was human but not fully divine.

This issue was difficult for the Church because it wanted to preserve its belief that Jesus was both fully human and fully divine. The Council of Ephesus stated the doctrine that Jesus was the Word of God made flesh and that he was both true God and true man. The council designated Mary as "mother of God" to stress the unity of the two natures—divine and human—in the person of Jesus. The council named this union "hypostatic" and said that it meant that the two different natures are not destroyed by this union. Jesus is really fully divine and really fully human.

It designated Mary as the mother of God, which elevated her to a central place in redemption. No longer was she simply a helper in God's plan, but her willingness to cooperate made human redemption possible.

## Theotokos: Mother of God

Mary was given her official Church title, *Theotokos*, mother of God, which gave authentication to the growing popularity of liturgy, hymns, prayers, and stories coming out of the Eastern world. After this decision, theology and beliefs about Mary increased. It was believed that Mary was taken up body and soul by God to reign in heaven. This event is known as her Assumption. The Church declared this belief to be true, and it has become an essential belief or Church doctrine.

The cultural flowering of the Middle Ages created images of Mary that evoked deep feelings about her. What was central to the art of the East a few hundred years earlier became much of the focus of Western art. The Madonna and her divine child captured the cultural imagination. Mary became mother of humanity. Writers and thinkers of the time, including Thomas Aquinas, built the intellectual and theological framework that allowed her to be celebrated in the Church. And celebrated she was—art, statuary, painting, stained glass, and architecture depicted her and helped to create a huge community devoted to her. Mary is what is missing for many, the feminine face of God.

# Apparitions: Here, There, and Everywhere

Apparitions of Jesus, Mary, the angels, and saints are a part of Catholic culture. There have been numerous visions or appearances of Mary around the world. Some of the most celebrated are her appearances at Lourdes, France; Fatima, Portugal; and Guadalupe, Mexico.

Apparitions require extensive investigation before being declared authentic. Such a ruling isn't binding. Instead, it means the Church does not believe its members will be harmed by such a belief. Declarations of authenticity do not constitute an article of faith. *Articles of faith* are teachings Catholics have to believe and are found in the Church's creeds. They include foundational beliefs such as the Trinity, Immaculate Conception, and Incarnation. After an article of faith has been declared, it becomes part of the unifying faith statement of the Church. Apparitions are considered sources of grace and are understood as helpful to the worship of God.

### S'ter Says

**Apparition** means becoming visible unexpectedly. Throughout the ages Catholics have found visible expressions of Mary at the most unexpected times and places. **Articles of Faith** are very basic beliefs not to be doubted. The Church is very careful to distinguish between a popular belief and an article of faith.

### Saints Preserve Us

**St. Gabriel, September 29, Patron of Communications Workers**

St. Gabriel the archangel was the angel who appeared to Zachariah to announce the birth of St. John the Baptist. He also announced to Mary that she would bear a son who would be conceived of the Holy Spirit. The name Gabriel means "man of God" or "God has shown himself mighty." The feast day for St. Gabriel is September 29, and he is the patron of communications workers.

## Lourdes: Healing Waters

Lourdes is a town in the southwest of France where Mary appeared to Bernadette Soubirous several times between February 11 and March 25, 1858. During this time, Bernadette reported seeing 18 different appearances of a very beautiful lady. The lady directed Bernadette to uncover a flow of water and to drink of it and to bathe in it. She said it would have healing effects. The lady then asked Bernadette to have a church built nearby. On her final appearance, she told Bernadette, "I am the Immaculate Conception." Four years earlier, the doctrine of the Immaculate Conception, which refers to Mary's conception in her mother's womb free from original sin, was declared an article of faith by the pope.

## Fatima: World Peace

Fatima is a small town in the middle of Portugal where, in 1915, three young children began to see a lady. She appeared standing on a cloud in an evergreen tree near a small cove. During her visits with the children, she talked intimately with them. On the sixth and final visit, she identified herself as the lady of the Rosary. She emphasized the importance of praying the Rosary daily as a devotion to the Immaculate Heart of Mary in order to bring about world peace. "If people do not turn to prayer," she said, "more war will break out." She asked for Russia to be consecrated to her Immaculate Heart. Four months after her warning, the Russian Revolution began. Many popes have honored the shrine at Fatima.

## Our Lady of Guadalupe: Patron of the Americas

The Lady of Guadalupe appeared in Mexico City in 1531 to an indigenous peasant, St. Juan Diego, recently canonized. Her image was imprinted on his cloak and hangs in the Basilica built in her honor. She has been named the patron of the Americas. Scientists from MIT have examined the image on the cloak and verified an interesting phenomenon that is part of the miracle. The reflections of the people who were present when the apparition first appeared can still be seen in her eyes. The cloth, made of a woven grass, remains in remarkable condition. Experts have noted that a similar cloth would have normally disintegrated by now. Our Lady of Guadalupe shrine is a popular pilgrimage for people from all over the world. Her story can be found in Chapter 23.

# Feasts and Devotions to Mary

There are 16 feasts of the Blessed Virgin throughout the liturgical year. In addition to these feast days, the months of May and October are dedicated to Mary and are the focus of many devotions. This section looks at 8 of her major feasts and the tradition of her monthlong celebration in May.

## Immaculate Conception of Mary: December 8, and Mary's Birthday: September 8

Many people mistakenly believe the term *Immaculate Conception* refers to Mary's sinless conception of Jesus, but it actually honors Mary's unique position of being conceived without original sin. It shows that she existed from her conception as prominent in God's redemption plan. She was born pure of heart and soul as a tribute to her unique place in salvation history. The Feast of the Immaculate Conception became a holy day of obligation in 1854.

---

**Epiphanies**

Muslims, like Christians, hold Mary in high esteem. In the Koran, Mary's mother prays "My Lord, I devote what is in my womb exclusively to the service of God, so accept this from me, for You are the all-hearing, the all-knowing." God "accepted her with a gracious reception and caused her to grow up beautifully" (3:37). Mary's mother was expecting to have a boy, and planned to dedicate him to the priesthood at the Temple in Jerusalem. Yet, "when she gave birth to [a girl], she said, 'My Lord, I have given birth to a girl … And I have named her Mary, and I commend her and her progeny to your protection from Satan the accursed'" (3:35–36). The angels, speaking to Mary, say, "God has chosen you and purified you and chosen you over the women of all peoples" (3:42). She is the only woman mentioned by name in the Koran, and Chapter 19 is named after her. The Koran sets Mary as the ultimate example of an ideal believer.

---

Mary's birthday falls 9 months later. This day honors Mary as God's gift to the people.

## The Annunciation: March 25, and the Visitation: May 31

Near the vernal equinox, the Annunciation marks the celebration of the conception of Jesus in Mary's womb. It occurs nine months before the feast of Christmas, the birth of Christ. The feast of the Visitation celebrates Mary's visit to Elizabeth immediately after the Annunciation when the baby in Elizabeth's womb, John the Baptist, stirred in recognition of the Messiah in Mary's womb.

## Mary, Mother of God: January 1

Mary, Mother of God is a feast first instituted in Jerusalem as early as the middle of the fourth century. Before Vatican II this was the Feast of the Circumcision of Our Lord. This feast day is also called the Solemnity of Mary. It followed the custom in Jewish law of presenting and circumcising the baby in the temple on the eighth day following birth. The feast focused on the obedience of Mary and Jesus to Mosaic law.

## The Assumption: August 15

The Assumption marks one of the oldest feasts of Mary and is an important date in the liturgical year. It celebrates Mary's body and soul being taken up into heaven. Liturgical processions began as early as 701 C.E. In some European cities, Mary's journey to heaven is symbolized by carrying her statue through town. Huge candles are taken to churches and lighted in a procession called *candelieri*.

## Our Lady of Guadalupe, Mother of the Americas: December 12

Our Lady of Guadalupe is the patron saint of the Americas and is key to understanding the Catholicism of the New World. On December 12, Mary is remembered as patroness of the Americas. She is the mother of all the people and, because she was once poor, has particular favor for them. On this day, her appearance to Juan Diego near Mexico City in 1531 is honored. Mary, as the universal mother symbol, is a reminder of the common relationship of all people. She offers her son, Jesus, to break through the old structures and categories of caste, class, religion, race, and gender by constantly reminding us that we are all children of the same God.

## May Altars

May is the month when Catholics pay special tribute to Mary. Most churches have a daily recitation of the rosary. Some parishes include a ritual popularly called a May Crowning. A typical May Crowning would include reciting the rosary, singing songs to Mary, a procession, and crowning of Our Lady's statue with a wreath of flowers symbolizing her virtues—to be imitated by the faithful. Prior to Vatican II, celebrations of the month of May were widespread. Each classroom in a Catholic school had a corner altar dedicated to Mary, with a statue and a steady supply of fresh flowers. Classroom time was often dedicated to saying at least one decade of the rosary, and singing at least one hymn. Altars were likewise set up in Catholic homes. Today the ceremony usually takes place in parish devotion outside of the liturgy. Honoring Mary has particular importance to young girls and women. It is a time when motherhood and feminine virtues are recognized and celebrated. Mary's popularity is growing among Protestant women, who like Catholic women, are seeking images of the feminine in religion.

Mary is one of the figures that Catholics are best known for. In this chapter, you have had a chance to learn a lot about her and the devotions that honor her. Part 4 describes other favorite Catholic devotions, sacramentals, and prayers. So if you have ever wondered what holy water, statues, mysticism, chanting, and a lot of other Catholic stuff is about, here is your chance to find out.

## The Least You Need to Know

- The stories of Mary were drawn from the rich cultural heritage of many sources.

- Mary holds a unique place in salvation, and devotion to her is profound among Catholics and others as well.

- Mary is revered as the mother of God.

- Our Lady of Guadalupe is the patroness of the Americas and brings with her a model for unity and peace.

# Part 4

# Imagination and Prayer

The imagination is a storehouse of all the sights, sounds, smells, sensations, and emotions we've experienced throughout our life. Imagination forms the lens through which we view life, and it forms our perspective on life. Imagination is also the place where God has traditionally spoken to the people, whether through dreams or from the insight gained in meditation.

In this part, we will look at Catholic imagination in terms of the words Catholics use, their music, and their everyday practices and rituals. Then we will focus on the central place where Catholic imagination and prayer are communally enacted: the Mass.

# Chapter 13

# Feeding the Imagination

## In This Chapter

- Why Catholics use statues, holy cards, and other Catholic stuff
- Standing, kneeling, blessing, and other sacred gestures
- How Catholics use the liturgical calendar to keep sacred time
- Is it superstition or Catholic imagination?
- What the Catholic funeral practices are

Catholic imagination is filled with images that reflect a Catholic understanding of the world as sacred, and reinforce the concept that the affairs of this life matter. In this chapter, we'll explore the use of sacramentals—"little" sacraments that help develop the Catholic imagination and feed a spirituality that is informing and shaping everyday experiences.

## Sacramentals: Little Sacraments

Almost everyone has a favorite object that belonged to a grandparent, parent, relative, or friend that he or she holds sacred. When you see such an object or use it, you remember the stories that go with it. Like pictures of admired ancestors, holy pictures and statues connect us to the memories

**Your Guardian Angel**

Consider marking a special occasion with a holy card. You can remember a baptism, a First Communion, a wedding, or a funeral with a personalized printed holy card from a Catholic bookstore.

we hold of those being pictured. They connect us to what that person was all about, particularly and perhaps most importantly to their values and how they lived their life.

The Church's sacramentals relate to God and to the saints and the values they upheld in life as members of the bigger "church family." They connect the faithful to the life and times of Jesus.

*Stained-glass window in a church, depicting the Annunciation. Christ the King Church, Nashville, Tennessee.*

*(Courtesy of H. L. [Dean] Caskey)*

# Catholic Stuff: Statues, Holy Cards, and the Saints Go Marching In!

You'll find statues everywhere in the Catholic world: in church, at home on the dresser, mounted on the dashboard, and even in the yard. A friend recalls growing up next door to "Our Lady of the Birdbath," a tribute to Mary that became a neighborhood attraction. You'll find statues in every Catholic Church—mainly on the side altars. They might represent the parish's namesake, such as Saints Peter and Paul, or St. Patrick, who is popular in Irish Catholic neighborhoods. Then there is Martin de Porres, St. Theresa, Michael the Archangel, Sacred Heart of Jesus, and more. Our

Lady of Guadalupe has almost become the national symbol for Mexico and is the center of many Mexican American parishes. The Infant Jesus of Prague—a representation of the Christ Child as an infant king—is a statue that is often adorned with robes reflecting the liturgical season.

*Crucifix prominently displayed over the altar. Christ the King Church, Nashville, Tennessee.*

*(Courtesy of H. L. [Dean] Caskey)*

LATIN CROSS    GREEK CROSS

CELTIC CROSS    TAU CROSS

*Four different styles of crosses.*

*(Courtesy of Bob O'Gorman and Mary Faulkner)*

Images of Jesus, Mary, and the saints are also found on holy cards—gold-edged playing-size cards that often have prayers or special devotions printed on the back. You'll often find them at Catholic funerals inscribed with the deceased person's name and dates of birth and death, to be taken with you as a reminder to pray for that person. Catholics often wear medals on chains around their necks. These coinlike replicas are formed with images of Jesus or saints. One particular medal has the words "In case of an accident please call a priest" inscribed on it. These and other items are often given as gifts at special occasions such as First Communion or Confirmation.

In addition to affirming God's immanent nature, there is another theology at work in the use of statues and sacred images. Catholics believe that God's community endures seamlessly throughout the ages. We've mentioned it before—the Church is a community of those who have died (saints), those who are here now (active members), and those who have died but are not yet prepared for heaven (the suffering). Prayers are offered to ask the assistance of the saints, to help the active members and to help the souls of the suffering finish their transition to heaven. We talked about how this is most joyously celebrated among Mexicans in Chapter 2 in describing the Day of the Dead festivals.

---

### Saints Preserve Us

**St. Christopher, Patron of Travelers**

St. Christopher is one of the most popular saints, and St. Christopher medals are among the most common sacramentals. Legend has it that Christopher was a giant of a man who made his living carrying people across a raging stream on his shoulders. One day his passenger was a small child who grew so heavy that Christopher feared they would drown. The child then revealed that he was Christ and that the heaviness was caused by the weight of the world he was carrying on his shoulders—hence his name, Christopher, which means Christ-bearer. Christopher is the patron saint of motorists and travelers and is invoked during storms. St. Christopher medals are typically affixed to the sun visor or dashboard of the car. After Vatican II, with the updating of the liturgical calendar, his feast day, **July 25,** was vacated—resulting in his not being officially recognized as a saint. Yet his popularity remains among the people.

---

## Church Bells Chiming

From the dreaded clang of your morning alarm clock to "church bells chiming on a Sunday morn," as the old song goes, bells get our attention. They wake us up and tell us something is about to happen. They also tune us up. They awaken the ears, and as the vibration travels to the brain the whole body is alerted. Bells are used in all churches to call worshippers together, and they are used throughout the week in other devotions.

Catholic Churches in many locations still ring bells three times a day to announce the Angelus—a Catholic prayer celebrating Mary saying yes to the angel, agreeing to become the mother of Jesus. The first ringing happens at 6 in the morning, the second at noon, and the third at 6 in the evening when it chimes for several minutes to signal the end of day. As the bell is ringing, Catholics may stop and say the following prayer.

The angel of the Lord declared unto Mary.
And she conceived of the Holy Spirit.
Hail Mary
Behold the handmaid of the Lord.
Be it done unto me according to your word.
Hail Mary
And the word was made flesh.
And dwelt among us.
Hail Mary
Pray for us, holy mother of God.
That we may become worthy of the promises of Christ.

Let us pray:

Lord, pour forth we beseech thee, thy grace unto our hearts that we, to whom the incarnation of Christ thy son was made known by the message of the angel, may be brought, by his passion and cross, to the glory of his resurrection, through the same Christ our Lord. Amen.

In his painting titled *The Angelus*, Jean François Millet depicts peasants in the field pausing and reflecting on the great mysteries of salvation and redemption (see the figure). In the foreground a man and woman stand praying in response to the ringing of the bells of the distant church. In the work, Millet portrays the peasant as one closest to God. The connection to the earth symbolizes connection to creation, and the figures are painted in a tone almost equal to that of the ground.

*Jean François Millet*, The Angelus.

*(Courtesy Alinari/Art Resource, New York)*

Today the Angelus might be rung only on special occasions. It still has the power to evoke deep feelings in those who grew up hearing it. At that time they would be hard put to not drop to their knees at its sound!

# Sacramental Gestures

From the swirling Sufi dancers of the Islamic religion to the more staid Congregationalists of New England, all religions, including Catholicism, have certain gestures or movements they use in worship. Almost everyone who visits a Catholic church and attends Mass comes away amazed at how much standing, kneeling, and sitting goes on. This section describes some of the gestures and movements that define Catholics.

## The Sign of the Cross

The sign of the cross is one of the first things Catholic parents teach their children, and it has made its way from the nursery into the wide world of sports. It would be rare indeed to watch a basketball game without seeing someone using this gesture before shooting a basket—and making it. Symbols have power!

The sign of the cross is made using the fingers of the opened right hand:

1. You touch your forehead as you say, "In the name of the Father"

2. You touch your heart as you say, "and the Son"

3. You touch your left shoulder as you say, "and the Holy"

4. You touch your right shoulder as you say, "Spirit"

5. You bring your hands together as you say, "Amen."

Most prayers begin and end with the sign of the cross. The priest also uses this gesture as he gives his blessing to the people. The sign of the cross expresses one of the basic truths of the faith: the existence of God as the Father, Son, and Holy Spirit—the Holy Trinity.

 **Your Guardian Angel**

Don't forget your blessings! Bless your food before you eat by making the sign of the cross over it and saying the grace prayer.

Other symbolic gestures include genuflecting on one knee (or two if the Blessed Sacrament is displayed) before taking your seat, as well as the standing, kneeling, sitting thing that catches visitors' attention. These gestures correspond to various parts of the Mass, and signal something of great importance or sacredness is happening—again, encoding religion in the body.

## Blessings for Everything!

We bless God for what he has done for us. In return we receive God's blessing. Catholics receive blessings from the priest, and the priest also blesses objects. Name an object (or any situation)—boats, cars, bicycles, horses, dogs, cats, crops, fields, gardens—and there's a blessing for it, a story to go with it, and a saint that's in charge of it! There's hardly anything that can't or doesn't get blessed.

Many parishes invite members to bring pets to church to be blessed on October 4, the feast of St. Francis. Stories of St. Francis's love of nature and all animals have captured the hearts and imaginations of people of all religious faiths. In farming communities, priests bless fields, tractors, and other equipment; in fishing communities, the boats are blessed; and in all communities, cars and homes are blessed.

Blessings are not just a Catholic practice. Probably most religions ask the divine to pay special attention in some way. Blessings acknowledge people's dependence on God and confirm their belief that God concerns Himself with their daily activities. Blessings connect Catholics more closely to God's *omnipresence*.

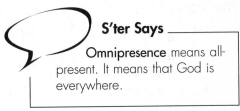

**S'ter Says**

**Omnipresence** means all-present. It means that God is everywhere.

When a priest or deacon gives a blessing, he uses holy water, which is water that has been blessed and set aside for sacred use. He might sprinkle the person or object and will most likely make the sign of the cross on the head of the individual being blessed. If he is blessing an object or a crowd of people, he will make the gesture of a cross in the air with his hand. He says something like, "May God bless you and keep you safe in the name of the Father, the Son, and the Holy Spirit. Amen."

The priest and deacon blesses all sacred objects before they are used sacramentally. The act of blessing reserves the object for use as a spiritual tool. From then on, those who use it treat it with respect. Blessings change consciousness about the object; they change the understanding of it and the treatment of it. Crosses, beads, medals, and other Catholic stuff are just plain objects until a priest blesses them.

## Hands, Knees, Heads, and Hats

Another sacred gesture involves the tradition of folding the hands together with fingers pointed upward as the common position for prayer. This hand position symbolizes that the one praying is focused on God. Some say the practice led to the shape of church steeples. Of course, prayer is acceptable in any posture at any time.

### For Heaven's Sake

Treat all sacramentals with respect when you're no longer using them. There is, for example, a protocol for retiring palm leaves from Palm Sunday. They are burned for distribution as ashes on Ash Wednesday.

As an earlier chapter described, Catholics bow before the altar, or genuflect if the tabernacle is on it, to honor it as the symbol of Christ and show respect for the presence of God. They usually do this just before taking their seats in church.

Kneeling is another Catholic practice, leading many visitors to remark on the ups and downs of a Catholic service. It's also customary to bow the head or even tip your hat when passing a church. The head is often bowed at the name of Jesus.

## Superstition or Sacred Tradition?

Sacramentals feed the religious imagination and open the heart. They make the connection to the sacred in a personal way that crosses the line between the transcendent and immanent sense of the sacred. They raise the awareness that God is everywhere. Involving the senses in worship opens other levels of awareness in addition to the usual listening to or reading sacred literature. One has only to attend a religious film or a play, listen to music, or visit an art museum to appreciate how aesthetics lift the spirit and help make the connection between life as it is and as it could be. They open the imagination where one can see a vision of what the reign of God might be like.

### Your Guardian Angel

Check your holy water supply. It is a Catholic custom to keep a bottle of holy water in the home. It can be used for blessing at the time of sickness and to protect the home against danger.

They change perception, nourish the spirit, and create a spiritual relationship between a person and his or her place in the world. Art and religious artifacts transmit values. No one would think of the famous paintings and sculpture of Michelangelo or da Vinci as superstitious, nor the music of Bach or Mozart or many other famous composers who first wrote and performed their music in church as part of the Mass. Sacramentals are just smaller representations of those aesthetics, and are infinitely more available.

# The Liturgical Calendar: Sacred Time

There are no digital clocks in the symbolic world, but there are times of the day marked by the sun and seasons of the year. Catholic time is measured by the events of Christ's life and corresponds to seasons of the year. It cycles around two major celebrations: the birth of Jesus at Christmas and his resurrection at Easter. For example:

- Advent begins the liturgical year with the first Sunday of Advent and goes to December 24.

- Christmas begins with the vigil of Christmas on December 24, goes through the Sunday after January 6, the feast of *Epiphany*, the feast of the Baptism of Our Lord.

- Ordinary time begins on the day after the Feast of the Baptism of Our Lord (First Sunday after the Epiphany) and continues through the day before Ash Wednesday.

> **S'ter Says**
>
> **Epiphany** is defined as a sudden intuitive perception or insight into the essential meaning of something. It marks the feast when the kings or wise men visited the Christ child in Bethlehem and honors their recognition of the Messiah. It is celebrated on January 6.

- Lent begins on Ash Wednesday and lasts until the Holy Thursday Mass of the Lord's Supper.

- The Easter *Triduum* begins with the Mass of the Lord's Supper on Holy Thursday and lasts until Easter Sunday.

- The Easter season begins on Holy Thursday and lasts for 50 days until Pentecost. Easter is celebrated on the Sunday following the first full moon after March 21, the spring equinox. This system of determining Easter's date comes from the way the Jews calculated the feast of Pass-over.

> **S'ter Says**
>
> **Triduum** is most often used when referring to the Easter Triduum that includes the three days prior to Easter Sunday: Holy Thursday, Good Friday, and Holy Saturday.

- Ordinary time continues the day after Pentecost and ends the day before Advent. Ordinary time refers to the times between the major seasons of Christmas and Easter.

In addition to the Sunday cycle shown here, there are two other cycles of feasts on the Church calendar. The second cycle is composed of the saints' days, one for almost every day of the year. The third cycle is made up of Mary's feasts. This cycle is "unofficial," but popular. It consists of the months of May and October, which are devoted to special celebrations of Mary. Additionally, there are more than 16 feasts throughout the year celebrating her, beginning with the Immaculate Conception on December 8 through the Assumption on August 15.

*The liturgical calendar of Church feasts shown on a wheel of the year.*

*(Courtesy of Bob O'Gorman and Mary Faulkner)*

## Celebrating the Seasons

Catholics celebrate the seasons by reading the Bible texts appropriate to the feasts. Generally, there is a reading from the Old Testament, an Epistle, and a Gospel at each Mass. The readings revolve on a three-year rotation. The color of the priest's vestments and the color of the various church decorations are changed according to the liturgical season. Naturally, the music of the Mass also changes with the season.

You've learned a lot about the sacred objects and practices of Catholics. In the next chapter, you'll find out about favorite Catholic prayers and sacred music.

**Your Guardian Angel**

Get a liturgical calendar to hang next to your regular calendar. The liturgical calendar connects you to the spiritual seasons of the year. Liturgical calendars indicate the Scripture passages for each Sunday and are available from a Catholic bookstore.

# Celebrating the Final Journey

The event unique to Christian faith is the Resurrection of Jesus Christ. Catholics first enter into this mystery in Baptism, dying to the old selves and being born anew in Christ. Throughout our lives we die and rise in various ways, embodying the Paschal Mystery of Jesus. The Church teaches that bodily death is not an end, but an ultimate passage to eternal life. In 1969, the *Order for Christian Funerals* was revised becoming a three-part liturgy. As presented in its ritual book, *The Order of Christian Funerals*, Catholics celebrate three phases of the funeral: a Vigil Service celebrated in the funeral home or the church, the Funeral Liturgy itself, and the Rite of Committal of the body at the cemetery.

The rites accept human mortality and death in the midst of life, ultimately one's own death, letting go, handing our dead and ourselves over to God. The rites also declare a belief in Christ, the Risen One who put death to death by his dying and rising to new life. Finally, the rites comprise a movement—an earthly journey from the place of death to the cemetery.

The vigil is a service of Scripture, a homily, songs, petitions/prayers, and a eulogy by family members or friends. Families may have the devotional prayer of a rosary. A priest or deacon conducts the Funeral Vigil.

For the Funeral Mass, at the church door, a pall (a decorated white cloth) as a reminder of the garment given at Baptism is placed by the family members over the casket. This symbolizes unity in Christ through baptism. The Mass is celebrated and at the end a "Song of Farewell" is sung before the body/casket and family leave for the cemetery.

At the cemetery, the Rite of Committal is celebrated. This includes a Scripture verse, prayer over the place of committal, the words of committal, intercessions to God and the saints, the Lord's Prayer, a concluding prayer, and a final prayer over the people. The body of the deceased is interred either in the ground or in a crypt. Traditionally, after the liturgies, families, relatives, and friends return to the parish for a reception.

The celebration of the funeral rites then expresses an acceptance, a belief, and a journey.

**Your Guardian Angel**

In 1963, the Vatican lifted the ban on cremation for Catholics.

## The Least You Need to Know

♦ Sacramentals are reminders of the sacredness of the everyday world and they cue Catholic memory and Catholic imagination.

♦ Involving the senses in religious worship is a particularly Catholic "thing." It encodes spiritual meaning into the body, both affirming and connecting to the presence of the sacred within self and other.

♦ Saints and sacramentals belong to the people. The Church rules on them, but that doesn't always mean you take the St. Christopher medal out of the car!

♦ The rituals of the Church follow the rhythm of the natural seasons according to the liturgical calendar.

# Chapter 14

# Catholic Prayers and Music: Tangible Poetry

## In This Chapter

- ◆ Some of the ways Catholics pray
- ◆ The history of the Rosary and how to pray it
- ◆ The Church's mystical tradition makes it into the third millennium
- ◆ Why Catholics pray all night

Prayer is like poetry offered to God. It opens us to our deepest level of being: our soul. Prayer is not simply an event, nor is it only words or actions. As we become mindful of God's presence in us and in all things, our whole life becomes a prayer. Catholics pray in many ways. In this chapter, we'll look at three long-standing prayer traditions: the Rosary, the mystical tradition, and the Liturgy of the Hours.

# Personal Prayer

Since the beginning of time, people have experienced a hunger, a deep instinctual need, to make sense out of life. This sensation creates the idea that there is something with which we long to make contact. This recognition is a prayer in itself. You could begin to define prayer as attentiveness to this primal urge.

Personal prayer represents an intimate, one-on-one relationship with God. It forms the foundation of spirituality. Although the Church has many formal community rituals and celebrations, the Mass being the most central of these, Catholics are urged to develop their personal prayer life.

The standard Catholic definition of prayer identifies four kinds of prayer:

- ◆ **Petition** is by far the most common type. Petition asks God for assistance in life's needs; it seeks God's intervention.

- ◆ **Gratitude** thanks God for blessings and gifts, both the asked for and the unexpected.

- ◆ **Adoration** expresses devotion, love, and recognition of a Catholic's absolute dependence on God.

- ◆ **Reparation** asks forgiveness, recognizes one's faults, and expresses sorrow.

The methods of personal prayer include the following:

- ◆ **Recitation,** such as the Rosary, litanies, the Way of the Cross, and other memorized prayers

- ◆ **Spiritual reading,** including passages from the Bible, particularly the Psalms

- ◆ **Recollection,** which is defined as taking a few moments throughout the day for a quick recall of God's presence in oneself and others

- ◆ **Contemplation,** including quiet time spent in inner reflection

- ◆ **Journaling,** or writing favorite passages and recording your interpretations and reflections on them

One way of praying is not better than another, and there is no one right way of praying. Traditional Catholic prayers include different types of prayers and different ways of praying. Prayer is personal and intimate. How one prays is not the point; that one prays at all is the more important concern!

# The Rosary

The Rosary is perhaps the signature Catholic devotion. If a filmmaker wanted to portray a character as Catholic, he or she might place a rosary in the actor's hands. Catholics often hang rosaries from the rearview mirror of their cars, and you'll know a Catholic at the end of his life because the rosary beads will be wrapped around his hands as he lies in his coffin; he will be buried with them.

The word *rosary* means "garland of roses." The rose is one of the flowers used to symbolize the Virgin Mary, and the prayer of the Rosary is very closely associated with her.

The rosary itself is a string of beads Catholics use to count the group of prayers known as the Rosary. The beads can be made out of wood, glass, gems, or even a knotted string. They range from very simple to very elegant in appearance. They are simply attractive objects until a priest blesses them. At that time, they become sacred and should be treated with respect.

**For Heaven's Sake**

Treat your rosary with respect. Don't wear a rosary as a piece of jewelry or use it as a decorative object. While they are attractive, remember that they have been blessed for use in prayer.

As a ritual, the Rosary involves two elements: mental prayer and vocal prayer. The mental prayer consists of a meditation on the mysteries of the life and death of Jesus Christ and his mother Mary. The vocal prayer consists of saying the prescribed prayers shown in the following section. Together these elements create a focused meditation, which helps to quiet the mind.

## Origins of the Rosary

A common Catholic story says St. Dominic (1170–1221), the founder of the Dominican order, received a vision of Mary in which she instructed him to encourage people to pray the Rosary to her as a means of invoking her aid. The Rosary was part of the monastic spiritual practices for centuries before Dominic. The practice of counting repeated prayers by using a string of beads, knots, or even pebbles in a bowl is in common use among Moslems, Buddhists, and other non-Christian religions.

Christian monks used beads to count the 150 psalms they chanted in Latin as part of their prayer life. Because some of the monks, as well as most of the common people, couldn't read Latin, they improvised a substitute for the 150 psalms. They began using beads to count 150 Our Fathers, divided into groups of 50. In time, Hail Marys were added to the prayer form. At that time, the Rosary was called Our Lady's Psalter, marking the 150 Hail Marys that corresponded to the 150 psalms.

---

### Epiphanies

How did St. Dominic get the credit for starting the Rosary? It seems that during the years 1470 to 1475 a zealous Dominican preacher, Alan de Rupe, preached all over Europe and told the story of Mary's appearance to Dominic and how she gave him the Rosary. De Rupe was a born exaggerator, or perhaps he realized the value of a good story as a preaching device. His claims were taken as truth. Regardless of whether the story of St. Dominic and the Rosary is true, it has become part of the legend of the Rosary and has linked inextricably the Dominicans with this favorite tradition.

---

## How to Say the Rosary

The Rosary is divided into five decades. Each decade represents a mystery or event in the life of Jesus. There are four sets of "Mysteries of the Rosary" (*Joyful, Luminous, Sorrowful, and Glorious*). These four "Mysteries of the Rosary" therefore contain, a total of twenty mysteries. The Joyful, Luminous, Sorrowful, and Glorious Mysteries are then said on specific days of the week (see each set of mysteries that follow). During private recitation of the Rosary, each decade requires devout meditation on a specific mystery. Here is how to say a rosary:

**Your Guardian Angel**

Any portion of the Rosary is a complete prayer! If you have time only for a single decade or even a single bead, it is still a prayer.

1. While holding the crucifix, make the sign of the cross and then recite the Apostles' Creed.

2. Recite the Our Father prayer on the first large bead.

3. On each of the three small beads, recite a Hail Mary, asking for an increase of faith, hope, and charity.

4. Recite the Glory Be to the Father.

5. Recall the first Rosary mystery and recite the Our Father on the next large bead.

6. On each of the adjacent 10 small beads, recite a Hail Mary while reflecting on the mystery. This completes a decade.

7. Each succeeding decade is prayed in a similar manner by recalling the appropriate mystery, reciting the Our Father, saying 10 Hail Marys and 1 Glory Be, and reflecting on the next mystery.

8. When the Rosary is completed, it is traditionally concluded with the prayer Hail! Holy Queen.

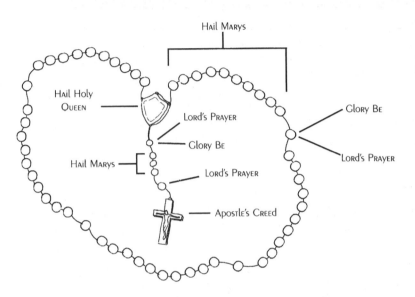

*The Rosary.*

*(Courtesy of Bob O'Gorman and Mary Faulkner)*

## The Prayers of the Rosary

The following prayers make up the Rosary. Note that Catholics often refer to The Lord's Prayer as the Our Father; it's just one of those Catholic things.

♦ **Our Father.** Our Father, who art in heaven, hallowed be thy name. Thy kingdom come; thy will be done on earth as it is in heaven. Give us this day our daily bread; and forgive us our trespasses as we forgive those who trespass against us; and lead us not into temptation, but deliver us from evil. Amen.

 **Your Guardian Angel**

Don't think you have to always say formal prayers. Your conversation with God is personal. Feel free to say what you need to say the way you need to say it.

♦ **Hail Mary.** Hail Mary full of grace, the Lord is with thee. Blessed art thou among women, and blessed is the fruit of thy womb, Jesus. Holy Mary, mother of God, pray for us sinners now and at the hour of our death. Amen.

◆ **Glory Be to the Father.** Glory be to the Father, to the Son, and to the Holy Spirit. As it was in the beginning, is now, and ever shall be, world without end. Amen.

◆ **Apostles' Creed.** I believe in God, the Father almighty, Creator of heaven and earth. And in Jesus Christ, his only Son, our Lord; who was conceived by the Holy Spirit, born of the Virgin Mary, suffered under Pontius Pilate, was crucified, died, and was buried. He descended into hell; on the third day he rose again from the dead; he ascended into heaven, sits at the right hand of God, the Father almighty; from thence he shall come to judge the living and the dead. I believe in the Holy Spirit, the holy Catholic Church, the communion of saints, the forgiveness of sins, the resurrection of the body, and life everlasting. Amen.

◆ **Hail! Holy Queen.** Hail! Holy queen, mother of mercy, our life, our sweetness, and our hope. To you we cry, poor banished children of Eve. To you do we send up our sighs, mourning and weeping in this valley of tears. Turn then, O most gracious advocate, your eyes of mercy toward us, and after this our exile, show unto us the blessed fruit of your womb, Jesus. O clement! O loving! O sweet Virgin Mary! Pray for us, O holy mother of God, that we may be made worthy of the promises of Christ. Amen.

## The Twenty Mysteries of the Rosary

You will often hear the word *mystery* used in the Catholic religion. It describes important beliefs about God, Jesus, and Mary that are part of the religion but cannot be substantiated outside of religious belief. Another way of saying it is that they are important expressions of the faith of the people. The power of contemplating the events in the life of Christ as mysterious is that you are accepting that you don't know everything there is to know about it in this moment. It opens the mind to receive spiritual insight.

**S'ter Says**

Mysteries are beliefs of the religion that are taken on faith. They are events in the life of Christ that are vital to the spiritual life of Jesus' followers.

The 20 mysteries of the Rosary are in four groups of five and represent joyful events, sorrowful events, glorious events, and luminous events in the life of Jesus and Mary.

**The Joyful Mysteries** (said on Mondays, Saturdays, Sundays of Advent, and Sundays from Epiphany until Lent)

1. The Annunciation

2. The Visitation

3. The Nativity

4. The Presentation

5. The Finding of the Child Jesus in the Temple

**The Sorrowful Mysteries** (said on Tuesdays, Fridays, and daily from Ash Wednesday until Easter Sunday)

1. The Agony in the Garden

2. The Scourging at the Pillar

3. The Crowning of Thorns

4. The Carrying of the Cross

5. The Crucifixion

**The Glorious Mysteries** (said on Wednesdays and Sundays throughout the year)

1. The Resurrection

2. The Ascension

3. The Descent of the Holy Spirit

4. The Assumption of Mary

5. The Coronation of the Blessed Virgin Mary

Pope John Paul II instituted a change in the Rosary. He added a fourth set of "mysteries" for contemplation, increasing the number from the 15 mentioned above to 20. The new mysteries focus on events of Christ's life.

**The Luminous Mysteries** (said on Thursdays throughout the year)

1. Jesus' baptism in the Jordan

2. Jesus' self-manifestation at the wedding of Cana

3. Jesus' proclamation of the Kingdom of God, with his call to conversion

4. Jesus' transfiguration

5. Jesus' institution of the Eucharist as the sacramental expression of the paschal mystery

## When Is the Rosary Said?

The Rosary is both an individual prayer and group devotion. The Church encourages the Rosary to be said as a family devotional practice during May and October, as well as throughout the year. May and October are months dedicated to Mary, and daily devotions using the Rosary are held in many parishes.

# Monasteries, Mysticism, and Contemplative Prayer

Christian *mysticism* and *contemplative prayer* began as early as the second century as Christians retreated to the desert to develop the spirituality of the emerging church. You might remember this from Chapter 8. It continued to be an important part of prayer life in the monasteries, and remains a vital tradition in the Church today. Of course, contemplation, mysticism, and even monasteries exist in other traditions as well.

**S'ter Says**

**Contemplative prayer** is a form of prayer developed in the monasteries. **Mysticism** describes the process of being contemplative. You are contemplative when you meditate and go within yourself to a quiet place where it is possible to experience God.

**For Heaven's Sake**

Don't worry! Be happy! Teresa of Ávila said, "Let go, and let God! Surrender the intellect to a higher power." Teresa felt strongly that we should learn to "get out of our heads," meaning that we should slow down our minds and learn how to experience God's love by feeling it, not just thinking or talking about it.

## Mystic Roll Call!

The mystical tradition has existed in every age of the Catholic Church: St. Augustine in the 400s; St. Hildegard of Bingen in the Middle Ages; St. Catherine of Siena in the 1300s; the English mystic of the 1500s, St. Julian of Norwich; a little later, St. Teresa of Ávila and St. John of the Cross; and in modern times, Thomas Merton. The mystic tradition of contemplation is still alive today in monasteries all over the world.

Monastic life lived in convents was one of the arenas in the Church where women were provided equal opportunity. It was their first chance to take an active role in the Church and society since the early years of the Church under the leadership of Jesus, where women were full participants in the inner circle. Convents became centers for learning, prayer, and good works.

---

**Epiphanies**

As a child, Catherine of Siena dreamed of dressing up like a man so that she could be accepted as a Dominican friar. From her earliest years, she knew she had a calling to religious life. She was born into a world that limited women in many ways, and although her parents opposed her vocation, they must have known their willful child would succeed in her goal. At 16, she entered the convent of the Sisters of St. Dominic. Her religious life centered on her numerous visions and ecstasies, and later she began writing.

---

## Monasticism: The Great Getaway

The basic idea of *monasticism* is seclusion or withdrawal from the world or society. The object is to achieve a life whose ideal is different from the dominant culture. Monasticism is found in every religious system that has attained a high degree of ethical development and is often organized around simplicity, commitment to specific prayers, fasting, hard work, and sometimes even self-denial. Underlying its practices is a deep commitment to preserving a set of ideals.

**S'ter Says** _____

**Monasticism** is the tradition of taking yourself away from the mainstream of society for the purpose of developing your spiritual practice. **Vows** are the promises made when one goes into a religious order. They are like wedding vows. The principal three are poverty (giving up private ownership to the community), chastity (giving up the right to marry and have intimate sexual relationships in order to devote to the Church), and obedience (submitting to the authority of superiors for assignments).

Monasticism had its beginnings in the early years of the Church, as Christians felt the need to make a strong commitment to each other and to create a safe structure in which to operate. They took *vows* concerning life together. The life of the early monastic was often one of extreme deprivation and hardship. In the 500s, monasticism came under the influence of St. Benedict, and the emphasis on self-denial was tempered. Today monastic life includes a principle of balance as part of its spirituality.

## Mysticism Today

In present times, responding to an apparent deep hunger for spirituality, Catholics are having a renewed interest in contemplative prayer, and now this practice is no longer restricted to the monasteries. A contemporary contemplative practice is called *centering prayer* and comes from the tradition of John of the Cross. It awakens people to the presence of God within and builds contemplative attitudes of listening and receptivity. This practice is a synthesis of the wisdom of Zen (Buddhism) and Hindu traditions of meditation with the contemplative tradition of Catholicism.

This type of prayer often follows four steps:

1. Reading of sacred Scripture

2. Reflecting on the Scripture

3. Focusing on a key image

4. Resting in contemplation

Approaches to meditation can be grouped broadly as contemplative and mindful meditation. Contemplative meditation focuses on a single point (often the breath) and stills the mind. Mindful meditation opens the mind to observe the flow of thoughts, feelings, and sensations passing through one's awareness without thinking about them. Regardless of the type practiced, meditation benefits the whole self (body and spirit). The body gains a deeper state of relaxation than that produced by sleep. It opens the mind to spiritual insight. It increases awareness, intelligence, and creativity. Meditation classes are taught in hospitals all over the country. It normalizes many functions such as blood pressure, lifts depression, quiets anxiety, improves the immune system, and speeds recovery from surgery. When imagery is involved, it has cured cancer and healed burns.

# Liturgy of the Hours

All over the world, people of all religious traditions are praying 24 hours a day, 7 days a week, all year round. The form these prayers take in the Catholic Church is called the Liturgy of the Hours, and represents the acknowledgment of the sacred relationship between God and creation.

The Liturgy of the Hours honors the inherent powers of nature contained in times of the day and seasons of the year. The oldest documents of civilization describe sacred times of sunrise, noon, sunset, and night as times when prayers were offered and hymns were sung. The Jews adapted these practices from their neighbors, using the Book of Psalms as the source of their daily prayers. Early Catholics followed the ancient tradition as a way of living the biblical command to "pray constantly." Great events in Christianity follow the maps of ancient sacred times: morning is the time of Resurrection, midmorning is the time of Pentecost, noon is the time of the Crucifixion, midafternoon is the death of Christ, and evening is the Last Supper.

The Liturgy of the Hours, along with the daily celebration of Mass, are part of the official prayers of the Church, which means that the clergy says them every day. In monasteries and convents this prayer is chanted in community according to its designated hours.

The Liturgy of the Hours is composed of hymns, psalms, Scripture, and prayers. The seven traditional Hours and their spiritual character follow with the contemporary names in parentheses:

- Matins or **Vigils** is the time of watching in the night. This prayer is celebrated at the midnight hour as one is enveloped in darkness in the silence of prayer and meditation while awaiting the coming of morning. (Office of Readings—said any time during the day)

- Prime or **Lauds** is the prayer at daybreak; thanking God for the first light, as at the beginning of creation, and for the light of Christ's resurrection. New beginnings, awakened innocence, joy, and optimism are expressed in the prayers. (Morning Prayer)

- **Terce** (Latin for third hour) is said at midmorning; the prayers call for strength as work begins and the day waxes strong. This hour is a reminder of Pentecost and the coming of the Holy Spirit, who strengthened the apostles.

- **Sext** (sixth hour) is prayed at noon when the sun burns directly overhead. One has become weary, and mindfulness of God is all but impossible. The prayer is a call for perseverance, and a reminder that Christ's crucifixion began at this hour. (Midday Prayer)

- **None** (ninth hour) is prayed at midafternoon and calls for more perseverance and strength to continue as one exceeds his or her prime and must keep going. The sun is descending. By acknowledging this hour of Christ's death, one touches finitude.

- **Vespers** is celebrated at day's end. The evening light bathes the world in gold, transfiguring it. One sees beyond the struggles of the day. This is the hour of wisdom and rest in thanksgiving after the work of the day. (Evening Prayer)

◆ **Compline** is from the Latin meaning "complete." It is the last prayer before retiring for the night. It foreshadows life's end and leads back to the darkness of night and the darkness of God's mystery. This prayer is a gentle daily exercise in the art of dying. (Night Prayer)

# Sacred Music

Music is worship; it is prayer. It is an essential element to Catholic worship. Music used in worship services is called liturgical music. During Vatican II, when the Church reviewed its music along with other practices, it stressed music's importance in the worship service and identified its necessity as an integral part of the Mass. The council promoted full participation of the faithful in the Mass, especially by way of its music. Vatican II represented a major shift from music that was in Latin and performed by choirs to a new music in English that is sung by the people.

## How Sacred Music Functions

In order for music to attain its liturgical purposes (to provide the listeners with spiritual sustenance), these qualities should be considered:

◆ **Aesthetic,** to connect the holy to the beautiful

◆ **Diversionary,** to eliminate boredom during tedious times during the Mass

◆ **Emotional,** to express hope and joy when words alone cannot do it

◆ **Enjoyable,** so that it is pleasurable to hear and perform

◆ **Involving,** so that it unites and draws people together into deeper participation in the Mass

◆ **Mood-setting,** to make the worship capable of addressing a wide range of human emotion

◆ **Revelatory,** so that it explores and reveals the religious experience

◆ **Text-enhancing,** to underscore the sacredness of certain texts

In most parishes, the choir director and the pastor work together to select music that matches the liturgical calendar and captures the meaning of the feasts.

In today's busy world, people are seeking peace of mind and many are going to the old tried-and-true spiritual practices as the ones we've looked at. Monasteries are opening their doors to laypeople, offering retreats and instruction in meditation. Praying the Liturgy of the Hours is one of the prayer forms that is becoming popular among laypersons impressed by its ability to calm the worried mind and put things back into perspective.

We've looked at some favorite Catholic prayers and practices. In the next chapter, you'll learn about some of the opportunities for spiritual growth in the Catholic Church as we focus on the key prayer of the Church—the Mass.

## The Least You Need to Know

- Prayer is one's personal relationship to God. It cannot be captured in any one prayer or contained in any one form.

- The Rosary is a popular Catholic prayer. Praying the Rosary is a spiritual practice that contains both contemplation and spoken prayer.

- Contemplation is a mystical practice that takes practitioners to their deepest center to experience their relationship with God.

# 15

# The Mass: The Catholics' Big Dinner Party

## In This Chapter

◆ What is a Catholic Mass?

◆ The two parts of the Mass and its seven activities

◆ What Catholics understand about Holy Communion

◆ How you can participate in the Mass

More than any other practice, the Mass marks Catholicism. You catch a glimpse of it on the news when the pope celebrates it, or when a celebrity marries, or at the funeral of someone famous, but for the most part it remains veiled in mystery. In truth, many Catholics don't fully understand what's going on behind the scenes at the Mass, but they enjoy participating in it anyway. This chapter looks inside the church doors at the somewhat mysterious Catholic worship service: the Mass.

# Celebration or Sacrifice: What Is the Mass?

Eucharist is the "official" term for Mass. Less commonly, it is called the Lord's Supper, the Breaking of Bread, or the Divine Liturgy, especially in the Eastern Church. All these names mean about the same thing and you can use the terms interchangeably. The most common name, however, is simply "Mass."

Catholics will sometimes refer to Mass as the "sacrifice" of the Mass, and other times the "celebration" of the Mass. It is both these things—a re-enactment of the sacrifice Jesus made for us by his death on the cross, and the celebration of his resurrection and continued presence among us through the sacrament of the Eucharist. The importance of the Eucharist for Catholics is their profound belief that Jesus Christ is not just a fact of history but is God's true presence with us now and always. Not simply present in memory or as a memorial, but sacramentally present in "matter and form."

**Your Guardian Angel**

If you are a person of another faith and are attending the Catholic Mass, it is acceptable to sit throughout the service. Or you can sit, stand, and kneel along with the other folks.

Mass is offered in most churches every day as well as several times each Sunday, and other special Holy Days throughout the year, when attendance is required. In fact, there is no hour of any day on this planet when a Catholic Mass is not being celebrated!

Catholics are renowned for the standing, kneeling, and sitting that goes on at Mass, to the confusion of newcomers. In the following discussion, you'll see that these actions aren't just intended to be aerobic exercises, but have meaning, designating the different activities of the Mass.

The Mass has two basic parts and a series of seven key activities:

**Part I: Instruction: The Liturgy of the Word**

- ◆ Gathering
- ◆ Proclaiming
- ◆ Explaining
- ◆ Praying

**Part II: Breaking the Bread: The Liturgy of the Eucharist**

◆ Offering

◆ Consecrating

◆ Communion

The New Testament story of the two disciples on the road to Emmaus the day of Jesus' resurrection (Luke 24:13–35) is reflected in the two parts of the Mass. In the first part of the story, Jesus walks with the disciples, but they do not recognize him. He gives them a hint by quoting the Jewish Scripture that tells about the coming of the Messiah. They still don't recognize him. Then he sits down to dinner with them, and he blesses and breaks bread, and they finally realize who he is. The two actions of Jesus in the story are enacted in Mass by the reading of the Scripture followed by the breaking of the bread. Let's begin at the beginning, with the first activity called the "gathering."

# The Liturgy of the Word

The first part of the Mass contains prayers, Scripture readings, and songs that change according to the feast of that day—following the cycle and seasons of the liturgical calendar. You can find the liturgical calendar in Chapter 13.

## Gathering: The People Arrive

Catholics are very much about community, and gathering perhaps best captures the essence of what the Mass is all about. After Jesus' resurrection, his followers gathered together for the purpose of keeping his work alive. The gatherings of the early communities continued and grew. Gathering remains the primary function of the Church. If Catholics quit gathering, the entire Catholic Church would cease to exist.

As Mass begins, the people stand. They acknowledge their need for God's help, and their inability to lead a "perfect" life, by saying a prayer together, called by its Greek name, the *Kyrie:*

> Lord, have mercy.
> Christ, have mercy.
> Lord, have mercy.

Next, the Gloria, a prayer praising God's greatness and the coming of the Lord, is either said or sung. It begins with the words of the Scripture the angels used to announce the birth of Jesus: "Glory to God in the highest!"

The priest then recites an opening prayer, which, like the Scripture readings, follows the cycle of the liturgical calendar.

## Proclaiming: The Word of God

After the priest's prayer, the people sit and several Scriptures are read by a layperson known as a lector. The first reading is often from the Hebrew Scripture or Old Testament.

Next, the congregation either sings or recites one of the psalms. Usually a lector or cantor recites or sings a verse, to which the people respond with a verse from the psalm.

The second reading follows with a passage from one of the New Testament letters. After this reading, the people stand and sing "Alleluia!" proclaiming the word of God will now be spoken in the Gospel message. Gospel means "Good News," so there is an air of celebration as we approach this New Testament testimony. While lectors read the preceding Scriptures, only the priest or a deacon reads the Gospel message.

## Reflecting: a Word to the Wise

After the Gospel, the people sit for the homily (or sermon) delivered by the priest or deacon in which comments on the various readings are given, relating them to every-day life. While the sermon in a Protestant church is often the focus of the service, in a Catholic Mass it represents a relatively small part, generally lasting about 10 to 15 minutes on a Sunday. During the weekday Mass, the homily, if one is given, is no more than 5 minutes.

---

### Epiphanies

Humorist and religious pundit Garrison Keillor likes to talk about the differences between Catholics and Lutherans on his weekly radio show, *A Prairie Home Companion*. He says it's easy to spot religious preferences in the neighborhood during the holidays. Catholics put their Christmas trees up on Christmas Eve and leave them up until January 6. Lutherans put theirs up on Thanksgiving night and take them down the day after Christmas! He could perhaps add the time allotted for the sermon to his comparison.

Following the homily, the congregation takes a short time to reflect quietly on what the priest has said. The people then stand to recite the Nicene Creed together. The Nicene Creed dates back to the early 300s and is the most widely used statement of the Christian Faith. It is common to Orthodox, Anglicans, Lutherans, Presbyterians, and many other Christian groups. It appears in Chapter 1.

---

### Epiphanies

In a recent homily on the passage "Blessed are they who hunger for justice ..." from the Sermon on the Mount, a priest suggested to the people of his parish that the Sermon on the Mount is a challenge to them to transform their world to Gospel values. He told stories about a visit some of the parishioners made to a parish in a poorer section of town during the past week. By doing so, he illustrated for the entire congregation that it was possible to begin to transform the world by putting up Sheetrock, cleaning up the park, and helping kids learn to read, and explained how meaningful and spiritual such activities were at their heart.

---

## The Prayers Go Out Over the Land

The prayers of the faithful, in which the people pray for the needs of the world, follow the Creed. A lector will usually read a short intercession to which the people respond: "Lord, hear our prayer." The prayers specifically mention the pope, other Church leaders, political leaders, and members of the congregation who may be in need of special blessing such as sick family members, and friends or relatives who have recently died. To each of these prayers, the people respond out loud with a phrase like "Lord, hear our prayer." The people then sit down for the offering. That concludes the first part of the Mass.

# The Liturgy of the Eucharist

The second part of the Mass is like a drama—a ritual presentation of Jesus' Last Supper. There are prayers, music, and the consecration of bread and wine, following the instructions given by Jesus. The priest stands at the altar, facing the people. Here, the words and actions remain exactly the same each day.

## There's No Free Lunch!

The Liturgy of the Eucharist begins with the presentation of the gifts. Members of the parish (quite often children or an entire family) acting as representatives of the congregation take the gifts of water and wine up to the priest at the altar. These gifts will be used in the ritual. This symbolic act connects the people to the ceremony, making them active participants. The collection plate is passed, and the people are invited to give an offering of money that supports the operation of the Church. Through this offering, the people's active engagement in the ceremony is further stated. The collection basket is then taken up to the altar where the priest receives it along with the other gifts, blessing them, offering them to God "as the work and fruit of our hands." Often the choir sings a hymn or a musician plays music.

**For Heaven's Sake**

Use your envelopes. Most parishes ask parishioners to pledge a certain amount of money for the year and to use printed envelopes for the collection basket. It is easier on the parish bookkeeper and on you at tax time.

The priest prays that God will "cleanse him of all iniquity" and symbolically washes his fingers that will touch the bread. The people pray that God will accept the gifts "for the praise and glory of His name, for our good, and the good of all His church."

## Blessing the Bread

This part of the Mass, known as the consecration, is the focus of all the prayers and activities that precede it. Bread and wine will be blessed or consecrated to become the body and blood of Christ. The congregation stands or kneels (depending on local custom), signifying the importance of the ritual. The church becomes very quiet, as people enter sacred time. As a preface to the Eucharistic prayer of consecration, the priest recites a short prayer of praise to God. A server may ring the altar bells three times as the people sing or pray the Sanctus:

> Holy, Holy, Holy Lord,
> God of power and might,
> Heaven and Earth are full of your glory
> Hosanna in the highest!
> Blessed is he who comes in the name of the Lord
> Hosanna in the highest!

The priest then begins the great prayer of petition and thanksgiving to God called the Eucharistic Prayer—the most important prayer of the Mass. During this prayer, the priest calls to mind the Last Supper; he takes the bread and says the words of consecration:

> "Take this, all of you, and eat it. This is my body which will be given up for you."

He elevates the bread above the altar to show to the congregation, and the altar server may ring bells signaling that the consecration had taken place. While looking at the Eucharistic bread, it is a common practice to silently whisper, "My Lord, and my God," or some other words of respect. When the priest sets the bread back down on the altar, he genuflects in respect. He then does the same with the chalice of wine.

Catholics believe in real presence—meaning that Christ is now actually present in the consecrated bread and wine. There is an atmosphere of deep respect, even awe, at this point of the Mass. The priest says one of many versions of the Eucharistic prayer. The following reflects the liturgical imagery of the ancient Church.

**Priest:** "Lord, you are holy indeed, the fountain of all holiness. Let your spirit come upon these gifts (bread and wine) to make them holy so that they may become the body and blood of our Lord Jesus Christ. Before he was given up to death, a death he freely accepted, he took bread and gave you thanks. He broke the bread, gave it to his disciples, and said, 'Take this all of you, and eat it. This is my body, which will be given up for you.' When supper was ended, he took the cup, and again he gave thanks and praise, gave the cup to his disciples, and said, 'Take this, all of you, and drink from it. This is the cup of my blood, the blood of the new and everlasting covenant. It will be shed for you and for all so that sins may be forgiven. Do this in memory of me.' Let us proclaim the mystery of faith."

**Your Guardian Angel**

During the "kiss of peace," don't be shy about expressing peace with those around you, even if you don't know them. Don't worry, you don't have to kiss them; a handshake will do.

**All:** "Dying you destroyed our death, rising you restored our life, Lord Jesus, come in glory."

**Priest:** "In memory of his death and resurrection, we offer you, Father, this life-giving bread, this saving cup. We thank you for counting us worthy to stand in your presence and serve you. May all of us who share in the body and blood of Christ be brought together in unity by the Holy Spirit. Lord, remember your church throughout the world; make us grow in love together with our pope and our bishop and all the clergy. Remember our brothers and sisters who have gone to their rest in the hope of rising again: bring them and all the departed into the light of your presence. Have mercy on us all; make us worthy to share eternal life with Mary, the virgin mother of God, with the apostles, and with all the saints who have done your will throughout the ages. May we praise you in union with them and give you glory though your son, Jesus Christ. Through him, with him, in him, in the unity of the Holy Spirit, all glory and honor is yours, almighty Father, forever and ever."

## Breaking the Bread

The people then stand to say the Lord's Prayer together and share the "kiss of peace" with each other (usually not an actual kiss, but a handshake or a nod of the head).

**S'ter Says**

**Host** is from the Latin *hostia,* meaning "victim," recalling the sacrifice of Christ. This term was used as one of several names for the Eucharistic bread in the Middle Ages.

The priest breaks the bread, now called the *host,* symbolizing Jesus' broken body on the cross, while the people pray the Agnus Dei: "Lamb of God, who takes away the sins of the world, have mercy on us."

In an act of respect, the priest invites the people to join him humbly praying: "Lord, I am not worthy to receive you, but only say the word, and I shall be healed."

The priest first eats and drinks the consecrated bread and wine and then invites the people to receive the sacrament. Those who are going to receive the Eucharist, usually most of the congregation, walk up the center aisle to the altar. They are given the option of taking the host in their own hand and placing it in their mouth, or letting the priest place it on their tongue, as was the tradition for many years. Eucharistic ministers often assist the priest by offering the hosts and the chalice of consecrated wine. Real wine is used, and it is not necessary to take it. The sacrament is complete without the wine. As the communicants return to their seats, they kneel in prayer and meditation. Often, music is played or a song is sung in the background during the distribution of Communion.

The priest completes the Eucharistic ritual by washing the chalice and placing any unused consecrated hosts in the tabernacle. These hosts may be carried to home-bound parishioners or taken to the hospital and given to the sick. The priest sits after Communion and the church is quiet for a time of reflection. When he rises, it signals the people to stand for the conclusion of the service.

At the end of the Mass, the priest blesses the people and dismisses them with the order, "Mass is ended! Go in peace to love and serve the Lord!" He sends them out into the world with a blessing, and the instruction to take Christ with them and make him known to whomever they meet. During his blessing, the people make the sign of the cross. The priest then ceremonially walks down the center aisle of the church preceded by the altar servers, while the people sing a final hymn. He usually stands outside and greets his parishioners as they leave the church.

# The Eucharist: Feeding the Flock

The main difference between a Protestant worship service and a Catholic Mass is the Eucharist. Not that Protestant churches don't serve Communion—many do—but Catholics believe that through the priest's consecration and through the people's belief, the bread and wine actually become the body and blood of Jesus. In participating in the Eucharist the people become one with each other and Christ——they become the sacrament of the Body of Christ. This ritual is referred to as *real presence.*

You recall, Eucharist, the formal name for the Mass, has two meanings: it is a memorial of Jesus' celebration of the Last Supper and a memorial of his sacrifice on the cross. Let's take a look at each of these meanings in more detail.

## Is It Real, or Is It "Memorex"?

The consecration ritual is very specific; it uses the same essential words and gestures each time it is done, in every church all over the world. Jesus told his followers to bless the bread and wine as he did and he would be there with them. As Catholics repeat the words used by Jesus at the Last Supper, they believe he is physically there with them. The Eucharist is a mystery, meaning it is taken on faith and can never be completely understood in the scientific way of knowing. It is possible, however, to know how memory works in our lives, to begin to see how it is even possible to believe in real presence.

When family and friends gather and remember a departed member of the group—particularly a person they cared a lot about—that person begins to come alive in the mind and imagination (where memory is recorded) of the people. As we talked about in Chapter 9, the memory, which occurs in the imagination, is real. Memories have chemical substance that flows through the body when it is activated—they become a physical reality.

The presence of Jesus, as he gathered with the disciples at the Last Supper, is recalled through the Eucharistic ritual. As the communal memory of the congregation along with other congregations all over the world recall the same memory, it grows in power. Participants enter that sacred space where the past and present connect, and in that sacred space, God is physically present and communicates with us. It is possible to physically and emotionally feel his love, support, and comfort. He is there with you, as he was with his followers at the Last Supper. Thus the real presence of Jesus is alive in the physical bodies of the people uniting them as the body of Christ. This explanation does not capture the whole mystery of the Eucharist, but the analogy can be helpful.

---

**Saints Preserve Us**

**Sts. Cosmas and Damian, September 26, Patrons of Druggists**

St. Cosmas and St. Damian (from Arabia in the Middle East) were brothers and were skilled in the science of medicine. They were filled with the spirit of Christian charity and never took money for their services. They were held in high esteem and greatly loved by the people of their town. When the persecutions broke out about the year 283, they were arrested because of their prominence. After undergoing various torments, they were finally beheaded.

---

## The Meaning of Sacrifice

We think of sacrifice as something we give up, even sacrificing a life for a cause, but as you look at the root word, it has a deeper meaning. It comes from Latin—*sacrum* meaning "holy" and *facere* meaning "to make." Sacrifice literally means to make something holy. Catholics use the word *sacrifice* when they talk about the Mass because they are bringing the gift of themselves to God at the altar to be made holy, to be blessed. The word "altar" comes from the Latin *adolere*, which means "to burn up." Fire purifies, and sacrifices have been enacted by burning, symbolizing purification or transformation, since the beginning of time. Thus, the sacrifice has come to mean change, even molecular change—transformation.

In a sacrificial ritual, we surrender to God; we give up the form in which we now exist, or the way we presently think about something, and willingly allow God to transform us. Jesus surrendered his will to God as he prayed in the garden of Gethsemane, as recorded in Matthew 26:39: "Yet not as I will, but as you will." The events that followed took him to his death on the cross and to his resurrection (transformation). By remembering Jesus' surrender, Catholics surrender themselves to the will of God during this act of Communion.

---

**Epiphanies**

The Eucharist ritual follows the Jewish tradition of remembering through story and ritual. Passover was one of the primary events in the Jewish story. It recalls the deliverance of the Jews from Egyptian slavery, and it is remembered with a ritual supper. This is the same Passover supper Jesus celebrated with his disciples as the Last Supper, the night before his death. Catholics believe Jesus declared that the sacrifice of his life would now achieve the deliverance of Passover to all. In declaring this, Jesus fused the memory of these events, Passover and the Last Supper ritual.

---

# Here's the Church, and Here's the Steeple, Open the Doors, and See All the People!

Catholics worship in a building called a church. As you enter a, you notice many sacred objects. From the holy water fonts on both sides of the entrance to the sanctuary lamp burning on the altar, there are many indications that you have entered sacred space. Catholic churches are generally quiet zones in our otherwise very busy and noisy lives, and it is the custom to observe silence when visiting a church. It is common practice for Catholics to visit the church when no service is going on and just sit in meditation in the presence of the Eucharistic bread in the tabernacle.

You'll see a long aisle with benches on both sides, leading to the sanctuary where the altar stands. The church has two basic spaces: the pews or the rows of benches with kneelers where the people worship, and the sanctuary where the priest, altar servers, and readers perform their respective tasks. The sanctuary and the pews face each other, and while the two spaces are defined as different, they interact. Let's go inside and take a look around.

## Sacred Spaces

If you haven't been inside a Catholic church, the first thing you will encounter as you enter a pew is the kneeler. A pew may be long enough to comfortably seat 10 or more people. Each row of pews will have a kneeler, a cushioned board of wood hinged on both ends and attached to the bottom of the pew. When it is time to kneel, you put it down so it rests on the floor. When you need to move in and out of the pew, you raise it on its hinge so that the aisle is clear.

The sanctuary is a large space with several key pieces of furniture. There is an altar in the center of the sanctuary, typically a waist-high table or slab of marble, about 5 to 10 feet long and about 4 feet wide. The surface of this table is smooth and polished, often with five Greek crosses engraved on its surface, one at each of the four corners, about six inches from both edges, and one in the center. It's covered with layers of cloth and will have candles burning during the liturgy of the Eucharist. Sometimes the candles are not on the altar but are placed around it. As you read earlier, the altar symbolizes Christ and connotes his sacrifice, or giving up of his will to God, and during the Mass, the followers will do the same.

The second item in the sanctuary is the pulpit, the stand from which the priest reads the Gospel and delivers the homily. The two parts of the Catholic Mass are celebrated around these two pieces of furniture. Finally, there is a third focal point: the presider's (priest's) chair. From here he directs the first part of the Mass—the Liturgy of the Word.

Either on a shelf behind the altar or on a side altar, you will find a little marble or metal box called a tabernacle. It is covered with a cloth, and the door is locked with a key. The Eucharistic bread that has been consecrated at Mass is kept there in reserve. The sanctuary lamp sits or hangs near the tabernacle and is always lit, signaling God's presence in the tabernacle in the form of the consecrated bread, Jesus' body. As mentioned before, there is always a crucifix visible near the altar. Additionally, the Easter candle is prominently displayed. There is more discussion of sanctuary furnishings and sacramentals in Chapter 13.

## Putting on Your Glad Rags

Those who participate at the altar during the Mass wear special ceremonial clothes. The priest's clothes (vestments) are the most elaborate and unusual. The different colors of the vestments correspond to the liturgical calendar and the seasons of the year. The rules that govern the proper form for the celebration of the Mass are contained in a book called the *General Instruction of the Roman Missal.* Here are some of the guidelines for the colors at Mass.

White and gold are used for important celebrations like Christmas and Easter. For funerals white is the regular color, representing Resurrection, although purple and black (worn in the past) are still used in more traditional parishes. Red is the color for the feast of the Holy Spirit (Pentecost), as well as for the celebrations of the lives of martyrs. Red is sometimes used for ordinations and installations and for church dedications and anniversaries. Purple is worn during more somber seasons such as Lent and Advent, as we prepare for the feasts of Easter and Christmas. Blue is often used instead of purple during the season of Advent, as it conveys hope, the main mood of Advent. Green is used at all other times.

Altar servers also wear special clothes, either a white alb (or gown), like the priest, or a black one called a cassock with a white vestment—a type of blouse—over it called a surplice. Generally the lectors, Eucharistic ministers, and ushers don't wear special uniforms.

*The Sanctuary. Christ the King Church, Nashville, Tennessee.*

*(Courtesy of H. L. [Dean] Caskey)*

## Who's Who at a Catholic Mass

Since Vatican II, the people are seen as participants in the Mass, not just observers. They make up the body of the assembled Church offering the Mass to God. The council document on the liturgy calls their role at the Mass "priestly." A priest presides, leading the congregation in offering worship to God. His words begin and end the Mass. He leads the prayers, reads the Gospel, and preaches the homily. He leads the praying of the liturgy of the Eucharist and says the words of consecration.

Often the priest is assisted by a deacon, or altar servers. Altar servers are boys and girls or men and women who assist by carrying items used in the service, such as the book containing the prayers and Scriptures. They may also ring the bells during certain times in the Mass. There are also readers called lectors who read the Old Testament and Epistles, and the prayers following the homily. In addition, there are men and women who distribute the Communion bread and wine, consecrated as lay Eucharistic ministers. Altar servers, lectors, and ministers of the Eucharist are prepared for their jobs by special instruction.

> **Your Guardian Angel**
>
> Being a lector at Mass can be a rewarding experience. The parish offers workshops to train lectors in public speaking and instruct them in the meaning of the biblical texts. Don't be afraid to volunteer!

Serving outside the sanctuary are choir members and ushers. The ushers greet and seat people and take up the collection. The key ministers in the whole service are the people.

## Guess Who's Coming to Dinner: Is It Just for Catholics?

All are welcome at a Catholic celebration of the Mass. If you're not Catholic and you attend a Mass, you should feel free to sit during the service or join in all the gestures and prayers if you are comfortable doing that. Typically, there will be a booklet available to help you follow the Mass.

Hopefully you'll forgive Catholics for what appears to be a lack of hospitality when it comes to receiving Communion. The Eucharistic ritual involves the actual belief that Jesus becomes present at the consecration. It is therefore reserved for those who formally profess this important Catholic belief. It seems that all families welcome guests, and yet some gathering times are reserved only for members. This reinforces their family bond. Catholic Communion is just that, a sign of Catholic unity.

While theologians and Catholic Church officials debate the possibilities for full Communion, many ordinary folks find themselves troubled by this separation, feeling the more unity Christians express, the closer all Christian churches will come to resolving differences, more closely modeling Jesus' words at the Last Supper: "that they may all be one." (John 17:21) Other Catholics want to maintain the existing rules around receiving the Eucharist to preserve its Catholic character, and to assure the bond of unity that is created by all who participate holding the same belief about its authenticity. When persons from another Christian denomination become Catholic, they are said to be received into full Communion. They are not rebaptized, but their participation in receiving Communion becomes the high point marking their transition into membership.

## The Least You Need to Know

- The Mass is the primary worship service for Catholics.

- The consecration and distribution of Holy Communion is the central ritual of the Mass.

- Catholics believe that the real presence of Jesus is actually contained in Holy Communion.

- Although the priest presides, the people offer the Mass along with him.

# Part 5

## Catholic Identity: How Are Catholics Wired?

We've looked at Catholics' biblical roots. We've looked at their sacramental life and practices such as incense, bells, and holy water. We've sampled their rich prayer life. Now in Part 5, we'll look at how they think and where they meet. When you consider the broad population base of Catholicism, what does it mean to identify Catholics as a tribe? Is there a process in which Catholic culture and thinking is formed? Is there a particular way Catholics engage the world? How does the Church maintain unity and diversity? Do Catholics all believe the same things? Do they all think alike?

In this part, we'll look at Catholic beliefs, examining some of the more controversial issues. We'll look at power within the Church: who has it, and who does not. And we'll discuss the powerful statement Catholics make about the reign of God through their tireless commitment to social justice. We begin, however, by looking at Catholics as a community.

# Chapter 16

# It's a Tribe

## In This Chapter

- ◆ The nature of Catholic community
- ◆ The parish: where the tribe meets, prays, and plays
- ◆ The parochial school: developing discipleship and citizenship
- ◆ The Church's social institutions
- ◆ Getting in and getting out of the tribe

Catholicism has a distinctive cultural and ethnic mark that is more than the sum of its rules and beliefs. In this chapter, we'll look at how this is formed through parish life and the role Catholic schools play in forming Catholics as citizens. After looking at where Catholic identity is formed and where it is lived out, we'll also look at how you get in and out of the tribe.

## Where the Tribe Meets

Up until recently, Catholics attended the church in their neighborhood and exceptions were few and far between. Although less true today, in the past the lines of parish distinction were as clearly drawn as those of voting districts.

Catholic priest and sociologist Andrew Greeley describes the ideal form of a Catholic parish as an "organic community." A Catholic parish is successful when the spiritual lives of the people are mutually nourished and able to grow there.

# Center for Belonging

The image of Church for Catholics is not in Rome, but down the block, on the corner. It's where you were baptized and where your older sister was married and where your grandparents' funerals were held. It is woven into your family history—that's what makes it organic.

Approximately one third of all Catholic churches in the United States have a Catholic school connected to them. While that number has fallen—nearly half had one just 30 years ago—the schools continue to be an important dimension of the organic sense of Catholic parish life. When the same beliefs and values are reinforced through Church, home, and in the classroom a strong unifying statement is made. The school is where faith is developed on a day-to-day basis for the young people, and the faith response of peace and justice can be fully explored.

In the predominately Protestant culture of America of yesteryear, Catholics were often not accepted into the larger community. They gained their sense of belonging by gathering in their parish churches. Although times have changed, the need for belonging remains a strong human desire. Parish life remains the primary spiritual home and the touchstone of Catholic identity. From that base, Catholics often belong to a variety of other organizations where they connect with others who have similar interests or spiritual goals.

Such organizations include the Christian Family Movement, Marriage Encounter groups, the Knights of Columbus, the Legion of Mary, programs for divorced and separated Catholics, Great Books clubs, Scripture study groups, Girl Scouts and Boy Scouts, the choir, various ministries to the sick and bereaved, and gatherings for seniors, to name just a few.

# Center for Prayer and Sacraments

The church is the heart of the parish and is where Catholics gather for the Mass. A variety of celebrations of Mass reflect the different character of parishes. For example, in Los Angeles, there are Masses being celebrated each Sunday in more than 50 different languages. Many Catholics still hold on to the Latin Mass, and a few parishes still offer it.

---

**Epiphanies**

Play and recreation are important to building community and remain integral to the spiritual and religious life of the parish. You might call it "sacred play." Indeed, many churches have a gymnasium for basketball and volleyball, as well as an auditorium ready for dances and other social events, such as variety shows or a haunted house at Halloween. Parishes sponsor golf or bowling leagues, card clubs, and quilting guilds. They offer ball fields, playgrounds, and grounds for church picnics. Positive social bonding is a religious and spiritual affair. Social life in the parish allows Catholics to experience God as the unifying force in human relationships.

---

The unique character of the parish is reflected in its music. Depending on the preferences of the congregation and the church leadership, a parish might offer anything from folk music to Gregorian chant. Certain parishes might even offer a rock Mass performed by the youth choir. Music helps to set the mood and environment, which is a key focus in today's Church. Some parishes extend this sense of celebration into choreographed lighting and sound. In addition, banners, sometimes made by the children or youth groups, decorate the church and mark the seasons.

The parish church is where sacramental life is celebrated through baptisms, weddings, and funerals as well as private devotions. Throughout the week, people often make a visit to the church for private prayer. Until recently the church doors were never locked. You could drop in at any time and expect to find a scattering of others sitting or kneeling quietly in prayer and meditation. Today, many city churches have had to make concessions to the times, but you can usually roust someone to let you in and you'll still find the faithful in prayer once you knock. On weeknights, novenas, benedictions, and seasonal devotions, such as the Way of the Cross during Lent, are held. All of these ceremonies and rituals work to create a sacramental identity that is communally shared.

## Launching Pad to the World

Ideally, the parish contributes to the political and cultural life of its city; and as we have seen, it is a viable force in national politics, too. The parish focuses the power of the people and can efficiently inform members on issues and organize them to affect political policies regarding issues as diverse as taxes, medical practices, abortion, wages, or capital punishment.

**Your Guardian Angel**

Send your kids to Catholic schools if you want to promote their social awareness. According to sociological studies, Catholics educated in Catholic schools are substantially more likely to be in favor of racial integration and tolerant of members of other denominations than are public-school Catholics.

In parochial schools, children are educated to be better Catholics *and* better citizens. Catholic education includes developing values and ethics—and integrating those principles into all areas of life. In a way, Catholic students learn their ABCs and 123s in order to make a better world, which for them means bringing about the reign of God. Weaving values into the wider culture isn't about imposing the Catholic Church on others (although this has been the case at times), but rather it is the embodiment of basic values based in Christian charity and justice. Catholic identity includes living the Gospel by being active in the world.

# Catholics' Social Face

The true measure of Catholic identity is how Catholics live their lives in the world. Jesus talked about bringing about the reign of God not simply as an idea to be expressed; it was an action to be taken. Jesus healed the sick, cared for sinners, and challenged the injustices in his society. His followers took on this mission from the start, as recorded in the New Testament in the Acts of the Apostles. The Church has expresses care for people in three primary ways: health care, education, and social services. Chapter 18, on social justice, is devoted to this focus of Catholicism.

## Catholic Health Care: More Than Chicken Soup for the Soul

From its earliest years in the United States, the Catholic Church has been vitally involved in health care, and currently, Catholic health-care institutions serve almost 80 million patients a year. Catholic hospitals constitute more than 10 percent of all hospitals in the country and receive about 15 percent of all hospital admissions.

**For Heaven's Sake**

You can't be a good Catholic and pass the buck. Catholicism is a religion of action in the world. Being a good Catholic requires hard work; you are expected to be involved in your church and in the community.

Both lay and religious men and women respond to the vocation of healing the sick and comforting the afflicted. Catholic hospitals employ almost 750,000 people, about 15 percent of all hospital employees in the country; their total payroll is in excess of $20 billion.

Most of the Church's health-care institutions are banded together in the Catholic Health Association (CHA), the largest single group of not-for-profit health-care providers. The CHA is organized to advance the health-care ministry through advocacy, education, research, and development. It supports and strengthens health ministries in the United States and speaks with one voice to address health issues.

## Catholic Colleges: Rocking the Cradle of Thought

In the United States, more than 200 Catholic institutions of higher education educate nearly 700,000 students. About 5 percent of these places are research universities, 10 percent are two-year colleges, and the remaining 85 percent are four-year universities and colleges, equally divided between liberal arts and more comprehensive institutions.

---

### Saints Preserve Us

**St. Vincent de Paul, September 27, Patron of Charitable Organizations and Prisoners**

St. Vincent de Paul was a spiritual advisor to a wealthy woman in France. He became aware of the plight of the peasants and began his missionary work to aid them. He founded many orphanages and hospitals, the Congregation of the Missions (the Vincentians), and the Daughters of Charity. It was said that his way with wealthy women greatly enhanced the success of his work. He died in 1660. The charity that bears his name, the St. Vincent de Paul Society, was founded in Paris in 1833. It operates all over the world today.

---

For the most part, Catholic colleges were founded by religious orders, such as the Jesuits, Dominicans, Franciscans, and Benedictines. As federal funding has required Catholic institutions to meet the test of independent control, most schools have moved to independent boards of trust that aren't controlled by the Church hierarchy. The religious orders have become sponsors, not owners. The faculty is diversified. Not only are there very few of the members of the sponsoring religious orders teaching, but being Catholic is not a necessary requirement for selecting faculty.

### Your Guardian Angel

You can get a full education at a Catholic college. The primary goal of Catholic universities, as most recently defined by Pope John Paul II, is to mediate faith and culture. They do this by developing cultural understanding through the arts, social sciences, and natural sciences, partnered with theology and philosophy.

# Catholic Charities: More Than Just a Handout

Catholic Charities is the largest private network of social service organizations in the United States. It works to support families, reduce poverty, and build communities. Catholic Charities provides emergency and social services ranging from shelters and soup kitchens to day-care centers, summer camps, centers for seniors, and refugee resettlement offices for more than 10 million people. Its annual budget exceeds $2 billion.

## Missing the Mark

The picture we paint in this chapter is the ideal, and while the ideal is met for the most part, that is not always the case. Putting Catholic values into action has sometimes been lost in translation! Throughout history and today as well, human failings can make a mess out of "doing the right thing." Even our best intentions are subject to human error. The fact that many people have suffered at the hands of a well-meaning Church cannot be denied. Examples abound.

While Catholic hospitals and charitable organizations provided safety for women and children, they likewise caused untold suffering by imposing misunderstood values. Women who were pregnant and not married were routinely "institutionalized" for their "own good" and for the "good of the baby." They were often lied to and pressured into signing adoption papers. Mothers and babies were separated cruelly, and continue to suffer because of these ill-designed policies. Practices have been changed for the most part, but the trail of broken relationships remains—and for the most part hasn't been addressed.

Another example involves the treatment of native people. Missionaries routinely took children out of their homes and "gave" them to other people or put them into homes across the country in the name of "Christianizing them." Not only were families destroyed, children were denied their language, customs, and spiritual practices. Stories of overly zealous nuns and priests and the resulting spiritual abuse have damaged many, and have likewise damaged the Catholic image and the Catholic soul.

As these stories are told along with stories of sexual abuse and cover-ups, they make the front pages. Some efforts at healing these breaches have occurred, and there's good reason to think they will continue, primarily due to publicity and financial damage to the Church. (You'll find more on this topic in Chapter 25.)

# Getting In and Out of the Tribe

The Church has a comprehensive process of initiation into the tribe. As we've seen, Catholicism is more a culture than an organization, which means that the word *initiation* is more accurate than the word *join*. There is a period of time in which the initiate gets to know the tribe and the tribal ways. The process is called the Rite of Christian Initiation of Adults (RCIA) and includes socialization, instruction, and ritual celebration that lasts a minimum of a year.

Entering the Church is an acknowledgment of the covenant relationship God has with His people. This Old Testament declaration of God's relationship to His creation proclaims that we are His and He will never forget that.

Sometimes, people may not find their covenant relationship with God fulfilled in the Church and they may choose to leave. And in rare cases the Church may find it necessary to sanction the actions of one of its members. This would happen when the action by a member publicly threatens the unity of the Church's teachings and beliefs.

## Joining Catholicism, Not a Quick Study

Catholics don't recruit. Ideally they invite an interested person to come to Mass and would be open to answering questions (maybe giving them a copy of this book!), but aggressive evangelizing isn't their style. The Rite of Christian Initiation of Adults, commonly referred to as RCIA, is the process for adults to become members of the Catholic Church. It begins with a time of instruction and bonding with the community, culminating in receiving the sacraments of initiation and full membership in the Church. You may remember from the earlier discussion of sacraments that this process sometimes includes baptism, confirmation, and the Eucharist, celebrated at the end of the process.

The RCIA came out of Vatican II, and reaches back in time to the early Christian communities for its model. The early communities emphasized bonding and a time for questions, instruction, and faith sharing, as well as preparation to receive the sacraments and admission into the Church, usually at the Easter Vigil.

This very old tradition outlines the process for today, and just as the early Church began with a time of getting to know one another, RCIA does, too. The Church family makes a commitment to welcome the stranger and create a caring, cohesive community of believers—for as long as it takes. It's up to the individual seeking membership to say when the bonding has happened.

For those who decide to move forward in the process, a period of inquiry begins, during which they meet with others from the parish in a more intimate way where stories are shared, questions answered, and basic beliefs of the Catholic faith are explored. It's common for the candidate to work with a personal sponsor, and they walk the journey together.

> **S'ter Says**
>
> **Catechumen** (from the Latin for "instructed") is one receiving instruction in the principles of Catholicism with a view to baptism.
>
> **Neophyte** (from the Greek for "newly planted") is a new Catholic who has just begun to live his or her life in the Church.

When the candidate feels ready and when the sponsor and the community agree it's the right time, he or she is enrolled as a *catechumen*, the title used to describe a person seeking instruction. During this more formalized time in the process, candidates usually participate in Sunday Mass, but leave after the homily (sermon) to go to their faith-sharing groups. At the appropriate time, generally the beginning of Lent, those who are ready to move ahead with the process will enter the final stages of preparation. Again, readiness is determined by group effort—the willingness of the candidate, the advice of the sponsor, and the acceptance of the community all help to determine readiness.

Normally, the Easter Vigil is the time when candidates receive the sacraments of initiation and are welcomed into full membership in the Church. After this, the new members *(neophytes)* enter a process of reflection on their experiences of receiving the sacraments, and are then assimilated into the parish.

Success of the RCIA depends on the parish community's participation. Without a genuine spirit of welcome, the process is vulnerable to becoming nothing more than a time of instruction. The caring of the community gives the rite vitality and life. This participation offers a challenge to some parishes, especially large congregations where members tend to be alienated from the sense of community themselves. The benefits of the program are twofold: the catechumen is provided a community experience, and the community is drawn together to offer one.

Here is a summary of the process:

- ◆ **Time of welcoming.** During this time, the candidate gets to know the community and experience the Gospel values it offers.

- ◆ **Acceptance as a candidate.** During a liturgical ritual of acceptance, the candidate expresses desire, and the community responds. This ritual is the entrance into a more structured process of instruction and faith sharing.

- ◆ **A time of development in the Catholic faith.** After the rite of acceptance comes this time of nurturing and growth in faith.

- ◆ **Election.** This formal, liturgical rite is usually celebrated on the first Sunday of Lent. The candidates express their desire to join the Church, and the parish ratifies their readiness to receive the sacraments of initiation.

- ◆ **Celebration of sacraments of initiation.** Usually held as part of the Easter Vigil, the elect are initiated through baptism, confirmation, and the Eucharist.

- ◆ **The honeymoon.** After their baptism, confirmation, and reception of the Eucharist, the newly initiated reflect on their experience of receiving the sacraments, and they are integrated into the community.

## Excommunication

*Excommunication* is one of those buzz words in popular culture, but it doesn't actually happen very often. It's a formal penalty the Church uses to exclude a Catholic from full participation in the Church. It is used rarely and only for serious reasons. It's not a moral condemnation, but a firm response to an action (usually a public one) that jeopardizes the integrity of the Church. Excommunication doesn't "kick" a person out of the Church, but it restricts that person's rights within the community.

The ultimate goal is to safeguard the community as well as encourage repentance and reconciliation. Excommunication is the strongest censure the Church can make, and at the same time, it extends the spirit of forgiveness.

Silencing is another example of official censoring, and is short of excommunication. It is generally reserved for people acting in an official capacity and misrepresenting Catholic doctrine. It is preceded by warnings after which the offending person is forbidden to speak publicly or publish for a period of time, perhaps 6 months to a year. It happens infrequently.

> **S'ter Says**
>
> **Excommunication** is an ecclesiastical censure depriving a person of the rights of Church membership and excluding that person from full fellowship in the community.

> **Your Guardian Angel**
>
> Excommunication does not have to be forever! It's a big deal and is used only in very serious situations. However, unlike a military court martial, it can be repealed. If the offense was a public one, it requires a public apology. If it was a private matter, it can be resolved with your confessor.

Unofficial censorship happens fairly routinely, just like it does in any organization—by being called on the carpet! Teaching positions can mysteriously terminate, speaking engagements can be canceled, and so on, until the message is received. Presently, many critics of the Church's stand on birth control, women's right to choice, women's ordination, and the possibility of marriage for clergy or celibacy by choice have received unofficial censoring.

## Maintaining Status: How Catholic Do You Have to Be?

As you may remember, we noted that 20 percent of Catholics leave the religion, and that the second-largest "denomination" in the United States consists of former Catholics. These statistics pose a couple of interesting questions: just what do people mean when they say they are Catholic? And what does it mean to leave the Church? Because of Catholicism's tribal nature and deep cultural identity, its character tends to remain with those who leave. It is rather like being a German American, Mexican American, Asian American, or African American: Catholicism gets into the blood!

From the perspective of the Church, you are Catholic unless excommunicated. From the perspective of the individual, you are Catholic as long as you still practice or in some way identify yourself as one. Practice means going by the six precepts of the Church that we listed in Chapter 4.

It is not unusual to hear people refer to themselves as Catholics when they have not attended church for 20 years or more. What about them is still Catholic? Most of the time, these people have maintained Catholicism's sacramental and communal sense of being in the world, and of relating to others—they keep their "Catholic wiring." They carry the Church within them.

## Broken Relationships: Recovering Catholics

Unfortunately, a number of people's experience with this religion has been damaging, so much so that the term "recovering Catholic" has worked its way into common language. For some people, this lingering connection has been so wounding that they spend a lifetime trying to heal from it. Others leave because they feel the Church isn't Catholic enough—others that it doesn't think big enough, is too narrow in its views.

When an institution such as a large company, a government, or a church has enormous power in the lives of people, the potential for an abuse of this power exists. We explicitly take up the matter of sex abuse in Chapter 25.

We've taken a look at the parish, some of the Church's organizations, its outreach, and its tribal nature. Regardless of how the Church identifies you—as a Catholic in "good standing" or a "backslider"—it is really your personal identity that is the important issue; you get to call the shot on this. How you choose to acknowledge or reject your alliance with the tribe differs with each individual. In the next chapter, we'll find out where Catholic teachings originate and how they become part of the traditions of the Church.

## The Least You Need to Know

- ◆ Catholicism is an organization with a distinct cultural character.

- ◆ The local Catholic parish is the place where most identify their Catholicism, and from there they engage the world.

- ◆ Catholic education has a good academic record and encourages students to take an active and informed role in society.

- ◆ The process for joining the Church as an adult is based in the early Christian communities. It includes a year of getting to know people, learning about the beliefs, and finally receiving the sacraments.

# Chapter 17

# The Teaching Church: More Than Just a Slap with the Ruler

## In This Chapter

◆ The two sources of Catholic teachings

◆ What is the Catechism?

◆ The dynamic relationship between bishops, theologians, and the people

◆ The educational process that "grows" theologians and other intellectually involved Catholics

The two primary sources of Catholic beliefs are the Bible and tradition. We talked about the Bible and the stories that are foundational to Catholicism in Chapter 7. In this chapter, we'll talk about the Church's role as teacher, the book that lists the essential teachings of the Church, and explore the process called theology from which new discoveries about truth emerge.

# The Sources of the Church's Teaching: Scripture and Tradition

To be a Catholic is to subscribe to a particular set of beliefs. This formal body of sacred knowledge called *Catholic tradition* is rooted in Scripture and contains the revealed truths collected throughout the long history of the Church. The pope and bishops interpret Scripture as well as rule on new insight—most of which comes from the pope, bishops, Catholic theologians, and scholars. There is a precise process of discernment regarding what will become Catholic tradition, and not everything popes, bishops, or others say is Catholic doctrine. Prayerful consideration is given to what will and won't become part of official teaching, and this is done for the purpose of maintaining unity.

## Keeping the Faith

Officially, Catholics are expected to believe in the Gospel of Jesus as interpreted by the Church and handed down in Catholic tradition. In reality probably no one believes every single Church teaching exactly the same way, and the Church doesn't "police" its members as to their personal beliefs.

> **S'ter Says**
>
> **Catholic tradition** is the body of sacred knowledge that constitutes official Catholic teaching or Catholic beliefs.

Faith is a gift from God, and faithful Catholics can (and do) disagree with official teachings, but they can't represent their personal beliefs as Catholic doctrine. Despite an emphasis on dogma and doctrine, the Catholic religion maintains its identity as a mystery based in the sacraments, and supported by its teachings.

## Tradition: More Shall Be Revealed

Catholics believe God continues to speak, and Catholic tradition is informed by what is called "ongoing revelation." Periodically, although not regularly, Church councils are called to update the system, set a new course for the Church, define a belief, or examine new information that will eventually produce new Church teachings. Vatican II, which you read about in Chapter 5, was a point when a new course was set. Specific teachings must be put into place to move that direction. This involves encoding council documents into Church law—also called Canon law.

In making judicial decisions, U.S. judges must consult existing rulings to see how previous judges have ruled in similar cases. This process is called establishing and following precedent—it assures continuity and keeps things from suddenly veering off course. At the same time, new situations can call for new interpretations. The Church uses a similar process in making decisions on articles of faith. Church leaders take new facts and circumstances into account while remaining faithful to what God has already revealed. Often it takes decades or even centuries of prayer and discussion before bishops are prepared to speak on a controversial matter. Tradition is not static, but for some it seems to move at the pace of a glacier, yet for others too fast.

Tradition is summarized in three places:

◆ The Nicene Creed

◆ Councils as collected in the council documents

◆ Encyclicals, or letters of the popes

This material is organized and printed in the text known as *The Catechism of the Catholic Church*.

## The Catechism

**Q.** Who made us?
**A.** God made us.

**Q.** Who is God?
**A.** God is our Father in heaven.

**Q.** Why did God make us?
**A.** God made us to know him, to love him, and to serve him in this world and to be happy with him in the next.

When asked these questions, every Catholic over the age of 40 will automatically give the very same answers. They learned them by heart in the *Baltimore Catechism*, the definitive religious textbook for all Catholic children in the United States from the end of the last century until the Second Vatican Council in 1960.

**For Heaven's Sake**

You don't have to read theology to be a good Catholic! Remember, Jesus didn't write any theology. He taught the people about God's love through his actions. He fed them, and he healed their illnesses. Through his attention, they were transformed. So if theology isn't your cup of tea, relax and read one of the many stories in the New Testament that tell of the works of Jesus.

The pope officially approved the new version in 1992, calling it *The Catechism of the Catholic Church,* and it's the principal resource for Catholic beliefs.

The *Catechism* is divided into four parts, and each contains a full discussion of beliefs and practices that correspond to its category:

- **The Nicene Creed.** What the Catholic Church believes.

- **The Sacraments.** What the Catholic Church celebrates.

- **The Commandments.** What the Catholic Church lives.

- **The Our Father.** What the Catholic Church prays.

**Your Guardian Angel**

Look beneath the surface for the meanings in the Bible. The teachings of Jesus changed people's lives, and they continue to have this power. He taught in parable form, meaning he told stories that had several meanings. People who have spiritual insight hear the deeper message.

You can check the Catechism for a clear answer to almost any question you might have on Catholic beliefs. Feel free to get a copy, even if you're just learning about the religion. The Catechism isn't difficult to read and is chock-full of helpful information. It is available online at www.scborromeo.org/ccc.htm.

# Theology: Faith Seeking Reason

Theology can be pretty intimidating to read, but when you boil it down to its essence, theology is talking about God. For most of history the Church has relied on classical theology—modeled on Greek philosophy. It uses logical concepts and abstract terms rather than stories or poetry, which is the way Scripture teaches.

St. Anselm, writing in the eleventh century, defined theology as "faith seeking understanding," and in all this time no one has come up with a better description. His definition recognizes that theology is grounded in faith, and recognizes that we are also creatures of reason and need a degree of reason to make faith accessible. The gap between these two worlds must be bridged at least as far as possible. At the same time, despite the great skills of these thinkers and human desire to "know," some faith experiences defy reason—they simply cannot be proven or understood by logic. Catholics treasure the mysteries of their faith, as much as the carefully thought-out beliefs, and regardless of its rich theological tradition, it maintains its essential character as a religion respectful of God's mysteries.

# Classical Theology

Christian theology actually began in the New Testament with the writings of Paul. Paul didn't have firsthand experience with Jesus, so his writings are "one time removed" from the experiences of those who knew Jesus. When Paul talks about what the disciples' experiences mean, he's doing theology. Paul uses philosophical reasoning, as he is speaking to the Greeks and Romans, whose language was formed in the classical way of thinking—rooted in scholars like Plato, Socrates, and Aristotle. It is less dependent on story and more on logical reasoning. As the early Church left its home in Judaism and began developing in the non-Jewish world, it moved away from story and relied more on philosophical statements or dogmas, which is what it does today.

---

**Saints Preserve Us**

**St. Anselm, Doctor of the Church, April 21**

In case you thought metaphysics was a New Age concept, you might be surprised to know St. Anselm, born in 1033, was considered to be a metaphysician. Metaphysics is the systematic investigation of the nature of ultimate reality. In contrast to physics, which tends to be concerned with more practical issues like building bridges or highways, it is concerned with otherworldliness and the nature of being. Anselm is best known for his systematic argument for the existence of God. He entered monastic life at the age of 27 and died in 1109. He has not been declared a patron of anything yet, although he is a Doctor of the Church. Maybe metaphysicians might want to adopt him!

---

Classical theology starts with a particular faith-based assumption about God. It then looks at Scripture for insight into how divine intervention has worked in the world, and then attempts to deduce what all that means to humanity. It did that for the practical purpose of calling the faithful to lead better lives, discerning what God wanted of the people.

A problem with classical theology is that it can build logical argument on top of logical argument until the conclusions are so far removed from anyone's life that they can become meaningless. Critics of classical theology good-naturedly describe this pitfall as a debate over how many angels can dance on the head of a pin! This isn't a fair appraisal, but describes the meaninglessness that "pure reason" divorced from people's lives can attain. Classical theology has been important to the development and understanding of faith, but since the later part of the twentieth century theology has followed a more contemporary approach—it is essentially a bottom-to-top way of looking at theological matters.

## Getting Grounded: Contemporary Theology

Contemporary theology, also known as "contextual" theology, begins with present experiences of the people (the context) and builds principles from there. One of the first expressions of contextual theology began in the middle of the last century in Latin America where it was known as "liberation" theology. It has given voice to many people whose experiences had not been adequately addressed in Church teachings. Today theologies have been written by blacks, women, Native people, and Asians, and even a theology of the environment has been developed using Scripture and Catholic tradition to discern a moral response.

The key difference between classical and contemporary theology is that the contemporary approach is grounded in a community of people who are experiencing a problem and looking to their faith for answers. Rather than building on abstract principles, contemporary theology starts with experience. In doing that it harkens us back to our origins in the teaching experiences of Jesus and the early communities, where a problem was recognized and the followers remembered the essential instruction of Jesus and acted accordingly; e.g., the poor were fed.

# Bargains from the Border: Liberation Theology and Base Communities

Contemporary theology became most prominent midway through the twentieth century in Latin America as a means of identifying the spiritual rights of the oppressed. Vatican II documents on social justice were heavily influenced by the experiences of the post-colonial Church as it was voiced in Latin America. Through the council document "The Church in the Modern World," this method of theology became the mode of contemporary theology.

The creative Latin American engagement with life and theology ignited sparks that flew through the whole Church and society at large. And after 500 years of imposed European traditions overlaying every aspect of their culture from art to theology, Latin America produced two major innovations: *liberation theology* and the birth of a new expression of Church community known as *base communities*.

## The Mirror of Change

In the 1960s, the model for theology was turned upside down. It happened when a crop of young Latin American seminarians studying in Europe met French, Belgian, and German theologians. Here's our rendition of how that meeting might have happened. Imagine for a moment that you are a young man living in a small village. You have attended the mission church and school all your life—serving at Mass, tending to the chores of the missions, and studying hard in addition to working in the fields and performing the endless chores necessary to help your family. Your hard work and arduous studies have finally paid off. You have been selected to attend the university and then experience the exquisite honor of going to Europe to read the works of the Church's greatest theologians.

Your family and the entire village are proud because they have all worked to help you attain this great honor. They probably feel that they may never see you again, but they are rejoicing in the service you will be giving to God and the people and your opportunity to "make something of yourself" by escaping the poverty of the village and the limitations of village life. A hometown boy makes good!

You have been prepared well by your teachers in Mexico City; you know what to expect, and you are looking forward to exploring not only the ancient and beautiful cities of Europe, but also the great classical texts of Augustine, Aquinas, Luther, and Calvin. As the first day finally arrives, you hurry to class along with other young men from all over Latin America. You are yet unaware of the radically different situation that awaits you in the huge mahogany-paneled library of the university. Rather than being given the beautiful, leather-bound, gold-leafed books to read, you and your fellow students have been singled out for a different experience.

You are handed a mirror and are instructed to look into it! What is going on? The teachers want to show you the power of discovering God by looking at yourself. The teachers ask: "What do your experiences tell you of the nature of God?" You wonder, "What could this mean?" You begin your study of theology by looking at your own reality. It is difficult: to look at your life is to face poverty, enslavement, domination, and inferiority. You are not proud to bring these harsh and shameful realities to the light of reflection. You fear looking into the mirror.

In contrast to the traditional theological training, these men in the 1960s received much more. They learned how to work with the people to help them transform their lives through theology. Their new teachers insisted that the authentic study of God needed to start with "the present realities." Reluctantly, the young men began to look into the mirrors they held. They saw their own faces and the faces of their people, the faces of enslavement and poverty. The process had begun. For hundreds of years, when the peasants complained about their condition, the Church taught them that to be poor was to be more "Christ-like." They were told to accept their situation.

Now they were being taught that their needs and the needs of their people were important, to be denied no longer. The reign of God was here and now. The seminarians were encouraged to search the Gospels for the saving message of "good news." They found it in the liberating message of the Gospel. Jesus had worked to end the oppression of the people. The word of God, for these young men and for the people they represented, became the promise of God's liberating action. Liberation theology was born.

These scholars returned to Latin America and, unlike their predecessors, did not impose classical theological teachings on the people. Instead, as their teachers had done, they began to listen to what the people were saying and search for a response in the Gospel. Over and over again, the Gospel told of good news for the poor and promised liberation. As the people realized that God had not abandoned them, the message began to heal the deep spiritual wounds caused by the Church and politics that they had lived with for many centuries.

Latin American theologians have contributed a substantial amount to the Church's social justice teachings, in the form of liberation theology. Their work set the tone for similar theologies to emerge that begin from the experience of the people: black theology, women's theology, Asian theology, as well as ecological theology, a theology that deals with the liberation of Earth itself. These theologies have begun to ask questions and make demands on the Church and the political structures to become more responsive to the needs of the people.

## Church in the 'Hood

Liberation theology is taking place in small, face-to-face gatherings of neighbors, where people talk about their lives and tell their stories. These gatherings are called base communities. The group then examines the Scripture for God's identification with their plight. A group might gather to discuss issues of poverty, disease, or poor wages in their community. The group would then turn to Scripture for instruction, perhaps drawing hope from the Gospel message of feeding the poor. They might also draw on a Church teaching to claim their moral right to a fair wage—reading papal encyclicals and statements from the bishops. Contemporary theology instructs the community to examine the systems and structures that allow the problems to exist.

In this regard, individuals are called to greater faith and to Christian action, and organizations are eventually called to examine the morality of their policies and likewise have the opportunity to grow in faith, and bring faith to action in transformed policies. They find new meaning in what they read and may be inspired to organize and take action.

This is a new sense of Church: a Church that is small and face-to-face, and a Church that expresses salvation not in the future sense of heaven, but in the here and now of everyday life. Base communities are addressing an issue of alienation in the United States parishes caused by large numbers and the desire for more intimate engagement with spirituality and faith, and many parishes are adapting this form.

---

### Epiphanies

Today there are more than a billion Catholics spread all across the globe (70 percent of them in Africa, Latin America, and Asia). There is perhaps no single institution as diverse as the Catholic Church. Yet most of its institutions were formed in the European tradition—this is especially true of its educational institutions. The call for the principle of catholicity today is for the institution to come to terms with its global character, and actively seek conversation with non-European educators, religious leaders, and students.

---

## Prophetically Speaking ...

Contemporary theology recognizes that not all people are having the same experiences. As people talk about their lives, questions arise about how and why they are facing a particular challenge. For example, the experience of multigenerational poverty exists in many communities despite the fact that people work from dawn until dusk. Awareness of this condition raises questions such as: Is it God's will that the people should be poor? Are folks being paid a fair price for their labor? What part does the local government play in the situation? What is the role of the Church in helping or not helping the people? Through this process the people form an economic, political, and spiritual analysis of their situation.

Both classical and contemporary theology speak with a prophetic voice, often calling accepted ways of thinking into question—including Church thinking. Pope John Paul II cautioned against using a Marxist analysis in liberation theology, and directed the followers to consult Scripture and seek solutions based in faith. Today's contemporary theology draws its vision from the Old Testament tradition such as Amos' appeal to "let justice roll down like waters, and righteousness like an ever flowing stream." (Amos 5:24)

# Stirring the Pot of Change

There is always a give and take going on between theologians and bishops, and contemporary theology can and does create tension with religious conservatives.

**Your Guardian Angel**

Theologians write theologies on any of a number of subjects: the nature of God, Jesus Christ, the Trinity, sin, redemption, the nature of the Church, politics, war, the economy, and ecology.

Theologians push at the establishment and when bishops feel they've gone too far, they issue warnings, tightening the reins. It's good to remember that even the highly respected theologian Thomas Aquinas was once silenced by Rome. Catholic thinkers are constantly developing theology; and as Scripture scholarship continues to improve, and more voices are heard, new insight and deeper meaning evolves. As the thousand-year-old definition reminds us, theology helps us understand faith, but it isn't a substitute for it.

Today the Catholic laity has become increasingly involved in studying, writing, and teaching theology, and many of these new theologians are women. Through diversity of experience and expression, Catholics demand more of their faith, and faith grows. However, the pope and the bishops alone are responsible for making the decision regarding official teachings, and as you might suspect, not every theology that is developed makes it.

---

**Saints Preserve Us**

Oscar Romero, Archbishop of San Salvador

Born in 1917, Oscar Romero was archbishop of San Salvador, El Salvador, and is remembered for his bold preaching on behalf of the rights of the peasants. Although he became the country's most respected and popular figure and was nominated for the Nobel Peace Prize, his decisive stand with the poor created a rift between him and the government. In 1980, a rightist death squad assassinated Archbishop Romero while he was preaching at Mass in the chapel of the cancer hospital where he lived. Many regarded his death as martyrdom. His cause has been introduced for canonization.

---

Theologians affect the Church teachings in three ways:

◆ **As communicators.** They listen and articulate the experiences of the people.

◆ **As connectors.** They connect the present-day stories to stories of yesterday—weaving the past to the present point in time.

◆ **As creative thinkers.** They see the "big picture." They listen to the people, and also have a broad knowledge of Church teachings. They connect the voice of the people (experience) with biblical teaching (story) and weave it into Church teaching (tradition).

## The Dynamic Triangle: The People, Theologians, and Bishops

The three groups of people who are involved in living, writing, and teaching contemporary theology are the people, the theologians, and the bishops. Imagine these three groups existing on points of a triangle. Ideally it would be a dynamic relationship, meaning communication would flow along the legs of the triangle between the points. The people's stories would be heard, solutions would be sought, discernment made, and the results woven into Church tradition. However, in reality this dynamism is often short-circuited.

The illustration is a model of its potential vibrancy in a process we call the *dynamic triangle of belief*.

Presently, communication has reverted to the classical one-way and top-down style—more like the ladder described in Chapter 6 and less like the dynamic triangle shown here.

**Your Guardian Angel**

Not every idea in theology becomes a belief of the Church. The theologians' job is to come up with new ideas and their expression; the bishops' job is to sort through them. It's the people who believe them.

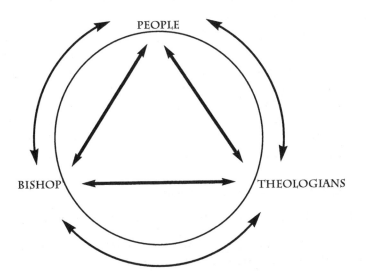

*The Dynamic Triangle of Belief.*

*(Courtesy of Bob O'Gorman and Mary Faulkner)*

The essential statement of faith is that the Holy Spirit exists in every relationship as the "glue" connecting all creation. Wherever people are, the Holy Spirit is present, bringing new insight and divine wisdom. The Holy Spirit connects the segments of the belief triangle, and it holds the potential for divine revelation and transformation for all.

This completes our look at the origins of Catholic tradition, and hopefully puts to rest the idea that Catholics all blindly follow one set of orders. In the next chapter, we'll look at Catholic social teachings and how they engage the world as agents of transformation, working for the reign of God.

## The Least You Need to Know

- There are two primary sources of Catholic teaching: Scripture, and the reflections on Scripture known as Catholic tradition. Unlike Scripture, which is closed, Catholic tradition can and does develop through a slow, prayerful process.

- The pope and bishops have guardianship over the articles of faith known as official Catholic teaching. They maintain unity and stability for this very large and sprawling Church.

- A dynamic relationship exists among the people, theologians, and bishops that feeds in new ideas—its dynamic quality is affected by the tone of Rome, but is ultimately informed by the Holy Spirit.

# The Catholic Church's Best-Kept Secret: Social Justice

## In This Chapter

◆ What's the difference between charity and justice?

◆ Breaking the taboo on dinner party topics: talking about religion, politics, and economics

◆ The nine defining themes of Catholic social justice

◆ How Latin America is at the head of the social justice class

## Lucy's Enlightenment

Lucy, a 15-year-old Catholic, had been saving money for an end-of-summer vacation with friends to the beaches of Southern California. She and her pals had had their hearts set on this trip for 2 years—pending parental approval, which they finally received. Lucy is an active member of St. Michael's youth group. It is here where the girls have become very good friends.

One summer evening the youth minister showed a challenging movie called *Behind the Swoosh: Sweatshops and Social Justice*. The movie immersed Lucy in the journey of a young Catholic soccer star, Jim Keady, as he took a year off and traveled to Indonesia to educate himself about the injustice of a multinational corporation's sweatshop. Introducing the movie, the young man said, "I am here today to tell you about my story …."

Keady had joined the staff of one of the hottest college soccer programs of the '90s fresh off their 1996 NCAA Division I National Championship. Along with coaching, he was studying for a Master's degree in theology and working on a paper examining the moral theology of labor practices. It was then he realized that his university was negotiating a multimillion-dollar contract with one of the corporations he had raised questions about—they were about to supply equipment and funding to all of the university's athletic teams. He spoke about the moral dilemma he was experiencing, saying he "personally did not want to be a billboard for a company whose business practices are unethical and promote injustice" (www.lrna.org/speakers/jimkeady.html).

The film was followed by a discussion and the idea of an "immersion" trip at the end of the summer for the youth group. They would visit a mission run by a group of Mercy Sisters and their Mexican women associates in a Maquiladoras community in Nogales, Mexico, just across the Arizona boarder. Lucy was hooked; she made a decision to abandon her dream vacation and use her savings to make this trip.

Why did Lucy choose to get involved? What gives young Catholics today the impetus to buck the system, even go against peers, and tackle such complex social issues?

Popular images of Catholicism generally include the papal entourages, St. Peter's Basilica, incense, stained-glass windows, and church bells; not much about social justice makes the papers. Lucy comes from a parish with a history of giving to second collections supporting causes such as Catholic Charities, the St. Vincent de Paul Society, and Pax Christi. It is a parish where love of neighbor and love of God connect. A banner in the back of their church quotes Dorothy Day, founder of The Catholic Worker: "We cannot love God unless we love each other." The people of this parish are aware of God's call to build a more just world. This chapter will explore the "best-kept secret" of the Catholic Church.

# Charitable Work and Social Activism

The push for social and economic responsibility by Catholic clergy and laity began in the late nineteenth century in the years following Vatican I. It was the result of two competing forces in the culture. The first was the industrial revolution with the rise of capitalism. The second was atheistic communism. The industrial revolution was creating huge inequity between the rich and poor, depriving workers of the essentials of life. Atheistic communism was threatening the Church's survival in many areas of Europe.

As you know, the Church began as communities dedicated to making people's lives better, and its continued attention to this mission is marked by the hospitals, schools, and other social institutions it has founded. However, by identifying and stating the specifics of social teaching, the Church stepped beyond charity to look at how injustice is built into the structures of society.

## Justice: A Community Effort

There is a difference between charity and justice—and both are necessary. Charity meets the immediate needs of people; justice looks at the structures that cause poverty. Hurricane Katrina provides a good example of how both levels must be addressed. In the wake of the storm, people required immediate assistance with food, shelter, and clothing. These needs were met by an outpouring of charitable donations. However, looking into the inequities that put a higher proportion of the poor at greater risk than others in the population raises questions of structural injustice. As these questions are explored, the answers often go back many generations.

Working for justice involves a group effort and eventually whole communities. It requires long-term commitment—not just a "second" collection. It begins by facing a problem, forming study groups, identifying issues, looking at government policies and practices, crafting public policy, lobbying, and promoting legislation. Charity is absolutely necessary to alleviate pain and suffering in the moment. However, it does not empower people to live full, authentic lives. Social justice addresses inequities in the system—it levels the playing field. The most effective and empowering social justice programs directly engage those who are in need of help in the process, giving them a voice in identifying the problem and in creating solutions.

## Bishop Lobbyists

The U.S. Catholic Bishops maintain an office in Washington not to lobby for special favors for the Church but to influence policy and legislation for low-income families, the homeless, and immigrants. In 1969, the Church established the Catholic Campaign for Human Development. It is organized (paraphrasing its mission statement) for the purpose of transforming lives and communities, focusing steadily on breaking the cycle of poverty in thousands of communities across the United States. The campaign operates with a twofold mandate:

- Funding low-income controlled empowerment projects
- Educating Catholics about the root causes of poverty

This second directive is rooted in the Catholic social tradition of helping people participate in the decisions and actions that affect their lives.

These programs are funded through an annual ("second") collection in Catholic parishes each year. Beyond the empowerment projects, the bishops' efforts have had a major impact in educating Catholics to form a broad approach to social justice—not just helping those in need, but advancing the kingdom. St. Michael parish and Lucy are an example of the fruits of this labor.

---

**Epiphanies**

During 2004, $9 million from the Bishops' Catholic Campaign for Human Development was awarded to 330 projects in 45 states, the District of Columbia, Puerto Rico, and the U.S. Virgin Islands. These projects include rural cooperatives in Appalachia, adult education for migrant workers, and community-based micro-enterprises that provide jobs in areas of high unemployment. Being Catholic is not a consideration in making these grants, nor is this a means of "churching" people but of empowering people to work on a local level to make changes in their lives for the possibility of authentic human development.

---

# Religion and Politics: Beyond Polite Conversation

A contemporary guide, *How to Make Polite Conversation at a Cocktail Party*, reminds us of the standard social wisdom regarding religion and politics saying, "Many people like to talk about pets, stocks, food, houses, and movie stars. Most won't really love to discuss salaries, politics, religion, or computers." Religion and politics top the list of controversial topics to be avoided in polite society, and most Americans heed the warnings and steer clear of them for fear of giving offence or inciting argument.

## God and Caesar

However, the connection among religion, economics, and politics has been a major topic for the Church from early on. When Jesus was questioned about it he politely responded, "render to Caesar what is Caesar's and to God what is God's."

(Luke 20:20–26) These words seem to have left the Church and society scratching their heads ever since. Some feel religion has no place in politics and they interpret the U.S. Constitution's separation of church and state that way. Others feel that matters of public policy and economics have intrinsic moral dimensions to which religion can and must speak. It would seem foolish to keep discipleship and citizenship in separate containers. Should not society be guided by compassionate principles that apply to all religions and cultures? Rigorous debate has to include social ethics. However, imposing a religion on others never works. It may not be a clearly defined line, but when it is crossed it becomes obvious quite quickly. A lot depends on the intentions of those who speak out.

---

### Epiphanies

Martin Luther King Jr. gave a sermon in which he talked about our "Drum Major Instinct"—the inborn need to be seen and recognized for our importance is something we all share. Our Drum Major Instinct can get us in trouble as individuals, as a nation, and as religious people. If we don't acknowledge it and keep it on track, it can easily be co-opted by worldly pursuits such as fame, fortune, and glory. He goes on to say, "Jesus gave us a new norm of greatness. If you want to be important—wonderful. If you want to be recognized—wonderful. If you want to be great—wonderful. But recognize that he who is greatest among you shall be your servant. *(Amen)* That's a new definition of greatness." *(Delivered at Ebenezer Baptist Church, Atlanta, Georgia, on February 4, 1968)*

---

We are always dealing with the essential human dilemma imposed by body and soul. As Martin Luther King Jr. pointed out, we all have that "Drum Major" instinct—that inborn desire to be important—to lead the parade. While a crusading spirit clouds what is needed for wise government, religion does offer politics and economics a vision of ideals. For the most part religion's highest function is to raise the issues, offer guidance, and call people to honesty and to their hearts in applying their ethics and values. The Catholic bishops have heard the call and answered it in this way, as you'll read in this chapter.

## Empowering the Laity

The most contemporary council statements of the Church on this relationship between discipleship and citizenship comes from Vatican II, in which it affirms the need to maintain a "rightful independence of earthly affairs" ("The Church in the Modern World," #36), limiting the Church's own direct control in matters of politics and economics. However, it calls the laity to take their role in relating religion and politics, teaching:

> "Let the lay [people] not imagine that pastors are always such experts, that to every problem that arises, however complicated, they can readily give a concrete solution, or even that such is their mission." ("The Church in the Modern World," #43)

So the Church calls the people to involve themselves in the messy world of politics and modern culture and become servants of the underserved, and thereby improve today's world. The Second Vatican Council offers the image of being on "pilgrimage," deeply committed to the road they walk and guided by the light of the vision of the Kingdom of God they are approaching.

# The Nine Themes in Catholic Social Teaching

The body of documents that make up Catholic social teaching have been written and circulated primarily in the last 100 years—beginning in 1891. There have been 12 so far. In addition, the U.S. Catholic bishops have issued two major statements on social issues, "The Challenge of Peace: God's Promise and Our Response" (1983) and in "Economic Justice for All: Pastoral Letter on Catholic Social Teaching and the U.S. Economy" (1986). We talked about how these letters make their way to the people through sermons and study groups earlier.

Drawing on the work of Thomas Massaro (*Living Justice: Catholic Social Teachings in Action*), here are nine central themes that emerge from these documents.

# Major Documents of Modern Catholic Social Teaching

| Latin title | English translation | Year of publication | Source | Major challenge it addressed | Major new message or idea |
|---|---|---|---|---|---|
| Rerum Novarum | The Condition of Labor | 1891 | Pope Leo XIII | Industrialization, urbanization, poverty | "Family Wage"; workers' rights |
| Quadragesimo-Anno | After Forty Years, or The Recon-Subsidiarity | 1931 | Pope Pius XI | Great Depression, Communism, and fascist dictatorships | Subsidiarity as a guide to government |
| Mater et Magistra | Christianity and Social Progress | 1961 | Pope John XXIII | Technological advances | Global justice between rich and poor nations |
| Pacem in Terris | Peace on Earth | 1963 | Pope John XXIII | Arms race, the threat of nuclear war | A philosophy of human rights and social responsibility |
| Gaudium et Spes | Pastoral constitution on the Church in the Modern World | 1965 | Second Vatican Council | Younger generations questioning traditional values | Church must scrutinize external "signs of the times" |
| Popolorum Progressio | The Development of Peoples | 1967 | Pope Paul VI | Widening gap between rich and poor nations | "Development is a new word for peace" |
| Octogesima Adveniens | A Call to Action on the 80th Anniversary of Rerum Novarum | 1971 | Pope Paul VI | Urbanization marginalizes vast multitudes | Lay Catholics must focus on political action to combat injustices |

*continues*

## Major Documents of Modern Catholic Social Teaching (continued)

| Latin title | English translation | Year of publication | Source | Major challenge it addressed | Major new message or idea |
|---|---|---|---|---|---|
| Justitia in Mundo | Justice in the World | 1971 | Synod of Bishops | Structural injustices and oppression inspire liberation movements | "Justice … is a constitutive of the preaching of the Gospel" |
| Evangelii Nuntiandi | Evangelization in the Modern World | 1975 | Pope Paul VI | Cultural problems of atheism, secularism, consumerism | The salvation promised by Jesus offers liberation from all oppression |
| Laborem Exercens | On Human Work | 1981 | Pope John Paul II | Capitalism and Communism treat workers as mere instruments of production | Work is the key to the "social question" and to human dignity |
| Sollicitudo rei Socialis | On Social Concern | 1987 | Pope John Paul II | Persistent under-development, division of world into blocs | "Structures of sin" are responsible for global injustices |
| Centesimus Annus | On the Hundredth Anniversary of Rerum Novarum | 1991 | Pope John Paul II | Collapse of Communism in Eastern Europe | Combat consumeristic greed in new "knowledge economy" |

*Major Documents of Modern Catholic Social Teaching, as it appears on pages 78–79 in Living Justice by Thomas Massaro (Sheed & Ward, an imprint of Rowman Littlefield Publishing, Inc., 2000)—used with permission.*

Additional information on Catholic Social Justice can be found at www.osjspm.org/cst/themes.htm

Following are the nine themes, along with a brief description.

## The Dignity of Every Person and Human Rights

Belief in the inherent dignity of the human person is the foundation of all Catholic social teaching. Human life is sacred, and the dignity of the human person is the starting point of a moral vision for society. This principle is grounded in the idea that we are made in the image of God and God is the ultimate source of our rights. God created us as the human family and these rights are located within our life together in community.

Being made in God's image means we are each the clearest reflection of God among us. He made us to be free from all slavery and exploitation from the earliest time of our conception to the last moments of a natural death. And so the Catholic Church takes an uncompromising position on slavery, abortion, euthanasia, and capital punishment.

## Solidarity, Common Good, and Participation

The Catholic approach to human justice is grounded in the absolute sanctity of creation, and considers the entire web of relationships that connect us to God, which include the natural environment, people, governments, and local communities. We are one human family. How we organize our society directly affects human dignity and the capacity of individuals to thrive or to suffer; and it either compromises us as humans or allows us to flourish. The obligation to "love our neighbor" has an individual dimension, but it also requires a broader social commitment including areas of economics, politics, law, employment, education, and more.

Our responsibilities to each other cross national, racial, economic, and ideological differences. Authentic development must be full human development, avoiding the extremes of underdevelopment on the one hand, and "super development" on the other. Accumulating material goods and technical resources will be unsatisfactory and debasing if there is no respect for the moral, cultural, and spiritual dimensions of the person.

Authentic human development requires equal participation. To be excluded from playing a significant role in the community is a serious injustice—it impedes full expression and full human development. This means restricted voting rights as well as race or gender discrimination in education and employment constrict full political and economic participation.

## Family Life

Family, whatever form it takes, represents the most basic unit of community. It is that intimate sphere where the human person is first nurtured into full life—biological, intellectual, and spiritual. Life is first of all nurtured in this social core. Thus the well-being of our entire society depends on healthy and stable family life.

In line with this value the Church lobbies for wise public policies, such as social welfare programs, adequate day care, medical leave, and other laws that contribute to the health of families.

> **S'ter Says**
>
> **Subsidiarity** means that government should be performed at the lowest level possible that can adequately do the job. Problems are best solved in the place where they arise. People are encouraged to resolve their conflicts themselves without referring them to higher authority.

**Epiphanies**

Abraham Lincoln expressed this notion of subsidiarity when he said:

The legitimate object of government is to do for a community of people whatever they need to have done, but cannot do at all or cannot do well, for themselves in their separate and individual capacities.

## Subsidiarity and the Proper Role of Government

The principle of *subsidiarity* means that government should be performed at the lowest level possible, as long as it can adequately do the job. Solutions that are closest to the people affected and which employ the smallest groupings and processes are to be preferred. If the needs in question can't successfully be met at the lower level, higher levels of government need to intervene.

The government has a positive moral responsibility. It is an instrument to promote human dignity, protect human rights, and build the common good. All people have a right and a responsibility to participate in political institutions so that government can achieve its proper goals.

The Church uses its voice to champion civil liberties and stand up against the intrusion of government as "Big Brother," spying on and intruding into the areas of community organization that the local people have the right and authority over.

## Property Ownership in Modern Society: Rights and Responsibilities

This principle balances two competing values in our society: the common good and the right to individual ownership of property. Catholic teaching opposes economic systems that hold back full human development, such as unresponsive regimes and those inspired by Marxism. At the same time it rejects the notion that a free market automatically produces justice. Competition and free markets are useful elements of economic systems; however, markets need to be kept within limits. Many needs and goods cannot be satisfied by the market system—meaning justice cannot be achieved by relying entirely on free market forces. When this happens, it's the task of the government and of all society to intervene and ensure that these needs are met.

## The Dignity of Work, Rights of Workers, and Support for Labor Unions

The economy must serve people, not the other way around. Work is intrinsic to being human, and through our work we can express our human dignity and achieve authentic human development. It is through our labor that we fulfill our vocation to become co-creators with God in the development of the world. All workers have a right to productive work, to decent and fair wages, and to safe working conditions. They also have a fundamental right to organize and join unions. Without this ability to combine their voices, workers are at the mercy of more powerful employers who can take advantage of them.

The Catholic Church supports an adequate minimum wage, safety and heath regulations of the workplace, and pension plans.

## Colonialism and Economic Development

Hunger and disease in any part of the world is a concern for all of us, as it tears at the web of creation. Catholic social teaching calls people to recognize, apply moral judgment, and take action against the causes of global poverty and underdevelopment. Catholic social teachings identify vast disparities between rich and poor. It boldly lays the problem at the feet of the sinful structures of world trade and finance that keep a majority of the people from their rightful opportunities for authentic human development.

Pope Paul VI's teachings centered on land reform in the Third World, equitable balance of production and exports, and aid to put more tools for self-improvement in the hands of underdeveloped peoples. The pope was not issuing a call for gifts but insisting on access to credit to make income-generating activities possible as a human right, and providing tools such as sewing machines for women's cooperatives in Africa and farm machinery for Central American villages.

Pope John Paul II followed suit as all three of his social encyclicals concerned global injustice and the uneven distribution of resources. His teachings made clear the crushing burden of international debt, the arms race, and concerns for a new economic domination, "neo-colonialism." The pope fingered two social sins that are at the bottom of misdistribution of resources and the inability to foster authentic global human development: the "all-consuming desire for profit" and the "thirst for power."

## Peace and Disarmament

Catholic social teaching is based in the absolute relationship between peace and justice, stating peace is the fruit of justice and is dependent upon right order among human beings. It promotes peace as a positive, action-oriented concept. In Pope John Paul II's words, "Peace is not just the absence of war. It involves mutual respect and confidence between peoples and nations. It involves collaboration and binding agreements."

Contemporary social justice teachings of the Church challenge the applicability of the age-old teaching, "the just-war theory." In a nuclear age it is hard to see how the theory's requirement assuring against disproportionate response and the targeting of civilians can be met given the current set of weapons in the world's arsenals. Pope John Paul II did not hesitate to scold the world powers for their premature resort to force in both the Gulf wars.

## Option for the Poor and Vulnerable

The term "the preferential option for the poor" emerged from the Latin American Bishops Conference in 1977. In 1987 Pope John Paul II entered it into the theological Canon, making it "gospel" in the Catholic vocabulary. In doing this he reversed the centuries-old perception of the Church's alignment with the wealthy landholders, a stand that had severely hindered its witness in the full human development of the poor. In identifying with the concerns of the poor, the Church interprets its entire mission as one of service to those in need of the means of authentic human development.

# Dorothy Day and The Catholic Worker Movement

Present-day teaching on world peace owes a debt to a great American Catholic witness to peace, The Catholic Worker, founded in 1933 by Dorothy Day and Peter Maurin; it is the flagship of Catholic peace policy.

Dorothy M. Day, who lived from 1897 to 1980, was an icon of the Catholic social faith in the twentieth century. A journalist, she converted to Catholicism, and her belief centered on a philosophy that stressed the value and dignity of each individual person. She founded an organization she called The Catholic Worker in which she attempted to make this ideal available to all who desired it. It is unlikely that any community was ever less structured than The Catholic Worker. Each community is autonomous. There is no board of directors, no sponsor, no system of governance, no endowment, no paychecks, no pension plans. Since Dorothy Day's death, there has been no central leader. The Catholic Worker was a Catholic presence that announced a concern for the poor and oppressed. In 1933, Day sold *The Catholic Worker* newspaper in New York's Union Square for a penny a copy. It has been in constant production since that time and is still sold at a penny a copy! Embracing voluntary poverty, Day worked tirelessly, establishing houses for the immediate relief of those in need and farming communes where each person worked to his ability and received according to his need. She modeled her organizations on early Christian communities. Day and her movement were a call to U.S. Catholics to reconnect to the Church history of caring for others.

Perhaps Day is best known for her proclamation of Catholic pacifism as the ideal response to war. Nonviolence was integral to her position, and her efforts at pacifism encouraged Catholics to change the social order by performing direct, albeit nonviolent, actions on behalf of peace and social justice. The pacifism of Dorothy Day and The Catholic Worker were at the heart of the American Catholic peace movement during the Vietnam War. The Catholic Worker movement spawned additional Catholic movements such as The Catholic Peace Fellowship and Pax Christi, U.S.A.

Dorothy Day reflected the Catholic's personal obligation of looking after the needs of fellow human beings as focused in the works of mercy. The works of mercy are seven charitable acts encouraged by the Church:

- ◆ Feed the hungry.
- ◆ Give drink to the thirsty.
- ◆ Clothe the naked.
- ◆ Visit the imprisoned.

- Give shelter to the homeless.
- Visit the sick.
- Bury the dead.

## Dorothy Day's Legacy for Today's Catholic Worker

The Catholic Worker has served as a prototype to many movements for social transformation in the Church. Here are a few that are currently transforming culture and might be of interest to you:

- **The Eighth Day Center.** In Chicago, various religious orders band together at this center to document major economic and political issues on a national as well as global scale. Similar centers exist all over the world. As international organizations, these centers are able to network broadly, quickly passing on information that will be used to bring about policy changes and create legislation in worldwide governments.

- **Volunteer groups.** One of the Church's best-kept secrets is that more than 300 Catholic organizations, such as the Jesuit Volunteer Corps, recruit college graduates for a year or two of service. Volunteers take their services into the community in the form of education in inner-city schools, job training, and finding housing for the homeless. At the same time, the volunteers live a community life of prayer and poverty, transforming their understanding of what it means to be in the world. More than 100,000 Catholics are involved in this work.

- **The Jesuit Center of Concern.** A policy think tank in Washington, D.C., the Jesuit Center researches the social implications of proposed legislation and thus provides a voice for justice in policy making.

- **The Wall Street Group.** Similar to the Eighth Day Center, Catholic religious orders have formed a Wall Street group that monitors the investments of their orders. They use their power as shareholders to call for corporate responsibility in the companies they have invested in.

# Conclusion: The Church Today

Before leaving this chapter, let's check back in on Lucy, the young woman who gave up her summer vacation to the beach to immerse herself in the lives of the people in

Nogales, Mexico. Lucy had a firsthand encounter with U.S./Mexican economic policy inequities. She witnessed the Mexican workers as they assembled goods at the U.S. factories for the U.S. market, at Mexican labor prices! As a result, Lucy is now working for changes in U.S. policy. She is typical of the youth in the Church who have responded to Pope John Paul's vision for them. They commit themselves to a life of service for the reign of God.

Some have voiced concern about the future of the Catholic Church. The radical changes at Vatican II left many disenchanted. Then came the sex scandals and cover-up by bishops, taking a further toll. Adding to the turmoil, the split between progressives and conservatives has created an ecclesial "red state"/"blue state" battle that defies gerrymandering! Thus, an outsider might be inclined to predict the Church's demise. But the insider knows that working for social justice is not only the best-kept secret, it's the best weapon against division as well. When Catholics roll up their sleeves, the slogan "Where doctrine divides, pursuing social justice unites" prevails. Its spirit is life-giving, and its mission statement—"let justice roll down like living water"—uniting.

## The Least You Need to Know

- Catholic social teachings are a call for justice in the world and a force for renewal in the Church. "The preferential option for the poor" identifies the Church's entire mission as one of service to those in need.

- The past 100 years has produced the most concentrated new teaching in Catholic history.

- The U.S. Catholic Church maintains governmental lobbies in the U.S. capital and in each of the states, not to promote its own welfare but as a witness of social justice.

- Pope John Paul II produced the most social teaching of any pope, and inspired a new generation of Catholics.

- The themes of Catholic social teachings are founded on the acknowledgment of the inherent dignity of every human person.

# The Teachings of the Church: Moving Beyond Sin

## In This Chapter

◆ Learn all about sin and forgiveness

◆ Making the case for virtue

◆ How sin continues to be a hot topic in the Church

◆ Appreciate the many teachings in the "seamless garment of life"

It's been said that sinning is easier to do in Catholicism than any other religion because Catholics have so many beliefs, rules, and regulations. For many years the Catholic Church focused its teaching and preaching on sin by listing every requirement or belief, and backing that up with the consequences each belief carried. "You better or else …" is often the first thing people think of when they hear the word *Catholic*, and this preoccupation with sin has been destructive.

Post–Vatican II Church morality emphasizes peoples' basic goodness and builds on it. It focuses on helping members foster biblical virtues by promoting loving, peaceful relationships and working together to bring the reign of God forward for more people to enjoy.

**For Heaven's Sake** _____

Don't think the Church is getting soft on sin! This is not the case. Instead, the Church focuses on developing virtue as a first line of defense against sin rather than using fear of punishment as a deterrent.

# Sin: Missing the Mark

Sin is a religious term. In the Old Testament, sin is understood as a break in the covenant relationship with God. It's the result of not following the will of God as we know it in our hearts. Although sin is often thought of as a violation against God, it is actually a violation against ourselves, our neighbors, and all creation. Most often, when the term *sin* appears in the New Testament, it is used in the phrase "forgiveness of sin."

In the past, Catholics saw sin primarily as disobedience to God and to "lawful superiors." Moral reflection is no longer centered on personal shortcomings but rather on the unconditional love of God. This change shifts moral reasoning from a reactive stance to a proactive one.

The new theology of sin teaches that sin enslaves, with the understanding that we are most God-like in our freedom. It is based on the belief that God wants us to live creatively and be free to grow to our full potential. Sin blocks our freedom to develop fully. Present teaching encourages Catholics to look at a wider context of social justice, because injustice limits the human spirit. If anyone is not free, no one is free. Catholics are encouraged to work for their own liberation and that of all others. Sin is that which violates human dignity and blocks freedom for others or ourselves.

## Categories of Sins: Specks and Logs

Traditionally, there were two different kinds of sin in the Catholic Church: mortal and venial. An analogy might be that a mortal sin corresponds to a felony, and a venial sin is like a misdemeanor. The biblical references to the difference in the magnitude of sin come from two passages. Matthew 23:24 describes the difference between a gnat and a camel; Matthew 7:3 discusses the difference between a speck and a log.

Mortal refers to the death a sin brings to the soul. It constitutes a serious rupture in a person's relationship to God and to the community. In order to restore this relationship, those who have committed a mortal sin go to confession and work with their confessor to heal the damages caused by their actions. Three things are necessary for a sin to be classified as mortal:

- It is a serious offense.

- The person must have full knowledge of the seriousness of it.

- It is committed with full consent of the will and with no coercion.

Venial sins are described as lesser offenses. However, any sin, like an illness in its early stages, can lead to more serious consequences if left unchecked. Paying attention to venial sins helps people locate troublesome patterns within themselves.

> **For Heaven's Sake**
>
> Guilt is a fire alarm. It tells you all is not right in your life. Find out what your part is in the problem. Forgiveness requires taking moral responsibility for your actions, and making the adjustments necessary to live in accord with what you know is right. When the fire is out, turn off the alarm!

Newer approaches to understanding sin should not lead to laxity, but instead to a deeper sensitivity to the human condition and the development of compassion. When the definition of sin is broadened to include all the ways in which we might be refusing God by limiting our engagement with life, it is not easy to draw up a list of sins as was once the practice. Although the commandments and the laws of the Church are still part of the process of moral discernment (the process of identifying right and wrong), they in no way represent the whole picture. There's more on this topic in Chapter 11, in the discussion of the sacrament of Reconciliation.

> **Your Guardian Angel**
>
> Check your terms. Guilt is feeling bad about something you've done. Shame is feeling bad about yourself. There is a big difference!

---

**Epiphanies**

The Bible often teaches with parables, stories, and metaphors, so the biblical images of everlasting fire are poetic warnings of what it would be like to be without God. Biblical images of hell abound: Matthew calls it a fiery furnace where people will "weep and gnash their teeth." (Matthew 13:42, 25, 30, 41) Mark says it is like Gehenna with its unquenchable fire. Mark (9:43) and Luke (16:19–31) tell the story of the rich man that explains hell as a place of eternal suffering with no alleviation of pain. Finally, the Book of Revelation (20:13) speaks of the "pool of fire."

---

# Human Sexuality: "Male and Female He Created Them"

Human sexuality refers to the state of being sexual, being in the world either as a female or a male. It includes anatomy, behavioral characteristics, bonding, and reproduction. Sexuality is a fundamental aspect of personal identity. Our sexuality enters into all aspects of our life and all personal interactions with one another and all aspects of self-expression and activity. There are no asexual or non-sexual human beings.

**Your Guardian Angel**

Think of your sexuality as part of your spirituality. God created human beings as male and female. Sexuality, then, is a gift of God. Sexuality and spirituality cannot be separated. Both are calls to intimacy, and therefore two sides of the same coin.

The role of the Church regarding sexuality is to help the faithful understand their sexuality and act in sexually responsible ways. This is an ongoing process of assessment and discernment that Church teachers have addressed from the earliest times. Increasingly in recent times, laypeople have added their voices to these teachings.

Vatican II called for the renewal of Church teaching in light of new knowledge from the physical and social sciences. In this section, we'll look at some of the issues in human sexuality that Catholics are struggling with today: birth control, homosexuality, and celibacy.

## Birth Control: The Church's Big Headache

Contraception refers to the ways in which men and women can prevent formation of a new life as a result of sexual intercourse. The Church's moral stand on contraception is based on important values regarding sexuality. One value is propagation, or having children and in that way participating with God in the continuous creation of life. Until the twentieth century, the Church rarely acknowledged other sexual values. All attempts to block sexual action from the intention to procreate were considered wrong, considered to be against *natural law.*

Vatican II introduced important changes on sexuality, and the mutual self-giving that is possible through sexual intercourse became a key value. Teachings began to recognize that sexual intercourse strengthens the unity and life-giving nature of the union between couples, and also recognized that married couples had both the right and duty to limit the size of their family to correspond to their situation and promote the quality of life.

Following Vatican II, Pope Paul VI gave a strict interpretation of these teachings in an encyclical titled *Humanae Vitae* (Latin for "of human life"), declaring, "Each and every marriage act must remain open to the transmission of life." *Humanae Vitae* set the Church spinning. Questions from bishops, theologians, pastors, and congregations abounded—and many still have not been answered.

Abstinence in rhythm with a woman's fertile cycle is the only acceptable form of birth control. The rhythm method, as practiced in the past, was often called "Vatican roulette" as an indication of how well it worked. However, sociological data reveal that approximately 80 percent of practicing Catholics do not follow the Church's official and authoritative teachings on birth control.

The issue of contraception continues to divide the Catholic Church. Many Catholics choose to employ artificial contraception, and report that their parish priests support them in the decisions they make in this matter, despite the Church's teaching.

## Natural Family Planning: It's Not Your Grandma's Calendar

There are young Catholics today who use Natural Family Planning (NFP), a more complex form of the Church-sanctioned "rhythm" method of birth control. This method is also known as the "sympto-thermal method." The woman observes and charts her temperature upon awakening, along with the consistency of cervical mucus and changes in the position and texture of the cervix. The charts allow couples to know with some degree of accuracy when the woman is fertile and thus when to abstain. The time of abstinence can be 7 or 8 days. This process, much more involved and accurate than the old rhythm method, is estimated to be 97 percent accurate before ovulation, the fertile portion of a woman's cycle, and 99 percent accurate after ovulation.

An added benefit to couples who use NFP is having fewer chemicals and preservatives in their bodies, such as result from the birth control pill. Those who have side effects or can't take the pill along with other medications also can benefit from it. Data also indicate that couples who use NFP have a divorce rate of only 5 percent—far below the national average. A couple was quoted as saying, "You have to communicate when you do this, and that seems to be one of the biggest stumbling blocks for couples. This requires you to talk about something very personal, which seems to make it easier to talk about other things."

## Homosexuality: Yes and No

For the most part, the Church has taken the position of "love the sinner, hate the sin" toward homosexuality. According to Church beliefs, to be a homosexual is not in itself sinful, but to practice homosexuality is considered immoral. The Church bases its belief in Scripture (Genesis 19 and 20:13, Romans 1:24–27, 1 Corinthians 6:9–10, and 1 Timothy 1:9–10) and moral tradition based on natural law reasoning. Natural law reasoning is a process the Church uses to examine human acts according to the "nature of things."

People within the Church have attempted to propose a Catholic approach to homo-sexuality. This approach would remain faithful to the traditional teaching about the two goals of sexuality (procreation and love) and at the same time be a genuine response to the nature of homosexuality.

They make the argument that because a change of orientation is out of the question (it is generally accepted that a person does not deliberately choose their sexual orien-tation), homosexuals should be given the same moral choices as heterosexuals: celibacy or permanent exclusive partnership. They argue that procreation can take place in adoption or other ways to give of self for the nurture of life in another. The Church, however, has not altered its position. Although it mandates understanding and compassion toward homosexuals, it holds a firm line against them acting on their sexual inclinations.

The Catechism of the Catholic Church (article 2357), while condemning homosexual acts and upholding its traditional teaching that "homosexual acts are intrinsically dis-ordered. They are contrary to the natural law. They close the sexual act to the gift of life." It concludes that "Its psychological genesis remains largely unexplained." Here the Church carefully distinguishes its condemnation of homosexual activity from a negative judgment of the "unexplained" orientation of homosexual persons.

Pope Benedict XVI has issued a document declaring that men who have "deep-rooted homosexual tendencies" or who carry on a "gay culture" may not be admitted to the seminary to become Roman Catholic priests. The document notes that if a man had "transitory" homosexual tendencies that have been "overcome" for at least 3 years, he may be admitted to the seminary. The document went on to say that this applies only to those seeking ordination and it would not be used to "defrock" men already ordained who do not meet this ruling. This ruling goes beyond the Church's practice of the last century that only required celibacy of all men desiring to be priests, regardless of sexual orientation.

The pope is concerned about the Church's already tarnished image and mindful of the splits that have been happening in the Anglican Church over the ordination of homosexuals.

---

### Epiphanies

St. Paul, writing in the early years of the Church, urged his congregations to consider celibacy. Scholars now tell us the reason for Paul's teaching was the Church's belief at that time that the end of the world was coming soon. Therefore, it was not the time to bring new life into the world. Additionally, for Paul, celibacy provided him unrestricted opportunity to be of service to the Church.

---

# The Seamless Garment

Cardinal Joseph L. Bernardin of Chicago called for the use of a consistent ethic of human life. This ethic would be applied to the issues of abortion, capital punishment, modern warfare, euthanasia, and socio-economic issues of food and shelter for all. His teaching recognizes the relationship between these social issues and the obligation to respect human life and dignity in all arenas. According to this principle, abortion and euthanasia (pro-life issues) and social ethics (human rights, peace, social justice, and capital punishment) must all be viewed in the same light. In other words, Cardinal Bernardin's teachings ask for moral consistency in what he has called the *seamless garment of life*. Let's take a look at each of these issues.

### S'ter Says

The **seamless garment of life** refers to Jesus' robe, which legend has it was seamless. In applying this ethic, one recognizes that protection of life is the basis for determining the morality of war, capital punishment, and abortion. In other words, under this ethic, it would be difficult to be in favor of capital punishment and against abortion.

# Euthanasia: Say No to Dr. Death

*Euthanasia* comes from the Greek and means "good death." Today, we use it to refer to intentionally ending the life of a terminally ill person. Other terms used to describe euthanasia are mercy killing, assisted dying, and recently, aid in dying. The 1980 Vatican *Declaration on Euthanasia* defines it as "an action or omission which of itself or by intention causes death, in order that all suffering may in this way be eliminated."

The issue of euthanasia boils down to the difference between taking an action to bring about death versus allowing a person to die naturally. *Killing* is a human act carrying moral responsibility for causing death. *Allowing to die* refers to withholding or withdrawing treatment so that the illness can run its course, the outcome of which may be death.

The Church teaches that one is not morally obliged to use "extraordinary means" to stay alive, for example, to have surgery, or chemotherapy, or radiation, or be force-fed, or live on a ventilator, or seek a transplant. All of these can be seen as "extraordinary." One is only bound to the ordinary: shelter, comfort, and food and water if eating and drinking are possible. The capacity of modern technology to ward off death brings more pressure to individuals, families, and caregivers; this and their inability to accept the inevitability of death are factors that contribute to the choosing of extraordinary and often futile treatment.

The Catholic Church recognizes life as a precious gift, humans as mortal, and God as supreme. Euthanasia violates the sanctity of life and the sovereignty of God by assuming ownership over life. The Church views the legalization of euthanasia as a threat to the common good; its teaching affirms the role of health-care providers as stewards of healing and caring. It upholds the hospice movement as a model for health care. Hospice sends health-care professionals into the homes of terminally ill people with the objective of making the people as comfortable as possible while they die a natural death without prolonging or hastening the process.

# Can War Be Justified?

The Just War Doctrine claims that, despite its destructive character, war is morally justifiable in certain circumstances and limitations. The doctrine has its roots in the Hebrew Scriptures and the Greek and Roman world. Augustine formulated it in the 400s when he stated that war is love's response to a neighbor threatened by force. Thomas Aquinas in the 1200s claimed the legitimacy of war waged in self-defense. These teachings came before the rise of modern warfare.

The Just War Doctrine has two purposes: first, it is a reminder that war is always a moral matter, not simply a political one. It requires serious consideration. Second, although the doctrine can judge certain circumstances for war as just, violence must be limited. The doctrine recognizes that regardless of its justification, war is a serious matter and must be mourned.

The eight criteria used to determine a just war are the following:

- ◆ It must be a just cause. Traditionally, to be a just cause, a war must have as its goal the protection of people from unjust attack, the restoration of rights that have been taken away, or the restoration of just political order.

- ◆ It must be led by a competent authority, which means that declarations of war must be made by competent authorities following established criteria, or due process. This principle has recently come under scrutiny.

- ◆ It must be a last resort after all possible peaceful solutions have been explored.

- ◆ It must involve comparative justice to remind both sides that neither is absolutely just.

- ◆ Its ends must be proportionate to its means: even a just war for a just cause cannot be pursued if the evils to be suffered significantly outweigh the good.

- ◆ It must have a right intention, which means it cannot be motivated by vindictiveness or hatred, but must be for the purpose of establishing a better and more peaceful existence.

- ◆ There must be a probability of success; if there is no possibility of winning and many people will be killed in the process, then it cannot be a just war.

The Just War Doctrine includes an additional principle of right conduct within war. Justice must rule conduct within war. Attacks against civilians are forbidden, and there must be ethical treatment of the wounded or surrendered.

The Just War Doctrine has been an important part of Catholic moral teaching. However, because of the development of nuclear weapons of mass destruction, theologians are now questioning whether war can ever be justified. In 1983, a pastoral letter by U.S. bishops, *The Challenge of Peace: God's Promise and Our Response*, reaffirmed the Just War Doctrine, but with the additional comments that in no cases could nuclear war, even limited nuclear war, be justified.

 **For Heaven's Sake**

Church teaching about war has said that because of the enormity of the destruction, nuclear war is not to be used under any circumstances.

The matter of establishing competent authority has also come under scrutiny. Many are unwilling to give the state the authority to determine whether justice is being served by war. Church teachers realize that governments are prone to interpret the situations in their favor, using the Doctrine of Just War to justify war. It falls to the Church community as a dedicated and informed body to be a voice for peace against the strong cultural presumption of violence as a solution.

# Abortion: When Life Begins

Few issues are more controversial or emotionally and morally charged than *abortion*. In this discussion, we're defining abortion as the intentionally induced termination of a pregnancy. Abortion is legal in some form in most countries in the world.

The controversy surrounding abortion hinges on identifying when life begins. At this time, scientists disagree regarding this very important point. The Church finds the most reasonable and prudent position is to accept conception, the moment when the sperm fertilizes the egg, as the beginning of human life. The Catholic Church opposes unrestricted abortion for the following three reasons:

- The Church sees God as the author of life and views the conception of a child as a gift to be welcomed into the community. The Catholic response to pregnancy is to care for both the mother and child.

- There is no clear scientific agreement to determine when life begins. The Church has taken the stand that it begins at the moment of conception.

- Because life is sacred and because there is no reason to believe it does not begin at conception, the fundamental value of life must be awarded the soul in the womb.

The Church believes no one possesses the right to take the life of the fetus. Although the right to choose is an important concept within the Church, it exists only before conception. Cases of pregnancy due to rape or to coercion or ignorance pose difficult problems for Church teaching. Objections posed by theologians and others look at the absolutist nature of the abortion rule, pointing out that it does not meet a norm of Catholic theology—that of critical nuance. Nuance means that circumstances count when weighing moral decisions.

The Church recognizes the difficulty of many women who are faced with the painful decision of whether or not to terminate a pregnancy. A seamless garment of life teaching about abortion would have us look at the social, cultural, and economic issues affecting the unequal status of women in the analysis. However, the official teaching remains that the only time abortion is permitted is when it is necessary to preserve the mother's life, which is covered under the concept of the lesser of two evils.

## Capital Punishment: A Call to Reconciliation

Catholic teachings hold to the sacredness of human life and teach that it must be respected from conception to death. Although Catholic teaching allows life to be taken through the Just War Doctrine and in cases of self-defense, Church leaders have increasingly brought the wisdom of capital punishment into question. The growing sense of the image of God present in all people presents a distinct spiritual obstacle to taking a life, even where serious injustice has occurred. Arguments against capital punishment are based in the following religious principles:

◆ Jesus' command to love your enemies and to be reconciled to them calls on society to find spiritual solutions.

◆ The Gospels provide bountiful evidence of God's absolute love for every person. Jesus did not avoid sinners in his ministry, but focused on the abundant mercy and gracious forgiveness of God.

◆ There is a fundamental Catholic belief in the potential for moral conversion present in all people, even the worst sinners.

For these reasons, many Christian churches have denounced capital punishment as incompatible with Christianity. Although the Catholic Church has been reluctant to condemn it in principle, most of the recent popes and bishops have spoken out against its use. Pope John Paul II made a strong social statement against capital punishment on his visit to St. Louis, where he personally met with the governor and requested that the sentence of a man condemned to die be commuted. His request was honored.

> **For Heaven's Sake**
>
> Be consistent! Catholic teaching has come to identify a "consistent ethic of life" that questions taking life in any circumstances, including abortion, just war, euthanasia, and capital punishment.

In 2005, the U.S. Conference of Catholic Bishops overwhelmingly approved a new statement of opposition to capital punishment, asserting that it contributes to a culture of death and violence in the United States. It was the bishops' first comprehensive statement on the death penalty in 25 years. They said their longtime opposition to capital punishment is being renewed and strengthened by new teachings and new support for abolition of the death penalty growing out of the *Gospel of Life* encyclical issued by the late Pope John Paul II. Citing John Paul's teachings, the bishops declared that "the death penalty is not intrinsically evil, as is the taking of human life through abortion or euthanasia," but "in contemporary society, where the state has other, nonlethal means to protect its citizens, the state should not use the death penalty."

"I think the abortion issue raised this up," Archbishop Sean O'Malley of Boston said. "As people began realizing that the dignity of human life was being diminished by abortion, it caused them to consider other ways in which the dignity of human life was being diminished."

Bishop Nicholas DiMarzio of the Diocese of Brooklyn said this document "is a call to reject the tragic illusion that we can demonstrate respect for life by taking life, that we can teach that killing is wrong by killing those who kill others."

The bishops drew a strong distinction between the Church's stance on capital punishment and its absolute opposition to abortion and euthanasia, stating that the death penalty was an issue on which "people of good will can disagree."

We've taken a look at the major teachings of the Church and gained an understanding of the process of how Church teaching evolves. In the next chapter, you'll learn more about the inside workings of the Catholic Church and about some of the career officers of the religious orders and the Church hierarchy.

## The Least You Need to Know

- ◆ Catholic moral teaching has shifted toward developing virtues and promoting loving response and away from what you are doing wrong.

- ◆ This shift promotes forgiveness and compassion which are intrinsic to Christianity.

- ◆ Catholics are questioning the Church's understanding of human sexuality and healing from some misunderstandings of the past.

- ◆ Catholics are urged to follow a consistent ethic of respect for all life in their teachings on abortion, euthanasia, capital punishment, social justice, and Just War theories.

# Chapter 20

# The Church: Moving from Steeple to People

## In This Chapter

♦ How does the Church structure work?

♦ What is a vocation? How would I know if I had one?

♦ Religious orders: who does the work of the Church?

♦ Can regular folks have vocations, too?

The Church is a top-to-bottom power structure, but many members are calling for more say in decision making and accountability from their leaders—but with change comes resistance. In our title we identify these two aspects of the Church as *people* and *steeple*, and in this present moment, it appears that the "steeple-people" are digging in. However, the vision of a more communal model of shared power, closer to the Church in its earliest years, doesn't go away. We'll take a look at the idea of "hierarchical communion" proposed at Vatican II and also learn more about the Church as it is today.

# A Call to Hierarchical Communion

The governing structure of the Catholic Church with power concentrated at the top has endured for more than 1500 years, but the Church has not always modeled the Gospel message. It has sometimes succumbed to the temptations of power and identified more with the militarism of its worldly benefactors than the spirit of its heavenly founder. As with all organizations, balancing is always being negotiated between the people and the structure that holds them together.

Vatican II laid out plans for a new model of Church where power would be shared, and at the same time the hierarchical order would be maintained. It's called *hierarchical communion*—it holds the promise of reaping the best of both worlds.

> **S'ter Says**
>
> Hierarchical communion, a term from the Church's Second Vatican Council, addresses the nature of the relation between the Church in Rome (the Vatican and the Pope) and the local churches all around the world (dioceses and their bishops). It indicates that the authority of the one is derived from and is dependent on the support (communion) of the other.

Let's use the illustration of a cone and a ball. The cone represents the hierarchical aspect; the ball represents its communal side. By putting the cone on top of the circle you have an image of a head wearing a dunce cap. By turning the image upside down you have an ice cream cone. The first image represents dominating the people as if they were dunces; the second represents the structure serving the people with a gift. What we suggest is that for Church, as "People of God," both hierarchy and communion are important, but authority is there as a gift of God for the purpose of serving the people—not to dominate them.

Hierarchical communion doesn't call for a different structure as much as a change in policy within the existing structure. Advocates of the Vatican II model want more emphasis on the communion side of the image. Changes from the council have been slow in coming, and much of what was suggested has faded into the background, at least for now. These differences of opinion are normal and therefore unavoidable in human affairs—they don't constitute cracks in the basic structure.

Balancing an organization the size of the Catholic Church is a monumental task. Many feel the Church is at one of those crucial times in its history where tension between the poles is high. Eventually, with prayer and honest dialogue, a third way can open that embraces opposing ideas. When this happens it is more than finding middle ground, it means going to higher ground. The term *hierarchical communion*, when it is extended to the whole Church, describes that kind of potential breakthrough.

# The Unified Church

You may remember from earlier discussions that a diocese is a group of individual parishes under the direction of a bishop. All decisions made by bishops eventually have to be in "communion" with Rome. This structure is somewhat similar to the United States, with Washington, D.C., presiding over the other states. Washington, like Rome, is the seat of government; each state has a governing structure and independence, but is under one set of laws—the Constitution of the United States. The Catholic Church is under one set of laws—Canon law.

## Who's Who in the Church

The decision-making power lies in the office of bishop. The pope is the "big bishop." He leads the other bishops and acts as their spokesman—and the "buck stops" at his desk. The source of the power exercised by the bishop of Rome comes from his role as head of the College of Bishops. The hierarchy of the Church consists of the following offices:

◆ **The pope.** The structure of the Church begins at the top, with the pope, the bishop of Rome. The College of Cardinals elects the pope.

◆ **Bishops.** Bishops are priests nominated by other bishops in their country and selected for office by the pope.

◆ **Cardinals.** The College of Cardinals is a group of approximately 120 bishops who have been elevated by the pope to the rank of cardinal. Membership in the College of Cardinals is divided between those who hold office in the Vatican (the *Roman Curia*) and those who are bishops of major cities in the world. For example, the United States has seven cardinals who head such dioceses as New York, Chicago, and Los Angeles. In all there are 13 U.S. cardinals; two have positions in the Curia and the others are retired.

> **S'ter Says**
>
> The **Roman Curia** is the bureaucracy that assists the pope in administering his duty of pastoring the Catholic Church. It was formally organized in 1588. It was last reorganized in 1988 by John Paul II.

◆ **Priests.** The bishop ordains priests who serve as pastors of the parishes.

◆ **Deacons.** Deacons are ordained by the bishop and serve in liturgical and justice ministries in a parish. Deacons can be—and most are—married.

Everyone below this level is considered part of the laity of the Church. An unofficial hierarchy has existed within the laity, but in the past few decades this is becoming a flatter structure. It might be represented in the following way:

♦ **Seminarians.** Those who are in training to become priests.

♦ **Nuns.** Women in religious orders.

♦ **Brothers.** Nonordained men in religious orders.

♦ **"Lay" professionals.** Directors of religious education, pastoral ministers, ministers of music, and chaplains, for example.

♦ All the rest of the folks.

In the spirit of Vatican II, every person has a role in all the mission of the Church, and none is more important than another. However, that is a bit like saying all people are equal, but some are more equal than others! The impetus is toward a more communal power structure, but at the risk of being repetitious, change comes slowly, which is true in societal structures as well as the Church.

## Bishops: Shepherds of the Flocks

A bishop shepherds his flock by presiding over feast day Masses and special ceremonies from his church, called the cathedral. He travels his diocese administering the sacrament of confirmation and leading special events such as the dedication of a church or the installation of a new parish priest. He administrates the business of the diocese and assigns priests to parishes, and they report to him.

The bishop supervises all the charities and educational institutions within his territory. He represents the Church in civic matters, and he is the principal teacher for his diocese. Just as the pope writes encyclicals to the whole Church, the bishop writes letters that teach and direct his people. Bishops are nominated by a group of other bishops from the same country. Following an elaborate process to determine eligibility for the office of bishop, the pope makes the final approval of all bishops.

## The Roman Curia

The Roman Curia is similar to the president's cabinet, but with greater power—members are appointed. It's headed by cardinals who handle such things as the appointment of bishops, decisions regarding worship, missionary efforts, and deciding who teaches and what is taught.

Many of the Church's decisions about teaching come from the office called the Congregation for the Doctrine of the Faith. This office was originally started in 1542 as the Congregation of the Holy Inquisition. In 1908, the name was changed to the Congregation of the Holy Office. In 1967, it received its present name. Cardinal Ratzinger was the head of this office from 1981 until 2005, when he became Pope Benedict XVI.

The relationship of the Curia to the pope is a hard one to nail down. The Curia makes decisions that are approved by the pope. Some are specifically approved; others are allowed to be published under his name without his explicit reading, depending on the seriousness of the issues being decided upon. Again, this can be compared to the authority given by the president to his cabinet members and advisors. The pope (like the president) has appointed these positions. He knows and trusts his appointees to carry out business in a way that represents the leader's general philosophy.

# Vocation: No Family Is Complete Without One

In Chapter 11, you read about the sacrament of Holy Orders; and here you'll take a closer look at the vocation to the priesthood. The word *vocation* means calling. For Catholics, vocation has been synonymous with a calling to Church service, and a lot of pride and respect is connected with being an "official" servant of the Church.

Those taking holy orders give themselves completely to the service of the Church as a full-time endeavor; except for deacons, they do not hold other jobs—nor do they marry. An ordained vocation is a significant commitment because it's for life, and this person will have influence over many people. Consequently, the time of preparation is lengthy and rigorous and can last from 5 to 15 years. People can be released from their vocation; however, both getting in and getting out require a formal process of discernment.

## Priests: The Guys on the Front Line

There are two kinds of priests, diocesan and religious orders. Diocesan priests work directly for the bishop and often head up parishes as pastors. Religious order priests belong to specific religious communities such as Dominican, Franciscan, or Jesuit, which are discussed in greater detail later in this chapter, and their jobs vary. Often they are teachers or

**For Heaven's Sake**

Don't think priests are the only ones with a vocation. In principle vocation to religious service starts at baptism, when one sacramentally "seals" his or her commitment to answer the call of Jesus to serve the Kingdom of God.

missionaries. A diocesan priest preaches, teaches, and administrates the business of the parish. He celebrates Mass, administers the sacraments, visits the sick, marries, and buries his parishioners.

Religious order priests belong to specific religious communities such as Dominicans, Franciscans, or Jesuits, organized around a specific work such as teaching or caring for the poor. The word "order" refers to receiving assignments or "orders" from the superior of the community, and also a spiritual submission members make to the group—similar to a marriage when a couple surrenders individuality in becoming a couple, thus giving the marriage priority. Assignments or jobs within a particular order vary, and reflect the declared spiritual mission of the order.

**Your Guardian Angel**

The proper way of addressing a bishop is "Your Excellency." The written form uses the title "Most Reverend." A cardinal is addressed as "Your Eminence."

# Religious Orders: Know Your Players

Catholic nuns and priests are usually referred to as the "religious," short for being members of the religious orders to which they belong. Religious orders are groups of men or women living in separate communities where they practice the particular form of spiritual life the order is dedicated to—such as education, health care, foreign missions, and so on. Most orders are celibate communities, in which the members join with the intention of staying for life.

Orders follow slightly different rules but most involve taking the vows of poverty, chastity, and obedience. Chastity refers to celibacy or virginity. Poverty generally means that all money is held communally. Obedience means the individual takes direction from his or her religious superiors regarding the nature of work assignments and living arrangements. Today some members of religious orders are employed in regular jobs, pay their expenses, and live on their own—but they maintain a strong sense of community.

There are two basic types of religious life: active and contemplative. Active religious members work in the world. Contemplative life describes those who choose solitude, silence, prayer, and penance. The contemplative tradition goes back to the second century and the communities that formed in the desert, as you may recall from Chapter 8. Contemplative spiritual life is lived close to the earth, and away from the world and worldly concerns; members are attuned to nature's rhythms. The essence of contemplative life is chanting the Liturgy of the Hours, where the passing of the day and night are marked by special prayers. Traditional religious orders and also new movements are increasingly open to incorporating single and married people. Some extend membership to non-Catholics.

## Becoming Monks, Nuns, and Brothers

The term *monk* refers to any member of a male religious community who lives a solitary life of prayer and contemplation. The word means "one who lives alone," referring to living away from the world—as religious life is always lived in community. Religious communities each have a unique character and sense of mission, but all are working toward the same general end—service to God. Some monks are ordained as priests, and some are not. Those who are not ordained as priests are considered part of the laity of the Church.

Preparation to become a monk, nun, or brother includes a time of spiritual formation in which candidates, called novices, spend the day in prayer and meditation, continue their education, and learn about the order they are preparing to join. They also spend time assessing their call to religious life under the guidance of a spiritual director.

When they are ready they take the vows of chastity, poverty, and obedience according to the traditions of the community they are joining. These are considered permanent vows.

There are more than 500 orders of nuns in the United States alone. Paradoxically, although the Catholic Church doesn't permit women to be ordained, it has been one of the first institutions in the culture where women were educated and became CEOs of institutions.

**Your Guardian Angel**

Some nuns take a new name when they enter the convent. It is correct to refer to a nun as "Sister" followed by her religious name, if you know it, or simply as "Sister" if you don't.

Brothers are male members of religious orders who take the vows of poverty, chastity, and obedience. Like nuns, they are lay members of the religious community, traditionally working in education and health care. In the post–Vatican II Church, brothers, like sisters, have expanded their work to better meet the needs of the times by moving into a wide variety of ministries, especially in the area of peace and justice needs.

## Benedictines: Behind Closed Doors

Benedict lived in the late fifth century and created a set of rules governing monastic life called the Rule of St. Benedict that has been followed by thousands of Christians for 1,500 years.

The Rule of St. Benedict teaches basic monastic virtues such as humility, silence, and obedience, as well as directions for balanced living. Benedict suggested times for common prayer, meditation, reading of sacred Scripture, and manual labor. He recommended moderation for his monks, believing in principles of sound health. He imposed limits to fasting and all-night prayer vigils that had become extreme in many monasteries. He recommended working with the hands about six hours a day and having leisure time for reading and common prayer.

The Rule of St. Benedict remains the backbone of Christian monasticism today, and many religious communities follow it, if not by the letter, definitely in spirit. Its recipe for prayer, fasting, and service assures the values of the Bible are lived in a balanced way. A person who joins the order usually remains in one place for life. Benedictines actually take a fourth vow, called "stability," to stay at this particular monastery for life.

**Your Guardian Angel**

Members of religious orders include the initials of the order (often its name in Latin) after their names. For example, the president of Loyola University Chicago is Rev. Michael J. Garanzini, S.J. Here "S.J." stands for the Society of Jesus, the official name of the Jesuits.

Benedictine Sisters are a female branch of the Order of St. Benedict and, amazingly, have been around since the 500s. They were formed by St. Scholastica, who was Benedict's sister. Their work includes agriculture, hospitality, education, skilled crafts, scholarship, counseling, and parish ministry. Many of their monasteries observe strict seclusion. The Benedictine Sisters came to the United States in 1846 and are actively involved in education and justice service ministries. Benedictines have the initials O.S.B. (Order of St. Benedict) after their names.

## The Rule of St. Francis

The Franciscan order is the common name of the Order of Friars Minor (O.F.M.) The members of this order follow the rule of life written by their founder, Francis of Assisi. They remain rooted in the call to a life of poverty, reflecting St. Francis's peaceful and gentle love of all, especially the poor. The rule was written in the early 1200s, and it embraces complete poverty not only for all its members, but also for the order itself. Over the years, Franciscans have negotiated a more moderate and practical interpretation of their rule, changing it to meet circumstances and pastoral needs more in tune with the times.

The Franciscan order originated in the late twelfth and thirteenth centuries along with many movements of laypeople as a counterpoint to excesses in the Church. They were seeking a return to the life characterized by the early Church of Jesus and his followers, feeling the Church was losing its sense of true mission. The Franciscans supported themselves by whatever trades they knew, devoting their lives to living the Gospel in simplicity and preaching its message to others.

---

### Saints Preserve Us

**St. Clare, August 11, Patron of Television**

St. Clare, born in Assisi, is said to be St. Francis's spiritual daughter because she very much followed in his footsteps. Born in 1193, she felt her calling from childhood. Under the guidance of St. Francis, she entered a Benedictine convent. She persisted in her desire to live an even more austere life, further separated from the world, and finally succeeded in founding the Poor Clares, or the Second Order of St. Francis. Her order soon spread across Europe. Clare inherited a great sum of money, which she gave to the poor, and she would accept no revenues for her monastery. She died in 1253 and was made a saint two years later. She was named patron saint of television because she was a woman of vision, and because she had visions!

---

## Dominicans: Telling It Like It Is

The Dominican order, officially known as the Order of Preachers (O.P.), was founded in 1216 by St. Dominic de Guzman. Dominicans, like Franciscans, emerged in response to the conditions in society and also within the Church.

The order spawned a couple of the most well-known theologians, Thomas Aquinas (1225–1274) and Catherine of Siena (1347–1380), who brought a social dimension to the order, infusing it with a concern for human rights. This concern is still very much a part of the Dominican life today. The Dominicans' outward focus is balanced by their strong tradition of inward-looking spirituality.

The Dominicans were established in the United States in 1805 and continue to be characterized by a commitment to poverty, prayer, and study. Dominicans publish periodicals, conduct schools of theology, and work in dozens of parishes, hospitals, and universities all over the world. The order now includes cloistered nuns and sisters in active ministry, as well as nonvowed members, who, in fact, are the largest number in the order. Although Dominican organizations function autonomously, they are united as the Dominican Family under the master of the order, who resides in Rome.

## Jesuits: The Pope's Foot Soldiers

Jesuit is the popular name for the Society of Jesus (S.J.), a religious order founded by St. Ignatius of Loyola in 1540. Among other religious orders, Jesuits were a fundamental part of the Catholic Reformation. Their motto is "For the greater glory of God." Ignatius, a military man, imbued the order with his fighting spirit. The Jesuits marched to Rome and put themselves at the disposal of the pope, declaring that they would not be "chanting the Office," like the other religious orders. Instead of chanting, which represented to them a passive type of spirituality, they declared that their work would be action for the advancement of Catholic doctrine and life. They vowed to go anywhere in the world the pope chose to send them. In addition to poverty, chastity, and obedience, Jesuits have a special fourth vow of obedience to the pope. Like the Dominicans and Franciscans, the Jesuits have a social ministry and have established many orphanages and other agencies for social assistance.

> **Epiphanies**
>
> The Society of Jesus, popularly known as the Jesuits, is the largest religious order in the Church. It numbers some 20,000 members on 6 continents and in 112 nations. Among these members are 14,000 priests, 2,000 brothers, and 4,000 men preparing for the priesthood. They serve under their general superior in Rome, who is appointed for life by and immediately accountable to the pope.

# Lay Vocation: What About the Rest of the Folks?

We opened this chapter by saying that Catholics traditionally used the word *vocation* to talk about priests, monks, nuns, and brothers. After Vatican II, the terms *lay vocation* and *lay spirituality* entered the Catholic vocabulary. The terms acknowledge and validate the faith journey of lay members, who are living their life according to spiritual principles, but are not professionals in the way the church traditionally defines it.

> **S'ter Says**
>
> In Catholic terms, **lay** refers to Church members who are not ordained. The ministry status of the laity has been greatly enhanced since Vatican II.

# There Is a Job for Everyone

Although the Church has always relied heavily on volunteers, laypeople were restricted from participating in the liturgical life of the Church. Today the following ministries reflect a growing process of laypeople sharing in the sacramental ministry as well as the governing of the Church:

♦ Eucharistic ministers are laypeople who distribute Communion during Mass as well as take it to the homes of the sick.

♦ Lectors read the first two readings of the Mass.

♦ Song leaders are members of the congregation who announce hymns, teach new songs, and lead congregational singing.

♦ Offertory gift bearers bring the bread and wine up to the altar.

> **Your Guardian Angel**
>
> Get active in your parish! It is a Catholic tradition to participate in service work, and there are many ways to do this at your local parish. Consider starting a new group that meets your needs and serves others. The main thing is to belong by being active.

♦ Altar servers are often young boys and girls who light the altar candles, hold the book for the priest to read from, ring the bells at the important times during the Mass, assist at Communion, and in other ways help with the celebration of Mass.

♦ Parish council members are elected by the parish to serve on the advisory council to the pastor in the operation of the church. Council members head up committees, such as the finance committee, the committee for the liturgy, and more. Laypeople also serve on diocesan pastoral councils.

♦ Social action enlists the aid of many volunteers. The parish may operate a shelter for the homeless, soup kitchens, or a food basket program. The parish might also spearhead education and social action on topics like capital punishment, abortion, peace, and justice.

The following represent traditional lay ministries, but with a new sense of their mission:

♦ Ushers greet people as they enter the church, show them to their seats, take up the collection, and generally assist the congregation during Mass.

◆ Ministers of hospitality welcome new members to the church and arrange the refreshments and coffee following Mass.

◆ Catechists teach the parish religious education classes.

**For Heaven's Sake**

Give everyone his or her due respect! No one's job is any better than anyone else's. Jesus was a carpenter, a day laborer. Peter was a fisherman. Luke was a doctor. Matthew was a tax collector. The women were homemakers, prepared food, and had leadership positions. Yet all had equal respect in the community.

◆ Youth ministers organize and gather the adolescent members of the church for social outings and spiritual reflection.

◆ Ministers of care are assigned to visit the sick and homebound.

◆ "Prayers" are the faithful who often attend daily Mass and are called on by the parish when it has a particular prayer to offer.

In addition, volunteers do myriad jobs ranging from cleaning the altar on a regular basis to providing transportation for elderly members.

## Faith in Action

To reinforce the connection between Church and world, some parishes have begun to hold ceremonies in which a person and their vocation is blessed. For example, during Mass one Sunday, the pastor called recent graduates of a nursing program to come forward. He prayed with them, saying: "God, you are the Great Physician, be present with these young people as they go about the work of healing. Bless these caps and stethoscopes, symbols of their service as a nurse." He then anointed the nurses' hands with holy oil.

**Your Guardian Angel**

Begin to think of your job as your spiritual vocation. You will be amazed at how much this thought can improve your attitude and your relationships with fellow workers. You are also more likely to receive the spiritual assistance or grace you need in overcoming difficult situations. Just try it for one day!

The updated version of Catholicism reflects the trend toward more respect and equality within the ranks, thus moving us all from steeple to people.

Having looked at what's happening today, in the next chapter, we'll revisit the Church's early years to gain a deeper understanding of its long history.

## The Least You Need to Know

◆ Vatican II drew the blueprints for a new model of Church with shared power, called hierarchical communion.

◆ Vocation is shifting back from a call to privilege and returning to a call of service.

◆ Religious orders have played an immeasurable role in shaping the Church since the second century, and they continue to do so today.

◆ The new model of the Church empowers the laity to play a more active role, and at the same time one's occupation in the world is now being recognized as ministry.

# Part 6

# The Church's History

Here we look at how Catholicism parallels the story of the Western world. We describe the different periods of history shaping the Church: its identification with the Roman Empire, the establishment of its centralized authority, its concern with unity, and how it became a European Church and then a truly world Church.

You'll learn about two big splits in the Church: first, between the Latin Church based in Rome and the Eastern Church based in Constantinople; second, between much of northern Europe and Rome, which resulted in Protestantism. You'll learn the story of Christianity's bloody arrival upon the shores of the American continent, brought by soldiers and missionaries, and finally, how the new religion incarnated in the Hispanic New World with the special assistance of the Brown Lady of Guadalupe.

# Chapter 21

# The Roman Establishment

## In This Chapter

♦ How the Church became the darling of the Roman Empire

♦ The price the Church paid for privilege

♦ The monasteries of Europe and the spread of the religion

♦ The rise of the Holy Roman Empire

Back in Chapter 6, we left the story of the early Church just as it was getting established. This chapter returns to those early days to describe some of the key players and important events in Church history. We resume the story in the fourth century with a look at two remarkable men, one an emperor and the other a bishop—with two remarkable mothers.

## From Underdog to Top Dog

As you may remember from previous chapters, the early Church was an outlaw religion. For the first 300 years of Catholicism, Christians faced the very real threat of having to choose their religion over their life, and many of them died for their faith. Despite these dangers, however, an unusual and interesting thing happened: the Church not only survived, but it also grew in numbers. The Church's core message of liberation appealed to a growing number of people inside the Roman Empire.

As the Church entered the fourth century, two men—and their mothers—would have a great impact on its development. The first was Constantine (288–337 C.E.), the Roman emperor who gave his protection to the new Church, effectively ending the persecutions. In the early years, the Church consisted of small communities of members who met in individual homes. Rituals were simple and intimate. This organization began to change when the important leader Constantine began to embrace the Church.

The second man to strongly influence the emerging Church was Augustine (354–430 C.E.), active just a few years later than Constantine. Soon after the Scriptures were recorded, Church leaders (known as "Fathers of the Church") began to write down their thoughts and reflections, and Augustine was the most significant figure in this theological tradition. One of the great systematic minds, he established the Church's intellectual foundation.

## Constantine: The Church Gets a Break

In the year 313, Catholicism got its first big break. Constantine from Gaul (which is modern-day France) took control of the Roman Empire and became its Emperor. He then made a decision that altered the course of history. He legalized the Catholic Church and supported it personally.

---

**Saints Preserve Us**

### St. Helena, August 18, Patron of Converts and Divorced

St. Helena was born in England. She married Constantius, an officer in the Roman army, and gave birth to Constantine. Shortly after her husband was given the title of Caesar and took over the governing of Gaul and Britain, he divorced her to marry another. Helena later converted to Catholicism and influenced her son regarding his favorable treatment of the Church. He made her an empress, and she used both her wealth and her power to help the poor and to build churches. At the age of 80, she went to Jerusalem to find the Holy Cross, the one upon which Christ was crucified. Legend says that she found it. She built a church there and used her considerable wealth to take care of those in need. She died in Rome in about 326.

---

Although Constantine himself was not baptized a Catholic until his death, two forces drove him to endorse this new religion. The first was the influence of his Catholic mother, and the second was a dream he had just before going into a battle at the Mulvian Bridge over the Tiber near Rome. In the dream he is said to have seen in the sky a flaming cross inscribed with the words "In this sign thou shalt conquer." He accepted the cross, Catholicism's major symbol, and won the battle. His victory became one of the most decisive moments both in the history of the Catholic Church and the history of Western civilization. Eventually, under his protection, Catholicism became the favored religion.

Constantine affected both the external and internal structure of the Church. First, his favors took the form of both land and tax incentives. Second, Catholics, no longer fearing persecution, stopped meeting in homes and started holding services in newly converted public buildings, a major work of his mother, St. Helena. Finally, he influenced the Church's internal structure by finding a way to settle disputes of faith.

### Epiphanies

Keep in mind that although the edict of toleration ended the Roman persecutions, the Catholic Church has been systematically oppressed in many other countries over its 2,000-year history. England in the sixteenth century, Ireland in the seventeenth, the United States in the nineteenth, and the Soviet Union in the twentieth are just a few places where the property, rights, and even lives of Catholics were threatened. As we'll see, there have been times when the Church has sanctioned similar behavior toward those who disagreed with it. The Declaration of Religious Freedom issued at Vatican II in 1965 held that religious freedom was both a natural and a civil right for all persons.

Constantine began the tradition of Church councils, in which members assembled to discuss differences and make decisions by majority rule. This method assured that the Church would always speak with one voice. He called the Church's first council, the Council of Nicaea (325 C.E.), which you learned about in Chapter 17. Constantine was an administrator who was familiar with both military and political organization. He gave the Church a political form, emphasizing the collective authority of the bishops. This structure gave the Church the stability it needed in the early years, which enabled it to grow, but the structure also gave the Church its authoritarian character, which has brought it much controversy.

Almost from the beginning, worldly considerations influenced Church structure, and it gradually adapted to the Roman world around it. Within the next 100 years, household Church communities became a thing of the past. The role of women in the Church, once so apparent during the time of Jesus, was all but eliminated as its all-male structure developed. Rather than being associated with service, Church office began to be associated with status and power.

Increasingly, Church and state finances mingled, and the Church became not just a vocation but a prosperous career for many people. Church leaders eventually lived like members of the secular aristocracy, often enjoying wealthy splendor. The simple communal meal that once characterized Catholic Communion gradually gave way to massive and ornate altars, where bread and wine were laid out ceremoniously. The separation between the priests and the people grew. In the centuries to follow, separation from the people, worldliness, and opulence would bring many problems to the Church.

On the other hand, there were positive changes that stemmed from the Church's relationship with the Roman state. The Church was able to exert a more humane influence on the empire. The state began to apply a more Christian understanding of social responsibility by feeding the poor and taking care of the sick. Most of all, the Church was able to grow and remain one communion that could transcend vast cultural differences—a cultural miracle that characterizes the Catholic Church up to today.

Although its decline had begun in the West, the Roman Empire was still vast and powerful, and Catholicism, now a favored religion, spread to its four corners. The Church suddenly began to acquire many new converts. When a chief of a tribe of people within the empire converted, his whole tribe came with him.

## Augustine: Lover and Loser

Like Constantine, Augustine was also greatly influenced by his mother. He was born in North Africa in what is now Algeria in 354 and grew up to become a writer, teacher, philosopher, and one of the most influential people in the Church's early history. His father was a pagan and his mother, Monica, was a Catholic. Augustine had an inquiring mind and explored many of the philosophies and theologies of his time before being drawn to Catholicism. Once a very worldly man, he founded a religious community as a safe haven from what he called "the decadent world," where he prayed and wrote extensively. He was made a bishop in Hippo (near present-day Annaba, Algeria) and worked tirelessly for the Church by preaching, writing, and administering. He believed in the power of education as a way to reclaim the soul's lost goodness. His vast body of writings on many subjects has been admired from his time through today.

Augustine left Christianity a mixed legacy. His deep love of the Church and of spiritual matters cannot be denied. He wrote beautifully and poetically about how the human spirit will only be satisfied when it falls in love with the will of God: "you have made us for yourself, O Lord, and our hearts will not rest until they rest in you." On the other hand, he was highly influenced by Plato's understanding of human nature and was caught up in a belief of the time called Manichaeism. Manichaeism taught that matter was separate from spirit and was in fact evil. It went even further to imply that there were two gods, one of good and one of evil. Although he eventually abandoned this philosophy and returned to the Church, he was never able to completely reconcile Manichaeism's dualism of good and evil. This led to Augustine's writings on original sin, which we discussed in Chapter 19.

---

### Saints Preserve Us

**St. Monica, August 27, Patron of Mothers and Widows**

St. Monica, the patron of mothers and widows, was born in 333. She married a pagan man described as having a "high temper." Her patience and gentleness influenced him, and he converted to Christianity before his death. Their son, Augustine, who was only 17 at the time of his father's death, was a bit of a playboy around old Algeria. Monica prayed long and hard and with great fervor for his conversion. When he left to go to Italy, she followed him and, along with St. Ambrose, the bishop of Milan, had a positive influence on him. However, it took another 15 years before he converted. In 387, she witnessed his return to God as he was baptized by his good friend Ambrose. Monica died soon afterward. Many a Catholic mother has prayed to St. Monica!

---

Augustine's most influential book was called *The City of God*. In it, Plato's ideas show up in Augustine's views about the relationship between the Christian community and the larger world. Augustine was also writing in response to the sack of Rome in 407. For him, this world-shaking event demonstrated the frailty of human endeavor. Only the soul endures forever in Augustine's view. His dualistic thinking showed up in his understanding of the relationship between the Christian community and the larger world. He believed that the Church should strive to form a "perfect society," a religious society separate from the material world around it. He believed humans' only purpose in life is to form this City of God on earth.

Augustine's idea of the relationship of religion to the state greatly influenced how the Church saw itself. It laid the foundation for medieval society, a society more concerned about the welfare of the soul than the welfare of the body. The difficulty resulting from Augustine's theories was the separation between the Church and the world around it. The Church adopted his beliefs on original sin and his views on separating spiritual matters from worldly concerns.

Even today, this dualistic view haunts Catholics as they sort their material and spiritual priorities. The redefinition of the relationship between the Church and the world was one of the primary shifts of Vatican II. Since Vatican II, the Church has made major efforts to improve its relationship with the culture around it.

# Christianity Comes to Your Hometown

For the most part, Western Europe of the 400s to the 800s was an unstable patchwork of towns, villages, and settlements, some of which were Roman and some of which were Germanic. The period was characterized by almost constant power struggles and fighting. Tribes coming from the northern and eastern areas of Europe were pouring into its settled parts searching for land and riches. By this time, the old Roman Empire had lost much of its power in the West and no longer offered the people protection against the invading tribes. In the Roman Empire's absence, the Catholic Church became the stabilizing force in Western Europe. The religion prospered and was characterized by its missionary work, building an elaborate system of monasteries and convents. These places provided safety, education, and support in an unstable time.

## Monasticism: Attraction Rather Than Promotion

Monasteries and convents brought Catholicism to non-Christian Europe. Monastic life is a tradition in the Catholic Church that goes back to the desert with St. Anthony and his followers in the third century. As early as 250 C.E., hundreds of Christians were living as religious "hermits" (monks) in the deserts of Egypt, Israel, and Syria. Antony (or Anthony) was converted to Catholicism (271 C.E.) and moved into the Egyptian desert as a religious hermit after hearing the words: "If thou wilt be perfect, go and sell all that thou hast." He is often spoken of as the "Father of Christian Monasticism." In 510 St. Benedict shaped monastic life under what is called the Rule of St. Benedict, which became the template for Western Christian monasticism.

> **S'ter Says**
>
> **Missionaries** are Church workers who are sent to foreign countries to do religious or charitable work. At times, they have been criticized for imposing values and beliefs on other cultures without an open exchange of ideas. In recent time, however, missionaries offer medical and educational assistance while working within the cultural beliefs of the people they serve.

Monasteries and convents housed communities in which religious life developed, away from "the world." Men who belonged to these early Church communities were often called monks; women were called nuns. From these communities came the *missionaries* who went out and lived among the tribes, helping to convert many tribal people to a new way of life.

The monasteries were cradles of art, sacred writing, and theological thought. As the invading tribes spilled down into Europe, the monasteries became safe harbors for the people and their culture. While continuing the work of conversion begun by the founding missionaries, some monasteries grew extremely wealthy and powerful. Their abbots (the name given to the head of a monastery) became some of the most influential figures in the area.

## St. Patrick: Three Cheers for the Irish

Missionary work was an important part of the early Church. If ever there was a giant among missionaries, it was St. Patrick. He is called the "apostle of Ireland" and remains its patron saint. Dates of his birth differ between 432 and 456, and his death is given as 461 or 493.

One of the best-loved stories about him says he drove the snakes out of Ireland. This story may be a reference to converting Ireland from the Druid religion, because snakes were one of the sacred druidic symbols. He used the shamrock to teach about the Trinity, which is why it is the sacred plant of Ireland. The Druids burned ritual fires throughout the countryside as part of their spring rites. Another legend says St. Patrick lit the Easter fire in defiance of this pagan custom.

The story goes that raiders from the sea captured St. Patrick from his home in Britain when he was 16. He was taken to Ireland, where he worked as a slave for the next 6 years. He eventually escaped and went back home to Britain. He became a priest and later a bishop. He was haunted by a dream in which he believed God was calling him back to Ireland. He eventually followed his dream and went back to the Irish and never left. He carried out massive missionary work, implanting the Catholic faith so widely and deeply in Ireland that it became one of the most Catholic of nations.

Many Christian texts were stored and copied in the monasteries of Ireland. For hundreds of years, the invading tribes from the "uncivilized" northern regions invaded Europe, eventually capturing and destroying Rome. Works of literature and art were hidden in the monasteries, thus preserving them from the invaders.

The term *Celt* has come to be associated with the Irish, but it refers to many of the people who lived across middle Western Europe.

| **Epiphanies** |
| --- |
| Did you know that the Irish are credited with saving Western civilization? Invading barbarians were destroying towns and villages throughout Europe, and the art and books of both the Greek and Roman civilizations were in danger of being lost. Many of them were hidden in the Irish monasteries, and so the boast has been made that the Irish saved Western civilization. |

Their conversion to Catholicism was gradual. The old Druid religion existed side-by-side with Catholicism in most of the Celtic lands for many years. Catholic churches were built on the old holy sites of the Druids, and often the names and images of the old gods were carved into the stone walls. The Celts retained the holy days of the old religions and rededicated them to Catholic saints. Ceremonies to acknowledge the new holy days were often similar to the ceremonies of the deities they supplanted. The holy days were celebrated with songs, dances, and ceremonies of the old religions. This process of appropriation was very common in the spread of Catholicism.

As the Church replaced Druids with bishops and priests, the people transferred their love and loyalty to them. Some of the magical world of Celtic mythology was translated into the rich Catholic stories of the lives of the saints. The Celtic religion had many goddesses, such as the Great Mother called Anna who would eventually be found in different forms in the various Celtic cultures of Europe. In Christian times, she lived on through the veneration of St. Anne in Brittany, St. Non in Wales, and St. Brigid in Ireland.

As a rule, Celtic and other indigenous religions held the female principle in equal if not higher regard than the male. You'll often hear reference to the Catholic Church as the "Mother Church," both in everyday language and in official documents. This designation represents the feminine or nurturing aspect of God. It refers to the Church as a womb in which the members grow and develop. The Church is the spiritual home, and home is the domain of the mother. The spirit of the Celtic people infused Catholicism with a sense of story, a love of song, and a strong community spirit.

Celtic monasticism was characterized by an independence of spirit and generally had little or no use for the politics of the Church in Rome. The clergy of the Celtic monasteries was able to get along well with the barbarian royalty. Their style was to mingle with the dignitaries, and they made every effort to respect local values. The intense era of Irish missionary activity throughout Europe lasted for roughly 100 years, from approximately 550 until 670.

In addition to the still vibrant churches in the East, two very different ideas of the Catholic Church existed side-by-side in central Europe during the first millennium. The Celtic version was an independent and decentralized form of Catholicism; the other Catholicism was a very Roman-centered Church, which saw itself as the authority in religious matters.

---

**Saints Preserve Us**

**St. Brigid of Ireland, February 1, Patron of Dairy Workers, Nuns, and Scholars**

Sometimes called the second St. Patrick, St. Brigid of Ireland was born in 450. She established communities all over Ireland, which helped the growth of the Church. Many miracles are attributed to her. One story says she once turned water into milk, which is why she is the patron of dairy workers. Her symbol, St. Brigid's Cross, is a straw cross, which is kept in the homes of Irish country people. This cross appears in pre-Christian art forms as well, giving substance to the idea that Brigid is an adaptation of the Celtic goddess, Brigit. Most likely, attributes of the pagan Brigit were transferred through folk memory to Brigid. Some scholars suggest that St. Brigid was the first bishop of Kildare, although this has not been proven. She is buried at Downpatrick with St. Patrick.

---

# German Christianity

In the countryside that would eventually be known as Germany, people lived in small villages and settlements and practiced pagan religions. The Catholic Church was extending its missionary efforts into the area. Boniface (673(?)–754), one of the leading missionaries of the time, was to Germany what Patrick was to Ireland a couple of hundred years earlier. He brought Catholicism to the German people.

Boniface was born in Devonshire, England, and from the age of 13, monks in a monastery in Exeter, which he later joined, educated him. One of the stories about Boniface tells of an encounter he had with a pagan chieftain. Boniface felled a sacred oak tree that the people believed belonged to Thor, the thunder god. When he was not struck dead, as the local people believed he would be, many of them converted. He built a church out of the oak tree. However, the pagans may have had the final say. A few years later when traveling near the same place, he and his 52 companions were attacked and murdered by a band of locals. His grave soon became a sanctuary where many gathered to pay respects to him.

Earlier missionary activity in Germany had left converts to Christianity without adequate support to maintain their faith in the outposts of civilization in which they lived. Boniface was able to bring support to these stranded Christians and bring many more converts to the Church. He did this by establishing monasteries that were centers for the faith, in which people were educated and instructed in the ways of the religion. He and his female cousin, Leofgyth, instituted a series of monasteries, which became anchors for the faith. These monasteries lasted for over 1,000 years, and many of them are still in existence today. The Church's missionary zeal did not confine itself to Germany, but was extended to Hungary, Russia, Denmark, Sweden, and all parts of Europe.

# From Rationality to Mysticism

The Roman world, influenced by the Greek culture, had carried many of the classical Greek thoughts and ideas, as well as its mysticism, into Europe. As the empire ended, so did the time of classic learning. The period that followed, known as the Dark Ages, lasted until the 1100s. However, it's important to recognize that many things lumped together under this period's moniker are not necessarily "dark." Catholicism prevailed, for instance, to become the popular religion of the land despite constant power struggles and wars.

During this time, the Church defined many of the practices and rituals with which it is so strongly identified today. For example, the Rosary was introduced, and statues and paintings of the saints sparked devotions. Feasts were celebrated with processions of colorful vestments, flags, and music. Morality plays and religious dramas were acted out publicly. Catholicism stabilized into the form it would keep for the next 1,200 years.

---

**Epiphanies**

Just as Ireland has Patrick and Germany has Boniface, many European nations have a missionary saint sent from the Eastern Church in Constantinople who first established Catholicism within their borders. Here are a few such saints with the approximate dates they began their missionary work:

- St. Severinus of Austria, 470
- St. Columba of Scotland, 560
- St. Ansgar of Denmark, 830
- St. Cyril of Russia, 860
- St. Methodius of the Czech Republic, 870
- St. Sigfrid of Sweden, 1000

---

# A New Empire Is Born

Roman culture continued to influence both politics and the Church's identity. Like the Roman Empire, the Church was headquartered in Rome and developed a centralized power structure. In the absence of the Roman state, the Church found itself existing as both a spiritual and often a civil authority, not entirely because it wanted political control, but because the people looked to it for leadership.

When Pope Leo III crowned Charlemagne emperor on Christmas in 800, the marriage between the Church and state became official. Charlemagne was the leader of a tribe in central Europe called the Franks. As he was crowned, he accepted the role of protector of the Church. The religious and political foundation for the later Holy Roman Empire was laid.

Let's summarize and clarify this important relationship between Catholicism and the Roman Empire. Initially, Catholics were outsiders and a threat to the Roman state. Then they became not only tolerated but also favored by Rome, which was losing its power to invading tribes at the time. The popes in Rome became the ones who could hold government together, and the Church began to exercise both civil and religious authority.

> **For Heaven's Sake**
>
> Don't confuse the Holy Roman Empire with the Church whose headquarters are located in Rome. The empire was a political structure. The Catholic Church and the kingdoms of Europe partnered for a thousand years, during which time the difference in roles between Church and state was often unclear.

When Charlemagne was crowned emperor, civil power and Church power again became separated—that is to say, there were again two distinct leaders, the pope and emperor, but there was still one agenda: to build Augustine's City of God. This new child of the marriage between church and state, called the Holy Roman Empire, would last 1,000 years. For centuries to come, Christian Europe was torn by wars between kings and princes. Contrary to the Church's intentions, the Holy Roman Empire never succeeded in bringing about the City of God.

By the time of the Dark Ages, the Church had adopted an authoritarian model and was wedded to the state. Problems of money, power, and authority infiltrated its structure. In the next chapter, we will look at the corrupt practices that resulted from these problems.

## The Least You Need to Know

- The organizational structure of the Church given to it by Constantine stabilized it and allowed it to grow.

- The indigenous tribes of Europe provided the Church with a rich, colorful heritage rooted in the earth.

- Monasteries were stabilizing influences on European culture, and spread the values of Christianity throughout Europe.

- The problems of power, money, and authority came with the Church's marriage to the Roman Empire.

# Chapter 22

# Division, Debauchery, and Reform: The Church's Second Millennium

## In This Chapter

- ◆ Catholicism splits in two
- ◆ Crusades, Inquisitions, and indulgences
- ◆ Martin Luther, Henry VIII, and the Protestant Reformation
- ◆ Catholicism reforms during the Council of Trent

The preceding chapter explained how the Catholic Church spread across Europe partnering with the political powers of the time. In this chapter, we'll look more closely at some of the problems that would haunt Catholicism for the next 1,000 years. We'll look at the reforms within the Church that brought it into modern times.

As the new millennium dawned, trouble that had been brewing for some time was about to boil over. First, the Greek Church split from Rome over differences in politics, ritual, and language (Greek versus Latin). Then a couple of protesters, one of them a friar (Martin Luther) and the other a king (Henry VIII), turned against the Church, taking big political portions of Europe with them. These events finally forced the Church to examine its practices and its role in the lives of the people. Although Church leaders instituted major reforms, the Church never again captured the unifying power it had. Let's take a closer look at these changes.

# Catholic and Orthodox: The Church's Y1K Problem

Besides Rome, there were major Catholic churches at Alexandria in Egypt, Antioch in Syria, and the well-known Church at Constantinople, as well as Jerusalem. Until the fifth century, these five regions of the Catholic Church, each headed by a *patriarch*, were considered to form a ruling "patriarchy." After this period the Church at Rome assumed supremacy as these churches maintained less and less unity.

> ### S'ter Says
>
> **Patriarch** is the chief bishop of the Church in a particular region of the world. The word is from the Greek *patriarches,* which means the father or chief of a race (*patria* is Latin for "clan" or "family"). In the Hebrew Scriptures, Abraham, Isaac, and Jacob, as the fathers of the Jewish family, are revered as patriarchs. Patriarchy, then, refers to the territory governed by patriarchs. Today, mainly the heads of the Eastern Churches use the title.

Although the first major separation in Catholicism didn't occur until 1054, tension had been building for several centuries. The Catholic Church in the East, centered in Constantinople, and the Catholic Church in Rome became locked in a power struggle over differences of language and theology. Rome's way of handling the problem was to excommunicate (expel) the Patriarch of Constantinople. In turn, the Patriarch of Constantinople excommunicated Rome, thereby breaking off from Roman rule. The rest of the churches which had developed in various eastern countries followed suit and as a group they became known as the Orthodox Church in Russia, Greece, the Ukraine, Romania, Turkey, and other parts of Eastern Europe.

Today, it would be difficult to identify the differences between them. With the exception of some Churches of the East, which reunited with Rome, they remain distinct. Efforts to reunite the Orthodox Churches and the Catholic Church continue.

# Catholicism's Dark Side

Although the Church felt the loss of its Eastern members, growth throughout the West more than made up for it, and the Church remained a major power in the Western world and found itself rolling in money and basking in power. Such a combination was extremely damaging for an organization whose mission was to proclaim God's reign and to do good works. The Church strayed far from its humble beginnings in the small town of Galilee where Jesus walked the dusty roads with the people and taught about his Father's love. We'll look at three particular practices the Church employed that took it further away from ministering to the people: the Crusades, the Inquisition, and the selling of salvation in the form of indulgences.

| Epiphanies |
|---|
| Simony refers to both the buying and selling of Church offices (the office of bishop, for example). This practice was originally condemned in the Acts of the Apostles, when Simon Magus tried to buy the apostles' power of blessing through the laying on of hands. Despite repeated efforts by the Church to extinguish this process, it was a recurring problem until the sixteenth century. Major offices of the Church, such as appointment to the position of cardinal, were bought by wealthy and influential political figures who wished to control Church decisions and finances. |

## Crusades: Holy War or War on the Holy?

Crusades are the name given to the "holy wars" launched by the Church mainly for the purpose of liberating the sacred places of Palestine from the Muslims, who are the members of the Islamic religion. Islam began to develop in Arabia under the direction of its founder, the prophet Muhammad. The spread of Islam after Muhammad's death in 632 has had no match in history. For the next 29 years, it expanded north of Arabia to Damascus and Jerusalem, east to Persia, west to Egypt, and farther on to the northern coast of Africa. By 715, Islam had reached Spain. The spread of Islam left the great centers of Eastern Christianity cut off from the Roman Empire. Lines were eventually drawn, and a peace was established that lasted for some time.

By the middle of the eleventh century, Islamic leaders closed the Holy Land to Christian pilgrims. The pope saw this action as an opportunity both to unite the Catholic princes of Europe against a common enemy and to liberate the Holy Land. He called for the first of a series of Crusades that stretched from the late 1000s to the late 1200s. Although the first of the Crusades did open up the Holy Land for Christian pilgrims, the net effect of the Crusades was destructive.

---

**Epiphanies**

Did you know that Islam is the fastest-growing religion today, with about a billion believers? Its population centers are in Indonesia (161 million), Bangladesh (100 million), Nigeria (100 million), and India (100 million). Its name comes from the Arabic word *Salaam*, meaning "peace." Membership requires surrender to God: "There is no God but Allah, and Muhammad is his prophet." This basic belief is accompanied by the practice of good deeds prescribed in their holy book, the Koran. Islam's history begins with Abraham of the Jewish Scriptures, and is monotheistic. In this regard, Judaism, Christianity, and Islam are akin to one another.

---

## Good Out of Evil

Despite the negative consequences of the Crusades, there was an unintended positive by-product for the West. There was a reconnection to the great learning of the ancient world and an influx of new ideas from the Islamic world, such as astronomy and chemistry. The Islamic world gave the West the Arabic number system and introduced the concept of zero, which made higher mathematics possible. In fact, *algebra* is an Arabic word.

One of the major beneficiaries of the rediscovery of classical learning was Thomas Aquinas. Taking the previously lost works of Aristotle, the great mind of the Greek Classical period, Aquinas incorporated his logical method into the theology of the Church. His methods of teaching, thinking, and talking about God have remained a bulwark of Church education up to the present time.

---

**Saints Preserve Us**

St. Thomas Aquinas, January 28, Patron of Schools

Thomas Aquinas (1225–1274) was born in Italy and was sent to the monastery of Monte Cassino at age 5 for education. He joined the Dominicans in 1244 and taught in Paris. Despite the fact that the bishop of Paris condemned him and had his works burned, he was named a saint in 1567. In 1880, Pope Leo XIII made him the patron of all the Church's schools and required all seminary students to study his thought as the one official philosophy of the Church. He is acknowledged as the greatest master of Church thought.

---

## Inquisition: Ask Me No Questions, and I'll Tell You No Lies!

People have questioned Church teachings since the Church began. Among the teachings that seemed to raise the most doubt were the beliefs in original sin, heaven and hell, Jesus' divine nature, the virgin birth, and the real presence of Jesus Christ in the bread and wine of the Mass. The Church did not always deal well with questions or dissent. It felt that heresy threatened its unity and the duty to keep the teachings of Jesus pure. Alignment with the political sector gave the Church the opportunity to use civil authority to employ physical force against dissenters, whom it identified as *heretics.*

The Inquisition was a court system set up by the Church for the purpose of tracking down heresies and punishing heretics. The word *inquisition* means "to question." Secular authorities had an interest as well. Both groups wanted to minimize dissent and disruption, and neither tolerated much diversity. The Catholic Church was still smarting from the loss of the Orthodox Church, and its ideal of one faith. In an attempt to hold it all together, the Church and the secular authorities joined to exert control over the religious world around them.

Priests of the Inquisition, led by the Dominicans, traveled throughout Europe preaching the faith. Following their sermons, they would ask the question: "Does anyone disagree with these Church teachings?" People were encouraged to come forward to report any wrong thinking or wrongdoing they might know about. Usually, no one would admit that they had any doubts about the religion themselves, but quite often they would declare a neighbor or enemy a heretic. Under torture, those who were accused and found guilty by the Inquisition were fined, imprisoned, and their lands and goods confiscated. If they refused to renounce their false beliefs, and often even if they did, they were cruelly tortured and killed.

The courts of the Inquisition were Church courts, and the crimes for which people were tried, specifically heresy and related offenses, were religious in nature. However, the power to punish was in civil hands. Those suspected of heresy by the Church were handed over to the civil authorities for punishment. In so doing, the Church attempted to stay above the consequences.

There were three distinct Inquisitions, spanning hundreds of years. Unfortunately, historical accounts of the Inquisitions are affected by a religious bias that hinders the gathering of accurate data. The avowed purpose of an Inquisition was to protect the faithful from heresy. Although the Inquisitions originally were launched against heretics, they later became directed against Jews and Muslims. In many areas of Europe, women became a favorite target of the Inquisition. In 1484, the pope issued an order that allowed an Inquisition of those suspected of witchcraft.

---

**Saints Preserve Us**

**Joan of Arc, May 30, Patron of France**

Joan of Arc was caught up in both the politics of France and England and the Inquisition. Born on January 6, 1412, in France, she heard the voices of St. Michael and St. Catherine from an early age. When she was 17, the voices told her to go to the king of France and help him recapture his kingdom, lost to the English. She was captured in battle, and the French did nothing to save her. After many months of imprisonment, she was tried by a local court and found guilty of heresy, sorcery, and adultery. The judges declared Joan's visions and voices to be "false and diabolical." Joan was burned at the stake on May 30, 1431. She was only 19 years old. Thirty years later, she was exonerated of all guilt by a court constituted by the pope. She was declared a saint in 1920.

---

The most notorious of the Inquisitions was the Spanish Inquisition, which began in about 1480, at the time Islam was driven out of the peninsula. Unlike the others, which were under ecclesiastical (Church) control, the Spanish Inquisition was an instrument of secular power, the Spanish crown. The goal of the Spanish Inquisition was to search out converted Jews and Muslims suspected of practicing their "old" religions. The Spanish Inquisition was used against political opponents. The Inquisition lasted in Spain for almost 400 years until the 1800s. The Spanish conquistadors exported the tradition to the New World and used it against the native people. They demanded loyalty to Spain and to the Church under penalty of torture and death.

---

**Epiphanies**

A remnant of the Inquisition called the Congregation for the Doctrine of the Faith exists in the Church today. (We talked about this group in Chapter 20.) It safeguards and promotes authentic Catholic teaching throughout the worldwide Church. It investigates controversy and holds extensive studies regarding questions surrounding matters of Church doctrine. It evaluates theological opinions and may admonish those regarded as incorrect or harmful to Catholic teaching. It also examines books and provides the authors the opportunity to defend themselves.

---

## Indulge Me, One More Time

Nobody knows when the practice of selling indulgences began, but it blossomed during the 1400s and 1500s.

*Indulgence* describes the remission of punishment due for sins. The Church assigned a spiritual value to certain practices or prayers to erase spiritual debt. If a sin were committed, an indulgence could be purchased rather than performed.. This practice was officially condemned in 1562, but not before it became the proverbial straw breaking the back of the Catholic Church. Indulgences are still a part of the Church today; however, they are not sold. The selling of relics was another corrupt church practice. Relics are pieces of cloth, hair, or bone that were believed to belong to one of the saints. They were displayed for money or sold.

# Problems, Protest, and Protestants

The Church, having partnered with the state in the Inquisition, employed increasingly more authoritarian means to thwart any diversity of thought or question of its dogma. Its use of power and control, albeit for the intended end of protecting the teachings of Jesus, had taken it far from its original mission.

Against this backdrop of corruption, a sound could be heard, a tap, tap, tap in Wittenberg, a small town in Germany. The sound came from a hammer banging against the large cathedral door. When the sun rose on that October morning in 1517, it shone upon a large piece of paper known as the *95 Theses* on which were listed 95 complaints against the Church. The man who wrote the paper and nailed it to the door was Martin Luther. It was not long before the document was discussed all over Europe, and the *Protestant* Reformation was born.

> **S'ter Says**
>
> A **Protestant** is any Christian belonging to a sect that seceded from the Catholic Church at the time of the Reformation. Lutheran, Episcopal, Methodist, and Baptist are some of the Protestant denominations.

On the heels of Luther's protest, Henry VIII, the king of England, broke with Rome and declared himself head of the Church of England. The differences in the beginning were political rather than religious, a quarrel between the king and the pope, which was not unusual in the Middle Ages. However, this quarrel went on to result in a permanent schism. Let's take a look at both of these influential men and how their actions affected the Catholic Church.

## Martin Luther: The Hammer Heard 'Round the World

Martin Luther, a German friar, began the Reformation. He was an Augustinian priest who was sent on a mission to Rome in 1510 and returned indignant at the corruption and worldliness of the Church. The following year, he became a professor of theological studies, a position he held until his death. Luther was particularly outraged at the selling of indulgences, which brought him to the conclusion that people are saved by faith alone. They could not earn salvation through actions or prayers. He attacked this practice and others in his *95 Theses*.

Luther followed his first list of complaints with his treatises of 1520, in which he questioned papal authority and other official Church doctrines. He was excommunicated in a document issued by Rome, which Luther promptly burned in the public square. Soon, the emperor summoned him. Luther defended his beliefs eloquently and refused to recant. He sought refuge in the castle of Wartburg where he translated the Bible into German. He organized the Lutheran Church and wrote essays, sermons, catechisms, and hymns, including the famous Protestant hymn, "A Mighty Fortress Is Our God." The creation of the Lutheran Church, which was formed around the teachings of Martin Luther, resulted in the Catholic Church losing its followers in a major portion of Germany.

## Henry VIII: Love and Marriage

The man known as Henry VIII was one of the most colorful rulers in the history of England. Henry wanted to divorce his wife and marry another. The Church refused to grant him the annulment, and he defied their authority by remarrying. He was excommunicated. In response, Henry instituted the Church of England and declared himself its head. As a result, Catholicism lost most of its English members. The Church of England, better known as the Anglican Church, exists as the Episcopalian Church in the United States.

Many other churches were founded in the 1500s in protest of the Catholic Church and its various practices. The emerging states of Europe were gaining power and wanted their independence from the old empire. They resented the fact that Church money from their regions was channeled into Rome. The Church and the state were so intertwined that political independence came at the cost of religious independence, and many wars would be fought throughout Europe for centuries because of it.

# Trendy Trent: Going to Reform School

Both Martin Luther and Henry VIII packed a big wallop, and the Catholic Church felt the sting of its losses. It realized that it had better make some changes, or it was going to lose even more members. The birth of Protestantism gave the push for the reform that many had been urging for hundreds of years. The pope finally called the Council of Trent. During the years 1545 to 1563, bishops of the Church met to clarify doctrines and to pass reforms that would redirect the course of the Catholic Church for the next 400 years. The results of this council essentially sounded the death knell for corrupt Church practices, and Church leaders got back to business—religious business.

## Scripture and Tradition Upheld

The Protestant Reformation sparked what is called the Counter-Reformation, in which the Catholic Church began to define its authority. It reaffirmed its stand that revelation is found in both revealed Scriptures and lived traditions. The Church had always claimed that a person couldn't interpret God's truth simply by reading the Bible. It has always believed God's revelation continues to unveil itself through the teachings of the Church. This idea, which was unacceptable to the Protestants, allowed bishops to continue to formulate Church teaching on more than just what was revealed in the Bible. The Church continued to decline to approve new translations of the Bible that were in the people's everyday language. This seemed to justify the Protestants' claim that the Catholic Church was afraid to have people read the Bible and do their own interpretation of God's will. The gulf between Catholics and Protestants was widening.

By the time the Council of Trent closed in 1563, it had dealt with many of the abuses cited by the Protestant Reformers, and it ended the corruption in the Catholic Church. The changes included a prohibition on the sale of indulgences, a crackdown on simony, a reformed liturgy, the establishment of seminaries for the proper training of priests, and more local control given to bishops. It turned its back on the world, not to turn around again until the most recent council, Vatican II.

## Lines Drawn: Them and Us

Catholicism was no longer the only game in Christendom, and by the end of the Council of Trent, firm boundaries were established between the Catholic Church and

Protestantism. There were five primary differences between them, and these differences remain in effect even today:

◆ Catholics maintain that moral authority comes from both Scripture and tradition. Protestants believe that Scripture alone holds moral authority.

◆ Catholics hold that Christ is truly present in the consecrated bread and wine of the Eucharist. Protestants, for the most part, see the Eucharist as a symbolic memorial of Christ's Last Supper.

◆ For Catholics, the sacraments are celebrations of the salvation achieved by Jesus Christ, which God offers us as a gift. Protestants believe that salvation comes through faith in biblical Scripture alone, and was accomplished once and for all time in the Calvary sacrifice of Jesus.

◆ Catholics believe in mediation, the establishment of a relationship with God through the efforts of another person. Christ and the church are the primary mediators. Protestants believe in an immediate and direct relationship with God, and shun intermediaries for the most part.

◆ Catholics keep the traditional seven sacraments: baptism, reconciliation, the Eucharist, confirmation, Holy Orders, marriage, and anointing of the sick. Protestants, de-emphasizing the role of a priest mediator, practice just two sacraments: baptism and the Eucharist.

# The Church Turns Its Face to the New World

The Protestant Reformation caused much of Germany and England to leave the Catholic Church. While the Church was losing its hold on Europe, Spain, a Catholic country, was opening up a new world. The New World provided an opportunity for the Church to establish the City of God one more time. That's what we'll discuss in the next chapter.

## The Least You Need to Know

◆ The ideal of one religion for all was shattered with the separation of the Orthodox Church.

◆ The involvement of the Church in money and power caused a loss of identity and integrity.

◆ The Protestant revolt spurred the reform of the Catholic Church.

◆ The Catholic Counter-Reformation assured the Church's survival as a religious institution and brought it into modern time.

# The Birth of the Church in the New Land

## In This Chapter

◆ The conquistadors meet the Aztecs

◆ Christianity in the Americas begins with an apparition

◆ A new race is born: the brown face of the Catholic Church

◆ Hispanic American Catholic heritage

In 1492, a Catholic Italian explorer named Christopher Columbus claimed America for Spain. Well, that's almost true. Actually, Columbus claimed America for both Spain and for God—in 1492, Spain's official religion was Catholicism. Thus, Catholicism in America and America itself share a common birthday.

Spain had just ended hundreds of years of war against Islam and was determined to solidify its kingdom. The Spanish believed in the unity of Church and state, and a strong alliance had been forged between the crown and the cross. In this arrangement, the Church sanctioned the activities of the state, and the state promoted the authority of the Church. This unity, combined with a high degree of military expertise, became

Spain's double-edged sword, and explorers carried this sword with them into the New World.

In this chapter, we'll take a look at the drama that was the establishment of Catholicism in the Western Hemisphere. We'll look at the religions that were already here and the effect that Catholic missionaries and soldiers had in the spread of Catholicism. This story involves missionaries, apparitions, exploitation, poverty, discrimination, and new beginnings. Indeed, a lot happened to Catholics and for Catholicism after October 12, 1492.

# Colonization: Ready or Not, Here We Come!

We often think of the New World as New England first and then the rest of the United States. However, the term *New World* describes the continents of South America and North America, including Central America and the Caribbean. Historically, the story of Catholicism in America begins in Mexico. Catholicism was exported from Europe on the same ships that brought the conquistadors. Conquistadors were the soldiers sent by Spain to conquer the people of the New World and establish European rule, which included European religion.

The indigenous people of the New World were architects of beautiful cities. They built canals, temples, and observatories. They knew mathematics and had accurate tools by which they measured the movement of the stars. They had a high degree of technological, artistic, religious, and scientific development. What they did not have, however, were the sophisticated tools of war that the Spanish and Portuguese brought with them. The finely tuned European war machine eventually overwhelmed the indigenous people of the Americas.

It is impossible to separate the spread of the Catholic religion from the effects of exploration and colonialism on the native cultures. Franciscan missionaries accompanied the soldiers into the New World. The soldiers and the priests each had their own agenda: to find gold for Spain and to baptize converts for Catholicism. This era of European expansion lasted for hundreds of years. During this time, the ideas, economies, and religion of Europe were transplanted to the New World.

## Europe Comes to Mexico

The first areas of the New World conquered by the conquistadors were the Caribbean islands, Mexico, and the countries of Central America. Critics of European conquest cite many incidences of inhumane treatment of the native people. Massacres and, in some cases, the complete annihilation of whole cultures occurred. The arrival of the Europeans and the imposition of their civilization left many of the original inhabitants poor, hungry, and suffering from the many illnesses brought by the explorers.

For the most part, the Church turned its back on the atrocities of the armies, accepted the legitimacy of conquest, and apparently had no trouble combining the practice of slavery with the practice of Christianity. It seems as though the Church was satisfied with the belief in the "natural" superiority of the Europeans to these strange, apparently "barbaric" pagans.

At the same time, Mexican historians have noted that it was the missionaries who extended the few acts of kindness and who challenged military practices. It seemed that although the "big" Church was indifferent—and by its indifference was a partner in the atrocities—the "little" Church took a stand against the prevailing practices.

One of the ways the missionaries attempted to assist the people was through the establishment of missions. Missions, not unlike the monasteries described in Chapter 20, were like small villages containing schools, churches, infirmaries, and shelter. Native language, customs, and religious beliefs were replaced with European language, manners, and values. In theory, the missions provided safe havens and were an attempt to socialize the native people into European culture. Many missionaries made little effort to understand the beliefs of the native people, to learn their language, or to engage their culture in any positive way. However, some missionaries did learn the language of the people and even adopted many of their ways.

## Saints Preserve Us

### Blessed Bartolomé de las Casas (1484–1566)

Born in Seville, Spain, he was a missionary to Latin America and the first priest to be ordained in the New World (1512). He was a Dominican who worked to improve conditions of indigenous people and to end their enslavement. The king of Spain named him Protector of the Indians. Bartolomé's efforts influenced the pope to declare that American Indians were rational beings with souls and their lives and property should be protected. His efforts led to the "The New Laws" adopted to protect the native peoples in Spanish colonies. He was the first bishop of Chiapas, Mexico. A scholar and historian, he has been called "the father of anti-imperialism and anti-racism." He knew Columbus and edited his journal. He is called Blessed, a step on the way to sainthood.

# The Beliefs of the Indigenous People

Europe met three main cultures in the New World: the Mayans, the Incas, and the Aztecs. According to historian and theologian Virgilio P. Elizondo in *La Morenita*, the Mayans had a well-developed culture and were great traders. The Incas had a closely knit society that ensured the equal redistribution of goods throughout the empire. The Aztecs were ruled by a monarch and had a hierarchical society. All three cultures were polytheistic, with both male and female deities, including an earth goddess and a sun god. The concepts of an underworld and an afterlife were present, and human sacrifice featured in all, to a greater or lesser degree. The Mayan pantheon was particularly interesting; the dual nature of their deity represented the duality of life and death, with stories of death and resurrection figuring prominently.

In the indigenous religion, Ometéotl, the name of "Great Spirit," was both the Lord and Lady of all creation. Ometéotl's feminine aspect was known by many names. She was the mother of earth, mother of the gods, mother of wisdom, and the heart of earth.

The indigenous religions had many similarities to the Catholicism of Europe, which, after all, had roots in the practices of the old tribal peoples. For example, both the religion of the Indians and the religion of the missionaries had sacred rituals, a calendar of religious feasts, a sacred language in which to speak to their God(s), and a well-defined priesthood with vestments, temples, and processions. The Indians also expressed their religious beliefs through poetry, song, and symbol. In the Indian religion, Elizondo explains, "nothing is unrelated." As we saw in the Old World, Mary intertwined with symbols of existing deities. The feminine aspect of the Indian's Great Spirit, Ometéotl, resurfaced in the coming of Christianity to the New World, as we will see later in this chapter.

# Spanish America

Even though the Aztecs did not possess the essential tools of war that the Spanish had, such as horses, steel weapons, and guns, they could have been a formidable force. However, it only took 6 years for Spain to conquer this major civilization. Three factors contributed to the success of the Spanish leader Cortés and the demise of the Aztec leader, Montezuma.

Many Indian tribes felt that the Aztecs' use of human sacrifice was a corruption of the religion of Quetzalcòatl, which was based on the dignity of life, simplicity, and prayer. Other groups of Indians especially disliked the Aztecs, who used brutal methods to hold their empire together, and they joined the conquistadors in a popular uprising against them.

---

| **Epiphanies** |
| --- |
| Hernán Cortés (1485–1547) was a Spanish explorer and conqueror of Mexico. In 1519, he was welcomed into the Aztec capital by Montezuma II (1466–1520), the last independent Aztec emperor. Montezuma mistook Cortés for the incarnation of the Aztec god Quetzalcòatl, whose return had been prophesied. Four years later, Montezuma was fatally wounded in a battle against the army of Cortés. |

A second factor giving Cortés an advantage over Montezuma was a religious one. In both the Mayan and Aztec cultures, the prophets had read many signs and had begun to prophesy the end of their civilization. The end had been predicted to occur in 1517 and 1519. In a very powerful coincidence (or perhaps as the fulfillment of their prophecy), Cortés landed on the Yucatan Peninsula in 1517 and arrived in their land in 1519.

A further prophecy given to the Indians by their priests predicted the return of Quetzalcòatl, a spiritual figure central to the religion of many Central American cultures. The prophecy foretold that he would come as a bearded white man out of the East. When the Indians saw Cortés, bearded and white, approaching from the east, many of them believed they were seeing the return of their god, and they began to follow him.

After Cortés took over the Aztec capital, the Franciscan priests met with the Aztec priests for a brief period of time. After the Catholic priests examined the religion of the native people with its blood sacrifices, they concluded that the religion should be destroyed. So Cortés and the soldiers not only brought down Montezuma, but they also plundered the temples. In their frenzy, they caused the massive destruction of all aspects of the Central American culture. Towns were destroyed, women were raped, and subjection and slavery were instituted. In the wake of the conquest, the oppression of the native people would last a long time.

The Incas and Mayans experienced similar fates. When the conquistadors arrived in modern-day Peru in 1532, they betrayed and murdered the Inca emperor, and were able to wipe out all resistance in just 5 years. The Mayan civilization was in an advanced state of decay by the time of the conquistadors, yet they still held out against the technologically superior Spanish for nearly 20 years (1527–1546), defeating them on several occasions. After they were overcome, both cultures suffered the same treatment the Aztecs had received.

# Missions and Conversion

As we stated earlier, the relationship of the missionaries to the people tended to be different from that of the conquistadors. The missionaries' underlying belief was that all people should have access to God. They believed the God of Jesus was the true God. However, they respected the people and defended them against the soldiers whenever they could. The native people came to see that the missionaries were sincere, simple men who literally walked barefoot among them. The missions became "sanctuaries" against the soldiers, and the missionaries protested the military's brutal treatment to the civil authorities.

> ### Epiphanies
>
> The Spaniards founded the first university in North America, the University of Mexico in Mexico City, in 1551. Also, the famous Texas landmark called the Alamo was once a Spanish mission.

*Frailes e Indigenas, a Representation of the Comparison of the Bible and the Aztec Codex (the Aztecs' sacred writings) by Spanish and Aztec Holy Men. Federico Cantù 1959.*

*(Courtesy of CONACULTA—I.N.B.A.—PINACOTECA VIRREINAL, Mexico City)*

However, in spite of an improved relationship between the missionaries and the natives and despite the missionaries' most zealous efforts, the missionaries still were unable to convert the Indian people to Catholicism in any significant numbers after 10 years. Broken and powerless, the native people weren't buying into the new religion!

# A New People Emerges

Although the Church failed at first in its efforts to convert the masses, some remarkable developments changed the face of Catholicism in the New World forever. Many who have examined the details of these happenings believe that they were a new incarnation of Christ. Let's take a look at these amazing events.

## The Brown Lady of Guadalupe

On December 12, 1531, a native peasant named Juan Diego Cuauhtlatoatzin had a religious experience that profoundly affected the development of the Catholic Church in the New World. It occurred as he hurried up Tepeyac Hill just outside of Mexico City on his way to Mass at a Franciscan mission. Suddenly, a vision of the Virgin Mary appeared before him. In his vision, she was a young Indian woman, brown and pregnant. As he saw her, she stood in front of the sun, but she did not obliterate its light. Rather, it glowed all around her, illuminating her. Her face radiated compassion, and she spoke to Juan, telling him she was the holy virgin mother of the true God. She spoke in Nahuatl, the Indian language of the conquered people. She told him that she wanted a temple to be built in her honor on the very spot on which she appeared. From the temple, she would help the people. She then sent Juan to the bishop to tell him of her request. He was refused admission and sent away. The Virgin sent him again and this time He was granted an audience. The bishop asked him many questions, and he told the story of the Virgin, right down to the smallest detail of his experience. The bishop did not believe him and asked for a sign that would prove it was the Virgin who had sent him.

**Your Guardian Angel**

Flowers and music often accompany apparitions of Mary. It is believed that these things are the supreme, most perfect means of communicating the presence of God. Likewise, honor is paid to Mary by bringing her flowers and through playing music, such as the many versions of the *Ave Maria* that have been composed for her.

Juan went back to the hill, where Mary appeared to him once again. He explained that the bishop wanted proof in the form of some kind of a sign. She told him to come back the next day and promised to give him proof. The next day Juan was detained due to the illness of his uncle. He was rushing to get the priest, and in his hurry, decided to not stop at the place where he had seen the apparition. As he passed by the place, Mary called out to him. He was embarrassed, but he stopped. She told him that his uncle would recover and that she would have a sign for him at the top of the hill. He went where she directed him to go and was astounded by what he found. There were exquisite roses where they should not be growing at this time of year. She told him to gather the roses inside his cloak and to show no one but the bishop.

Juan went to the bishop, and the bishop asked to see what he was holding inside his cloak. As Juan opened his cloak, roses spilled out onto the floor. The bishop was amazed. But even more astonishing was the exact image of Juan's vision of the Virgin that had been imprinted on his cloak. The bishop fell to his knees in prayer.

Elizondo tells us the appearance of the Virgin Mary had profound significance for the Indian people. In discussing the symbolic meaning of the appearance, he goes on to say that perhaps most important was that the mother of God came to them not as a Spaniard but as one of their own. Her skin was brown, the exact color that the conquerors told them was "inferior." Unlike the typical European images of her, the Virgin was obviously an Indian woman of native Mexican heritage.

It was significant to the Indian people that the Lady stood in front of the sun. The Sun God was the main god in their pantheon. Her position in front of it showed that she came as a new representation of the divine, growing out of that which came before her. In this way, she connected the symbols of the old religion to the new religion of Christianity.

There were further symbols, as well. The Lady's dress was a pale red, the color of the blood sacrifices of the old religion and the color of the blood of the people that had been spilled by the conquerors. Red is also the color of the East, and it represented new beginnings to the people. Her blue mantle told them she was of royal descent, possibly a deity. The stars in her mantle echoed the prophecy given 10 years earlier that told of a comet signaling the end of their civilization. Perhaps most significant was the black maternity band stretched across her belly, in the center of which was the Aztec cross. The Lady was clearly offering her child to the New World. This vision would come to be understood as a new incarnation of Christ in the Americas.

Word of the Lady's appearance spread rapidly across the land. Crowds began to gather at the bishop's home to see the cloak that held her image. It was placed above the cathedral altar and later in the shrine that was built on the site of her appearance, as she had requested. The "Brown Lady" became the new symbol of the Mexican people and a new symbol for Catholicism as well.

The image of Our Lady of Guadalupe, as she is called, fused European Christianity with the spirit of the native people. Because the Indian people could see themselves in her, their own spirituality could translate into Christianity. To this day, the image remains brilliant in the Basilica in Mexico City, which was built on the site of the original appearance of the Lady. Millions of people visit this site every year.

As brilliant as the image hanging in the basilica is, it lives even more intensely in the hearts of the people. The merging of symbols in this image—the Aztec Sun God and the God of the Christians in the womb of the Virgin Mary—transformed both Catholicism and the indigenous religions. For the Indians, the new religion of Catholicism was no longer seen as something foreign, but as something growing out of their own religion. They believed they had entered the next phase of their spiritual story. Rather than seeing the end of their civilization, they saw a new beginning. For Catholicism, this image offered an opportunity for renewal.

## *La Nueva Raza:* The New Race

In the beginning, the Church opposed what they referred to as the Guadalupe incident, fearing that it was a ploy by the native people to reinstate their own religion. Although the grassroots Franciscan missionaries understood the importance of the devotion to Guadalupe, the Franciscan intelligentsia fought it vehemently. However, the archbishop reaffirmed his official support of the devotion. He had ordered the building of the basilica, and he was convinced of the importance of the image.

*A picture of Our Lady of Guadalupe as imprinted on the cloak of Juan Diego in 1531.*

*(Norberto Mujica)*

In the long run, the Church could not deny the remarkable effects the Lady of Guadalupe had on its mission to spread the word of Christ to the people. Unlike the first 10 years of the Spanish presence in the New World, the second 10 years were marked by the conversion of a phenomenal number of Indian people to Catholicism. It was as though the Mexican culture sprang back to life. Festivals, pilgrimages, and dances are still a huge part of Mexican Catholicism today. A mingling of cultures amongst the Spanish, the African slaves they brought over, and the indigenous Indians occurred. From this mixture, a new race of people was born called *La Nueva Raza*.

> **S'ter Says**
>
> **La Nueva Raza,** the new people, is a Spanish phrase that describes both the mixing of the Spanish, African, and Indian blood, spirituality, and culture, and the resulting new culture that was produced.

The "official" Church waited many years before ruling on the miraculous nature of Juan Diego's vision. In 1754, a little over 200 years after the vision, the pope knelt in front of a painting of the Virgin and declared Our Lady of Guadalupe the patroness of Mexico. He instituted a Mass and prayers in her honor. What this meant to the people, in effect, was that the Virgin's appearance had become "dogma." Pope John Paul II canonized St. Juan Diego on July 31, 2002. His feast day is December 9.

---

**Saints Preserve Us**

**St. Martin de Porres, November 3, Patron of Hairdressers**

St. Martin de Porres (1579–1639) was born in Lima, Peru, the son of a Spanish gentleman and a freed African slave. He is one of the few saints of color recognized by the Church. At age 15, de Porres became a Dominican lay brother and became known for his rugged humility. God worked extraordinary wonders through him. He spent his life in service to his community both as a barber and a farm laborer. It was said that God rewarded Martin for his humility with the gift of great spiritual wisdom. Bishops sought his advice, and he resolved many theological problems of the day. St. Martin de Porres became the patron saint of hairdressers because hairdressing was one of the duties he performed for his brothers in the friary to which he belonged.

---

# Cultural Contributions to Today's Catholicism

Firmly planted in the New World, the Spanish and Portuguese culture flowered, as did the Church. The scope of the lands these countries would come to control was immense. It stretched thousands of miles from the tip of the South American continent, across Central America, the major islands of the Caribbean, and from Florida across the South and Southwest to the western shores of California. The heritage of these Catholic lands continues to exist today in place names such as St. Augustine, San Antonio, Santa Fe, and San Francisco.

This heritage goes beyond names on a map. Today, Catholicism exists in large numbers among Hispanic Americans, who are estimated to actually comprise nearly 50 percent of the total United States Catholic population. As the number of Latin American Catholics increases, the face of Catholicism in the United States is changing. The Catholic Church, once dominated by Europeans, struggles today to understand the hearts and minds of these "new people." Communal by nature, and still remembering the poetic-symbolic religion of their ancestors, these people embody a spiritual aspect of religion that offers balance to the more "rational" side of the European Catholic Church.

According to the official 2000 Census, there are 35.3 million Hispanics (or Latinos, as they are termed in the census) in the United States, or 13 percent of the total population. They are 38 percent of the U.S. population under age 18. Since 1990, the nation's Hispanic population has increased 58 percent, up from a total of 22.4 million in 1990. In 2020, the Hispanic population will be approximately 52.7 million. In 2040, this number will grow to about 80.2 million. In 2050, with a population of approximately 96.5 million, Hispanic Americans are projected to constitute 25 percent of the U.S. population, one out of every four U.S. Americans.

The Hispanic people have a strong sense of family and family values. They bring particular religious and cultural practices to the United States Catholic Church in the form of liturgical rituals that strengthen family values.

The *Posada* is a ritual enacted at Christmas in many Mexican American parishes in Texas, Chicago, California, New Mexico, and elsewhere. It involves a house-to-house procession in which a couple, playing the role of the two Galileans, Joseph and Mary, walk through the streets, knocking on doors seeking shelter. Over and over again, they are refused. After the young couple has been rejected a number of times, someone finally listens to what they are saying and offers them a place to stay. As they are received into a home, there is much joy and celebration.

> **S'ter Says**
>
> **Posada**, the Spanish word for "shelter," is used to describe a house-to-house procession at Christmastime in which the drama of the Galilean couple Joseph and Mary is enacted.

The two key themes of this Gospel reenactment are the rejection of the poor and the joy that comes to those who open their home and heart to the ones whom others have rejected. In a remarkable connection, this faith ritual relates beautifully to the current Mexican American experience. Risking their lives by crossing the border to find work to feed their children, Mexicans meet rejection. Like the holy couple who is carrying the child Jesus, the hope of the future, with them, they do not give up.

As in the ritual enactment of the Posada, the second important part of this real-life Mexican Posada involves a request to the people of the United States to open the border, share their wealth, and receive the gift of joy that is the completion of the ritual.

In this chapter, you've met some of the indigenous cultures that were living in the area now known as Central America and Mexico and have heard how Catholicism arrived in the New World. In the next chapter, you'll see how Catholicism spread in the north through European immigration.

## The Least You Need to Know

- There were well-developed cultures on the American continent when the Europeans arrived.

- The colonization and evangelization of North America and South America was accomplished with pain, death, and a great loss of native culture.

- The appearance of Our Lady of Guadalupe transformed the European assault into a new revelation of the face of God.

- Hispanic American Catholics play an important role in shaping the new face of the Catholic Church in the United States.

# Chapter 24

# Catholics Earn Their Citizenship

## In This Chapter

- Catholics and the American Revolution
- Five million Irish sail into U.S. ports
- Germans keep their language and faith
- The Catholic Church becomes American
- Crises of faith and citizenship

In this chapter, you'll see what happened north of the border in the New World. At first, the 13 original colonies barely noticed Catholicism. Soon, however, following an enormous wave of immigration, Catholics became major players in the construction and expansion of the United States. The reaction of the established Protestants to the immigrants was not altogether favorable, and Catholics suffered a great deal of prejudice and discrimination. They reacted by building a fortress Church and developing a strong Catholic identity of separatism.

As time went on, their prosperity in the middle of the twentieth century allowed them to become part of mainstream America and to become champions of democracy. The reward was the election of the first of their own, John F. Kennedy, as president. Before they were able to bask in this new glory, however, his assassination, the Vietnam War, the cultural revolution, and Vatican II's redefinition of Catholicism put American Catholics in a tailspin. This chapter explores these developments.

# Catholicism and Colonial America: There Goes the Neighborhood!

Catholicism's journey took a very different route north of Mexico. The first English colonists were Protestant: Puritan, Quaker, and Anglican, not Catholic. At the time of the American Revolution in 1776, the proportion of Catholics in the British Colonies was estimated to be less than 1 percent. Slowly but surely, however, Catholicism entered mainstream American life.

## Breaking Into the Protestant Club

The colonial adventure began in 1607, when a small number of colonists, mostly from England, settled in the new land. They had endured the difficult migration across the Atlantic and survived the challenges of the first years of homesteading.

At the same time, another situation was all too rapidly becoming apparent in the marketplace of Boston and other ports along the Eastern seaboard: a marked increase in the number of French Catholic traders selling furs. All over the coast of eastern Canada and northern Maine, French trappers and their families were arriving, bringing their version of the Catholic story with them. They brought Catholicism to the northern regions where they trapped and moved down the trade route of the Mississippi River to the port of New Orleans. Like the Spanish in the southern part of the continent, the French intermarried with the native population, sowing their culture and religion into the native soil.

No doubt, the British Protestant population felt squeezed between these two sets of unwanted "invaders," the Spanish and the French. In this unfriendly and somewhat hostile environment, Catholicism, for the most part, was met with prejudice, fear, persecution, and eventually laws that discriminated against it. Indeed, discrimination and prejudice against Catholics would have a long history in Britain's original colonies and throughout much of modern American history. The Protestants were there first, and the Catholics were forced to earn mere acceptance, to say nothing of respect. For instance, early copies of *The New England Primer* were filled with images that would persuade any young reader that the Catholic Church was the Devil incarnate.

---

**Saints Preserve Us**

### Blessed Kateri Tekakwitha (1656–1680)

Kateri Tekakwitha had a Christian Algonquin mother, and her father was a chief of the Mohawk. She converted to Catholicism and was rejected by her people. She ran away to the Christian Indian village of Sault Ste. Marie, near Montreal. She dedicated herself to Christ and led a life of holiness and austerity. She died at the young age of 24. She was known as "Lily of the Mohawk," and the faithful have credited her with many miracles. She has been beatified, meaning that she is called "blessed," which is a step in the process of becoming a saint.

---

# Catholics and the Revolution

Back home in England, in an effort to civilize the Irish and rid the country of its popish religion, Britain had strengthened its penal laws. These laws discriminated against Catholics, even to the point of forbidding the celebration of the Mass. England extended these laws to its colonies in America. Catholics, although few in number, were forbidden to own land or hold office in the New World. Without land, they could not build churches or schools. In spite of the prejudice they faced in colonial America, however, Catholics joined their Protestant neighbors in the revolution. They had a specific interest in it because the British penal laws threatened their religious survival. They became fervent supporters of independence.

Once the Revolutionary War was won and the U.S. Constitution ratified in 1789, the Catholic Church had the freedom to officially establish its first diocese, which it did in Baltimore, Maryland. The Catholic Church in America then elected its first bishop, John Carroll.

As Catholics began to own land and start businesses, they came to be regarded as good citizens, and as a result, their Protestant neighbors more readily accepted them. For the first time, Catholics felt welcome in the new United States. All that would change, however, during the nineteenth century, when Catholic immigrants began to arrive in record numbers, upsetting what had been a delicate balance among the new country's citizens.

# Coming in Droves: The Immigrant Experience

The words *foreign*, *Catholic*, and *poor* became synonymous in the minds of the original Protestant settlers. The relationship of "native" Protestants to "foreign" Catholics entering the United States in the nineteenth century was similar to the way our body tries to fight against what it perceives as disease: by rejecting foreign matter that enters it.

The story of immigration is told in the population statistics. During the century after 1790, the Catholic population grew from a mere 1.1 percent to a significant 14.4 percent by midcentury. Most of these immigrants were Irish or German, and they tended to congregate in the cities. The number of foreign-born Catholics in major U.S. cities was staggering:

◆ Philadelphia: 30 percent

◆ New York: 49 percent

◆ Chicago: 50 percent

◆ St. Louis: 60 percent

Catholic Hispanics, French, Irish, and Germans immigrated to the United States in significant numbers during the first part of the 1800s. Italy, Poland, and Eastern Europe sent even more Catholics at the end of the 1800s and the beginning of the 1900s. More than two million Italians and more than a million Poles and Eastern Europeans came to the United States between 1900 and 1925. These immigrants formed ethnic neighborhoods and parishes often staffed by the clergy and nuns who accompanied them in their migration. They built schools, convents, hospitals, and orphanages. These "ethnic" neighborhoods still characterize cities such as Chicago, St. Louis, and New York.

Due to American farmers' need for harvesters between the 1920s and 1960s, Mexican Catholics increased their migration to the United States. In the 1970s and 1980s, Catholic refugees from Vietnam, Cambodia, Laos, Guatemala, El Salvador, Nicaragua, and Haiti came to the United States as a result of political unrest in their home countries.

## Potatoes, Poverty, and Discrimination: The Irish in America

The Irish potato crop failures in the late 1840s sent huge waves of Irish, most of whom were Catholic, to the United States. In a relatively short period of time,

Ireland's population was reduced by half. Thousands died of starvation at home, and many more died in the "coffin" ships that brought them to America. More than five million Irish emigrated to the United States in the nineteenth century.

Political cartoons, rampant discrimination, derogatory literature, and even physical assaults occurred. By the end of the century, acts of political and economic discrimination were prevalent. For a time in Philadelphia, the bishop had to close all the Catholic churches, dispensing people from their Sunday obligation in order to protect his flock from physical harm. Protestants were attacking and burning the churches in reaction to the Catholics' challenge of the use of the Protestant version of the Bible in the city's schools.

---

### Epiphanies

After the Protestant Reformation, English-speaking Protestants used their translation of the Bible known as the King James Version. As we discussed in Chapter 7, the Protestant Bible differs somewhat from the Catholic version. Public schools of the day used the King James Bible and prayed Protestant prayers, sang Protestant hymns, and required attendance at Protestant services. This situation made Catholic children feel like second-class citizens.

---

A national political party, popularly known as the Know-Nothings, was formed in the middle of the nineteenth century to oppose Catholics and other foreigners. During the immigration of Italians and Poles at the turn of the century, the infamous Ku Klux Klan widened its scope of bigotry to include Catholics.

Despite the difficult situations the Irish faced in settling in their new home, they survived and strongly influenced the character of the Catholic Church in America, not only by their sheer numbers, but also by their indomitable spirit. They brought a love of family, a sense of humor, and a deep respect for the clergy. Since they lacked other political representation, they elevated their priests to the status of the old tribal chieftains of their beloved homeland.

## Sauerkraut and Sausages: Germanic Education and Liturgy

German Catholics also had a strong influence on the course of Catholic history and culture in the United States. At one time, the German immigrants instituted a movement whose purpose was to make German a second language in the public schools. When this movement failed, they sought an alternative. They began to promote and champion what was then only a small movement—the Catholic school system—to preserve their language and culture.

An abiding question for the Church during this time of growth and adjustment was just how much it should participate in the dominant Protestant American culture. There were those Catholics who favored assimilation and those who fought to keep the Church separate. The hierarchy spent much time in its national meetings debating the "school question"—that is, whether or not Catholic children could be educated in the "common" or public schools. By the end of the century the question was decided at the Third Council of Baltimore (1884). With German agitation and support from Rome, the council decided that every parish had to build a Catholic school and that parents had to send their children to the Catholic school under the sanction of mortal sin.

If you were a German-speaking Catholic, you were allowed to become a member of a German-speaking parish, which might lie outside the normal parish boundaries for your home. By 1912, there were more than 1,600 *national parishes*: 346 German, 336 Polish, and 214 Italian. Today, as a remnant of this policy, you might find two Catholic churches standing side by side: one that served an English-speaking Catholic congregation and the other that served a German-speaking one.

> **S'ter Says**
>
> A **national parish** is a parish that is not based on geographic boundaries, but which belongs to an ethnic group. Such parishes, where English was the second language, were common in the United States during the years of immigration. Officially, these are called "personal parishes."

Another contribution made by the German Catholics were the monasteries in the heartland of Indiana and Minnesota, where the vibrant Catholic liturgy was kept alive in this country. The German tradition of monasteries goes back over 1,000 years to the time of St. Boniface.

## Poles: Pierogi and Patriotism

Large-scale Polish immigration to the United States began in the 1870s. The early settlers attended Irish or German Catholic parishes until they could found their own. Soon, however, they established lay committees to raise funds and lobby the bishops to provide Polish parishes and schools. With the parish came other Polish organizations providing insurance for illness and death, promoting Polish religious observances, and sponsoring youth activities.

Polish financial contributions were among the highest in the U.S. Catholic Church. In 1870, there were about 15 Polish parishes; by 1930, there were more than 800. By 1920, there were more than 400 Polish American Catholic schools, and more than two thirds of the Polish American children attended them. The role of the Polish priest was that of the undisputed religious and civic leader. He was spiritual leader, temporal leader, teacher, legal counselor, business advisor, and mediator between the immigrant and American society. In the parish schools, classes were generally taught in Polish, and English was taught as a foreign language.

U.S. Church authorities exercised strict control over national parishes. They demanded title to all property and the authority to assign priests. This denial of lay participation in decision making conflicted with the Polish experience of Catholicism back home. It also conflicted with their dreams of American democracy. A foreign, mainly Irish, clergy and hierarchy controlled the most important Polish institution in America, the parish church. Despite Polish pleas for the appointment of Polish American bishops, it was not until 1908 that the first Pole was ordained bishop. He was an assistant to the archbishop in Chicago.

## Italians: Pasta and Festa

In 1870, Rome, the last vestige of the Papal States, fell, and the pope retaliated by forbidding Italian Catholics to participate in national politics. The Vatican denied recognition to the kingdom of Italy. With the accompanying political, social, and economic unrest, millions of Italians left their homeland. By 1900, more than 100,000 Italians were migrating annually to the United States. Four fifths of these immigrants were from southern Italy, and 75 percent of those who came were working-age males. For the most part, these immigrants were poor and illiterate.

---

**Saints Preserve Us**

**St. Frances Xavier Cabrini, November 13, Patron of Immigrants**

Born into a farming family in Italy, the youngest of 13 children, St. Frances Xavier Cabrini (1850–1917) founded a religious order called the Missionary Sisters of the Sacred Heart of Jesus. She sailed to New York with Italian immigrants in 1898 and opened Columbus Hospital there. She became a citizen in 1909 and took her works of mercy to all parts of the United States. At the time of her death, 3,000 of her nuns lived in 70 convents. She founded more than 50 hospitals, schools, and orphanages. She is the first American citizen to be canonized a saint, and she is the patron of immigrants.

**Your Guardian Angel**

You can attend the annual *festas*, commemorations of the patron saints of particular villages or areas of Italy, in many United States cities. They are popular, citywide celebrations. Perhaps the best known is the feast of San Gennaro in New York, which runs for 11 days in September and attracts over three million visitors.

The Irish-dominated Church in the United States saw its task was to turn these Italian immigrants into church-going, law-abiding Catholics who would demonstrate to U.S. Protestants the compatibility of Catholicism and American patriotism. Their aim was assimilation. Few Italian priests migrated to the United States, and those who did were generally not accepted by the American bishops, who regarded them as incompetent and avaricious. It wasn't until 1954 that the first Sicilian-born bishop was ordained in the United States. It was mainly the Italian religious orders, such as the Franciscans and the Scalabrini Fathers (a special order that was founded in 1887 to minister to immigrants), who served as missionaries to the Italian Americans.

The assimilation goals of the U.S. Catholic Church succeeded with the Italian immigrants. They stand in marked contrast to many Italians in Italy, who are not regular churchgoers and are at times downright anticlerical. They take great pride in the many Italian American Catholic men and women who serve the United States as mayors, governors, cabinet members, and members of the Supreme Court.

---

### Epiphanies

On January 31, 2006, Samuel Alito became the fifth sitting Catholic justice on the Supreme Court, making Catholics a 55.6 percent majority on the Court. Alito joined Chief Justice John Roberts appointed in 2005, Justice Antonin Scalia appointed in 1986, Anthony Kennedy appointed in 1988, and Clarence Thomas appointed in 1992. The first Catholic justice, Roger B. Taney, was appointed Chief Justice by Andrew Jackson in 1836; the second, Edward Douglass White, appointed in 1894, became Chief Justice. Others are Joseph McKenna, 1898, Pierce Butler, 1923, Frank Murphy, 1940, Sherman Minton, 1949 (became a Catholic after retiring from the Court), and William J. Brennan, 1956, the only sitting Catholic justice until he was joined by Scalia in 1986.

---

## African Americans: Soul Food, Clapping, and Justice

Catholicism is the largest religion in the world for people of African descent, and there are more than 200 million black Catholics worldwide. However, Catholics make up less than 6 percent of the African American population. Presently, there are 2.3 million black Catholics in the United States. The history of African American

Catholics goes back to the oldest Spanish settlement in the United States: St. Augustine, Florida in 1565.

The Church's relationship with its African American members has not always been ideal. The Church's position on slavery was disturbingly conservative and cautious. For example, the bishop of Philadelphia during the time just before the Civil War stated that he regretted the consequences of slavery, but at the same time, he cautioned his church members that the public law must be obeyed. Catholic landowners, including priests, owned black slaves as early as the 1600s. The practice was not widespread, but it continued until the end of the Civil War. On the positive side, the pope sent missionaries to the United States from England to open the schools and seminaries to black membership. Also, some bishops, like the bishop of Cincinnati, used his religious authority to call for emancipation.

**For Heaven's Sake**

You're making a mistake if you think that Africa hasn't played an important role in the Catholic Church from its beginning. Sts. Augustine, his mother Monica, Benedict the Moor, Moses the Black, Cyril of Alexandria, and Simon of Cyrene, who helped Jesus carry his cross, were all African. So were three popes!

By the late 1800s, the black Catholic population was approximately 200,000 out of a total black population of 7 million. There were 20 churches, each with its own primary school, and 65 other schools. The schools were staffed primarily by two orders: the Oblate Sisters of Providence in Baltimore, Maryland, founded by Elizabeth Lange, and the Sisters of the Holy Family in New Orleans, Louisiana, led by Henriette Delille and Juliette Gaudin.

Father Patrick Healy, Ph.D., born in 1830 of an Irish father and a mother who was an emancipated slave, was the first freeborn African American priest. This remarkable man became the president of Georgetown University in 1868. Born in 1854, Father Augustine Tolton was the first slave-born priest in the United States. Because no American seminary would permit his entrance, he was educated and ordained in Rome. Upon completion of his studies, he was supposed to be sent to work in Africa. In a surprise decision and possibly to test the United States' claims of being an enlightened nation, Rome sent him to America. He served in a parish in Quincy, Illinois, and later in Chicago.

Although still underrepresented in the Church leadership, today African Americans are visible in all areas of the U.S. Catholic Church. The highest concentration of African Americans is in Louisiana and in the Baltimore–Washington, D.C., area.

African Americans make up 15 percent of the Louisiana Catholic population, 13 percent of Maryland's Catholic population, and 7 percent of New York's Catholic population. There are 250 African American priests and 13 bishops in the United States, one of whom was a recent president of the U.S. Conference of Bishops.

Their presence, and the presence of many other black leaders (deacons, sisters, seminary professors, and heads of religious communities), has created many positive results. Their lively liturgies are a joyful expression of the African soul. Their commitment to justice is a living example of the Church "walking its talk" on a variety of social issues.

As a result of the efforts of these black scholars and others working for racial equality in the Church, a hymnal entitled *Guide Me: The African American Catholic Hymnal* (G.I.A. Publications) was published in 1987. That same year, the first black Catholic congress in the twentieth century was held in Washington, D.C. These have become annual events. Shortly afterward, Catholic bishops issued a pastoral letter on racism titled "Brothers and Sisters to Us," and the black bishops issued their own pastoral letter on evangelization, "What We Have Seen and Heard."

Perhaps the ministry valued most by the African Americans is the Church's commitment to inner-city Catholic schools. Big-city dioceses heavily subsidize education for African Americans who make great sacrifices to enroll their children. Religious affiliation is not a requirement of acceptance into these schools. In fact, the number of Catholics enrolled is less than 30 percent in some schools. Nor are these schools seen as a means of recruiting new Catholics. They are a perfect fit between a Catholic Church that values good teaching and African Americans who value good education.

# A Checkered Church Solidifies

If you look at a penny, you'll find imprinted upon it the Latin phrase *E Pluribus Unum*, "one people out of many," which became the motto of the United States. If the Catholic Church in the United States minted its own pennies, they might read *E Pluribus Unum Catholicum:* "one Catholic Church out of many people." The U.S. Catholic Church faced a major challenge, namely to maintain an essential Catholic identity characterized by oneness under Rome within a culturally diverse America. This Catholic identity was fed by a diversity of ethnic customs, with an emphasis on emotional practices and devotions of the faith, such as celebrations of Mary, feast days of saints, novenas, public processions, and benedictions. Immigrant Catholicism was characterized by dependency on clerical authority and strong ties to Rome.

The Catholics' first experience in the United States was a positive one. In the American Revolution, they won their freedom of religion and the right to own property. They ended the nineteenth century in great numbers, but were rejected by the larger society. The Catholic reaction was to develop a siege mentality and form a cultural fortress within the cities. The Irish had broken the ground of immigration in the new country. The next waves of immigrants, the Germans, the Italians, the Poles, and the Eastern Europeans, benefited from this sod busting, but they also inherited the anti-Catholicism that was so strong in this century.

---

### Epiphanies

Al Smith, a Democrat, was governor of New York. In 1928, he became the first Catholic to run for the presidency. He lost to Herbert Hoover in a campaign marred by anti-Catholic bigotry. The slogan "A vote for Smith is a vote for the Pope" was frequently heard. Born on the Lower East Side of Manhattan, Smith used to joke that he graduated from the Fulton Fish Market. Smith made a commitment to religious liberty and freedom of conscience.

---

## Catholic Prosperity

Although Catholicism prospered, it still remained separate from the mainstream. Instead of merging into the public American world, Catholics built a parallel world of Catholic-run hospitals, orphanages, and welfare agencies that provided food, heating fuel, clothing, and money. There were homes for the aged, schools from elementary through university levels, professional organizations, social charities, and even Catholic cemeteries.

During the 1950s, a Catholic building boom exploded across America. Catholic churches and schools filled the land from Maine to California. In numbers never before experienced in the history of the Church, Catholic parents sent their sons and daughters into religious service as priests, sisters, and brothers. They became the workforce that built the strong identity of the Catholic tribe in the United States. Upward of 70 percent of Catholics attended church every Sunday, and one half of all Catholic children were educated in parish schools. In the evenings, families across the country gathered around their radios to listen to Father Peyton broadcast the family Rosary. Bishop Sheen delivered his weekly TV message to millions of Catholics (and Protestants). The Catholic Church was comfortable in the 1950s.

Every Catholic classroom in the United States displayed an American flag, a picture of the president of the United States, and a picture of the pope. Class began with prayers, followed by the Pledge of Allegiance and four verses of "My Country 'Tis of Thee." Students were taught that good citizenship was an important part of good Catholicism. There was an optimistic spirit and a sense of well-being that went with being Catholic in America. An entire generation had climbed out of the poverty of the immigrant years and could now put money away for their children to attend Catholic colleges. The spirit of the day seemed to say to Catholics that they surely were in the right place at the right time. It fostered their belief that they were citizens of the one true country and that they held the one true faith.

## The Loss of Innocence

In 1960, in a history-making event, John Fitzgerald Kennedy became the first Catholic elected to the highest office in the land, which further fanned the embers of Catholic faith. The odds of Kennedy, a Catholic, winning the nomination and then the presidency of the United States were poor to say the least. Anytime a Catholic aspired to public office, anti-Catholicism showed itself to be lurking just below the surface. Although Catholics had certainly achieved a respectable number in the population, they could not elect a president by themselves. Any candidate would have to win a considerable Protestant vote to make that happen. Protestants feared that a Catholic's allegiance to the Church in Rome superseded allegiance to the United States Constitution.

In a famous speech to the Houston Ministerial Alliance, candidate Kennedy convinced his audience that this fear was unfounded. Although elected by the most narrow of margins, it showed the world that Catholics had "made it," even if just barely. Kennedy was bright, attractive, and promised Americans that life would be good. In so doing, he redeemed a generation of older Catholics from the humiliation of Al Smith's brutal defeat in 1928.

Bubbling beneath the surface of society, however, were stewpots of unrest. As those pots began to boil over in the decade of the '60s, the certainty of the 1950s gave way to questions for all Americans. This experience would ultimately affect Catholics as well. The changes during this decade challenged accepted notions of what it meant to be a United States citizen and what it meant to be a Catholic.

Kennedy's assassination after just 1,000 days in office—along with the assassinations of other political and religious leaders, including Martin Luther King Jr., Robert Kennedy, and Malcolm X, in the years that followed—abruptly ended the innocence of the time and set the nation spinning. For Catholics, it was an especially tough time. The changes in society seemed to go against every tenet of their faith: the use of drugs, protest against the government's involvement in Southeast Asia, the sexual revolution, the advent of the birth control pill, and the possible legalization of abortion. The expectation that they would be the new carriers of America's promise to become the "New Jerusalem" was being sorely tested.

# Catholics Come of Age

Jack Kennedy broke through the religious barrier and seemed to free Catholics' access to higher office. If you examine the lists of the candidates at the top of the ticket during the '60s, '70s, and '80s, it seems that it was almost a requirement to include a Catholic on the ticket: Tom Eagleton, Sargent Shriver, James Miller, and Geraldine Ferraro are all examples of prominent Catholic candidates. The numbers of Catholics in the president's cabinet continued to grow, and their leadership in Congress increased.

Social research showed that Catholics were among the best-educated people in the United States. They were capturing major executive positions in business, and they were moving to the suburbs. What had been a poor, immigrant, illiterate, disempowered minority who had built a Catholic fortress was now truly becoming an organization of the first citizens of the land.

In the 1960s, however, Catholics received a double whammy. Vatican II was called to take a serious look at the definition of the Church. It created questions in the minds of many Catholics. In so doing, it knocked out a major pillar they had come to rely on: the notion that their Church was the perfect, one true Church. In the political arena, antiwar and anti-patriotic demonstrations in the form of burning flags and draft cards knocked out the other pillar that held up many citizens: the idea that the United States was the perfect state. These two blows shook the U.S. Catholic identity. The 40 years since the crumbling of these pillars has been a tough time of reconstruction.

## Movin' on Up

For Catholics, moving into the suburbs meant moving away from the tight-knit, ethnic neighborhood parishes. In the suburbs, Catholics lived side by side with "other" Americans. Often, the parochial school did not follow them to their new suburban parishes. This happened for a couple of reasons. Although Catholic wealth increased dramatically, the cost of building new schools increased even more dramatically. In addition, the suburban public schools that served these Catholics were extremely well financed and clearly superior to the ones in the cities from which the Catholics had come. Catholics who now had their sights set on upward mobility would turn to these public schools for the sake of socially and financially bettering their offspring. It became clear that post–Vatican II Catholicism would no longer be primarily fostered in a Catholic classroom.

## The Transference of Leadership: The Baton Is Passed

Not only did the profile of parishioners change in the 40 years following Vatican II, but so, too, did the leadership. The council introduced a new word to Catholicism: "ministry." In the 1960s and 1970s, as the clerical and religious leadership began to digest Vatican II, people saw a new opportunity for service in the Church. Nuns, whose work had largely been confined to education and health care, went back to school and retooled themselves for work as *pastoral ministers*, rather than schoolteachers. In their absence, both the teaching core and the leadership of Catholic parochial grade schools and high schools shifted to the lay members of the Church.

> **S'ter Says**
>
> **Pastoral ministers** is the term used in the Catholic Church since Vatican II to describe church workers who have taken on various roles that once were filled by priests.

Throughout the Church's history, a wide gap had existed between the clergy and the people. Vatican II seriously challenged this division between the sacred and the secular. Consequently, a great number of priests and sisters reexamined their state of life and the basis on which they had made the choice to "leave the world." Priests left the priesthood, and sisters and brothers left the religious life in great numbers. In 1965 there were 60,000 priests in the United States and in 2000 there were 45,000, despite an increase of 20 million U.S. Catholics. The post–Vatican II climate affected the new supply of leadership coming into the Church as well. Enrollment in seminaries by the end of the 1960s plummeted in a more dramatic fashion than the stock market crash of 1929. In 1960 there were 41,000 U.S. seminarians. By 2000, that number was down to 3,400. On the other hand, while in 1960 there were very few laypeople preparing for professional Church ministry, in 1985 there were 10,500, and by 1996 that number had almost doubled. In 2000 there were over 35,000 lay Catholics enrolled in programs preparing for professional Church ministry, more than 10 times the number of seminarians preparing for the priesthood!

These pastoral ministers perform many of the works that were exclusively done by priests and nuns in the past. While Catholic schools have less and less influence on the increasing number of Catholics, the actual works of pastoral ministry have multiplied. Many of these ministers work in the new youth programs of the parish. More lay ministers work with the sick and dying. Many parishes have bereavement ministers who contact the family as soon as news comes of a death and help that family grieve the loss and prepare the funeral celebration. In fact, lay ministers now make up the majority of professional Catholic chaplains in hospitals. And, of course, many of these lay professional ministers administer and coordinate the spiritual and physical operation of the over 3,000 U.S. Catholic parishes that do not have a resident pastor. All of these pastoral ministers are in addition to the 150,000 lay teachers and administrators in the Catholic elementary and grade schools.

The nonordained serve at the level of diocesan leadership as well as in such positions as chancellor (manager of the bishop's office), chief financial officer of the diocese, and judges in diocesan church courts. Women comprise more than 85 percent of this leadership. Administrative and pastoral responsibilities in the post–Vatican II Church in the United States have become virtual female arenas.

## The Least You Need to Know

- A checkered American Church characterizes the growth of Catholicism in the United States.
- Immigrants from Ireland, Germany, Italy, Poland, Mexico, and many other countries have contributed their cultural traditions to the U.S. Catholic Church.
- *E Pluribus Unum Catholicum:* "one Church out of many people" would be a good motto for the Catholic Church in the United States.
- The results of Vatican II are more participation in the Church by greater numbers of people.
- Catholic identity today is shaped more by parish life as a whole than the parish school.

# Part 7

# A Look to the Future

Finally, we look at the Church of the future from the spirit unleashed at Vatican II. We focus this future through the classic marks of the Church—*one*, *holy*, *catholic*, and *apostolic*—to see how these enduring qualities speak to the Church and to the culture. We look at inequity between men and women, divisions between culture and the earth, competition between European values and values of a worldwide Church, and the power struggle between the institutional Church and Church as community. We look at who the U.S. Catholics of 2025 will be.

Additionally, we take a hard look at the festering wound of sex abuse that has plagued the priesthood for more than a generation, now lanced by the laser light of the media. Taking a Taoist view, we see this as both crisis and opportunity.

We're optimistic about the future. We see the rich resources of the Church's lived tradition as bread for the journey.

# Catholic Sexuality: The Church's Dirty Little Secret?

## In This Chapter

- ◆ Sex scandals: how could this happen?
- ◆ Clerical culture: secrecy and power
- ◆ The heritage of questionable theology
- ◆ The reality of Catholic's sexuality

Beginning 35 years ago as a whisper, and now reaching a deafening crescendo, sex scandals have damaged the faithful, clergy and laity alike. Broken trust cuts away at the structure and threatens the faith of the people. The Church finds itself skating on the edge of financial bankruptcy.

This chapter looks at the abuse and the attempted cover-ups by Church leaders to try to answer the underlying question: how could this happen? In search of insight, we'll look at the history of Catholic sexuality and the development of a clerical culture to see its relation to a climate of abuse. Out of this catastrophe, the people are claiming a new sense of ownership of their religion.

# Sex, Lies, and Vatican Tapes

In the closing years of the twentieth century, and continuing into the twenty-first, we have been blasted with news about sex scandals within the Church. One couldn't open a newspaper or turn on the television without hearing of further discoveries of pedophilia by priests and cover-ups by bishops. These problems eventually led to the unprecedented resignation of a senior cardinal of the U.S. Catholic Church, Bernard Law of Boston.

The Church has always taken a hard line regarding sexuality: Catholics can't divorce, use birth control, or seek an abortion (regardless of the circumstances). However, this time the moral camera is on the clergy rather than folks in the pews.

In addition to thousands of lawsuits filed against the U.S. Catholic Church, reports of further abuses pour in from the four corners of the world. As victims and parents began to come forward and expose these violations, they were assured by their pastors and bishops that the offender would be effectively dealt with by the Church. They were told to "trust the Church." However, what became apparent in the civil investigations as the scandal unfolded was a pattern of cover-up in diocese after diocese. The figures continue to rise, and few Catholic dioceses in the United States are free of accusation.

## "Safe" Sex: Cover-up by Bishops

Focus shifted from the victims and priests to the bishops. Catholics believe their clergy is a special breed—well educated, dedicated, and a cut above the regular guy—and are used to leaving Church business to the "professionals."

However, in June of 2002, the leadership broke usual form and called their own meeting to discuss the problem and discern an appropriate response. In doing so, the timeless code was broken and a new note sounded: people were holding their leaders accountable.

## Is Sex Abuse a Catholic Issue?

What makes such an incomprehensible set of crimes possible? The exact social or genetic factors aren't fully known. Nor are the long-term results of these abuses on the victims known, although experts have testified to the extensive damage and the slow, painful time of recovery.

One question that gnaws away at the hearts of many is whether or not sexual abuse is a Catholic issue. Is there a particular climate in the Church in which sexual abuse was able to incubate, grow, and eventually become systemic?

The sexual abuse of children has been a part of life for thousands of years. Different societies at different times in history have identified it and dealt with it in different ways. Experts agree that certain components are common to the history and profile of all kinds of abuse, including sexual abuse. The agreed-upon ingredients are:

♦ power inequity

♦ secrecy

♦ previous abuse (most abusers have been the victims of abuse).

# Our Legacy: Dualism and the Mind/Body Split

As we gaze into the rearview mirror, we see a man in a hair shirt, another wearing the robes of bishop, and a third in monk's clothing. They are Anthony, Augustine, and Aquinas. These three men, spanning time from two centuries after Christ up into the 1200s, formed the Church's understanding of human sexuality, patriarchy, hierarchy, and finally celibacy, all of which shape the character of the Church's *clerical culture*. From the beginning of the institutional Church, sexuality was rooted in the split between body and spirit, resulting in a suspicion of the body's innate sinfulness, distorting the basic understanding of human sexuality.

> **S'ter Says**
>
> **Clerical culture** is the beliefs, customs, practices, and behaviors of the clergy who live a life distinct from the laypeople.

## The Soul of a Cleric: Anthony and Augustine

Many of the Church's ideals regarding spiritual life were developed in the Egyptian desert during the third century, under the influence of Anthony (251–356), the founder of Christian monasticism. You read about this in Chapter 8, so we'll just remind you that desert spirituality involved men and women living away from the world in separate communities in which they practiced celibacy and virginity, along with a life based on prayer and fasting. They believed spiritual transcendence depended on subduing the flesh. Thus, spiritual perfection was based more and more on celibacy. As time went on, these celibate communities became the primary source for clergy from which popes and leaders were then selected.

Augustine (354–430), following Anthony's teachings, articulated the Church's primary rationale for both celibacy and marriage. Augustine reasoned that original sin was passed through the genitals during sexual intercourse. Out of this philosophy, the Church became fixated on genital sexuality and failed to see intercourse in the context of love, devotion, and family life. Marriage was seen as a necessary but lesser state, reserved for those who could not control their "lower" nature. It took a backseat to the celibate life. Thus the foundation was laid for marriage and also for the clerical culture, a culture reserved for men separate from the world of families and children.

## Celibacy's Slippery Slope

Celibacy was not an easy mountain for the Church to climb. For the first several hundred years, clergy exercised the right to choose marriage and family. A first official step toward mandatory celibacy occurred as early the Council of Nicaea, in 325, when a papal decree was issued insisting that there was to be no marriage after ordination. Candidates for the office of bishop who had wives and children were required to sign a statement protecting the Church from any inheritance claims.

A thousand years passed in the Western Church, and the struggle to achieve mandatory celibacy continued. In the tenth and eleventh centuries, papal documents pretty much solidified its practice in the Western Church. The religious world of the clergy separated further from the world of marriage, and their involvement in family life was limited to the experiences of the clergy's own childhoods. They did not experience sex as part of a complex set of relationships between human beings based on love and caring for one another. They saw it as an independent act disconnected from anything other than procreation.

## Spawning Ground for Sin Legislation

Thomas Aquinas (1225–1274) became the next key theologian, upholding the teaching on sexuality exclusively for procreation by adding Natural Law Theory as the new basis for moral reasoning. The crux of Aquinas's theory is that natural laws exist governing all creation, including the activities of animals and humans. By observing nature, we are able to determine God's will and live in harmony with it. The Church used Natural Law Theory to arrive at its conclusion that there can be no artificial interference in sexual intercourse. Thomas, basing his theory in Aristotle's philosophy, believed there were universal moral absolutes.

A fundamentalist Natural Law has obvious limitations. For example, through its application the Church deduced that although fornication, adultery, incest, and rape were serious sins, they did, in fact, preserve the "natural order" (they could result in procreation) and thus were lesser sins than artificial interference during sexual intercourse (birth control) or masturbation.

## Sex Education: "Thou Shalt Not ..."

The primary message was about keeping sex "under wraps." Under wraps, of course, meant bridled, harnessed, boxed, or subdued in some fashion. The Catholic link between sex and sin was thus forged: the body was declared sinful and spirituality was considered otherworldly—characterized by an ethereal quality of sexlessness. In ruling on sexual matters, the Catholic Church has continued to adopt a Natural Law ethic to guide its members on sex, contraception, and homosexuality. It continues to interpret the primary purpose of sex as procreation and anything that prohibits this natural outcome of sex is seen as a barrier to the fulfillment of the sexual purpose. Thus contraception, oral and anal sex, masturbation, and homosexuality are all understood as activities that prevent procreation from happening and are condemned as unnatural.

**Your Guardian Angel**

Catholic sex education still is focused in "don't." Religious educators are calling for a comprehensive theology to be written on Christian sexuality that would be directed toward understanding human sexuality. They see sex education as a lifelong process affirming the sacredness of love, the body, and sexuality.

Vatican II brought a development to Church teaching on sexuality, placing value on the bonding through mutual self-giving that intercourse creates for couples.

Our legacy of "pure" soul and "vile" body influenced Church theology from the get-go. Just as the association between sin and sexuality was made early in Church history, the link was infused early into the young Catholic's life: everything sexual was sinful.

These teachings remain as trickle-down attitudes from parents and teachers and continue to have influence over younger generations of Catholics. For the Church officials, sex was a series of isolated individual acts—lusting, kissing, petting, intercourse—each bearing its own moral price tag. It wasn't taught (perhaps it hadn't been discovered yet, in the pre-Kinsey world) that sexuality intrinsically belonged to being human, that to break off bits and pieces of sex was like chipping off a piece of Michelangelo's David to teach about art. So few learned how to be sexual beings.

# Clericalism: The Secret Culture

Going back to the question we asked earlier about whether sexual abuse is a Catholic thing, perhaps a clue to the answer can be found in one word, *clericalism*. Clericalism describes the power and influence of the clergy. In its extreme it results in a clerical culture, a composite of the beliefs, customs, practices, and behaviors of a particular class of people who live a life distinct from the larger society, in this case the clergy.

In the Catholic Church, this culture is set apart from the general membership. Formation for the priesthood occurs in seminaries, where young men are separated from their families and friends to spend the next four to eight years in a spiritual incubator. The purpose of seminary formation is to cultivate a special or distinct way of life different from the culture left behind.

The clerical culture has spiritual power over the members. It is in this culture that the Church's rules are made and from which it sets its norms. The clergy's decisions have enormous influence over the larger membership, yet it has no accountability to them. No accountability secures secrecy.

## The Power of Secrecy

The enormity of this secrecy recently came to light when U.S. bishops were required to turn their records over to the civil authorities. Many in the public were shocked to realize the Church existed outside society's laws. Church authorities were not always required to report cases of abuse. Even when they were, the clout of their sacred power was so great that civil authorities hesitated to act; they were more apt to go along with bishops who promised they would take care of this business. Many centuries of clerical culture conditioned both the clergy and the people to accept this privileged discretion with few questions.

The clerical collar is a symbol of trust with sacred power. Catholics have great love and respect for their priests and bishops. For the most part, the clergy lives up to their reputation. That is why Catholics as well as many others were shocked to discover these enormous transgressions. What happens when the priest, wearing the sacred symbol of priestly position, has a very "human" sexual problem? Commonsense questions such as this escaped the imagination for a long time because these men were regarded as living above the world, removed from the mundane. Secrecy has power.

## Bishops: Stewards and Shepherds

Bishops are both shepherds of the flock and stewards of the Church. Looking back over the events of the last few years, this conflict of interests sits at the heart of the cover-ups; it represents a decision to protect the institution at the expense of the children. The effects of this decision—which was not made just once by one bishop, but over and over again by many bishops—is immeasurable.

At the same time that the actions of Church authorities were being investigated, a similar dynamic exploded in the corporate culture and news of financial scandals shared the spotlight with the Church pandemonium. Although these corporations wield a lot of power over our financial lives, the Church claims eternal power over our souls. In short, for believers the stakes are much higher. But in both cases, the dynamics are the same—a cover-up to protect the institution at the expense of the people.

Sexually abusing children is an emotional or mental sickness. It requires treatment. Covering it up, leaving children in danger, giving parents false information, and denying priests the help they need indicates moral decay.

## Peeking Under the Cleric's Robe

Celibacy, a requirement for the priesthood, is surrounded by controversy. As the heat builds regarding sexual abuse in the Church, there is a strong temptation for those who oppose mandatory celibacy to jump on the scandal and attempt to co-opt the emotional charge to help energize their cause. The Church has rightfully made the point that there is no direct correlation between celibacy and sexual abuse. While this is true, there is the tendency of those who advocate for celibacy to refuse to look to see if anything might be discovered about child abuse in the clerical culture. Yet below the surface of these two opposing theories exists the possibility of a deeper connection between celibacy and abuse, the link between celibacy and power.

Celibacy is the glue by which the clerical culture is held in place. A pious but powerful image of the priest that has endured over time is that he is "in the world, but not of the world." Yet the great poet T. S. Eliot wisely reminds us of our humanness in his poem "The Hollow Men," in the line "Between the idea and the reality ... falls the shadow." Celibacy is an idea, an ideal. It has seldom (perhaps never) been practiced perfectly. Yet the Church has presented priestly celibacy as a *fait accompli*, as if it were perfectly lived.

Catholics seldom get a sermon preached where the priest begins with a statement like, "Boy, isn't this sex thing a bear?" Rather, the discussion about sex focuses on the people in the pews. Many feel that it would be better if we knew that the priests were having problems living up to their ideals and that we were all in this together. We'd know up front that they are sexual beings, too, and stop thinking of them as super-human. We'd know what we were dealing with, and we could help each other more. More importantly, parents might be less likely to place children in what might become a dangerous situation, if we were not so naïve on this issue.

Yet priests do struggle with celibacy. They sometimes win the struggle and sometimes lose and submit to a variety of clandestine sexual relationships: with women, with men, and apparently with children. Does this struggle mean there is a relationship between celibacy and sexual acting out? No, but understanding the struggle allows us to shed light on the situation and then be able to recognize and deal with deviancy. When sex is surrounded by lies, cover-ups, shame, and guilt, an unhealthy climate begins to build—sex and secrecy isn't generally a good mix.

When the institutional Church has something to lose, be it its own image of itself, the trust of the people, or the power that is secured through secrecy, the tendency for denial is great. The decision to sweep this volatile situation under the rug is like storing nuclear waste in the refrigerator: it has a half-life that won't go away.

## Protecting Patriarchal Power

There are no women present in the clerical halls of Rome where the decisions are made. There are no children running down the stairways, needing supper, or leaving grimy little handprints on the art. Which goes to say that the attitudes, definitions, and rules about life and, pertinent to our present discussion, the rules about sex, are formed by celibate men who are isolated from the world of women, children, and family men. Further to the point, decisions about sexuality have not changed significantly since the fourth century. The rules were made when people still thought the world was flat and the question of whether women were human was debated in religious and intellectual circles. Clerical celibacy assures that women, children, and family men remain quietly outside the inner circle. To be "outside the circle" means you have no power. In this case, it also means no access to law-making. Celibacy has power.

# Sexual Imagination (Thou Shall ...)

Catholic sexuality among the Church officials seems confusing at best, somewhat disturbing, and downright destructive at times, as we are currently bearing witness to. And sex education has been responsible for implanting ideas about the sinfulness of sex to the exclusion of sex as bonding and nurturing.

How does this perplexing sexual story play out in the Catholic bedroom? At first thought, it would seem to follow that Catholics would be hopelessly messed up. However, that does not seem to be the case. According to research by sociologist and Catholic priest Andrew Greeley, Catholics have good sex—in fact, better than the rest of the U.S. population—measured by everything a sociologist can measure. Catholics place a high emphasis on family, and generally hold women in high regard. In light of the weird messages that have pervaded Catholic teaching and the popular image of sexually repressed Catholics, how can this be?

## The Paradox: Lousy Laws, Good Sex

The paradox lies in the rich Catholic tradition of sacramental ritual, the penchant for smells and bells that is intrinsically Catholic. (See Chapter 9.) Ritual transmits meaning at a deeper level than written or spoken teaching. While the hierarchy relies heavily on Catholic tradition (that body of knowledge we've talked about) to discern truth, the people have traditionally put more emphasis on ritual than on the other forms of Church teachings. While Anthony, Augustine, and Aquinas carry the *rational* tradition of theological writing, it is directed primarily to the intellectuals in the Church. A sacramental tradition based in symbol and ritual imparts spiritual truth to the folks in the pews.

Smells and bells, along with other sensory stimulants such as vestments and banners of bright colors, oils, candles, and pageantry, form the basis of sacramental life. They are the symbols of ancient people, encoded with their inborn sense of the sacredness of life and the earth. As Catholics are sprinkled, rubbed with oil, and otherwise anointed throughout life, they are being spiritually encoded with the understanding that the body and spirit are one. This spiritual and sensory liturgical life sharply contrasts to the dualistic theology that separates spirit and body and it negates conflicting messages that tell us the body is sinful.

Remember, only 10 minutes of the weekly Catholic Mass is dedicated to transmitting the Word through preaching. The rest is all sacramental ritual. Beliefs transmitted through ritual sink deeper into the soul than the written word—they deliver a stronger teaching.

A question begging to be asked is: "Why, then, aren't Church leaders positively influenced by the rituals they perform?" A possible answer is that they probably are, at least on an intellectual basis. But already distrustful and intolerant of their own physical nature, perhaps they theorize on ritual rather than experience it. At the bottom, people, enlivened by earth-based liturgy, live a religious life that is not separate from the physical body, sex, and family life.

## The Least You Need to Know

- Sexual abuse by priests is one element of the recent sex scandals, and the cover-up by bishops is a second and more destructive element of the scandals.

- Not everything is known about the causes of abuse; however, it is known that power inequities and secrecy are factors.

- While Church history gives a picture of a flawed understanding of the body and spirit, the sacramental life celebrates the presence of the spirit in the body.

- The Church is called toward being a community, where the primary concern of the institution is to assure the safety of the whole flock.

# Face-to-Face in the Third Millennium: The Church Looks to the Future

## In This Chapter

◆ A new name for a "new" Church

◆ Challenges the Church faces in the new millennium

◆ Strengths and values that transcend time

◆ Who are the people of the "new" Church?

Ecclesiastes reminds us that there is really nothing new under the sun. However, every age seems to have its own version of the same old human story; each page brings a "unique" set of challenges and with them come opportunities. In this chapter, we'll take a look at four challenges the Catholic Church faces as it moves on into the third millennium. At the same time, there are resources and traditions within the Church that can meet these new situations with creativity. We'll look at those resources, too.

# Recap: Past, Present, and Future

Pope John XXIII told the Church to turn and face the culture, to embrace it, and learn from it. His advice represented a complete reversal from the past—it sounded a new note in Catholicism, the beginning of a whole new symphony. The new journey required a new self-image. For many years, the Church thought of itself as the City of God; it was above the terrain of this world. The image was one of separation—separation between the Church and the world, between members and clergy, and between Catholics and other faith communities. The Second Vatican Council retrieved an old biblical image, Church as the "People of God," an inclusive vision of community, recognizing we're all in this thing together.

It is no small thing to change one's image. In a 2,000-year-old institution of a billion people, it's a massive undertaking. It affects every interaction between the institutional Church and members, and likewise with the larger world community. John XXIII's vision was both prophetic and harkened back to earlier times. While simple in concept, it is profoundly complicated to accomplish, no surprise that it meets resistance and takes time. And there are the natural concerns that change brings, the need for stabilization to make sure things don't completely fall apart.

The Church has four enduring qualities that have held it together for 2,000 years. During that time it has seen many changes. These qualities assure its transcendence into a new time and place. You may recall them from the old catechism, the four marks of the Church: *one, holy, catholic and apostolic.* In this chapter, we'll look at how these essential qualities guide the Church as it turns to face the world and fully engages the global culture of this time in history.

## The Tectonic Plates Shift

Pope John XXIII's directive is part of a shift in consciousness that is occurring throughout Western culture; it's called a *paradigm* change. Paradigms are models, or basic ways of understanding reality; maps, as it were, on which humans attempt to organize life. For a variety of reasons (including lobbying by the Holy Spirit) these core assumptions about life are periodically called into question—and when enough people hold the same questions long enough the map is redrawn. When a paradigm changes, it's like an earthquake: not necessarily destructive, but definitely rearranging the landscape! Paradigm shifts in

> **S'ter Says**
>
> A **paradigm** is a model, or a very clear example of something. It helps us to frame our thinking. To change our paradigm requires a major shift in how we see things.

Western history include the ending of tribal life, the building of city-states, the demise of many monarchies, and the advent of democracy.

Paradigm shifts within the Church are on a somewhat parallel course with culture. The Church began as a spontaneous loosely formed movement within communities; it shifted to a hierarchal institution, and is now uniting these two aspects in the model, People of God. As you've seen throughout this book, there is a dance going on between the Church and culture—they shape and are shaped by one another.

While the paradigm shift began in the field of physics, it is changing our understanding of reality in all areas of human development, including medicine and social sciences. And this realization that matter is no longer the spiritless thing we thought it was makes it possible for the rational world of science and the symbolic understanding of faith to look each other in the eye and shake hands.

The new paradigm is one of connectedness. It breaks through the dualistic thinking that has characterized Western thinking since early times. The new map no longer separates the sacred from the world, matter from spirit, or clergy from the people. The following table shows how four principles—authority, power, order, and the divine—change with the new paradigm. Many theologians understand the principles of the new paradigm to be the same as those reflected in the teachings of Jesus. They believe that it takes us past the dualism that has impeded many from grasping the true Christian message.

Here is how Christian principles look when translated into nondualistic principles.

| Old Paradigm | New Paradigm |
| --- | --- |
| Either/or | Both/and |
| Institution vs. Private | Mutual |
| External vs. Internal | Cooperative |
| Transcendent vs. Immanent | Omnipresent |

We'll look at the four marks of the Church mentioned earlier, drawing on the new paradigm principles of quantum physics as a way of understanding that all reality exists both in the material sense (concrete) and potential sense (spirit).

# The Church Is One

*The Catholic Teaching:* in the *Catechism of the Catholic Church*, we are told that unity is the essence of the Church. The Church is unified through its source in the Trinity, through its founding in Jesus Christ, and in soul through the Holy Spirit. All people and cultures are gathered in this unity as the People of God—bound together by love.

*The Challenge:* to come to terms with its feminine nature.

## The Church's Unified Vision

As we've seen from the beginning, the Catholic Church has pursued a vision of unity. The quantum worldview brings with it the potential for realizing that vision by making the presence of Holy Spirit in all people and in all human endeavors obvious. Realizing that God exists in the "differences" allows us to let go of the fear of diversity that has clouded the vision. It tunes us to the mystery waiting to be revealed in each encounter.

## Unified Vision Interrupted

The unified vision cannot come into being when many members of the community stand outside the circle. Western society's heritage is patriarchal, which, as you have learned, means male leadership. The Church was organized according to the society of its time, and women have been excluded from decision-making leadership since the second century. As the secular culture moves closer to equity between the sexes today, the Church is woefully behind the times. However, it has a history of female leadership and an opportunity to step ahead of the crowd. Society is searching for religious values to help shape these new roles. Equity does not mean simply putting women in leadership positions; it calls for a transformation of the organization to reflect the values of both men and women. Such an institution would be much more communal and less hierarchical.

## Women in the Wings

The Church has a powerful resource in its history of female leadership. From the early years when convents and monasteries first developed to the present time, there has been a strong Catholic tradition of religious women (nuns) making their own decisions and setting their own policies. In modern times, women have continued that tradition as CEOs in education and health-care systems, making Catholic women among the first in Western culture to occupy executive roles.

If you were to look at college and university presidents in the 1950s, you would find very few females, but those you would find would very likely be Catholic nuns.

Today, women remain a primary resource for the continuing life of the Church. They are in the forefront of religious scholarship. The majority of students in the ministry programs at Catholic colleges and universities are females. At many Protestant seminaries, it is Catholic women who make up an increasingly large proportion of the student body, studying theology and pastoral ministry, as chaplains and religious educators. They are preparing to be leaders and decision makers in the Church, and already parishes in the Catholic Church are without a priest, and women are pastoring them. Yet ordination is the gateway to decision making in the Church. And as these women prepare for a variety of ministerial responsibilities, some are preparing for ordination. At this time, however, the doors of the Catholic seminaries, and ordination, remain closed to them.

---

### Epiphanies

Sister Mary Madeleva, C.S.C., president of St. Mary's College in Notre Dame, Indiana, was a champion of women's education in the Church. In 1949, she presented a groundbreaking paper in which she proposed an educational reform program for American nuns. Until this point, they had been put into the burgeoning Catholic schools before they had a chance to finish their own education. The pope called the major superiors of religious women to Rome and urged them to offer programs of professional education and spiritual formation before sending sisters to their assignments. This movement changed the identity and set the direction of Catholic nuns, making them some of the best-educated women in the country.

---

## Letting Justice Roll Down

From its first council in 325 C.E. to the present, there have been 21 councils in which beliefs and policies for all its members have been established. However, no woman has ever had decision-making authority at any of these definitive church meetings. The Church does have precedents and resources for dealing with change regarding cultural and societal inequities. In the past, when the U.S. Catholic Church refused to admit black students to the seminaries, the Vatican opened Roman seminaries and ordained these men.

Strides toward partnership were made after Vatican II, and women have been allowed to participate in several official ministries. The new Code of Canon Law (1983) made provisions for the expansion of women's roles in the Church, opening the following positions to women on the diocesan level: diocesan chancellors (the chief operating officer of the bishop's staff), auditors, assessors, defenders of the marriage bond, promoters of justice, judges on diocesan courts, members of diocesan synods, and financial and pastoral councils. It also allowed women to become pastoral administrators in parishes that have no priest. However, ordination is still prohibited.

Papal statements since Vatican II have continued to uphold the ban against women's ordination, and Pope John Paul II closed the discussion on it. At the same time, groups of women and men, including both lay and clergy, are holding a vision of unity, advancing the Church toward the "tipping" point. They do this not out of a sense of rebellion, but as a genuine expression of the Holy Spirit. They belong to the Church not because they have to, but out of choice. Many feel that Rome's refusal to enter into discussion may actually be moving the Church toward a deeper transformation than simply ordaining women.

# The Church Is Holy

*The Catholic Teaching:* the Church is holy—not that all members are holy, but through the abiding presence of the risen Christ who dwells among us. The path is open, and the journey is toward manifesting the love and goodness that has been laid out.

*The Challenge:* to come to terms with its own spirituality.

As Church members refuse to be defined in a "pay, pray, and obey" way with the emphasis on rules and regulations, it moves toward a more spiritual understanding of the human journey. Indeed, studies tell us that almost one half of the people in the United States meet at least monthly in some sort of a small group that defines its purpose as a spiritual quest. This is a startling shift from a few years ago, representing a transformation not only of our sense of community but also of our sense of the spiritual. With greater material consumption now than in all preceding centuries put together, the call to spirituality has never been sounded more loudly.

## Spirit on the Rise

People who don't belong to a church or formal religion talk about being on a spiritual quest. A trip to any bookstore yields shelves of material about spirituality, and retreats, seminars, and workshops on spirituality abound. Coursework at any given

Catholic university shows a decided proliferation of classes on inner growth and self-discovery as well as spirituality and the spiritual classics, such as Hildegard of Bingen, Catherine of Siena, Teresa of Ávila, John of the Cross, and others in the Catholic mystic tradition.

The overlap of psychology and spirituality is inevitable. The word *psyche* itself means soul. Psychology, like the other sciences, separated from religion for a time; but it is reclaiming its original work of helping people discover their souls and connect to the inner dwellings of the spirit. Whether the message is coming from the human potential movement as self-actualization or the U.S. Army as "Be all you can be" doesn't matter. Beneath the slogans is a desire to develop the self and to incorporate the spirit.

### For Heaven's Sake

Don't forget, "Christ is present in all things"; so say the Jesuits. The new interest in spirituality draws Church members back to their Catholic identity in the sacraments. As they reconnect to their sacramental roots in the physical elements—earth, air, fire, and water—consciousness of the presence of the sacred in all creation is awakened and senses are sharpened.

# The Church Is Catholic

*The Catholic Teaching:* all nations form but one community. This is so because all stem from the one stock which God created to people the entire earth, and also because all share a common destiny, namely God. His providence, evident goodness, and saving designs extend to all against the day when the elect are gathered together in the holy city (from the Catholic Catechism: 311).

*The Challenge:* to come to terms with its catholicity.

You might recall from an earlier discussion that the four marks of the Church were first written in Greek, and later transcribed into Latin, as it became the official Church language. We noted that the term "catholic" remained in its Greek form as the official name—*katholikos, kata* or "toward," plus *holos* or "whole." Catholic is often translated as universal, meaning the Church is for everyone and it is found all over the world. This is true. But "toward the whole" has a different meaning. Let's explore the difference between these two understandings from a quantum perspective.

## Universal: All Over the Map

Today, there is no corner on the globe where Catholicism is absent. What was once an essentially European Church now finds itself surpassed in size by the Church of Africa, Asia, and the Americas. Together, these areas of the world add up to 75 percent. Europe represents the other 25 percent. Clearly, Catholicism is no longer a European Church. Yet at the beginning of the twentieth century, more than 75 percent of the Catholic population was in Europe, as it had been for centuries.

Global ministry has long been a major part of the Church—Jesus' last words to his followers were "Go, make disciples of all nations." (Matthew 28:19) Catholics have set up schools and hospitals, and created diplomatic alliances all over the world in an effort to bring the Church to other cultures. However, in doing this, missionaries often went with the understanding that bringing the Church to the people meant converting the people to the European understanding of the Church, rather than finding Christ in the lives of the people. This method resulted in the destruction of many cultures.

This old understanding of "catholic" as a universe drew lines of distinction between itself and the larger world and does not challenge the existing membership to learn and grow—to expand and embrace. The new way is respectful of other cultures, learning from the people and seeing all of us belonging to unified divine creation.

Distinction between different religions is not being erased—it is important to identify and to preserve the beliefs and practices of people. Again, the changes that are happening aren't external, they're internal. Transformation is happening as our perception of who we are in relationship to others is transformed.

## Speaking a Universal Language

The Holy Spirit came to the apostles and disciples on Pentecost, filling them and sending them out into the world. When the disciples spoke to the people, each group could understand in their own language. It is important to note that the people didn't necessarily understand the language the apostles were speaking, but rather the other way around. It was as if the apostles were speaking the people's native tongues. The story is saying it's up to the messenger to transmit the message in the language of those being addressed. This happens naturally through the language of symbol— where we see our likeness. The deeper understanding of "catholic" is "toward the whole." It means opening to embrace, not forming a closed circle.

The Church is being drawn to higher ground where it can *become* sacrament, finding common expressions of the sacred within different cultures—bridging the gap. The new missionary, whether talking with friends and neighbors or to those across the world, speaks from a deeper understanding of Christianity, an ability to relate through the symbols of faith, rather than a strictly literal understanding of the Christian message.

New missionary efforts adapt to the culture they have come to serve—outreach respects local autonomy. New religious orders and clergy are drawn from the cultures of the people they serve, and native people are increasingly selected as bishops and archbishops. In 1978 there were 3,714 Catholic bishops; in 2002 there were 4,439. The bulk of that increase can be attributed to Africa. Rather than becoming the means of instilling European values, indigenous religious leaders relate to specific needs of the local people. The Mass thus becomes a celebration of diversity. Colors, fabrics, flags, and other sacramentals relate to the symbols of the people, rather than the overlay of European symbols. Church architecture is no longer imported from Europe, but instead churches are made of local materials, designed by the people according to the styles of their culture.

The new Church heralds the end of colonialism and the beginning of a new era. For this "new people," the Gospel message is grounded in the political, economic, social, and spiritual realities of the local area, rather than exclusively those of Europe. Perhaps most importantly, in a transformed understanding of the Church's mission— to bring the "good news"—the Church offers itself as a symbol of the coming together of people, loving one another and sharing resources as the early apostolic communities did. It does this by expanding itself to embrace others, to celebrate diversity, to enlarge their own understanding of the Gospel.

# The Church Is Apostolic

*The Catholic Teaching:* The whole Church is apostolic, in that it remains, through the successors of St. Peter and the other apostles, in communion of faith and life with her origin—and in that it is sent out into the whole world. All members of the Church share in this mission, though in various ways. "The Christian vocation is, of its nature, a vocation to the apostolate as well." Indeed, we call an apostolate "every activity of the Mystical Body" that aims "to spread the Kingdom of Christ over all the earth." (from the Catholic Catechism: 377)

*The Challenge:* to come to terms with its Mystical Body.

Most Catholics are more familiar with the term apostolic as "apostolic succession," describing papal lineage, connecting the office of the pope to Peter. However, the term "apostolic" applies both to the Church's institutional leaders and to the members of the Christian community. It describes the experience of a community of people who have an unbroken line back to the first communities and to the experiences of Jesus when he was with them in human form. This apostolic group is devoted to keeping Jesus alive in their community.

These two concepts of Church, expressed in Chapter 4 as The Big Church and the Little Church, really are two aspects of the same thing, following the same pattern we have seen throughout history. The Church as institution can overshadow the Church as community—cathedrals being more visible to the passersby than the people within them. Rather than seeing itself as supporting the community, it has viewed the community as supporting the institution—after all, cathedrals cost money. A quantum understanding of Catholicism connects these two separate functions again, seeing them as vital, and necessary, equal partners.

## Partnership: From Power Over to Empowerment

The renewed Church involves partnership with power and decision making that reaches back to apostolic time. It reclaims the understanding of common power that was the original "good news" to the early communities. As the Church shifts from the mechanical world to the quantum world, it is shifting from the hierarchical to relational power, where the people again have access to decision making.

The institutional Church's power and its notion of absolutism have gotten it into trouble more than once. The traditional response put forth by the hierarchy to any objections (as mentioned earlier) is "The Church is not a democracy." Opponents agree, adding, "nor is it an aristocracy or a dictatorship." Instead, it is a community. As the Church moves forward, the structure will have to include both a way of talking with the people and a way of listening. This feedback loop will make decisions more communal. We've shown some of the ways this is already happening, as well as the resistance. In doing that we are identifying both poles; agreement will come by finding middle ground. Or, as we have been saying, agreement will come by going to higher ground.

## Sharing the Bread

The Church has a powerful resource within its tradition to accomplish partnership. This resource is Jesus, the man who came out of Galilee 2,000 years ago and gathered together communities for sharing, a purpose that was ritualized in the Eucharist.

Jesus, a Jew, honored the rituals of his religion, but did not teach in the Jewish temple. He taught his followers through the everyday experiences of the world in which they lived, showing people how to honor the "kingdom within." As he taught them to go within themselves and connect with God, he transformed their understanding of power. In every action, in every word, in every way, he told his followers that they had the power, saying "The Kingdom of God is within you."

Jesus also changed the flow of power in another significant way. He did not direct his teaching to the Temple authorities, as you might have expected him to do. He did not tell them they should treat the people differently, which would still be a top-to-bottom flow—it would still leave them looking outside themselves for their spiritual identity. Jesus did what would be called an end play in football jargon—he told the people to understand themselves differently, thus reversing the flow of power, turning the 4,000-year tradition of patriarchy upside down, and instituting a time of partnership.

> **Your Guardian Angel**
>
> Prayer is an equal opportunity event! According to Vatican II, the new image of the Church as the People of God challenges any notions of spiritual elitism, which have been fostered by differences between clergy and laypeople. The spirituality of the common people is not to be considered in any way lesser than priestly, religious, or monastic spirituality.

The challenge to build partnership models in the Church of the next millennium is a challenge to the people, as well as the leaders. As the paradigm within the Church shifts, the challenge to its members is to understand themselves differently—to accept their power and take responsibility as full partners. The challenge to the leaders is the same, but in reverse. It is to understand leadership differently and take responsibility for sharing power.

The ultimate survival of the Church, of course, depends on the generations to come. Following our theme of quantum Catholicism, the question is: how will the Church of the future meet the challenges of the next generation?

# The New Generations: Passing the Cup

No one can tell the story of Catholicism's future, but we do know it lies in the hands of the next generations. Who are these young people? How are they responding to Catholicism? When we look to the Catholic future, it might be helpful to do a quick survey of the present.

**Pre–Vatican II Generation** are Catholics who came of age prior to Vatican II and comprise approximately 22 percent of Catholics born before 1943. They've upheld the institutions of twentieth-century Catholic life and they exhibit a loyalty to the institutional Church.

**Vatican II Generation Baby Boomers** were born between 1943 and 1960 and are more likely to follow their yearning for fulfillment regardless of whether they find it in the institution or elsewhere. They comprise about 43 percent of the Catholic population and are largely responsible for the spiritual movement we described earlier.

**Post–Vatican II Generation: Anglos & Latinos** were born between 1960 and 1980 and have almost no lived experience of the pre–Vatican II Church. They are estimated to be 41 percent of the adult Catholic population.

---

### Epiphanies

The "Next Gen"—sometimes called Gen Y, Echo Boomers, or Millennium Generation—have left the nursery and are arriving on the scene. They're between the ages of 5 and 20 and of greater numbers than any previous generation—being themselves a baby boom brought on by the baby boomers! They're more racially diverse than previous generations. In the United States, one in three is not Caucasian. One in four lives in a single-parent household. Three in four have mothers working outside the home. As a point of reference for those of us who are boomers and older, these kids began using computers in nursery school.

---

## Post–Vatican II Generation: Anglos

This generation is largely made up of the descendants of the European immigrants. Many are seeking family and beyond that, a community. They describe an ideal community not unlike the New Testament family whom Jesus identified when he was asked who his brothers and sisters were. He replied, "Those who hear the word of God and do it."

This generation has a healthy irreverence and skepticism of all institutions, including the Church. They recognize God's presence in the broadest sense and see God in all communities, all religious traditions, and all races. Their God is not bound to one sexual identity. This generation is more comfortable crossing cultural barriers than any of its predecessors.

They share a bond of diversity, and tolerance is their ethic. For them, church is not an end in itself but a symbol, and they refuse to idolize it. This generation has not been schooled in religious education in the traditional ways. Many are unfamiliar with the *Catechism*, and their heroes and role models are not found in the lives of the saints. They are unfamiliar with the history of the Church. The symbols are drawn from the pop culture; life's meaning is conveyed to them through music, movies, sit-coms, and comic book characters. A large portion of this pop culture, by this genera-tion's own admission, is meaningless, yet a part of it does carry meaning and even creates inspiration. They seem to be asking for the Church to help them in sorting out the mix.

## The Latino Generation

A particular portion of this generation are young *Latinos* who, like their Anglo coun-terparts, are in their 20s and 30s, and come from as many as 22 different countries of origin. Many are white, some are black, and most are in between. They are a global culture. Some of their families have been in the United States for centuries; some have only recently arrived. They are the descendants of the conquistadors and the Indians of the New World culture.

More than being simply bilingual, they are rediscovering their roots and inventing a new bicultural identity, meaning that they exist in both worlds without losing the sense of who they are. They weave a complex web of relationships with their elders, with other cultures, and with one another. They show no signs of assimilation or Americanization. Rather, their strong identity influences the culture.

### Epiphanies

The terms **Hispanic** and **Latino** are used interchangeably to define a diverse people. The terms refer to Mexicans, Caribbeans, Cubans, Puerto Ricans, Dominicans, the Andean people, and people from the American Southwest. The diversity of the Hispanic community is its strength. The religious spirit of these people blended with the Catholic faith. Their spirituality is expressed in love of God, love of neighbor, and love of self; this love binds the people together fashioning *el pueblo de Dios*, the people of God.

For the most part they are Catholic and their faith is more unstructured then their parents'. As one member put it, "We respect and honor Catholic traditions, yet are not bound to the old practices." Their Catholicism is cultural as well as religious, and it is integral to their Hispanic identity. They are aware they come from a rich culture and history, and they want to celebrate it. In a marked contrast to their Anglo fellow young Catholics, they draw a strong part of their religious values and identity from family. They often grew up living together with aunts, uncles, cousins, and grandparents, all attending church together.

# Quantum Generation: Generation Q: Identity Chosen, Not Commanded

As the Church enters the new millennium, it does so with a generation for whom all things are alive, filled with spirit, and connected. We might call this new generation of Catholic youth the *Quantum* Generation. They seem to have been born with a global consciousness, having inherited a global vision of what it means to be human, and are carrying the values that can bring in their vision.

Those in the Church who work with these young people say they are looking for ways to be involved and that it is important that they feel invited. They want to be with others of like values. They don't have the traditional structure of growing up their parents and grandparents had, and they want to form that kind of relationship. The Church is attractive to them for that reason, but they have to be invited. They have a spiritual hunger, and they seek a place to nourish it. If the Church is to reach them it will have to be perceived as having something important to give. Service to others is important to them, and they are willing workers when offered the opportunity.

---

### Epiphanies

Demographically, about 60 percent of Catholics under 20 are Latinos and Latinas, many of whom were not born within the U.S. borders. A good number of these kids live in the West and Southwest, not the Catholic institutional bastions of the Northeast and Midwest. They are big-city dwellers for the most part. It is less likely for them than their grandparents that both their parents are Catholic and that they were married in a Catholic church. Also unlike their grandparents, 50 percent of whom attend Mass once a week, only 25 percent of their parents do. Only about 60 percent of their parents are registered in a Catholic parish versus almost 80 percent of their grandparents.

---

The third millennium presents major challenges. The story of the Catholic Church will be lived and written by the Church's greatest asset: the next generation. From our point of view, its spirit is strong and it is in good hands.

---

**Epiphanies**

One of the most successful programs for the young is Theology on Tap. It is an opportunity for the young to gather to share their faith concerns, along with a meal and company. The format is generally a series of evening events that are simple and relaxed: gathering in a restaurant, listening to a presenter, and then sharing. These programs are popular in many dioceses around the United States.

---

# Incarnation: Celebrating Life

The Creator of this vast universe took form as a tiny baby, and walked among us. He delivered a simple message that spoke of loving and a love demonstrated by feeding each other and caring for the needs of the world. It is ironic to think that his arrival into the human story should be interpreted as anything but encouragement and an indication that this is a good place and we are good people. It is hard to believe that the very folks who most celebrate his coming, even name themselves after him, might miss the point.

During a recent U.S. presidential election, the slogan "It's the economy, stupid!" circulated. A way of adapting that phrase to this situation might be: "It's the Incarnation, idiots!" For a long time, the Church has been focused on the Resurrection. It claims special status as the Church of the Risen Lord. In doing that, it puts more of an emphasis on God's otherworldliness. Not a bad thing for a religion to do. However, balance calls us to look more closely at the Incarnation. Not just to settle questions about whether Jesus saved us, paid our bill on sin, or showed us how to live; those kinds of theological debates go on forever. Who can really know the mind of God? Balance might come in a simpler, easier way. What does any family do when a baby is born? They celebrate. It might be time to celebrate the Incarnation, rather than attempt to figure it out.

# In Conclusion

In that spirit of celebration, we conclude the third edition of this book, with gratitude to all who have read the first two editions, and many who have written to us to let us know what was missing, as well as what they really liked. Over the last three years, the book has given us the opportunity to meet many people and hear about their faith struggles and victories. The old way was to think we were all separate, and that at the time of death, some would be sent one way and others a different way—and we all had our fingers crossed! In listening to the people, it becomes clear that we are all in this thing together and we sink or swim as a community. As imagined differences fade, as rank and privilege erode, we see ourselves reflected in one another's eyes—we move closer to the promised wholeness.

In the introduction to this book we promised to do our best to make the title come true: Understanding Catholicism. Hopefully we've done that. However, Catholicism is a complex religion. It is symbolic, full of sacrament and ceremony, and when you enter that realm you are in for some surprises. Things are not always the way they seem, nor are they totally understandable. Paradox rules!

One way of understanding Catholicism is to understand it as a living faith. Faith doesn't have a hardcore forever and ever definition, but is characterized by qualities or graces such as conviction, trust, belief, confidence, and more, and it comes in manageable doses as you go. It's good to remember the Church is a pilgrim people—and this is a Church on a journey. To completely comprehend faith would be attempting the impossible—to be God. The Catholic Church probably stands the tallest and makes its strongest statement when it answers some of the most difficult theological questions by humbly saying, "It's a mystery."

## The Least You Need to Know

- Catholicism is a living faith—a mystery transmitted through ongoing revelation.

- The Church of the future moves beyond dualism, healing the separations of the past: mind/body, male/female, matter/spirit, unchanging/changing, and moving toward wholeness.

- In order to thrive, the new Church is less bound by fixed dogma and rules, and more connected through its common vision. This open spirit allows it to grow and expand naturally.

- Young Catholics are drawn to the Church out of the need for a genuine experience with religious values—they are eager to work for justice, and want doctrine and ritual.

- The emerging Church is reminiscent of the early Church in that its great diversity is its strength.

# Glossary

**abortion, clinical**  Intentionally bringing about the termination of a pregnancy to cause the death of the fetus.

**absolution**  The power the priest has through the sacrament of reconciliation to extend God's forgiveness to contrite people.

**altar**  From the Latin *altare*, akin to Latin *adolere*, which means to burn up. An altar is a raised structure on which the Eucharistic elements are consecrated in the sacrifice of the Mass and incense is burned in worship.

**angels**  Purely spiritual creatures with intelligence and free will, acting as messengers and protectors in service to God.

**apostolic**  One of the four classical marks of the Church, which characterizes the connection of the Church for all time to the tradition and experience of the first followers of Jesus, the apostles. The term designates the authenticity of the tradition.

**Ascension**  Jesus' return to heaven after his death and resurrection to be reunited with God and to prepare a place for his followers.

**Assumption**  When the Blessed Virgin Mary's earthly life was completed, she was taken up body and soul into heaven, where she shares in the glory of her son's resurrection.

**baptismal font**  Large container for holy water often made of marble and placed at the entrance of the church that is used in the sacrament of baptism.

**base communities**   Small groups led by laity who gather together for Scripture reading, discussion, Communion services, and community action; this movement started in Latin America.

**belief**   An expression of faith accepted as true even in the absence of scientific proof; it may or may not be part of official Church teachings (see *dogma*).

**Bible**   The sacred texts of both the Old Testament (or the Hebrew Scriptures) and the New Testament (the material written after the time of Jesus).

**Bible vigil**   Post–Vatican II Church ceremony during which the Bible is honored on the altar and passages are read and reflected upon.

**bishop**   The highest order of ordination in Church hierarchy; this person is ordinarily in charge of a group of parishes called a diocese.

**Canon** (biblical)   The word is used to designate those writings that came to be accepted as authentic biblical texts; it also is used to designate the most solemn part of the Mass, including the consecration of the bread and wine—the "Canon of the Mass."

**Canon law**   From the Latin "rule," the rules governing the Church. One refers to Church law as Canon law.

**capital sins**   Not actual sins, but thoughts and behaviors that the Church has determined to be the human conditions that are dispositions toward sinning. They are pride, covetousness, envy, anger, lust, gluttony, and sloth.

**catacombs**   A system of tunnels beneath the ground outside of Rome and other ancient cities, often used by early Catholics as hiding places when they were being persecuted. Many saints are buried there; they are visited as sacred sites.

*Catechism*   The book containing the official teachings of the Catholic Church for the instruction of children or adults interested in the Catholic faith.

**cathedral**   From the Greek *cathedra*, meaning "bishop's chair" or "throne," cathedrals are churches in which a bishop ordinarily celebrates the sacraments.

**catholic**   The word from the Greek *kata* or "toward" and *holos* or "whole" is one of the four classical marks of the Church. In its original Greek sense it expresses the ideal of Jesus that "all" are to be embraced as God's people. From its Latin translation, it means universal, an emphasis as extending all over the earth, as a Church for all; all its believers follow a set of common beliefs and practices.

**celibacy**   Promise made by those entering religious service to abstain from sexual relationships.

**ceremony**   A formal practice or custom established as proper to honor a special occasion.

**Christ**   The Greek word for "anointed"; kings were anointed in the Old Testament. Applied to Jesus as the anointed one of God.

**Christian**   Term first used (disparagingly) to describe the followers of Christ in Damascus as early as 40 C.E. Later adopted by these followers in the second century.

**Church**   A specific community of the faithful, usually determined on a territorial basis, local or regional, that carries on the mission of Christ in the world to reconcile humankind to God.

**clergy**   Those ordained to perform the sacramental functions of the Church.

**clerical culture**   The beliefs, customs, practices, and behaviors of the clergy, who live a life distinct from the laypeople.

**clericalism**   Describes the power and influence of the clergy.

**cloister**   Place of religious seclusion for prayer and meditation.

**College of Cardinals**   A group of select bishops that offers counsel to the pope, elects new popes, and governs in times between popes. They are the chief administrators of the Church. They are the bishops of major dioceses and/or head up the various Church agencies. The pope appoints them.

**colonization**   A process by which one country occupies another for the purpose of economic exploitation.

**communion of saints**   An expression of unity linking all the people of God, living or dead, through all ages, into one eternal community.

**contemplative**   A meditative form of prayer developed in the monasteries.

**council (ecumenical)**   A worldwide assembly of bishops called together by the pope for the purpose of setting policy and making decisions.

**covenant**   An agreement used in the Old Testament to describe the relationship between God and the people. It establishes that God will not abandon the people even if they fail to live up to their side of the agreement.

**creation**   The unfolding of all God's plans. Creation is in a state of movement toward an ultimate perfection as destined by God.

**cross** Two planks of timber, one placed across the other; an instrument of execution in Roman times. Jesus was put to death on a cross in a practice known as crucifixion.

**crucifix** A cross that holds the image of Jesus crucified, used for devotion in Catholic churches and homes.

**Crusades** Military expeditions undertaken by the Christians of Europe in the eleventh to the thirteenth centuries for the recovery of the Holy Land from the Muslims.

**dogma (doctrine)** A formally stated official belief of the Catholic Church concerning faith or morals.

**dualism** The view that reality consists of two basic opposing elements, such as mind and body or good and evil.

**ecclesial** or **ecclesiastical** Pertaining to the Church.

**ecumenical** Of worldwide scope or applicability, concerned with promoting unity among churches.

**encyclicals** Letters written by the pope to instruct the people.

**epiphany** A sudden intuitive perception or insight into the essential meaning of something.

**Epiphany** The feast when the kings or wise men visited the Christ child in Bethlehem. It is celebrated January 6. The birth and the baptism of Jesus are considered epiphanies.

**Eucharistic ministers** Parishioners who assist the priest in the distribution of Communion during Mass.

**evil** That which motivates or results from morally bad or wrong choices.

**excommunication** Censure by Church authorities excluding a Catholic from participation in the sacramental life and from the exercise of any Church office.

**existentialism** Twentieth-century philosophical movement emphasizing a person's radical aloneness, personal freedom, and personal responsibility for decisions in one's existence.

**Extreme Unction** Former name of the sacrament now called "Anointing of the Sick." "Extreme" refers to the deathly condition of those who are receiving it, and "Unction" means "anointing with oil."

**faith**   Our belief in the basic goodness of God's plan for us. In faith, we believe and act as if what we hope for will be granted. It also refers to the acceptance of Church teachings or the content of those teachings.

**First Communion**   Reception of the sacrament of the Eucharist for the first time.

**free will**   The human experience that governs our actions and gives us the freedom to make choices regarding our full expression of God's love.

**globalization**   Understanding all the world as a community and seeing the interconnectedness of people, economies, and resources.

**God**   The supreme divine being, the Creator of all that is, the fullness of being and of all perfection. God is without beginning and without end. God is love, the binding force in all that is.

**Gospel**   The good news that Christ has come. The Gospel, as read at Mass, is taken from the biblical books of Matthew, Mark, Luke, and John.

**grace**   From the Latin *gratia* or "gift": the gift of God's life in our souls, which moves us toward right choices.

**heaven**   State of fulfillment after our life on earth where we are in God's presence for eternity.

**hell**   State of our existence without God; once understood as the eternal fires in which the damned suffered forever.

**heretics**   Catholics who engage in any deliberate, persistent, and public denial of some article of revealed truth of the Catholic faith.

**hierarchical communion**   A term from the Church's Second Vatican Council addressing the nature of the relation between the Church in Rome (the Vatican and the Pope) and the local churches all around the world (dioceses and their bishops). It indicates that the authority of the one is derived and is depended on the support (communion) of the other.

**hierarchy**   Literally, "a holy order": the term refers to Church government by the ruling body of clergy organized into orders or ranks, each subordinate to the one above it; also, it designates a graded or ranked series of Catholic values.

**Holy Orders**   The process of ordination by which a man becomes a deacon, priest, or bishop to minister to people's spiritual needs and safeguard the rules and regulations of the faith.

**Holy Spirit**    The third person of the Trinity—Father, Son, and Holy Spirit; God's eternal presence to us opening our hearts and minds, guiding us in our actions, and otherwise assisting us on our journey.

**homily**    A sermon centering on Scriptural text.

**holarchy**    A holarchy is a hierarchy of holons.

**holon**    Comes from the Greek *holos*, "whole," and *on*, "part" or particle. This means that it is both a thing unto itself and part of something bigger at the same time. For example one is a person; let's say a son, who is also a part of something larger—a family. A family is a whole in itself, but also a part of a neighborhood. A holon asserts its individuality in order to maintain the order of a structure, but it also submits to the demands of the whole structure in order to make the system viable. This duality is similar to the particle/wave duality of light.

**host**    One of several names for the Eucharistic bread. From the Latin *hostia*, meaning "victim," it recalls that Christ was sacrificed for us.

*Humanae Vitae*    Latin for "of human life," this is the document written by Pope Paul VI continuing the ban on the use of artificial birth control.

**Immaculate Conception**    Dogma that Mary was conceived in her mother's womb free from original sin to enable her to be a pure vessel through which Jesus would be brought into the world. Do not confuse with "virgin birth," which refers to Jesus' conception in Mary's womb without Mary giving up her virginity.

**immanence**    God's presence here and now that can be experienced by humans.

**Incarnation**    The event in which God took human form and entered the human journey.

**indulgences**    Prayers or actions performed to remit the afterlife punishment for sins.

**infallibility**    A dogma stating that the pope speaks without error, on behalf of the Church, in union with the bishops when he proclaims an article of faith or morals.

**Inquisition**    Official investigation by the Church of suspected heresies.

**intercessor**    Christ's function as the mediator between God and the people. This term is also applied to his mother, Mary, because she was a necessary link in God's plan to send His son as an intercessor. Saints act as intercessors, too.

**Jesuits**    A religious order established in the 1500s by St. Ignatius of Loyola, dedicated to work for the pope. Their official name is the Society of Jesus.

**Jesus**   Hebrew name meaning "God saves," expressing both the identity and the mission of the Son of God born of the Virgin Mary.

***La Nueva Raza***   Spanish phrase, "the new race," describing the mixing of the Spanish, African, and Indian blood, spirituality, and cultures resulting in all of the cultures being changed.

**laypeople**   From the Greek word *laikos*, meaning "of the people." Church members who are not ordained.

**liberation theology**   An array of theologies that articulate the faith journey from the perspective of the people's experience of their struggles.

**liturgical practices**   Church services and ceremonies, readings at Mass, Communion, the sacraments, prayers, rituals, and celebrations.

**liturgy**   The prayers and rituals of the Church.

**magisterium**   The Church's teaching function.

**martyrs**   Those killed for their faith. Martyrdom automatically results in sainthood; that is to say, a martyr's soul goes directly to God.

**Mary**   The mother of Jesus, the Son of God.

**mechanical view of the universe**   Sees the universe as nonliving, something the Creator wound up like a clock, set in motion, and left on its own.

**miracle**   An event that breaks the laws of nature; an extraordinary happening that gives us a glimpse of God at work in the world.

**missionaries**   Religious workers sent to foreign countries to do religious or charitable work.

**missions**   Agencies such as schools and hospitals established and maintained by the Church in areas new to the Church's influence to assist people to meet their everyday needs.

**modernism**   A heresy condemned by the pope in 1907 referring to modern scientific thinking, which believed that truth changes.

**monasticism**   Tradition of taking oneself away from the mainstream of society for the purpose of developing spiritual practice.

**monstrance**   Ornate golden vessel containing the Blessed Sacrament under the form of bread, pressed between two pieces of clear glass. It sits on the altar for Eucharistic devotions.

**moral** (noun)  A concisely expressed belief or rule stating what we believe is right or wrong.

**moral law**  A sense of right and wrong that is part of an inborn and informed conscience. It is based in the understanding of a rational order established by the Creator that gives us guidance in making moral choices.

**mysteries**  Beliefs taken on faith, which can never be fully understood by reason.

**mystic**  From the Greek word meaning "mystery," this term describes a person who engages in the practice of meditation from which he or she experiences a relationship with God and gains spiritual insight.

**mysticism**  Going within yourself to a quiet place where it is possible to experience the mystery of God.

**myth**  A story that tells the beliefs of a group of people regarding their origins, history, and destiny. Myths transmit truths.

**national parish**  A parish not based on geographical boundaries, comprised of an ethnic group who celebrate the liturgy with special attention to their native customs.

**Natural Family Planning**  A practice that requires a couple to restrict intercourse to naturally occurring times of infertility within the woman's cycle. It works with the nature of human sexuality by respecting the biological reproductive imperative rather than attempting to alter it through barrier and chemical methods. The Church endorses this method of birth control.

**natural law**  The way the natural world works. It makes itself known to us by our awareness of the natural order of things. It represents a commonsense understanding of the world.

**novena**  From the Latin *novem*, meaning "nine," this is a devotion repeated nine successive days.

**omnipresence**  One of the characteristics used to describe God; it describes God's presence everywhere.

**ordination**  Entrance rite into the order of deacon, priest, or bishop.

**original sin**  An inherited state of weakness that we endure because of being separated from our original state of unity with God. It is part of being human.

**Orthodox**  Describes the Greek or Eastern Churches that are not under the direction of the pope.

**paradigm**   From the Latin for "to compare." It is a model of something. It designates the set of assumptions, concepts, values, and practices that frame a culture's vision. To change our paradigm requires a major shift in how we see things.

**parish council**   A post–Vatican II development in the Church's governing structure made up of church members who are elected or chosen to plan ministries and secure the resources for the parish.

**parochial schools**   Elementary and high schools supported by the parish, which provide a general education and instill Catholic ethics and values.

**pastoral ministers**   Church workers who have taken on various roles that once were filled by priests or nuns.

**patriarchy**   A family or organization controlled by men. The opposite is matriarchy, which means women are in charge and are the head of families. Much of patriarchy has its roots in Catholicism.

**pedophilia**   Sexual activity of an adult with a child.

**Penitentials**   Handbooks of penances from the sixth to the twelfth centuries prior to the institutionalization of confession as a sacrament that provided a code of sexual behaviors among very diverse early medieval societies.

**Pentateuch**   The "book of the five scrolls" known as the Old Testament Torah. Moses commanded that the Torah law be placed in the Ark of the Covenant to be kept safe during the wilderness journey of the Hebrew people.

**Posada**   From the Spanish for "shelter," this term describes a house-to-house procession at Christmas in which the drama of Joseph and Mary is enacted.

**priests**   Ordained clergy of the Church.

**prophetic tradition**   Old Testament warnings about the consequences of actions. Some of the prophets were Isaiah, Jeremiah, Amos, and Micah.

**Protestant**   A Christian belonging to a sect that seceded from the Catholic Church at the time of the Reformation. Lutheran, Episcopal, Methodist, and Baptist are some Protestant denominations.

**pulpit**   From the Latin *pulpitum*, this is a staging platform from which the priest proclaims the Gospel reading of the Mass and preaches the homily.

**purgatory**   A state of the soul after death in which it progresses toward its final union with God. The soul in purgatory can be aided in this journey through prayers and good works of the living.

**quantum spirituality**   The call to recognize the unity of the world and be involved with it creatively.

**quantum worldview**   Holds that everything is made up of both particles (solid) and waves (energy) and that these two states exist at the same time within each "individual" piece or "quantum." This is an understanding that everything is connected by way of a unifying field of energy. It is in contrast to the mechanical worldview that perceives a separation between the physical and spiritual worlds.

**RCIA**   Stands for the Rite of Christian Initiation of Adults. It is a process of entrance into the Catholic Church.

**real presence**   A dogma that Christ is present in the sacrament of the Eucharist, physically and spiritually feeding the body and soul.

**reason**   Our ability to know the existence of God with certainty through our hearts and minds.

**Reconciliation**   The sacrament by which sins are forgiven and we are reconciled with God and absolved from guilt. A common name previously was confession or the sacrament of penance.

**relics**   Any part of the physical remains of a saint or items such as clothing that have touched the body of a saint.

**religion**   From the Latin *religare*, meaning "to bind back," religion is concerned with making connections between the sensate world and that which exists beyond. Religion operates from a faith basis rather than reason.

**religious liberty**   A Vatican II doctrine affirming the natural right to be free of coercion in one's religious beliefs.

**Renaissance**   The rebirth in Europe of the classic Greek and Roman architecture, painting, sculpting, music, and literature during the fourteenth, fifteenth, and sixteenth centuries.

**Resurrection**   The faith event of Jesus' rising from the dead on the third day after his crucifixion, demonstrating his victory over sin and death and the eternal life that is available to people.

**revelation**   A source of knowledge available to us beyond the reach of normal knowing; it is divine insight or inspiration by which God speaks to people of the divine plan.

**ritual**   See *ceremony*.

**Roman Curia**   Bureaucracy that assists the pope in administering his duty of governing the Catholic Church.

*Roman Ritual*   Liturgical book of the rites and blessings commonly performed by the clergy. Since Vatican II this book has been called the *Book of Blessings.*

**sacramental principle**   Sees divine presence in everything; a vision of the world that glimpses God in and throughout all things, every person, all communities and movements, events, places, objects, the world at large, and the entire cosmos. It is a foundational principle in Catholic religion.

**sacramentals**   Objects used to connect Catholics to spiritual experiences. Rosaries, candles, bells, and statues are common Catholic sacramentals.

**sacred Scripture**   The sacred writings of the Old (Hebrew) and New (Christian) Testaments that are believed to be inspired by the Holy Spirit and written by human hand.

**salvation**   God's loving action through Jesus that guides us and moves us toward what is good for us and away from that which would harm us.

**seamless garment of life**   An ethic recognizing all created things are connected to and by the Creator in a whole and unbroken relationship. It requires a consistent ethic of respect for the value of life across the board in the areas of access to food, shelter, health care, education, capital punishment, war, abortion, and euthanasia.

**seminary**   From the Latin *semen* (meaning "seedbed" or "nursery"), a theological school for training priests.

**sexual abuse**   Forcing unwanted sexual activity by the use of threats or coercion.

**"signs of the time"**   Phrase used by Pope John XXIII in opening Vatican II that told the Church to look at the world and to learn from it.

**simony**   Refers to the sin of both the buying and selling of Church offices.

**sin**   Behaviors or intentions that are against God's will for us. It has been described as "missing the mark" or falling short of our potential.

**social justice**   A concept holding that all members are free to participate fully and receive the just benefits in the society in which they live.

**soul**   Our individual spiritual self, the breath of life, the indwelling of the Holy Spirit. Not separate from the body, but integral to it, it connects us to God, to one another, and to all of creation. Our souls live on when our physical lives are finished.

**spiritual director**   One trained to work with people spiritually, much like a psychologist works with someone emotionally.

**tradition**   Church teachings that have developed over the years based on the teachings handed down from Christ and the apostles.

**transcendent**   Beyond the ordinary range of human experience or understanding. The full nature of God is transcendent.

**Triduum**   The liturgy celebrated on the three days prior to Easter Sunday: Holy Thursday, Good Friday, and Holy Saturday.

**Trinity**   The mystery of faith expressing one God in three persons. The divine persons—the Father, Son, and Holy Spirit—do not share the one divinity among themselves, but each is a distinct personality of God, whole and entire.

**Viaticum**   Latin meaning "on the way with you," the name of Communion when it is being given to a dying person.

**virginity**   In ancient times, a state of independence or autonomy, referring to a woman who made her own decisions. When used to describe Mary, it means she said yes to God of her own free will, acting independent of any influence or coercion. Commonly, it means a woman or man who has never had sexual intercourse.

**virtues**   Right ways of acting, habits that guide us in the way of good sense and good faith and govern our relationships with others.

**visit**   Catholic custom of stopping in to the church for a few minutes during the day to say a quick prayer.

**vocation**   From the Latin *vocare*, meaning "call," this term refers to a calling to the priesthood, religious life, or other spiritual paths.

**vows**   Binding promises made when one goes into a religious order. The principal three are poverty (giving up private ownership to the community), chastity (giving up the right to marry and have an intimate sexual relationship in order to devote oneself to the Church), and obedience (submitting to the authority of one's superiors for assignments).

**Western world**   Lands west of Istanbul, Turkey. Lands to the east of Istanbul are called the Eastern world.

# Appendix B

# Recommended Reading

Allen, John L. Jr. *The Rise of Benedict XVI: The Inside Story of How the Pope Was Elected and Where He Will Take the Catholic Church.* New York: Doubleday, 2005.

Cahill, Thomas. *Pope John XXIII.* New York: Viking Press, 2002.

Carroll, James. *Toward a New Catholic Church: The Promise of Reform.* Boston: Houghton Mifflin Co., 2002.

Copeland, M. Shawn. "Tradition and the Traditions of African American Catholicism." *Theological Studies* 61, no. 4 (December 1, 2000): 632.

Cozzens, Donald. *Sacred Silence: Denial and the Crisis in the Church.* Collegeville, MN: Liturgical Press, 2002.

Dokecki, Paul R. *The Clergy Sexual Abuse Crisis: Reform and Renewal in the Catholic Community.* Washington, D.C.: Georgetown University Press, 2004.

Dolan, Jay P. *In Search of an American Catholicism: A History of Religion and Culture in Tension.* New York: Oxford University Press, 2005.

Dumestre, Marcel J. *A Church at Risk: The Challenge of Spiritually Hungry Adults.* New York: Crossroad/Herder & Herder, 1997.

Elizondo, Virgilio P. *Galilean Journey: The Mexican-American Promise*, 2nd ed. Maryknoll, NY: Orbis Books, 2000.

Faulkner, Mary. *Supreme Authority: Understanding Power in the Catholic Church*. Indianapolis, IN: Alpha Books, 2002.

Gibson, David. *The Coming Catholic Church: How the Faithful Are Shaping a New American Catholicism*. San Francisco: HarperSanFrancisco, 2003.

Greeley, Andrew. *The Catholic Revolution: New Wine, Old Wineskins, and the Second Vatican Council*. Berkeley, CA: University of California Press, 2004.

———. *The Catholic Imagination*. Berkeley, CA: University of California Press, 2001.

Groome, Thomas. *What Makes Us Catholic: Eight Gifts for Life*. San Francisco: HarperSanFrancisco, 2003.

Kennedy, Eugene. *The Unhealed Wound: The Church and Human Sexuality*. New York: St. Martin's Press, 2002.

Lakeland, Paul. *The Liberation of the Laity: In Search of an Accountable Church*. London: Continuum International Publishing Group, 2004.

Ludwig, Robert A. *Reconstructing Catholicism*. Eugene, OR: Wipf & Stock Publishers, 2000.

Meara, Mary J. F. C., Jeffrey A. J. Stone, Maureen A. T. Kelly, and Richard G. M. Davis. *Growing Up Catholic: An Infinitely Funny Guide for the Faithful, the Fallen and Everyone In-Between*. New York: Broadway Books, 2000.

Papesh, Michael L. *Clerical Culture: Contradiction and Transformation*. Collegeville, MN: Liturgical Press, 2004.

Steinfels, Peter. *A People Adrift: The Crisis of the Roman Catholic Church in America*. New York: Simon & Schuster, 2004.

Swidler, Leonard. *Toward a Catholic Constitution*. New York: Herder & Herder, 1996.

Weigel, George. *The Courage to Be Catholic: Crisis, Reform, and the Future of the Church*. New York: Basic Books, 2002.

Whitehead, Evelyn and James. *The Wisdom of the Body: Making Sense of Our Sexuality.* New York: Crossroad/Herder & Herder, 2001.

Wills, Gerry. *Papal Sin: Structures of Deceit.* New York: Doubleday, 2001.

———. *Why I Am a Catholic.* Boston: Houghton Mifflin Co., 2002.

# Encyclopedia and Catechisms

Bunson, Matthew, ed. *2003 Our Sunday Visitor's Catholic Almanac.* Huntington, IN: Our Sunday Visitor, 2002.

*Catechism of the Catholic Church*, 2nd ed. Washington, D.C.: United States Catholic Conference, 2000.

*The Companion to the Catechism of the Catholic Church.* San Francisco: Ignatius Press, 1994.

Flannery, Austin P., ed. *Vatican Council II: Volume 2: The Conciliar & Post Conciliar Documents.* Collegeville, MN: Liturgical Press, 1998.

Glazier, Michael, and Thomas J. Shelley, eds. *The Encyclopedia of American Catholic History.* Collegeville, MN: Liturgical Press, 1997.

Glazier, Michael, and Monika K. Hellwig. *The Modern Catholic Encyclopedia.* Collegeville, MN: Liturgical Press, 1994.

McBrien, Richard P. *Catholicism: New Study.* San Francisco: HarperSanFrancisco, 1994.

McBrien, Richard P., ed. *The HarperCollins Encyclopedia of Catholicism.* San Francisco: HarperSanFrancisco, 1995.

*New Catholic Encyclopedia*, 2nd ed. (15-vol. set). Waterville, ME: Gale Group, 2002.

O'Collins, Gerald, and Mario Farrugia. *Catholicism: The Story of Catholic Christianity.* New York: Oxford University Press, 2003.

# Catholic Beliefs and Practices

The Vatican has produced a *Compendium of the Social Doctrine of the Church*, published in the United States by the United States Conference of Catholic Bishops, Washington, D.C. 2005.

Anderson, Bernhard W. *Understanding the Old Testament*, 4th ed. Paramus, NJ: Prentice Hall College Div., 1986.

Beaudoin, Tom. *Virtual Faith: The Irreverent Spiritual Quest of Generation X*. Hoboken, NJ: John Wiley & Sons, 2000.

Berry, Thomas. *The Great Work: Our Way into the Future*. New York: Harmony/Bell Tower, 2000.

Boff, Leonard. *Ecclesiogenesis: The Base Communities Reinvent the Church*. Maryknoll, NY: Orbis Books, 1986.

Burns, Gene. *The Frontiers of Catholicism: The Politics of Ideology in a Liberal World*. Berkeley, CA: University of California Press, 1992.

Cooke, Bernard J. *Distancing of God*. Minneapolis, MN: Fortress Press, 1988.

Dulles, Avery. *Models of the Church*. New York: Image Books, 1991.

Elizondo, Virgilio P. *Guadalupe: Mother of the New Creation*. Maryknoll, NY: Orbis Books, 1997.

———. *La Morenita*. Liguori, MO: Liguori Publications, 1981.

Greeley, Andrew. *The Catholic Myth: The Behavior and Beliefs of American Catholics*. New York: Collier Books, 1997.

Happel, Stephen, and David Tracy. *A Catholic Vision*. Minneapolis, MN: Fortress Press, 1988.

Haughton, Rosemary. *The Catholic Thing*. Springfield, IL: Templegate Publishers, 1980.

Hellwig, Monika K. *Understanding Catholicism*. Mahwah, NJ: Paulist Press, 2002.

Holland, Joe. *Modern Catholic Social Teaching: The Popes Confront the Industrial Age 1740–1958*. Mahwah, NJ: Paulist Press, 2003.

Massaro, Thomas, S.J. *Living Justice: Catholic Social Teaching in Action*. Lanham, MD: Sheed & Ward (an imprint of Rowman & Littlefield Publishing, Inc.), 2000.

O'Murchu, Diarmuid. *Quantum Theology: Spiritual Implications of the New Physics*. New York: Crossroad/Herder & Herder, 1997.

Sawicki, Marianne. *The Gospel in History: Portrait of a Teaching Church: The Origins of Christian Education*. Mahwah, NJ: Paulist Press, 1988.

———. *Seeing the Lord: Resurrection and Early Christian Practices*. Minneapolis, MN: Fortress Press, 1994.

Sodano, Angelo, and Renato Martino, Pontifical Council for Justice and Peace. *Compendium of the Social Doctrine of the Church*. Washington, D.C.: United States Catholic Conference, 2005

Wessels, Cletus. *The Holy Web: Church and the New Universe Story*. Maryknoll, NY: Orbis Books, 2000.

Wills, Garry. *Bare Ruined Choirs: Doubt, Prophecy and Radical Religion*. Garden City, NY: Doubleday, 1972.

# Catholic History

Bokenkotter, Thomas. *A Concise History of the Catholic Church*. New York: Doubleday, 2003.

Carroll, James. *Constantine's Sword: The Church and the Jews: A History*. Boston: Houghton Mifflin Co., 2001.

Coffey, Kathy. *Hidden Women of the Gospels*. Maryknoll, NY: Orbis Books, 2003.

Davies, Oliver, and Fiona Bowie. *Celtic Christian Spirituality: An Anthology of Medieval and Modern Sources*. New York: Continuum, 1999.

Davis, Cyprian. *The History of Black Catholics in the United States.* New York: Crossroad/Herder & Herder, 1995.

Dolan, Jay P. *In Search of an American Catholicism.* New York: Oxford University Press, 2002.

Gilkey, Langdon Brown. *Catholicism Confronts Modernity: A Protestant View.* New York: Seabury Press, 1975.

Küng, Hans. *The Catholic Church: A Short History.* New York: Modern Library, 2003.

Morris, Charles. *American Catholic: The Saints and Sinners Who Built America's Most Powerful Church.* New York: Vintage Books, 1998.

O'Gorman, Robert T. *The Church That Was a School: Catholic Identity and Catholic Education in the United States Since 1790.* Washington, D.C.: The Catholic Education Futures Project, 1987.

O'Murchu, Diarmuid. *Reclaiming Spirituality: A New Spiritual Framework for Today's World.* New York: Crossroad/Herder & Herder, 1998.

Pennick, Nigel. *The Sacred World of Celts: An Illustrated Guide to Celtic Spirituality and Mythology.* Rochester, VT: Inner Traditions Intl. Ltd., 2000.

Thompson, Mary R. *Mary of Magdala: Apostle and Leader.* Mahwah, NJ: Paulist Press, 1995.

# Catholic Culture

Brinkmeyer, Robert H. *Three Catholic Writers of the Modern South.* Jackson, MS: University Press of Mississippi, 1985.

Donovan, Daniel. *Distinctively Catholic: An Exploration of Catholic Identity.* Mahwah, NJ: Paulist Press, 1997.

*El Dia de los Muertos (The Day of the Dead).* San Antonio, TX: Institute of Texan Cultures, The University of Texas at San Antonio, 1991.

Giles, Paul. *American Catholic Arts and Fictions: Culture, Ideology, Aesthetics.* New York: Cambridge University Press, 1992.

Icher, François. *Building the Great Cathedrals.* New York: Abradale Press, 2001.

Kennedy, Eugene C. *Tomorrow's Catholics Yesterday's Church: The Two Cultures of American Catholicism.* Liguori, MO: Liguori Publications, 1995.

Massa, Mark Stephen. *Catholics and American Culture: Fulton Sheen, Dorothy Day, and the Notre Dame Football Team.* New York: Crossroad/Herder & Herder, 1999.

Smith, Huston, David Wakely, Thomas Moore, and Ismael Fernandez De La Cuesta, eds. *Gregorian Chant: Songs of the Spirit* (book and CD). San Francisco: Bay Books, 1996.

Walker, Barbara G. *The Woman's Dictionary of Symbols and Sacred Objects.* San Francisco: HarperSanFrancisco, 1988.

# Catholic Prayers and Saints

Alberione, James. *Queen of Apostles Prayerbook.* Boston: St. Paul Editions, 1976.

Altemose, Sr. Charlene. *Why Do Catholics?: A Guide to Catholic Belief and Practice.* Burr Ridge, IL: WCB/McGraw-Hill, 1990.

Bauer, Judith A., ed. *The Essential Mary Handbook: A Summary of Beliefs, Practices, and Prayers.* Liguori, MO: Liguori Publications, 1999.

Bielecki, Tessa. *Teresa of Ávila: Mystical Writings.* New York: Crossroad/Herder & Herder, 1994.

Cannato, Judy. *Quantum Grace: The Sunday Readings: Lenten Reflections on Creation and Connectedness.* Notre Dame, IN: Ave Maria Press, 2003.

Chittister, Joan D. *The Rule of Benedict: Insights for the Ages.* New York: Crossroad/Herder & Herder, 1992.

Cohen, J. M., trans. *The Life of Saint Theresa of Ávila by Herself.* New York: Viking Penguin Books, 1957.

Delaney, John J. *Dictionary of Saints*. New York: Doubleday, 1980.

Ebertshäuser, Caroline H. *Mary: Art, Culture, and Religion Through the Ages*. New York: Crossroad/Herder & Herder, 1998.

Faulkner, Mary. *The Complete Idiot's Guide to Women's Spirituality*. Indianapolis, IN: Alpha Books, 2002.

Heywood, W., ed. *The Little Flowers of St. Francis of Assisi*. New York: Vintage Books, 1998.

Hoever, Hugo. *Lives of the Saints*. Totowa, NJ : Catholic Book Publishing Co., 1990.

Sandoval, Annette. *The Directory of Saints: A Concise Guide to Patron Saints*. New York: Penguin Books, 1997.

Tetlow, Joseph A. *Ignatius Loyola: Spiritual Exercises*. New York: Crossroad/Herder & Herder, 1992.

Tobin, Greg. *Saints and Sinners: The American Catholic Experience Through Stories, Memoirs, Essays and Commentary*. New York: Doubleday, 1999.

Trouvé, Marianne Lorraine. *Favorite Prayers and Novenas*. Boston: Pauline Books & Media, 1997.

Warner, Marina. *Alone of All Her Sex: The Myth and the Cult of the Virgin Mary*. New York: Knopf, 1976.

# Internet Resources

**Catholic Information Center on Internet**
www.catholic.net

**The Holy See**
www.vatican.va

**Natural Family Planning**
www.billingsmethod.com
www.ccli.org

**Official Catholic Sites on the Web**
www.georgetown.edu/centers/woodstock/links/links_official.htm

**Religious Orders**
http://employees.csbsju.edu/roliver/orders.html

**Catechism of the Catholic Church (search)**
www.scborromeo.org/ccc.htm

# Index

## A

Abba, definition of, 97
abbot, definition of, 281
abortion, 11–12, 256–257
Abraham, 73
abuse, 4, 25, 212
    sexual, 329–338
    Voice of the Faithful and, 28–29
active religious life, 264
Acts of the Apostles, 87
A.D., 71
Adam, 72
adoration, 178
Adrian VI, pope, 44
Advent, 173
Africa
    and Catholicism, 319
    Catholic population of, 23
African American Catholics, 35, 318–320
    Mass, 17–18
*Agnus Dei*, 198
air, 69
    as Holy Spirit, 119
Alan de Rupe, 180
alb, 202
Alexandria, 288
algebra, term, 290
Alito, Samuel, 318
allowing to die, definition of, 254
All Saints Day, 16
All Souls Day, 16

altar, 105, 201
    definition of, 200
    reverence for, 172
    Vatican II on, 55
altar servers, 203, 269
    clothing of, 202
Ambrose, saint, 279
Americas
    Catholic population of, 20–22
    church history in, 299–310
    patron saint of, 158, 160
The Angelus, 168–170
Anglican church, 294
Anglos, in post–Vatican II generation, 350–351
animals, patron saint of, 171
Anne, saint, 282
annulment, 142
Annunciation, 159
Anointing of the Sick, 148–150
Anselm, saint, 222–223
Ansgar, saint, 284
Anthony of Egypt, saint, 107–108, 280, 331
Antioch, 288
anti-Semitism, 90–91
Apocalypse, 87
Apostle's Creed, 182
apostolic
    Church as, 347–349
    definition of, 39, 348
apparitions
    definition of, 157
    of Mary, 156–158, 305

Aquinas. *See* Thomas Aquinas
archdiocese, 45
Aristotle, 290, 332
Ark of the Covenant, 74
Artemis, 155
articles of faith, 157
Ash Wednesday, 118
Asia, Catholic population of, 23
assimilation, 316, 318
Assumption, 40, 160
Augustine of Hippo, saint, 154, 184, 254,
    276, 278–280, 319, 332
Australia, Catholic population of, 23
authority
    and just war, 255–256
    protecting, 336
awareness, sacramental, 129
Aztecs, 35, 302–303, 306–307

## B

Baby Boomers, 350
Baltimore
    Catechism, 52, 221
    Third Council of, 316
Baptism, 70, 134–136
    origins of, 136
baptismal font, 134
Bartolomé de las Casas, blessed, 301
base communities, 224–227
B.C., 71
B.C.E., 71
Beatitudes, 47–48
Belgium, Catholic population of, 22
bells, 168–170
Benedictines, 266
Benedict of Nursia, saint, 185, 266, 280
Benedict the Moor, saint, 319
Benedict XIII, pope, 44
Benedict XV, pope, 44
Benedict XVI, pope, 44, 253, 263

bereavement ministry, 325
Bernardin, Cardinal Joseph L., 253
Berrigan, Daniel, 32–33
Berrigan, Philip, 32
Bible, 81–93
    African American, 17
    Catholic beliefs on, 87–89
    definition of, 82
    on Hell, 250
    interpretation of, 222
    Protestant Canon versus Catholic, 86, 315
    term, 71
    Trent on, 295
    Vatican II and, 56
birth control, 250–251
bishops, 142
    addressing, 264
    and death penalty, 257–258
    definition of, 107
    in hierarchy, 261–262
    number of, 347
    and pope, 40–41
    on racism, 319
    and sex scandals, 330, 335
    and social justice, 233–234
    and theologians, 229–230
    and Vatican II, 54
black vestments, 202
Blessed Virgin. *See* Mary
blessing(s), 171
    bread, 196–197
blood, baptism by, 136
blue vestments, 202
Boniface, saint, 283
Bono, 30–31
Boston, Catholic population of, 22
Brazil, Catholic population of, 21
bread
    blessing, 196–197
    breaking, 198
    sharing, 348–349

Brennan, William J., 318
Brigid of Ireland, saint, 282–283
brothers, 262, 265
Brown, Dan, 25–26
Butler, Pierce, 318

# C

Cabrini, Frances Xavier, saint, 317
Canada, Catholic population of, 20
candelieri, 160
candles, 120–121, 201
Canon
    definition of, 47
    determination of, 86–87
Canon law, 47, 220, 261, 344
Cantù, Federico, 304
capitalism, atheistic, 233
capital punishment, 257–258
cardinals
    addressing, 264
    in hierarchy, 261
care, ministers of, 270
Carroll, John, 313
cassock, 202
Castro, Fidel, 21, 43
catacombs, 105–106
Catechism, 12, 221–222
catechists, 270
catechumen, definition of, 214
Catherine of Siena, saint, 184–185, 267
Catholic
    Church as, 345–347
    definition of, 13
Catholic Campaign for Human
    Development, 233–234
Catholic Charities, 212
Catholic Church
    in Americas, 299–310
    as apostolic, 347–349
    as catholic, 345–347

characteristics of, 128
    definition of, 12–13
    future of, 23–24, 327–354
    hierarchy of, 45
    history of, 273–325
    as holy, 344–345
    Jesus and, 101–103
    as listener, 56–58
    as mother, 282
    as one, 342–344
    oppression of, 277
    as People of God, 54, 340, 349
    schism in, 288
    structure of, 259–271
    teachings of, 219–230
Catholic education
    African Americans and, 319
    colleges, 211, 304
    German immigrants and, 315–316
    on sex, 333
Catholic Health Association (CHA), 211
Catholic health care, 210–212
Catholic identity, 1–64
Catholic imagination, 111–122
    feeding, 165–176
    sexual, 337–338
Catholicism
    basic actions of, 10–12
    basic beliefs of, 5–9
    elements of, 67–80
    sensuous side of, 109–161, 337
    spirit of, 5–6
    spirituality of, 25–36
catholicity, principle of, 227
Catholic Peace Fellowship, 243
Catholics
    characteristics of, 6
    differences from Protestants, 296
    diversity among, 8–10, 15–24, 31–36
    former, 216
    identification of, 3–20

maintaining status as, 216
populations of, 20–24
recovering, 216
as tribe, 207–217
Catholic Worker movement, 232, 243–244
C.E., 71
celebration, Jesus and, 103, 353
celibacy, 63, 144, 253
and abuse, 332, 335–336
in religious orders, 264
Celts, term, 281
censoring, 215–216
centering prayer, 186
*Centesimus Annus*, 238
ceremony, definition of, 70
CHA. *See* Catholic Health Association
chalice, 143
Chardin, Pierre Teilhard de, 57
charitable organizations, patron saint of, 211
charity, 49, 212
versus justice, 233
Charlemagne, emperor, 285
chastity. *See also* celibacy; sexuality
in religious orders, 264
Chavez, Cesar, 33–35
Chicago, Catholic population of, 21, 314
choir, 204
chrism, in Confirmation, 138–139
Christianity
development of, 102–108
key stories of, 97–101
structure of, designing, 106–107
Christian, term, 102
Christmas, 98, 173
Christopher, saint, 62, 168
church
big versus little, 45, 348
in New World, 301
building, 201–202
definition of, 12–13, 58

development of, 102–103
as sacrament, 125–127
cilice, 27
citizenship, Catholics and, 36, 311–325
*The City of God* (Augustine), 279
Civil Rights movement, 52
Clare, saint, 267
Clement XII, pope, 44
clergy
and abuse, 329–338
Celtic, 282
shortage of, 63–64
Vatican II and, 324
clerical culture, definition of, 331
clericalism, 334–336
definition of, 334
clothing
for Mass, 202
Vatican II and, 62–64
collection, 196
College of Cardinals, 42
colleges, Catholic, 211, 304
collegiality, 41
colonialism, 241–242, 300
color, of vestments, 202
Columba, saint, 284
Columbus, Christopher, 299
Committal, Rite of, 175
common good, 239–240
communal worldview, 78
communications workers, patron saint of, 157
communion, hierarchical, definition of, 260
community, 128
and anointing of sick, 149
Compline, 188
confession, 62, 144–147
confessional, 146–148
Confirmation, 137–139
origins of, 138

Congregation for the Doctrine of the Faith, 44, 263, 292
conscience, 48–49
  Vatican II on, 60
consent, in marriage, 140–142
Constantine, emperor of Rome, 276–278
Constantinople, 288
contemplation, 107–108, 178
contemplative meditation, 186
contemplative prayer, definition of, 184
contemplative religious life, 264–265
contraception, 11, 250–251
Cortés, Hernán, 302–303
Cosmas and Damian, saints, 200
councils, 52, 343. *See also* Vatican II
  of Baltimore, 316
  definition of, 53
  Ephesus, 155–156
  of Nicaea, 5, 277, 332
  of Trent, 8, 295–296
Counter-Reformation, 295–296
courage, 49
covenant, 73–74
  and marriage, 139–142
creation stories, 72–73
cremation, 175
Croatia, Catholic population of, 22
Crosby, Bing, 30
crosier, 143
cross, 116
  Brigid's, 283
  Helena and, 276
  sign of, 170
  types of, 167
crucifix, 116, 167
crucifixion, 100
Crusades, 289–290
Cuauhtlatoatzin, Juan Diego, saint, 305–306, 308
Cuba, Catholic population of, 21
culture, Vatican II and, 56–58

Curia, 262–263
  definition of, 261
Cyril of Alexandria, saint, 319
Cyril of Russia, saint, 284
Czech Republic, Catholic population of, 22

**D**

dairy workers, patron saint of, 283
Damasus, pope, 86
Damian, saint, 200
Dark Ages, 284
*The Da Vinci Code* (Brown), 25–26
Day, Dorothy, 232, 243–244
Day of Atonement, 74
Day of the Dead, 16
deacons, 142, 203
  in hierarchy, 261
  types of, 143
death, 16–17, 175
death penalty, 257–258
Declaration of Religious Freedom, 277
Deer Dance, 18
Delille, Henriette, 319
Desert Fathers and Mothers, 107–108
desire, baptism by, 136
developing world, Catholic population of, 23–24
Dia de los Muertos, 16
dignity of person, 239
DiMarzio, Nicholas, 258
diocese, 45
disarmament, 242
divorce, 141–142
Doctor of the Church, Anselm, 223
Dominican Republic, Catholic population of, 21
Dominicans, 267–268, 291
Dominic de Guzman, saint, 179–180, 267
druggists, patron saints of, 200

Druids, 281–282
Drum Major Instinct, 235
dualism
 and abuse, 331–333
 Augustine on, 279–280
 Platonic, 76

# E

Eagleton, Tom, 323
earth, 68, 118–119
Easter, 100
 Triduum, 173
 Vigil, 121
Eastern Orthodox Catholicism, 12, 288
ecclesiastical, definition of, 12
Echo Boomers, 350
ecological theology, 226
economics, Catholic Church and, 234–235, 241–242
ecumenism, Vatican II and, 58–60
education. *See* Catholic education
Eighth Day Center, 244
Eliot, T. S., 335
Elizabeth of Portugal, saint, 141
Elizondo, Virgilio P., 302, 306
El Paso, Catholic population of, 22
enculturation, 16
envelopes, parish, 196
Ephesus, Council of, 155–156
Epiphany, definition of, 173
epistles, 84
Escrivá, Josemaría, 26
Estevez, Ramon, 33
Eucharist, 199–200. *See also* Holy
Communion; Mass
 liturgy of, 193, 195–198
 ministers of, 203, 269
 term, 136–137

Europe
 Catholic population of, 23
 conversion of, 280, 283
euthanasia, 254
*Evangelii Nuntiandi*, 238
evangelists, roles of, 84–85
Eve, 72
evil, 7
excommunication, 215–216
 definition of, 215
Extreme Unction, 148

# F

faith, 49, 71–75, 354
 in action, 270
 articles of, 157
 definition of, 112
 Luther on, 294
 and science, 57
 and teachings, 220
 and theology, 222
Falsani, Cathleen, 31
family life, 240
fasting, 61
Fathers of the Church, 276
Fatima, 158
fear of the Lord, 138
Ferraro, Geraldine, 323
fifties, 52, 321–322
fire, 69, 120–121
First Communion, 136–137
*flor de muerto*, 17
France, patron saint of, 292
Franciscans, 266–267, 303, 307, 318
Francis of Assisi, saint, 171, 266
Franks, 285
free will, 74
fundamentalism, 89
funerals, 175

## G

Gabriel, saint, 157
Galilee, 96–97
Galileo, 56
Garanzini, Michael J., 266
gathering, 193–194
Gaudin, Juliette, 319
*Gaudium et Spes*, 237
Generation Q, 352
Generation Y, 350
Genesis, 72–73
Gennaro, saint, feast of, 318
genuflection, 6, 170
German Catholics, immigrant experience of, 315–316
Germany, Catholicism in, 280, 283
gestures, sacramental, 170–172
gladiators, definition of, 105
globalization, and Catholic Church, 346
Gloria, 194
Glorious Mysteries, 183
Glory Be, 182
*Going My Way*, 30
gold vestments, 202
good, common, 239–240
Gospels, 84, 87
    Synoptic, 85
government, role of, 240
grace, 7, 49
    sacraments and, 126–127
gratitude, 178
Greek influence, 75–76
Greeley, Andrew, 208, 337
green vestments, 202
Guadalupe, Our Lady of, 35, 158, 305–307
    feast of, 160
guilt, 7, 249
    Bono on, 31
    confession and, 147

## H

Hail Holy Queen, 182
Hail Mary, 181
hairdressers, patron saint of, 308
healing
    Anointing of the Sick and, 148–150
    Lourdes and, 157
    meditation and, 186
health care, Catholic, 210–212
Healy, Patrick, 319
heathen, term, 69
Hebrew Scriptures. *See* Old Testament
Helena, saint, 276–277
Hell, 250
Henry VIII, king of England, 293–294
hierarchical communion, definition of, 260
hierarchy, 107, 260
    protecting, 336
    Rome and, 77–78
Hildegard of Bingen, saint, 184
Hispanic, definition of, 351
Hispanic Catholics
    cultural contributions of, 308–310
    young, 351–352
historical books of Bible, 87
hocus-pocus, definition of, 116
Holocaust, Church and, 59
holy, Church as, 344–345
holy cards, 167
Holy Communion, 70, 136–137
    fasting before, 61
    host, definition of, 198
Holy Orders, 142–144
Holy Roman Empire, 284–285
Holy See, 41
Holy Spirit
    air as, 119
    in Confirmation, 137–139
    gifts of, 139
    on Pentecost, 100–101

holy water, 119–120, 171
homily, 194–195
homosexuality, 252–253
Hoover, Herbert, 320
hope, 49
hospitality, ministers of, 270
host, definition of, 198
Hours, liturgy of, 186–188, 264–265
*Humanae Vitae*, 251
human life, teachings on, 239, 253–358
human rights, 239
    Dominicans and, 267
human sexuality. *See* sexuality
hypostatic union, 156

Inquisition, 291–292
Institute of Hispanic Liturgy, 21
Ireland, Catholic population of, 22
Irish Catholics
    immigration experience of, 314–315
    St. Patrick and, 281–283
Islam
    Church and, 59, 91–92
    crusades and, 289–290
    growth of, 290
    and Mary, 159
Israel, Catholic population of, 23
Italian Catholics, immigrant experience of,
    317–318

# I

Iceland, Catholic population of, 22
Ignatius of Antioch, saint, 13
Ignatius of Loyola, saint, 129–130
imagination. *See* Catholic imagination
Immaculate Conception, 158–159
immanence, definition of, 114
immigrants, Catholic, 309–310, 312–320
    patron saint of, 317
Incarnation, 353
Incas, 302–303
inclusive language, 58
indigenous peoples
    of New World
        beliefs of, 302
        Church and, 300–310
        Our Lady of Guadalupe and, 305–307
        treatment of, 212
    of Western Europe, influence of, 78–79
indulgences, sale of, 292–295
industrial revolution, 233
infallibility, papal, 40–41
    definition of, 40
Infant of Prague, 167
initiation, 213

# J

Jerusalem, 99–100
Jesuits, 32, 268, 345
    Center of Concern, 244
    definition of, 33
Jesus, 95–108
    bowing at name of, 172
    and Catholicism, 101–103
    core ideas of, 102
    death of, 98–100
    historical, 96–97
    as Jew, 97
    and new church, 348–349
    pronouns for, 96
    and ritual, 113
    and sacraments, 123–131
Joan of Arc, saint, 292
job, as vocation, 270
John, Gospel of, 85–86
John of the Cross, saint, 184, 186
John Paul II, pope, 4, 39
    and anti-Semitism, 92–93
    background of, 43–44
    and Bono, 31
    on capital punishment, 257–258

on Catholic colleges, 211
in Cuba, 21
and Guadalupe, 308
on Hell, 7
on Holocaust, 59
on liberation theology, 227
and Opus Dei, 27
and papal election process, 42–43
and Poland, 22
and Rosary, 183
on teachings, 242
John the Baptist, 136
John XXIII, pope, 52–54, 340
journaling, 178
Joyful Mysteries, 182–183
Judaism, 59, 71–75, 90–93
Church and, 92
and Jesus, 97
separation from Christianity, 104–108
Judeo-Christian, definition of, 68
Julian of Norwich, 184
justice, 49
versus charity, 233
*Justitia in Mundo*, 238
Just War Theory, 33, 242, 254–256

## K

Kateri Tekakwitha, blessed, 313
Katrina, Hurricane, 233
Keady, Jim, 232
Keillor, Garrison, 194
Kennedy, Anthony, 318
Kennedy, Jacqueline, 54
Kennedy, John F., 36, 60, 322
Kennedy, Robert, 322
killing, definition of, 254
King, Martin Luther, Jr., 235, 322
kneeler, 201
kneeling, 172

Know-Nothing party, 315
Koran, 159, 290
*Kyrie*, 193

## L

labor
Cesar Chavez and, 34
dignity of, 241
*Laborem Exercens*, 238
labor unions, 241
laity
empowerment of, 235–236
Vatican II and, 324
vocation of, 268–270
Lange, Elizabeth, 319
language, inclusive, 58
*La Nueva Raza*, 307–308
definition of, 308
Last Rites, 148
Latin, Vatican II on, 55, 61
Latin America
Catholic population of, 21, 23
cultural contributions of, 308–310
liberation theology in, 224–227
Latin Church, 12
Latino, definition of, 309, 351. *See also*
Hispanic Catholics
Lauds, 187
law, 11–12, 74–75, 83
Law, Bernard, 330
lay, definition of, 268. *See also* laity
lay professionals, 262
leadership, Vatican II and, 324
lectors, 203, 269
Lent, 173
Leofgyth, missionary, 283
Leo III, pope, 285
Leo XIII, pope, 290
letters, Bible, 84, 87

liberation theology, 224–227
life, teachings on, 239, 253–258, 353
*Life Is Worth Living*, 32
Lillis, Harry, 30
Limbo, 135
Lincoln, Abraham, 240
literal interpretation, 88–89
liturgical, definition of, 11
liturgical calendar, 10, 173–174
liturgy
    of the Eucharist, 193, 195–198
    of the Hours, 186–188, 264–265
        Vatican II on, 55–56
    of the Word, 192–195
Lord's Prayer, 103, 181, 222
Los Angeles, Catholic population of, 21
Lourdes, 157
love, Jesus on, 97
Luke, Gospel of, 86
Luminous Mysteries, 183
Luther, Martin, 293–294

# M

Madeleva, Mary, 343
magisterium, definition of, 39–40
Mandela, Nelson, 43
Manichaeism, 279
Maquiladoras, 232
marigolds, 17
marital problems, patron saint of, 141
Mark, Gospel of, 85
marriage, 139–142
    mixed, 58, 141
Martín de Porres, saint, 308
martyrs, 104–106
    definition of, 105
Marxism, 227, 241
Mary, 151–161
    apparitions of, 156–158, 305–307
    birthday of, 158–159
    feasts and devotions, 158–160, 174

    history of, 154–155
    Mother of God, 155–156
        feast of, 159
    not worshipped, 152
    Our Lady of Guadalupe, 305–307
    popularity of, 152–154
    as virgin and mother, 153–154
Mass, 10, 191–204
    African American, 17–18
    Funeral, 175
    Nuptial, 140
    participants in, 203–204
Massaro, Thomas, 236
Matachina Dance, 18
*Mater et Magistra*, 237
Matins, 187
Matthew, Gospel of, 86
Maurin, Peter, 243
May Altars, 160
Mayans, 302–303
McKenna, Joseph, 318
*mea culpa*, 61
media images, 25–26, 29–31
mediation, 126–127, 296
meditation, 186
mercy, works of, 243–244
Merton, Thomas, 59, 184
Methodius, saint, 284
Mexican-American Cultural Center, 21
Mexican Catholics, 307–308
    population of, 20
    rituals of, 16–17
Mexico, Catholicism in, 300–301
Micah, 53
Millennium Generation, 350
Miller, James, 323
Millet, Jean François, *The Angelus*, 169
mind/body split
    and abuse, 331–333
    Augustine on, 279–280
    Plato and, 75–76

mindful meditation, 186
minimum wage, 241
ministers
    of care, 270
    of Eucharist, 203, 269
    of hospitality, 270
    pastoral, 324–325
    youth, 270
ministry, 324
Minton, Sherman, 318
miracles, 6
    Jesus and, 99
missionaries, definition of, 280
missions, 301, 304
miter, 143
monasticism, 107–108, 184–185
    Benedictine, 266
    Celtic, 282
    definition of, 185
    in early church, 280–281
    and ecumenism, 59
    German Catholics and, 316
Monica, saint, 278–279, 319
monks, definition of, 265
monotheism, 74
Montezuma II, emperor of Aztecs, 302–303
morality, models of, 11–12
morality plays, 284
moral law, 74
mortal sin, 248–249
mortification, 27
Moses, 74
Moses the Black, saint, 319
mother(s)
    church as, 282
    of God, Mary as, 155–156
        feast of, 159
Muhammad, 289
Murphy, Frank, 318
music, 17, 61, 188–189, 209
    sacred, function of, 188

Muslims. *See* Islam
mysteries of Rosary, 180, 182–183
mystery, 79, 123, 354
    definition of, 182
mysticism, 107, 184–186, 284
    definition of, 184

# N

national parish, definition of, 316–317
Native Americans
    Kateri Tekakwitha, 313
    parish, 18–20
Natural Family Planning (NFP), 251–252
natural law, 251
    Aquinas on, 332–333
neophytes, 214
New Orleans, Catholic population of, 21
New Testament, 82, 84–86
New World. *See also* Americas
    Church in, 299–310
    term, 300
New York City, Catholic population of, 22, 314
Nicaea, Council of, 5, 277, 332
Nicaragua, Catholic population of, 20
Nicene Creed, 5, 195, 222
Noah, 73
Non, saint, 282
None, 187
nonviolence, 243
North America, Catholic population of, 23
"Nostra Aetate," 91–92
novices, 265
nuclear war, 255
nuns, 262, 265
    addressing, 265
    as pastoral ministers, 324
    patron saint of, 283
    Vatican II and, 324

# O

obedience, in religious orders, 264
Oblate Sisters of Providence, 319
Oceania, Catholic population of, 23
*Octagesima Adveniens*, 237
offertory gift bearers, 269
O.F.M. *See* Order of Friars Minor
oil
    in anointing of sick, 149
    in Confirmation, 138–139
    holy, 119–120
Old Testament, 59, 71, 82–83
    Catholic Church and, 90–93
O'Malley, Sean, 258
Ometéotl, 302
omnipresence, 124–125
    definition of, 171
one, Church as, 342–344
O.P. *See* Order of Preachers
Opus Dei, 25–28
order, term, 264
Order of Friars Minor, 266–267, 303, 307, 318
Order of Preachers, 267–268
Order of St. Benedict, 266
orders, religious, 264–268
Ordinary time, 173
O.S.B., 266
Our Father. *See* Lord's Prayer
Our Lady. *See* Mary

# P

*Pacem in Terris*, 237
pacifism, 243
pagan, term, 68–69
pall, 175
palm leaves, 118–119, 172
Pan de Muerto, 16

papal. *See* pope(s)
Papal States, 42
paradigm
    definition of, 340
    shift in, 340–341
parish, 207–210
    national, 316–317
parish councils
    definition of, 55
    members of, 269
parishes, 45
parochial schools, 52, 208, 210. *See also*
  Catholic education
    African Americans and, 319
    decline of, 323–324
    German Catholics and, 315–316
participation, 239–240
partnership, 348
Passover, 200
pastoral ministers, 325
    definition of, 324
paten, 143
patriarch, definition of, 288
patriarchy
    protecting, 336
    Rome and, 77–78
Patrick, saint, 22, 281–282
patron saints
    of Americas, 158, 160
    of animals, 171
    of charitable organizations, 211
    of communications workers, 157
    of dairy workers, 283
    of druggists, 200
    of France, 292
    of hairdressers, 308
    of immigrants, 317
    of marital problems, 141
    of nuns, 283
    of prisoners, 211
    of retreats, 130

of scholars, 283
of schools, 290
of stonemasons, 106
of television, 267
of travelers, 168
Paul, saint, 102, 136, 155, 223, 253
Pax Christi, 243
peace, 242
    Fatima and, 158
    prayer for, 32
    sign of, 197
penance, 144–147
Pentateuch, 83, 87
Pentecost, 67, 100–101
People of God, Church as, 54, 340, 349
permanent diaconate, 143
Peter, saint, 39
petition, 178
pews, 201
Peyton, Father, 321
Philadelphia, Catholic population of,
    314–315
Philippines, Catholic population of, 22
Pius XII, pope, 43, 59, 93
Plato, 76, 279
play, 209
Poland, Catholic population of, 22
Polish Catholics, immigrant experience of,
    316–317
politics, Catholic Church and, 234–236
poor, option for, 242
Poor Clares, 267
Popemobile, 43
pope(s), 38–44. *See also* John Paul II
    Adrian VI, 44
    Benedict XIII, 44
    Benedict XV, 44
    Benedict XVI, 44, 253, 263
    Clement XII, 44
    Damasus, 86
    election of, 42–43

in hierarchy, 261
infallibility of, 40–41
and Jesuits, 268
John XXIII, 52–54, 340
Leo III, 285
Leo XIII, 290
Paul VI, 44, 241–242, 251
Pius XII, 43, 59, 93
*Popolorum Progressio*, 237
Posadas, 309–310
    definition of, 309
poverty, 35
    in religious orders, 264, 266–267
Prague, Infant of, 167
prayer, 177–189, 270. *See also* Rosary
    of faithful, 195
    hand position for, 171–172
    personal, 178
    Vatican II and, 61–62
Pre-Cana sessions, 141
precepts of the Church, 46–47
priests, 142
    abuse by, 329–338
    and celibacy, 335–336
    clothing of, 202
    in hierarchy, 261, 263–264
    ordination of, 142–144
    shortage of, 63
    Vatican II and, 324
Prime, 187
prisoners, patron saint of, 211
proclaiming, 194
propagation, 250–251
property ownership, 241
prophets, 53–54, 87
    liberation theology and, 227
Protestants
    characteristics of, 296
    in colonial America, 312–313
    definition of, 293
    and Lord's Prayer, 103

and Mary, 160
Reformation, 293–294
and sermon, 194
and worship, 114–115
province, 45
prudence, 49
psychology and spirituality, 344–345
pueblos, 18–20
pulpit, 201
purgatory, 16
purple vestments, 202

## Q–R

*Quadragesimo Anno*, 237
Quantum Generation, 352
Quetzalcòatl, 302–303

Ratzinger, Joseph Alois, 44, 263
reading, spiritual, 178
real presence, 197, 199
recitation, 178
recollection, 178
reconciliation, 144–147
recovering Catholic, 216
red vestments, 202
reflecting, 194–195
refugees, Catholic, in United States, 314
relics, 293
religion, definition of, 69, 112
religious liberty, 59–60, 277
religious orders, 264–268
reparation, 178
*Rerum Novarum*, 237
responsibility, 60
retreats, patron saint of, 130
Revelation, Book of, 87
revelation, ongoing, 220, 295
Revolutionary War, Catholics and, 313
rhythm method, 251

Rite of Christian Initiation of Adults (RCIA), 213–215
Rite of Committal, 175
ritual, 68–70
definition of, 70, 112
sensuous elements of, 111–122, 337
theology of, 113–117
Roberts, John, 318
Roman Catholicism, 12
Roman Curia, 262–263
definition of, 261
Roman establishment, 275–285
Roman influence, 77–78, 99–100, 104–106
Rome, 39, 42, 107
Romero, Oscar, 227
Room at the Inn, 58
Rosary, 158, 179–184
how to say it, 180–181
origins of, 179–180
prayers of, 181–182
Vatican II and, 56
when to say it, 184
*Roukh*, 119
rules, 11–12, 45–49
rules of orders
Benedictine, 266
Franciscan, 266–267

## S

sacramental awareness, 129
sacramental principle, 124–125
sacramental(s), 117, 165–170
definition of, 112
sacrament(s), 10, 133–150, 222
church as, 125–127
definition of, 112
Jesus and, 123–131
sacrifice, 200
human, 302

St. Louis, Catholic population of, 314
St. Peter's Basilica, 41
saints. *See also specific saint*
    feast days of, 174
    martyrs, 104–106
    Vatican II and, 62
sanctuary, 201
Sanctus, 196
San Ildefonso Pueblo, 18
Scalabrini Fathers, 318
Scalia, Antonin, 318
scandals, 4, 25, 212, 329–338
scholars, patron saint of, 283
Scholastica, saint, 266
schools, patron saint of, 290
science, Church and, 57
Scripture. *See* Bible
seamless garment of life, 253–258
seasons, 174
Second Vatican Council. *See* Vatican II
secrecy, power of, 334
sectarianism, definition of, 31
seminarians, 262
   and homosexuality, 253
   Vatican II and, 324
seminary, 144
sensuousness
   and ritual, 111–122
   and sacraments, 133–150
   and sexuality, 337–338
Septuagint, 88
sermon, 194–195
serving, Jesus and, 103
Severinus, saint, 284
Sext, 187
sexual abuse, 329–338
   factors in, 330–331
sexuality
   Catholic
      positive aspects of, 337–338
      problems with, 329–338

   education on, 333
   and sin, 250–253
   and virginity, 153–154
shame, 249
Sheen, Fulton, 32, 321
Sheen, Martin, 33
Shriver, Sargent, 323
Sigfrid, saint, 284
sign of peace, 197
Sign of the Cross, 170
silencing, 215, 227
Simon Magus, 289
Simon of Cyrene, 319
simony, definition of, 289
sin, 145–146, 247–258
   as missing the mark, 248–249
   term, 248
sisters. *See* nuns
Sisters of the Holy Family, 319
sixties, 322–324
   Catholicism in, 51–64
S.J. *See* Jesuits
slavery, Church and, 319
slippery slope, 11
Smith, Al, 320
social action, 232–234, 269
social justice, 210, 231–245
   Vatican II and, 57–58
Society of Jesus. *See* Jesuits
solidarity, 239–240
*Sollicitudo rei Socialis*, 238
song leaders, 269
Sorrowful Mysteries, 183
Soubirous, Bernadette, 157
Spain, and Americas, 299–310
Spanish Inquisition, 292
spiritual directors, 130, 265
spirituality, 25–36, 344–345
   lay, 268
   and sexuality, 250

spiritual reading, 178
stability, in religious life, 266
statues, 166
Stein, Edith, saint, 92
Stephen, saint, 106
stonemasons, patron saint of, 106
subsidiarity, principle of, 240
superstition versus tradition, 172
surplice, 202
Swiss Guards, 42
symbol, definition of, 127–128
sympto-thermal method, 251–252
Synoptic Gospels, 85

## T

tabernacle, 74, 202
Talmud, 83
Taney, Roger B., 318
Taos Pueblo, Catholic church, 19–20
teaching(s), 247–258
    development of, 219–230
    Jesus and, 103
    social, themes in, 236–242
    sources of, 220–222
Teilhard de Chardin, Pierre, 57
television, patron saint of, 267
temperance, 49
Ten Commandments, 45–46, 222
Terce, 187
Teresa of Ávila, saint, 184
testament, definition of, 82
theology, 222–224
    classical, 223–224
    contemporary, 224–227
    dynamic triangle and, 229–230
    liberation, 224–227
    of ritual, 113–117
    roles of, 228–229
Theology on Tap, 353

Theotokos, 156
Thomas, Clarence, 35, 318
Thomas Aquinas, saint, 156, 227, 254, 267, 290, 332
Tolton, Augustine, 319
Torah, 83
tradition, 65
    definition of, 7, 220
    loss of, 60–64
    versus superstition, 172
    and teaching, 220–221
    Trent on, 295
transcendence, definition of, 114
transitional deacons, 143
travelers, patron saint of, 168
Trent, council of, 8, 295–296
tribe, Catholics as, 207–217
Triduum, definition of, 173
tuna casserole, 61

## U

U2, 30
Uganda, Catholic population of, 23
United States
    Catholic history in, 311–325
    Catholic population of, 21–22
    Supreme Court, Catholics on, 318
universal, Church as, 345–347
*Universi Dominici Gregis*, 43
University of Mexico, 304
ushers, 204, 269

## V

Vatican City, 4, 37–50, 317
Vatican II, 8–9, 51–64, 323
    and deacons, 143
    generations after, 350–352
    and loss of tradition, 60–64

on marriage, 140–141
on religious freedom, 277
on sexuality, 251
venial sin, 248–249
Vespers, 187
vespers, definition of, 18
vestments, 202
Viaticum, definition of, 148
vigil lights, 120
Vigils, 187
Vincent de Paul, saint, 211
virginity, Mary and, 153–154
virtues, 49
Visitation, 159
visitors, behavior for, at Mass, 192, 204
vocations, 143, 263–270
    definition of, 263
    lay, 268–270
    shortage of, 63–64
    Vatican II and, 324
Voice of the Faithful (VOTF), 28–29
volunteer groups, 244
vows
    definition of, 185
    of orders, 264, 266
vulnerable, option for, 242

wisdom books of Bible, 87
Wojtyla, Karol. *See* John Paul II
women
    in early church, 277
    and future of Church, 342–344
    Inquisition and, 291
    and mysticism, 184
    and ordination, 63, 144
    and pastoral ministry, 325
    and theology, 227
Word, liturgy of, 192–195
workers
    Cesar Chavez and, 34
    dignity of, 241
works of mercy, 243–244

X, Malcolm, 322

yada, 71
Yom Kippur, 74
youth, 349–353
youth ministers, 270

# W–X–Y–Z

Wall Street group, 244
war. *See* Just War Theory
water, 69
    in baptism, 134–136
    holy, 119–120, 171
Wenceslaus, saint, 22
Western Rite, 12
Western world, definition of, 76
White, Edward Douglass, 318
white vestments, 202
Wills, Garry, 119

Niles Public Library

OCT 0 5 2006

Niles, Illinois 60714